RECONSTRUCTING
THE ACADEMY

DISCARDED
JENKS LRC
GORDON COLLEGE

RECONSTRUCTING THE ACADEMY

WOMEN'S EDUCATION AND WOMEN'S STUDIES

JENKS L.R.C.
GORDON COLLEGE
255 GRAPEVINE RD.
WENHAM, MA 01984-1895

EDITED BY ELIZABETH MINNICH,
JEAN O'BARR, AND RACHEL ROSENFELD

THE UNIVERSITY OF CHICAGO PRESS
Chicago and London

LC
1756
.R43
1988

The essays in this volume originally appeared in various issues of
SIGNS: JOURNAL OF WOMEN IN CULTURE AND SOCIETY.
Acknowledgment of the original publication date can be found on the
first page of each essay.

The University of Chicago Press, Chicago 60637
The University of Chicago Press, Ltd., London
© 1978, 1980, 1982, 1983, 1986, 1987, 1988 by
The University of Chicago
All rights reserved. Published 1988
Printed in the United States of America
92 91 90 89 88 5 4 3 2 1

Library of Congress Cataloging-in-Publication Data
Reconstructing the academy.
   Selection of essays originally appearing in Signs.
   Includes bibliographical references and index.
   1. Women—Education (Higher)—United States.
2. Women's studies—United States.— 3. Women's colleges—
United States. I. Minnich, Elizabeth Kamarck.
II. O'Barr, Jean F. III. Rosenfeld, Rachel. IV. Signs.
LC1756.R43 1988   376'.65'0973   87-35846
ISBN 0-226-53013-2 (alk. paper)
ISBN 0-226-53014-0 (pbk. : alk. paper)

The paper used in this publication meets the minimum requirements of
American National Standard for Information Sciences—Permanence of
Paper for Printed Library Materials, ANSI Z39.48-1984. ∞

CONTENTS

ACKNOWLEDGMENTS

We would like to thank the many people whose hands and minds gave support to the publication of this book. As always, we would like to thank the journal's staff, Mary Wyer and Anne Vilen, for coordinating the editing and production of this book; Marguerite Rogers and Janet Woolum, for their careful composition of the bits and pieces of information that glue the essays into book form; and the students who populate the *Signs* office with energy and enthusiasm, lending each her own skill to the task of building new knowledge about women, in particular, Amy Thomas, Marjolein Kars, Diane Everett, Barbara Condon, Leigh Alvarado, and Alice Poffinberger.

INTRODUCTION

Simone Weil, denied entrance to the Ecole Normale Supérieure, wrote that she fell into deep despair over loss of the "transcendent realm only truly great men enter and where truth resides" (*Simone Weil: An Anthology*, ed. Siân Miles [New York: Weidenfeld & Nicholson, 1986], 5). For centuries, the exclusive academy controlled not only access to "true" education but also the definition and validation of reason itself. And since, following Aristotle, reason was taken to be *the* specifically human characteristic, women's exclusion from the "transcendent realm" of the academy both resulted from and reinforced the patriarchal view that women were less than fully human. As Simone de Beauvoir observed, women seemed to be locked out of transcendence not by being female but by the meaning attached to "being female."

Fortunately, women did not accept these restrictions. They sought to enter the academy and, when they finally did so, used what it offered them to change their own lives and often those of other women as well. Higher education became a route to a less overtly restricted life. The academy itself did not change for these early women, but despite its continuing silence about their lives, their histories, their thoughts and creations, they found ways to use it for their own purposes.

These women won a place for us in the academy—yet our presence is by no means reflected accurately, or adequately, at all levels, nor are all groups of women equally represented. Having overcome some of the barriers to our physical presence, we are working now to be fully present, not by transforming ourselves but, rather, the academy—for the failures of education lie there. It was a great and noble struggle to achieve access; now, we must work to make the rooms we have entered suitable for all, not merely for the gentlemen of the club, and not only for the white ladies, either. If we would be fully present, we must all truly belong.

In this volume, Elisabeth Young-Bruehl's essay opens the critique of the dominant tradition passed on by the academy. It is a tradition that both inspired our dreams and wounded our sense of

I

self. Young-Bruehl takes on the assumptions about reason, about thinking, about the life of the mind that seemed both neutral and transcendent as long as the dreams held sway. In considering women as philosophers, she reclaims for women the almost lost notion that philosophy is an overarching and foundational love of wisdom rather than expertise on a particular tradition of reasoning. That is, she does not simply say, "Women too can be philosophers," which leaves the definition of philosophy untouched. She says, "Women *are* philosophers," simultaneously breaking open definitions both of philosophy and of women. The realization that notions of reason and of maleness have been conflated and that the consequent gendered reason has been placed at the center of definitions of what it means to be human not only clarifies one deep and dangerous way in which women were defined by and for men but also points us toward the need to reinterpret reason—and so, of course, education as well. Such revelations are keys to unlocking the door of the academy if we are to enter, and then to leave, whole.

Feminists who are critiquing and re-creating all of the disciplines within the academy turn fundamental critiques such as Young-Bruehl's into strategies for action. Margaret Andersen's review essay on the thought and practice emerging from now widespread efforts to transform the curriculum demonstrates clearly how rich and complex that work has been. Andersen's work complements the earlier analysis of women's studies by Marilyn J. Boxer. While feminist scholarship challenges disciplines individually, and women's studies programs nurture the growth of new, interdisciplinary teaching and research, the feminist critique of the whole also continues—for the qualities that informed the exclusiveness of the academy have framed institutional structures and practices as well.

At issue is the question: How best can we, as women, as educators, work on, as well as within, the traditional academy? Such work cannot be easy on any level. Susan Hardy Aiken et al.'s article on one curriculum transformation project brings Young-Bruehl's philosophical and Andersen's and Boxer's theoretical-practical overviews into sharp, concrete, particular focus. Every project must, after all, take place in a particular institution and be run by particular individuals. There is no one formula for institutional change, and Aiken et al. do not offer one. By going in depth into their own experiences of trying to teach their colleagues, they remind us that there are choices about how to proceed every step of the way; that we can make mistakes, and learn from them; that we must make our own plans, taking into account not only what all academic institutions within the dominant tradition have in common but also what each has that is individual and who we are as individuals as well. When the theoretical is put into practice, it cannot simply be applied or it will fall into dogmatism and become either tyrannical, in its discounting of individual and particular realities, and/or ineffective because of ignorance of such realities.

Feminists are not immune to such errors, of course. Zinn et al. remind us that working within the academy can easily mean that feminists accept or introduce false universals so that we, too, mystify exclusivities, whatever our intent. And Gail Pheterson's descriptions of the ways in which our past experiences with oppression disrupt our ability to share a common goal is deeply personal precisely even as it grounds itself in political realities. We are warned in these two essays that an uncritical inclusiveness may be limiting, that inclusion is not an end in and of itself, but, rather, inclusiveness is the ground on which we transform. How, and with whom, we proceed to work for inclusiveness is thus of central importance.

Such connections between ends and means, theory and practice, require also the grounding of our work in a knowledge of our educational history. The history of our physical exclusion, which informs all of these essays, is the focus of Sally Schwager's essay. Her review gives us the context in which we work—a context needed as much for individual strategizing as for theory grounded in, and so capable of, helping us affect our always historically rooted realities.

We need to remember that "women's education" has been, and remains, a richly ambiguous phrase. Does it mean education as it has always been, extended to women? Does it mean education designed precisely for women? If the latter, is the design predicated on past or present or on transformative understandings of gender? Or, to put the question in institutional terms, does women's education point to a focus on women within coeducational institutions or push us toward validation of institutional separatism? If the latter, what are the reasons for the separation? Is it that women require special help and support because we start out behind, weaker in some critical way? Or is it that, as long as coeducation perpetuates the old misleading dream, separate institutions alone provide space for the strengths of women? The articles by Mary J. Oates and Susan Williamson, M. Elizabeth Tidball, and Joy Rice and Annette Hemmings bring us up to date on these issues, building on the thinking about women's education and women's colleges that was reengaged in the late sixties and seventies as a result of the rush to coeducation when previously all-male preserves finally opened to women. We are reminded of how powerful the dream of "the best" education has been, and how conflated with maleness, as we reconsider the arguments for women's colleges. How do we want to define the success of any form of education?

In one of its most recent versions, the argument for separate educational institutions for women has also promoted, or seemed to validate, the idea that role models are very important for young women. The presence of larger numbers of women on faculties and in the administrations of women's institutions is cited as one reason women seemed to be empowered by studying even a still male-dominated curriculum. Thus, the presence of women on campuses in all roles has come to be sought not only as a matter of professional equity but also as necessary in order to provide role models for students. It matters who teaches us, whom we see in roles of power and authority. The teachings of the academy have always gone far beyond those contained in the formal curriculum.

However, the question of what inclusion means and should mean remains complex. The articles reexamining the case for women's colleges are not only complemented but challenged, as well, on the issue of role modeling by Berenice Fisher's work. Fisher's article involves us in a careful reconsideration of what we are doing when we valorize role models, questioning even the familiar idea of "modeling" as a way of teaching. She asks us to be very careful that we do not inadvertently subvert our own best intentions through lack of critique and through insensitivity to the implications of theory for practice. Is there not, for example, an unacceptable reimposition of hierarchy implied in prescribing role models? And what vision of moral autonomy is embedded in the highly ambiguous term "model," considered as both noun and verb? Our relationships with each other in the context of the academy-in-transition are especially meaningful, even central, in the effort to reconstruct the academic environment.

As we continue to rethink the relations of women to each other, we cannot afford to turn away from the issue of relations between women and men. One troubling and emblematic example of those relations is the sexual harassment that women confront on campuses and in the workplace. We have finally named, and hence become able to act effectively against, sexual harassment. As a result, we have also come to realize that many of those who thought women should no longer be excluded from higher education glossed over the whole issue of sexuality—perhaps because early paternalistic advocates for "separating the sexes" made so much of it, and perhaps because we needed to break free from overdetermination of women as sexual creatures.

Yet sexuality as historically, culturally, and politically constituted cannot be ignored. We are now forced to know that males do prey on females "even" in the academy, enacting and reenforcing the twisted relation of gender to sex and sex to sexuality as expressions of the power basic to male dominance. We now know that the distinction between gender, as cultural construct, and sex, as physiological fact, while simple and very useful, is not enough, in and of itself, to help us rethink and change the old sex-gender system. The claim that human sexuality derives directly from "Nature" and hence is not open to change may indeed be one of the most political claims made. This volume includes Phyllis Crocker's early piece on sexual harassment in the academy as part of the on-going effort not only to deal with the abuse of power that harassment represents—to help us *do* something about such utterly unacceptable behavior—but also to name one specific way in which the inclusion of women in higher education is a challenge to fundamental premises that inform Western ideas about the construction of the sexes. These informing "facts" have long been hidden and mystified as "natural," in the case of sex difference, and "private," in the case of sexuality. The phenomenon of sexual harassment, once named, exposes the persistence of cultural rationalizations about male entitlement to female bodies.

We may be in the academy; we may be bringing feminist scholarship into the curriculum; we may be changing ways of teaching and working; but that does not mean we have eliminated the sex/gender hierarchy. It is expressed in sexual harassment just as it was in our exclusion, and both reduce us to our male-defined bodies. Again we are reminded that even our physical presence in the academy is a profound challenge to the dominant tradition. Simply by being there, we are seen as provocative. Achieving access is not, cannot be, enough.

* * *

These are the complex theoretical and stubborn practical issues that we encounter as we try to change the academy. But it would be a mistake to assume that we enter and struggle within an academy that is monolithic. In fact, today the academy is being shaped by many forces, including powerful intellectual developments that, like feminist scholarship, are affecting some of its long-term assumptions and structures. Linda Alcoff's essay helps us understand some of those developments by joining feminist scholarship, particularly that issuing from cultural feminism, with post-structuralism, comparing and contrasting them in an effort to see how/if these two powerful new developments in thought may be complementary. For example, both seem to Alcoff to share in the effort to dismantle the dominant tradition's obsession with overarching principles. She sees post-structuralism offering important conceptual tools to this aspect of the feminist critique. However, analyzing what feminism, in its turn, offers post-structuralism, she notes that without generalizations on a large scale, we cannot get to the level of political analysis. However particular and contextual our work is (and it must be in order to take account of the lives, thoughts, and works of women in all our diversity), feminism also calls on us to analyze the all-embracing structures that shape our different lives, and then to be willing to generalize about them.

Alcoff's article is, then, helpful in illuminating the present intellectual ferment within the academy, engaging other critiques with feminist work to mutual benefit. In so doing, it picks up the work of Young-Bruehl, extending the analysis of the informing assumptions of the academy to the contemporary scene. It does so in the spirit of conversation, that particular commitment of women-as-philosophers, and so also helps break the old academic privileging of the adversarial, argumentative mode of thought, speech, and writing.

This collection as a whole, then, hopefully points us toward conversations about our future. Feminist scholarship is no longer simply a criticism of or compensation for old errors, nor is it an isolated specialty practiced only by a few. It can and should enter critically into all efforts not just to extend but also to redefine knowledge. Yet, in so doing, feminist scholarship does not become just one among many new voices. It retains its commitment to critique all knowing. Women and women's studies are now included in the academy, and feminist scholarship is spreading throughout the curriculum. But we do not yet have a transformed academy, as we do not yet have a transformed world, in which all humans can be properly included. As we insist not only on being in, but also on being fully present as, ourselves, to and for each other, we set the terms for that transformation—and continue the quest to understand ourselves, others, and understanding.

* * *

We are coming to know our past and to comprehend our present, but what about the future? Now that we have some points of access, now that the doors are open even if the rooms inside are not yet furnished to make all people equally at home, what do we expect the next barriers to full inclusion to be? We have no essays in this volume that speak directly to that question, and, of course, we have no answers ourselves. Still, we have already learned several important lessons that provide some views on what is to come. We can expect a continuing need for the feminist critique of the dominant tradition and all that was born within and of it. We will need to continue critiquing our own work as well; we learned to think and act within the very tradition we wish to open, enrich, and change. The reflexivity of thought that allows us to think about our thinking is essential to our enterprise, lest we slip inadvertently back onto the very track we thought we had refused. But reflexivity is not enough; we can still feel trapped.

To inform our thinking at all levels, we need to remain in conversation with multiple others, not just those with whom we find discourse easy. We need to listen to informed and thoughtful critics and stay in touch with lives outside of the academy in this culture and in others. We need to act as well as think, and to act in different arenas. We cannot think well for long without the call back to particular realities action requires and gives us. We need the sharp moments of self-understanding through contrast and commonalities that cross-cultural work can bring.

With critique, reflexivity, conversation, action, and cross-cultural understanding, we give ourselves a web that is complex enough to hold us while restraining us from spinning off on our own single thread, trying to span the abyss with too weak a weaving, or creating a pattern that is not open to differences. But, of course, even all of that is still not enough. We speak here of re-creating a whole tradition, a whole culture, polity, world. Let us, then, as we work, also be gentle with ourselves. We cannot do it all, even together, in a short time.

When we ask and are asked, why do we do it? what is our vision? we say many things—our dreams are as diverse and multihued as we. But perhaps we can say that we do not want to dream one new vision to replace the old. We recognize the danger in that. We want to open space for the dreaming of humanity, no longer forced to masquerade as "man," and a particular sort of man at that. Humankind cannot know itself until women know themselves. As Adrienne Rich wrote, "I suggest that not anatomy, but enforced ignorance, has been a crucial key in our powerlessness" (*Blood, Bread and Poetry: Selected Prose 1979–1985* [New York: Norton, 1986], 2).

In refusing all that locked us into destinies not of our own choosing—not of our own at all—we are indeed expressing a vision. It is in part a vision the academy has long claimed to serve—that of loving wisdom. What we bring to that quest is the familiar and particularly stubborn conviction that wisdom cannot be sought only by an exclusive few conversing behind walls only with each other. The love of wisdom calls on us to go beyond narrow expertise just as it pushes us to ground the general in particularity, in contexts. It asks us to remember that beyond the search for knowledge as it is construed within professionalized fields of inquiry, we are called to seek a stronger, more inclusive, and far more challenging comprehension of who we are. We do so to learn how we have chosen to live and think and create and to learn new ways—for the sake of all, and for our shared earth.

THE EDUCATION OF WOMEN AS PHILOSOPHERS

ELISABETH YOUNG-BRUEHL

It is unfortunate that, for reasons of personal and cultural habit, when we think about ourselves as askers of questions, thinkers, or, using the generic title, as philosophers, lovers of wisdom, we think of ourselves as selves. That is, we think: *I* am thinking—first person singular, one person solitary, an interiority, a mental machine.

Of course, it is fortunate that we—women—ever do think of ourselves as thinking; and in this light, the matter of *how* we do so seems secondary. For there is a great deal in our personal and cultural histories suggesting that thinking is not our province, not our privilege, not even our possibility. So great, indeed, is the weight of prejudice about women's abilities and achievements as thinkers that we often look to the lives of thoughtful women with questions not about how they thought of their thinking but with questions about how they thought at all, how they managed *not* to be as this great weight of prejudice prescribed.

Biographies of women often have about them an air of amazement. They are infused—particularly when they are written by women—with an

The title and topic for this essay were suggested by the sesquicentennial committee at Mount Holyoke College, where it was delivered as a lecture in October 1985 to celebrate the college's sesquicentennial. My thanks for their comments on an earlier draft to the members of the Mount Holyoke Project on Gender in Context.

This essay originally appeared in *Signs*, vol. 12, no. 2, Winter 1987.

exclamation: She did it! Institutions for the education of women originate—even when they are circumscribed by visions of educated women as ideal helpmeets for educated men—from the imperative form of the same impulse: You can do it! Despite everything and almost everyone outside, here you can do it! In most stories of exemplary women who have managed to do what was not expected of them, and in most stories of institutions that have tried to make the exception more of a rule, the focus is on sources of support. In every exemplary woman's drama, there will be a cast—usually a very limited cast—of encouragers, and in every institution's story there will be exemplary leaders who encourage a cast of encouragers.

Because women find it no easy matter to think at all, they are more inclined to be aware of (even if not openly acknowledging of) their supporters than men, who, after all, are supposed to be able by nature to set up in the thinking business as solitary entrepreneurs. For women—I want to argue—the supportive others are always there, and always there *in thinking*.

Thinking, we usually assume, goes on in our heads. It involves a control center that produces thoughts. Thoughts, then, flow forth like a stream unless somehow blocked or distracted. That is, we have perceptions passively or actively received, and ideas innate or acquired, which are all by some ruling mental fabricator or organizer fixed for flow into languages of various sorts that allow us to express ourselves. Thoughts are made or crafted or commandeered. Simple.

I want to question this notion, this enthralling picture, of thinking as a kind of mental organizing of mental material or mental troops; but since I want to question also what this picture means for women, for women who are trying to think, I want to raise my question contextually. So let me continue for a few minutes like a manifesto.

We live as women in a revolutionary era for women: it is a time of nothing less than the first concerted effort by women to question and change definitions of our sex and gender—our femaleness and femininity, our proper place and purpose—that have been proposed, with variations, throughout the history of patriarchies. We live in and with a mass movement that has grown in the post–World War II period from an aspiration to a reality; from a vision particular to a segment of the Western intelligentsia to an achievement known to and contributed to by people all over the world. The feminist movement is truly an Internationale for the first time in history.

It is certainly obvious that, as a movement hoping to secure socio-economic and political equality for women, the feminist movement is still in its infancy. The changes in women's statuses that it has brought about are everywhere insecurely instituted and under constant threat—in bedrooms, at breakfast tables, in marketplaces, clinics, courts, and political forums—from those who resist change, wish to roll it back, and even sometimes from those who are working for it.

But I think that it is reasonable to claim that although the movement has miles to go in the matter of rights, it has already made a revolution by adding to the query, What do women want? the question, How and by whom have women's wants been determined? It is one thing, for example, when a psychological study is conducted to try to assess differences between women and men, and quite another when the assumptions—the perceptual and conceptual biases—that shape such a study are themselves the object of study.

I do not consider this example to be isolated or academic. The shift it exemplifies is crucial and, I think, novel, even though it is certainly the case that, throughout the history of women's struggles for emancipation, analysts of the female condition have understood that prejudice predetermines and perpetuates institutions of inequality as much as institutions of inequality reflect and confirm prejudice; that habits of thought organize social relations as much as social relations organize habits of thought. Proclamists of emancipation have also understood that lasting change requires both reform of our ways of ordering our lives in all spheres and intellectual critique. The classics of the feminist movement have won their positions as perennials because their addresses to institutionalized inequality have been combined with studies of prejudice.

But what is new in the postwar era is that the institutions and intellectual disciplines that shape the form and content of education—by which I do not mean simply schooling—are being critically reshaped. Studies of prejudice are no longer reported by voices in the wilderness; they are broadcast in the metropli of consciousness, in educational settings of all sorts. "The whole pyramid of discrimination," as Juliet Mitchell has written, "rests on solid extra-economic foundation—education."

When intellectual critique is reflexive and self-critical, that is, when it both questions *and* questions how its questions have been and are being posed, then intellectual critique is truly philosophical. What is going on now, as the feminist movement's critique reaches into the root systems of prejudice against women, is the education of women as philosophers. But when I say this "as philosophers" I mean not as professional philosophers or even as heiresses to traditional philosophical inquiry. What I do mean will take me a little while to say.

*   *   *

Within our European tradition, philosophizing began in an era of cultural ferment. All around the Mediterranean Sea, peoples who had lived in relative isolation encountered each other as traders and soldiers, adventurers and empire builders. Among the sixth-century B.C.E. Hellenes settled on the Ionian coast, at the edge of an empire (the Persian) being swept with a fervor called Zoroastrianism, there lived thinkers now known collectively as the pre-Socratics. These men began to ask whether the world in all its rich diversity is not really made up of one primal stuff, or moved by one regnant power, or ruled on one principle. At the same time, among the Israelites (settled uncertainly in their Promised Land), prophets and priests, heirs of Moses, wrote texts declaring that one God created the world and rules over it. In both of these traditions, for all their differences, the ruler was conceived as the orderer, the world-mind.

Many and diverse are the ways in which the search for a *monos*, a one, transcendent or imminent, has taken place since this foundational era of our history. Each renewal of the search has summoned up the original search reflexively, asking whether and how the monisms of the founders were true. Is the one Anaxagoras's *Nous* (Mind)? Heraclitus's *Logos*, Parmenides' Being? Is it Plato's Good? or Aristotle's telic Unmoved Mover? Is the one God the God of the Jews? or the Christians? or perhaps even the Ahura-Mazda of the Zoroastrians?

In another period of great cultural ferment and contact among peoples—peoples not just of the Mediterranean but of the then circumnavigated globe—there grew up alongside this reflexive questioning that had been the impulse of many renaissances other forms of reflexivity. In the European era known as the Enlightenment, people began to question how the *human* mind conducts its philosophical and religious searches. Are all the monisms, so seemingly diverse, mere variations of a single Truth? A Truth for Man? Could it be that all the different monisms are themselves manifestations of one universal human Mind?

These were the questions of Enlightenment cosmopolitanism, but there were also questions in the Enlightenment that marked a second new form of reflexivity, quite different from the cosmopolitan one that ushered in mental monism. Is it possible that people's minds, rather than being fitted for knowing the single Truth and hindered from such knowledge only by local differences of customs and languages, are and always have been destined to know only themselves? Do minds know only the walls of their prisons—the walls of diverse, historically determined prisons? Perhaps (so this form of questioning went) human beings are condemned to mind-bound truths and forever precluded from any Truth with a capital *T*. These questions were focused on the nature of mental activity, as were the cosmopolitan questions; but they did not reach beyond mental activity to a monistic Mind of Man. On the contrary, they opened the way for notions of cultural diversity, mental relativism—the basic ingredients of what might be called the intellectual French Revolution.

This second form of Enlightenment reflexivity is apparent in many kinds of nineteenth-century studies of what we today call "difference":

anthropological studies of "primitive" non-European peoples; sociological studies of nonaristocratic peoples of various classes; historical studies of nonvictorious peoples suppressed in the triumph of European civilization; philosophical inquiries into the history of ideas, *Geistesgeschichte*, including suppressed ideas. But it is certainly the case that before Marx and Freud were heeded, most of these studies contained more or less explicit assumptions about the evolutionary truth of the predominating modes of civilization—that is, they acknowledged the different but then measured it by the standard of the successful, the ideal mind: given time, evolution will reinstate the Truth.

Feminist writers participated in this great upheaval and expansion of horizon, but often quite ambiguously. The ambiguity of their critiques centered in their attitudes toward reason. From the time of Mary Wollstonecraft until the time of Simone de Beauvoir, feminists noted that women do not think as men do—that their minds are not male minds, educated like male minds. Women, it was understood, have been kept in economic, social, and political conditions that deprived them of the rationality of men. Mary Wollstonecraft and Simone de Beauvoir both—in the eighteenth century and in the twentieth century—lamented that women have been kept from rationality and from the transcendent capacities of reason. One of the key aspirations of feminism, to put the matter in other words, was to free women from their circumscribed mental worlds and let them enter into male rationality, participate in it as equals.

To this aspiration, postwar feminism has addressed probing questions about whether it is not, in effect, a reinstatement or reaffirmation of the monistic Enlightenment ideals, one Mind of Man or one evolutionarily ideal mind. Recent feminists have said—to speak baldly—why emulate male rationality? Male rationality, after all, has been supplying reasons—for centuries—for the oppression of women; why emulate it? Male rationality has judged women's mental abilities—as well as their physical abilities—inferior; why emulate it? This questioning is coordinated to an inquiry that Jane Martin has summarized well in her *Reclaiming a Conversation:* "Since the early 1970s, research has documented the ways in which such intellectual disciplines as history and psychology, literature and the fine arts, sociology and biology are biased according to sex. This work has revealed that on at least three counts the disciplines fall short of the ideal of epistemological equality for women: they exclude women from their subject matter, distort the female according to the male image of her, and deny value to characteristics the society considers feminine." The phrase "epistemological equality" does not mean equal participation in male rationality; it means equal acknowledgment for male and female minds, lives, and histories.

The first level of critique launched by feminists from Wollstonecraft to de Beauvoir against the prejudice that women cannot think was launched against the prejudice itself. Once this critique had cleared a space, and once women in large numbers had begun to speak and act in public on "the woman question," its sequel came. Questions were raised, are being raised, about how thinking or reason is thought about. Do the predominant modes of thinking about thinking exclude or suppress not just groups of people but types of activity—that might or might not be specific to those excluded groups? Maybe the definitions of thinking laid down by men—so this critique suggests—exclude what women do. Thus the old feminist question has been re-posed: Do men and women think differently? And the answer to it is: yes. Sometimes now the answer is: yes, and furthermore, women's thinking is *better*. But at any rate, the message of this critique is clear: no longer are women or their thinking to be judged by the standards of male rationality.

When I spoke earlier of the feminist movement's critique reaching to the roots of prejudice and the consequent education of women as philosophers, I did not mean—as must now be obvious—as philosophers in the monistic tradition. I meant as continuers and radicalizers of the reflexive critical mode that has slowly brought the monistic tradition into question. But before I try to continue the story of what this questioning means for women, I want to consider one further crucial intellectual obstacle that the feminist movement's critique has met and tried to overcome. If, as I have claimed, the Mind or Reason has been at the center of religious and philosophical monism, how did women's alleged inferiority come to be associated with her anatomy?

There are many ways to approach this question. Let me choose just one—the broadly historical—as an example. Ever since the Enlightenment, there have been speculations that the era in which Greek philosophy and the Israelite and Zoroastrian religions were born was an era of transition in the eastern Mediterranean from matriarchal to patriarchal societies, from Earth Goddess religions to religions in which male deities or a male deity dominated. Recently, this speculation has intensified and been supported with archaeological evidence and reinterpretations of literary evidence. If this transition did take place, then monistic thought can be seen as male intellectualization triumphant, in the sense that as men placed themselves in rulership over women, they placed the mind in rulership over the body. That is, women became defined by and associated with the body that the mind ruled. Monism, to put the same point differently, involves suppression: for the one to rule, it must rule something other, which is conceived as nonmental—either animally all-body or ethereally extramental, whorish, or saintly.

Such a broad historical speculation is not, in any strict sense, provable, any more than are corollary psychoanalytic speculations about why men began to dominate women and to dominate rationally their own bodies, to regulate their erotic pleasures. The importance of such speculations has been and is that they have helped establish a distinction that is central to feminist critique: the distinction between sex and gender, or between anatomical differences and differences of socialization, education, and political power. Anatomical differences are, so this distinction implies, perennially matters of fact, but, as facts, they are never without valuative interpretation or manipulation; they are never contextless.

The distinction between sex and gender was crucial to Simone de Beauvoir's work. It was she who gave the postwar feminist movement its orienting maxim: Women are not born, but made. But the issue of anatomical difference has not disappeared from the theoretical scene; indeed, it haunts it. Again and again, either in a sexist mode (like contemporary sociobiology) or in a woman-affirming mode, these differences have been brought back as the essential ones and as the sources of mental differences. Women, that is, have been said to have genetic endowments or brain lateralizations productive of mental differences, or an essential, timeless "corporeal ground" (in Adrienne Rich's phrase) productive of mental differences. In the current phase of feminism, each and every way that anatomical difference has been evaluated or "genderized" is up for questioning: do the evaluations reflect or transcend the old forms of male/female, mind/ body hierarchical dualisms? Simone de Beauvoir's own version of the mind/body dualism has been rigorously criticized, particularly insofar as she thought that women, to be free, to be rational, ought to transcend their reproductive capacity and not have children, or insofar as she thought that women who accepted themselves as women, as anatomically female, would desire only other women.

Let me put this development more generally. It has been widely acknowledged that accepting the male/female, mind/body dualisms in a merely reformative spirit, that is, either by reversing the values of the dualisms and elevating female over male and body over mind, or by attributing to females the mind power of males at the expense of their bodies, means foreclosing a deep critique of those dualisms.

When I say that the feminist movement's critique has brought about the education—the beginning of the education—of women as philosophers, I mean that we all, regardless of the terms we use, struggle at this philosophical bedrock. Twentieth-century philosophy, in its most radical modes, has been struggling in a crisis known as "the end of metaphysics." And that means the end of enthrallment by tradition-long metaphysical forms of thought such as the dualistic forms I noted. But what we can see in the last decade is the beginning of a merger of philosophical questioning and feminist questioning. That is, we can also see the very beginning of the education of philosophers as feminists.

Now that the pluralistic reflexive critical tendency within the European tradition and the feminist critique have begun to relate to each other explicitly, many developments are possible. Once the framing dualisms of the tradition are grasped as part of the problem—and we, as critics, are aware that our own critiques are historically bound up with, intertwined with, the very foundational thought forms we wish to criticize—the reconstruction of our history and the envisioning of future possibilities become very rich, complex projects. With what thought forms are you criticizing inherited thought forms?—this is the omnipresent question. It could produce a mire of methodologism and it could produce new feminist factions, but I do not think these are the likely outcomes.

When inherited thought forms are grasped as enthrallments of the imagination, *all* of their ingredients are up for critique. And I think this job will prove too compelling to be reduced to battles over method or to permit rigidification of theoretical and practical experimentation. And, besides, once the European tradition has ceased to enthrall our minds, it and its particularities—the differences of moments within it, the efforts at rebellion or nonconformity it has been laced with—become newly interesting, and so do all of the traditions which it is *not*; in time and space, we can hope that the feminist inquiry will become more global, more comparative, more concrete, more subtle. Minds and bodies, not the mind and the body; men and women, not the male and the female; masculinities and feminities, not the masculine and the feminine; sexualities and genderizations— the plurals will come forward, and the past will be viewed as a resource, not just as a tragedy. We will see, as Adrienne Rich once wrote, "the damage that was done and the treasures that prevail."

*   *   *

It is in this context, or with this hope, that I want to return to the statement with which I began. When we think of ourselves as thinkers, we tend to think of ourselves as selves, I said, as first person singulars, solitaries, interiorities, mental machines.

In our own period of great cultural ferment and contact among diverse peoples—in the period of world wars and, since the Second World War, worldwide shared sense of planetary peril—both the mental monism of the Enlightenment and the mental pluralism of the Enlightenment with its monistic evolutionary bias have been under question. What is at philosophical issue are images of the mind in which one part or function predominates, either structurally or evolutionarily, and (ideally) produces one kind of thought, one kind of truth, one form of rationality.

Within the Western tradition, the critical assault upon such images has come, I think, not just from philosophy proper but from the practice of psychoanalysis. And these two critiques have gained strength from various forms of sociopolitical critique of what Foucault has called "totalizing discourse" that show the exclusionary import of such images; that show how they exclude non-European modes of thought, classes and races not educated in and for rationalism, and, finally, women whose thinking is derided as feminine, irrational.

Let me focus my attention for a moment on the psychoanalytic critical strand. Even though Freud's metapsychological formulations were indebted to, embedded in, traditional divisions of the mind into hierarchically arranged parts as well as to traditional notions of one mental function maturing over time into natural dominance over others, his key insights all point to a new venue. The mind or psyche has structures, but these are in constant interaction; id, ego, and superego are not separate faculties or compartments; they are definable only in dynamic relation to each other. And unconscious, preconscious, and conscious are not like steps going up, each to be left behind as the next is achieved. Our mental processes are, to speak simply, conversational. We are not solitary when we think; we are full of voices.

These voices are representations of both our drives or instincts and their worldly encounters, from the first ones in our parents' care to the most recent, from the early ones with objects and words to the later ones with ranges of others and with our cultural heritage in all its many forms. These voices represent in us all we have desired and all desires we have desired to have or not to have; they represent all the linkages and severances we have made among our desires and all the interpretations of our desiring with which we order ourselves, setting and resetting, repeating and extending, boundaries on the confusing and never entirely lost initial boundarilessness of our natalities. Reason does not rule over instinctual desires in this conception; desires are the reason for reason and reason is the reasoning of desires. Reason without desire is empty, as desire without reason is blind. Even when the two are in tension, in conflict, neither wins.

Freud distinguished between primary unconscious or unarticulated mental processes to which we have very little access and secondary mental processes, conscious processes to which we do have access or of which we are self-conscious. The latter include differentiating, connecting, and categorizing of things, events, words, and also what we generally call thinking. There is, obviously, a dualistic conception here, but primary and secondary processes are not rigidly distinct or hierarchically related in structural or evolutionary terms. Freud made it quite clear that if conscious secondary organizing processes become severed from the primary processes of the unconscious and the desirous id, they are in danger of running unhealthily empty or being actually ruled by the severed-off processes, just as an adulthood, if it is built too firmly upon repressed childhood instincts, is in danger of running into depression, paralysis, or distortion of thinking. Freud himself valued scientific thinking as the most advanced and valuable form of secondary-process thinking, but he was keenly aware that the conversation of primary and secondary processes in, for example, poetry is responsible for poetry's universality and power, just as he was aware that a clinician listens not to secondary-process mentation but to the complex conversation of processes that is free associational speech.

The value of the idea that our mental life with others and with ourselves is conversational—that it is a constant interconnecting of all sorts of representations of our experience and also potentially an extension of our experience as we hear ourselves and others and reflexively interpret ourselves in and through novel conjunctions or conversational moments— the value of this idea is that, if we take this idea seriously, *live* this idea richly, we cannot become what I have called mental monists. And the corollary to this impossibility is that we cannot become prescriptivists of the mental realm.

By these claims I mean several things. First, we cannot assert that any one form or process of mental life is to be cultivated to the exclusion of others or that any one structuring of mental life is absolutely superior. Second, we cannot hope to organize the social world in order to structure the conversation of mental processes, including the conflictual conversations, for our mental life does not reflect directly or reproduce unmediatedly the social world—it is not in any simple way causally related to the social world.

*   *   *

Let me say what these statements imply by returning to the monistic tradition, which, I said, has been questioned within philosophy and by feminist inquiry into the roots of prejudice. Throughout the Western philosophical tradition, since the time of the pre-Socratics, Plato, and Aristotle, we can observe a tendency to establish corollations between images of the mind and ideal images of social-political organization. Plato, for example, asserted that the mind has three parts—reason, spirit, and appetites—and that the ideal *polis* should have three classes—philosopher-kings, guardians, and artisans or laborers. Aristotle asserted that the mind matures over time so that reason actualizes its potential to rule over the irrational parts of the mind, and that city-state organization, analogously, matures over time so that it grows closer to the ideal of a naturally superior male class ruling over inferior men, youths, and, at the bottom of the hierarchy, reasonless women and slaves. In the developed Christian tradition, the mind is ruled by a divine part—the *lumen naturale*—as the creation is ruled by God, and as the state should ideally, by divine right, be ruled by kings. Many variations on these notions have existed, some of which seem to come from introjections into the mind of idealized political arrangements, and some of which seem to be projections of analyses of the mind into visions of ideal political arrangements. At any rate, the philosophical *esprit de systeme* has the effect that images are constructed that protect the hegemony of a part of the mind and also legitimate a mentally superior ruling class or person. Mental monism and legitimations of political domination have mutually supported one another.

With respect to this habit of construction, the idea of our minds as conversations poses two challenges. First, it refuses the hierarchical tendency in the habitual constructions by insisting that all mental structures and processes have their importances relationally but not in relations of, so to speak, unrotating authoritarian rulership. The idea of our minds as conversations is, to use sociopolitical terms, radically democratic, anti-authoritarian; and thus it is no surprise that it should percolate in the philosophical tradition at a moment when radical democracy is an ideal and when forms of authoritarianism have been more cruel than at any other time in history. The image of our minds as conversations is, I think, crucial to progressivism in political theory: it implies that mental and political democracies can be mutually supporting, in accord with the traditional constructing technique but not in accord with the traditional constructions.

But, second, the idea of minds as conversations refuses the homology between mind and sociopolitical organization by insisting that the primary processes of the unconscious do not directly reflect or recapitulate any existing sociopolitical relations and cannot be the basis for envisioning any such sociopolitical relations. Unless you believe that there is such a thing as a collective unconscious, there is no homologue in the sociopolitical sphere for the unconscious and primary processes (though there are certainly processes awaiting an adequate group psychology). And what this means is that the individual lives and the particularities of individual internal conversations of people will always defy political theoretical constructions, even democratic ones, that are prescriptive.

It seems to me that some contemporary feminist visions are continuations of the long habit of constructing idealized sociopolitical forms as corollaries to images of the mind—and vice versa. For example, among those feminists who advocate for the future some form of matriarchy or some form of lesbian nation as the means for overthrowing or separating from patriarchy, there is an assumption that "natural" female thinking or feminine mental virtues are superior and should dominate over male rationality. Thus emotionality, intuition, maternal or nurturing thinking, or even the "primary narcissism" of mother-daughter (or woman-woman) bonds should rule in mental matriarchy, or mental gynarchy. The tradition of corollating mental images and political images is simply turned upside down.

This kind of upside-down construction has been criticized by other feminists, and their main critical approach has been psychoanalysis, because it points to what is left out of such a reversal: the conversation of primary and secondary processes, and, specifically, any appreciation of how the Freudian "discovery" of the unconscious asks us to respect the irreducible differences among us. But the entire habit of construction, I think, also needs philosophical critique, and the education of women as philosophers is the way to such a critique.

Psychoanalytic attention to the conversation of mental process and the general philosophical critique of mental monism that I have been noting as emergent have in common their skepticism toward any form of what Jacqueline Rose has called "utopianism of the psyche." The common caution about such utopianism asks that inversions of traditional habits not replace traditional habits as one ruling group replaces another in a political revolution that stops short of a cultural revolution, a critique of rulership, a change of attitude toward rulership. But even on the level of cultural revolution, this common caution asks that we not assume that social or political changes—for example, changes in the structure of the nuclear family, which is one of the primary locuses for the transmission of patriarchy—imply changes in peoples' psychic structures in any *direct* way. If shared parenting, one of the most frequently advocated social goals, is seen as the way to break up a social syndrome of the reproduction of mothering (in Nancy Chodorow's phrase) and to bring about the autonomy which too much embeddedness in relationship has kept unavailable to women, then this common caution asks that advocates of shared parenting not neglect processes of the psyche that may very well go on in *any* kind of parenting. It does not seem possible, for example, for there to be child rearing without unconscious communication between rearer (male or female) and child, a conversation that would not be conflict free even among angels. This is so (in psychoanalytic terms) both because all children *need* parenting and because we all have in us a plurality of psychic purposes—id purposes, ego purposes, superego purposes—that will conflict to some degree even in the healthiest of us as we outgrow our childhood instinctuality. And it is also so because parents bring their own purposes—often their own narcissistic loves—to the raising of their children. Autonomy is always a struggle—though there is certainly every reason to work toward making it a struggle worth waging.

*   *   *

Let me try to indicate what these reflections on "psychopolitical" constructions imply by beginning again in a different key. The simplest way in which mental monism as a prescriptive ideal translates into our everyday life is apparent, I think, in the goal to which we are so often urged to direct ourselves: we are to seek an "identity."

It seems to me that the quest for identity is particularly strong—in our Western societies at least—among women. It is the self-imposed equivalent of what social rites of passages traditionally have been for males: entrance ways into adulthood, into manhood in the sexual sense, into extra-familial love and work. It marks the need for individuation and autonomy in female terms: the need for definition achieved rather than accepted, chosen rather than enforced, made rather than born. Identity has become, for many women, the personal translation of emancipation: the political *made* personal, not suffered like a decree or a fate.

Our need for identity is our need not to be dictated to, dominated—not to be, as Simone de Beauvoir expressed it, always the Other, to others or to ourselves. The quest for this identity is in many ways laudable in sociopolitical terms. But it seems to me that it can also run contrary to—or involve suppression of—our internal conversations, and especially the unwelcome conflicts in them and the archaic voices in them that are kept (as D. W. Winnicott once put it) "in a state of uncommunication." To put this matter another way: identity—unity, cohesion—at the price of further repression or denial is an achievement awaiting an explosion. It can be a form of mental monism consciously chosen but nonetheless itself exclusionary.

These remarks about prescriptivism could be understood as implying a critique of feminism's sociopolitical emancipatory goals; but I want to make it as clear as I can that this is not what I intend. What I am trying to suggest is that all of the voices or purposes that are our minds must be heard in order for us to achieve not *an* identity but a more communicative form of life—the possibility of conversational reconciling, both in ourselves and with others. This, I take it, is the psychotherapeutic hope: making the unconscious or id voices conscious does not mean eliminating them; it means becoming reconciled to them and allowing them many other ends, a plurality which may include the ends of social and political revolution and which certainly will include the goal of thinking in many modalities. As Anna Freud once put this hope (in an unpublished letter): "What we are actually trying to do in education and in therapy is to sort out the individual's purposes and to make room for ego (reality) and superego (morality) purposes where the individual had felt hopelessly under the sway of id (instinctual) purposes."

The education of women as philosophers that I have been describing and invoking is an educational and therapeutic hope phrased as a conversation with a tradition at the moment of its internal crisis: the unsilencing of its suppressed voices and the breakup of its inhibiting monistic formations. From it will come support for thinking in the very processes that thinking traditionally has been said to transcend, or over which thinking has been said to rule.

*　*　*

At the beginning of this reflection I claimed that, because women find it no easy matter to think at all, given the weight of prejudice against them as thinkers, they are much more aware of (even if not openly acknowledging of) their supporters, those who have encouraged them to do what so much in our tradition holds they cannot or should not do: think. The supportive others, I said, are always there *in our thinking*.

What I meant by this claim is that the exemplary women who have in the past done what was not expected of them have never been entirely absent from our memories or the historical record. Women's history and biography writing are projects to make this heritage more richly and widely known and to recover the parts of it that have been neglected or distorted—often distorted by the kinds of mental habits I have been discussing. These are projects for redressing injustice and for giving our history a foundation that prevents future injustices. But I also meant that we all have in us voices that are supportive. We all have, for example, the voices of our own initial curiosities about the world and about the so-called facts of life, our first efforts at explaining to ourselves such perplexing matters as the origins of ourselves or the origins of our younger siblings. The education of male and female children as "good" children in narrow and often sexist terms, which it is the business of higher education to question, usually consists of dulling this curiosity with moral or rational strictures, not allowing it to meet freely with the "ego (reality) and superego (morality) purposes" that connect us to ourselves and to others. But the original curiosity remains—even if, under the worst circumstance, the curiosity is tyrannizing because distorted or denied. And it can remain as the primary-process spur to and contribution to all future intellectual activity.

Between prohibitions upon childhood questioning and denigrations of women's thinking, there is an obvious link: the assertion of adult power over children and the assertion, by individuals or in the general cultural discourse, of power over women are both forms of obedience training. This link is, I think, what makes the link between psychoanalysis and philosophy so important for our later lives. But between the exemplary women who inhabit our memories and imaginations, and our own curious childhood selves there is also, I think, a link: we turn to exemplary intellectual women with our still-active early desires to know, as well as with our later resurgences of this desire in different forms, including those forms that we have come to feel are obstructed because we are female. We internalize exemplary men and women, and we need "ego ideals" of both sexes, but it is women who were marginalized and continued thinking with whom we associate our own marginalized desires to know.

*   *   *

The culturally transmitted thought forms and habits of construction I have been examining are the intellectual manifestations of obstacles that have deep roots—in our culture and in ourselves. Both restoration of women's voices suppressed in the history of the cultural discourses and restoration of the pluralities of voices inside us that have been threatened with monism in our upbringings and in our encounters with the cultural discourses require analysis of those thought forms and habits of construction. Higher education for women is the outward and visible sign that this analysis is under way, that a cultural revolution is advancing. The inward and spiritual grace of this revolution will take longer—for it is a deeper matter. I have tried to suggest that the education of women as philosophers is the framing of its guiding questions.

College of Letters
Wesleyan University

AN ANALYSIS OF UNIVERSITY DEFINITIONS OF SEXUAL HARASSMENT

PHYLLIS L. CROCKER

This article evaluates definitions of sexual harassment adopted by undergraduate institutions for use in grievance procedures and policy statements.[1] The analysis focuses on three areas: the purpose of these definitions, their range and effect, and ways they can be improved. By scrutinizing the implications and trends in official statements developed by university administrations, we can identify issues for further attention.[2] More questions will be raised than answered; but the preliminary and tentative nature of the conclusions reflect the fact that the full extent and implications of this stubborn, pervasive, and complex problem are still being uncovered.

This analysis is based on taking seriously the academic community's perception that the relationship between student and professor is the key to a satisfying and successful college education. The Yale College Bulletin announces that Yale "presents students with a great breadth of learning and gives them access to scholars who are engaged not only in

Abiding appreciation for their assistance, support, and patience goes to Ruth Borenstein, Anne E. Simon, Kent Harvey, and Catharine A. MacKinnon. The original version of this paper was prepared for L. Miranda and Associates, Bethesda, Maryland.

1. Literature on this general topic of sexual harassment in higher education is compiled in Phyllis L. Crocker, "Annotated Bibliography on Sexual Harassment in Education," *Women's Rights Law Reporter* 7 (Winter 1982): 91–106.

2. This paper will not consider the crucial process of devising a definition of sexual harassment, a process which will influence the university community's acceptance and use of the definition.

This essay originally appeared in *Signs,* vol. 8, no. 4, Summer 1983.

communicating knowledge but also in discovering it."[3] Sexual harassment in education is so abhorrent because this special formative relationship between teacher and student is abused and exploited by professional self-interest in sex and power aggrandizement.[4]

Definitions of sexual harassment are important because they can educate the community and promote discussion and conscientious evaluation of behavior and experience. Students learn that certain experiences are officially recognized as wrong and punishable; professors are put on notice about behaviors that constitute sexual harassment; and administrators shape their understanding of the problem in a way that directs their actions on student inquiries and complaints.[5] A definition can set the tone for the university community's response to sexual harassment. Superficiality of concern can be transparent—either in a definition so restrictive and technical that it prohibits complaints or does not include many women's shared experience of victimization, or in one so vague that it loses its educational value. It is vital that a definition fully and firmly express official scorn and outrage at sexual harassment and that it be accompanied by a policy and grievance procedure which appears to, and can, identify and remedy sexual harassment complaints and punish offenders. Students and faculty will be more inclined to treat the issue seriously if the definition and accompanying procedure signal that the administration is committed to addressing the problem.

No definition will be absolutely complete—it is extremely difficult to encompass every dimension of a problem we are still learning about. Attempting to address the complexity of the issue by introducing elaborate distinctions merely creates an overly legalistic and mechanistic formula that allows for excuses and technical loopholes. A definition should be intended as a guide, not a set of standards for proscribed behavior.

Perhaps, too, no definition will satisfy everyone in the university community: many will be threatened and defensive; others will find it unnecessary, restrictive, silly, even morally offensive; but still others will welcome recognition of an ugly and pervasive problem.[6] The fundamental importance of any definition is that it challenges many assumptions that have flourished in academia (and in the rest of society) for a

3. *Bulletin of Yale University* (New Haven, Conn.: Yale University, 1980), p. 13.

4. This argument underlies the legal consideration of sexual harassment in education. Alexander et al. v. Yale University, 459 F. Supp. 1 (D. Conn. 1977), affirmed 631 F.2d 178 (2d Cir. 1980). See also Phyllis L. Crocker and Anne E. Simon, "Sexual Harassment in Education," *Capital University Law Review* 10 (1981): 541–84.

5. This analysis focuses on sexual harassment of women students by male faculty (including administrative personnel). Sexual harassment of students by students is a widespread problem that can severely damage and restrict a student's educational opportunities. When ignored, it is a backhanded way of allowing the denigration of women students to continue while claiming concern for stopping it.

6. These differences in response raise the question whether any definition could ever equally and fairly address the concerns of all groups, and if not, why not.

long time. What is now being defined as illegal and/or unethical has been taken for granted, considered acceptable, and even thought of as liberating, therapeutic, educational, or a right of status.

How then do universities define and categorize the experience of abuse? At present, a wide range of definitions exists, from the restrictive guidelines of the American Psychological Association—which condemn "deliberate or repeated comments, gestures, or physical contacts of a sexual nature that are unwanted by the recipient"[7]—to the broad guidelines of the National Advisory Council on Women's Educational Programs—which prohibit "the use of authority to emphasize the sexuality or sexual identity of a student in a manner which prevents or impairs that student's full enjoyment of educational benefits, climate, or opportunities."[8] A number of colleges have adopted the definition of sexual harassment promulgated by Yale in 1979: "An attempt to coerce an unwilling person into a sexual relationship, to subject a person to unwanted attention, or to punish a refusal to comply. . . . [This includes] a wide range of behavior from actual coercing of sexual relations to the forcing of sexual attentions, verbal or physical, on an unwilling recipient."[9]

Recently, many colleges and universities (e.g., Rutgers University, Cornell University, and the universities of Minnesota and Wisconsin) have adapted the Equal Employment Opportunity Commission guidelines on sexual harassment in employment:

> Unwelcome sexual advances, requests for sexual favors, and other verbal or physical conduct of a sexual nature constitute sexual harassment when:
> 1. Submission to such conduct is made either explicitly or implicitly a term or condition of an individual's employment or admission to an academic program,
> 2. Submission to or rejection of such conduct is used as the basis for decisions affecting an individual's employment status or academic standing, or
> 3. Such conduct has the purpose or effect of substantially interfering with an individual's performance on the job or in the classroom, or creating an intimidating, hostile, or offensive work or study environment.[10]

7. "Ethical Principles of Psychologists," *American Psychologist* 6 (June 1981): 633–38. The section "Professional Relationships" is applicable to clients, supervisees, students, employees, and research participants.

8. Frank Till, *Sexual Harassment: A Report on the Sexual Harassment of Students* (Washington, D.C.: National Advisory Council on Women's Educational Programs, 1981), p. 7.

9. The University of Delaware, University of California at Santa Cruz, Brown University, and Tulane University all follow Yale's definition. The definitions discussed in the text will not be separately cited. All references are current as of February 1981. Copies of grievance procedures are available directly from the institutions.

10. The Equal Employment Opportunity Commission guidelines were adopted on

All these definitions have two positive and critical features in common: they recognize a wide range of behavior and experiences as sexual harassment and they acknowledge a potentially broad impact and effect on victims. The first part of this analysis will examine each of these aspects in light of the ways in which definitions name and identify women's experiences, codify violations, warn potential perpetrators, and promote community consciousness. The second section will consider the limiting and potentially dangerous aspects of these definitions.

* * *

The variety of behaviors defined as sexual harassment by Rutgers University includes "unwelcome sexual advances, requests for sexual favors, and other verbal or physical conduct of a sexual nature"; Yale delineates a continuum from "actual coercing of sexual relations, to the forcing of sexual attentions, verbal or physical." Stating a range of occurrences is valuable: it makes faculty aware of a broad spectrum of actions for which they are accountable (not just one or two specific acts); it alerts students that they do not have to tolerate a number of different experiences; and it officially acknowledges the fact that abuses ranging from verbal comments to rape can occur and have a damaging impact.[11]

It is critical to recognize initially that sexual harassment includes nonphysical actions such as sexually suggestive comments; it is not limited to pinches, pats, leers, or grabs. As current statistics document, verbal advances and statements about physical appearance constitute the most frequent types of sexual harassment.[12] Individual students can also

---

November 10, 1980, and published in the Code of Federal Regulations, vol. 29, sec. 1604.11. The use of these guidelines implies that relationships in employment and education are the same, that an employer and employee interact just as a professor and student do. This assumption needs to be carefully examined.

11. One effect of defining a range of types of sexual harassment is to distinguish between actions immediately identifiable as wrong and those which must be evaluated in context. However, all attempts by the university to classify "objectively" the seriousness of an offense or limit the victim's experience simply add to and reinforce the original injury. Fundamentally, sexual harassment is an expression of a teacher's disregard and disrespect for a woman's intellectual development and integrity. The moment a professor leers, pinches, or requests any sexual "favor" the student is injured; their relationship is damaged irreversibly. The student is told, in no uncertain terms, that the professor is interested in her body and in his sexual gratification, not in her academic or intellectual growth. The injury is compounded by any subsequent negative impact on the student's academic performance or on any evaluation of the student by the professor.

12. Donna Benson and Gregg Thomson, "Sexual Harassment on a University Campus: The Confluence of Authority Relations, Sexual Interest, and Gender Stratification," *Social Problems* 29 (February 1982): 236–52; Kenneth Wilson and Linda Kraus, "Sexual Harassment in the University" (Greenville, N.C.: East Carolina University, Department of Sociology and Anthropology, 1981, Mimeographed).

be sexually harassed by derogatory remarks that a professor makes to a group of students (e.g., in the classroom).

All universities readily agree on the most egregious abuse of power, influence, and authority. Yale defines it as "coerced sexual relations or punishing a refusal to comply." Stanford University states that "coercive behavior with suggestions of reprisals or rewards that will follow the refusal or granting of sexual favors constitutes gross misconduct and need happen only once." While statistics thus far indicate that rape and threats of retaliation are the least frequently reported forms of sexual harassment on campus, these figures also clearly document that such offenses occur, probably more frequently than many are ready to accept.[13] By clearly and adamantly condemning this conduct, university administrations can refuse to allow the issue of sexual harassment to be trivialized. If there is official agreement that sexual harassment includes behavior already culturally identified as reprehensible, then charges cannot be easily dismissed as the grumblings of dissatisfied students. A serious problem with the conceptualizations noted above, however, is the relationship of rape to threats of retaliation: in Yale's guidelines, threatening behavior is labeled as serious an abuse as rape; in Stanford's rape is either outside the category of the "most serious" violations or included only if accompanied by a verbal threat. The implication is that rape without threats is a *lesser* offense than verbal threats without rape. Additional dangers inherent in the view that threats are the only clear-cut forms of sexual harassment will be discussed below.

In addition to specifying a range of punishable behaviors, these definitions also recognize the effect harassment has apart from its specific influence on a grade or a recommendation. For example, Rutgers University's guidelines state that sexual harassment "has the purpose *or effect* of substantially interfering with individual performance . . . or of *creating an intimidating, hostile or offensive work or study environment*" (my emphasis). Stanford refers to "repeated and unwanted sexual behavior which *adversely affects the working or learning environment*" (my emphasis). The inclusion of these phrases indicates a critical recognition that harassment can, whether intended or not, affect not only one student's relationship to one professor, but her relationship to and performance in all her academic studies.[14] Yet the wording of the Rutgers definition leads one to question who will judge what constitutes "substantial" interference. While a definition need not provide a clear answer, the qualifying words are cause for concern. The term "substantial" implies that a standard exists by which a victim's perception of interference can be

13. Benson and Thomson; Wilson and Kraus estimate that 53,169 women are victims of physical assault by their professors each year.
14. Benson and Thomson; Till (n. 8 above); Linda Kraus, "A Situational Analysis of Sexual Harassment in Academia" (M.A. thesis, East Carolina University, 1981).

evaluated—and that the standard is a nonvictim's perception of the same incident or experience. But what does that mean for a sexually harassed student who must measure the degree of interference? Does it mean that there is an "acceptable" level of interference—to be determined by someone who does not know the pain, humiliation, fear, and loss of self-confidence and integrity so commonly felt by women who have been sexually harassed? What if the effect of an event that disrupted her education is judged to be trivial? Who determines how "substantial" the impact on her must be? While close attention to one qualifying word may seem unwarranted, its presence in the definition at least calls for an investigation into the reasons for its inclusion.

Potentially, the behavior of one professor toward a group of students is sexual harassment if it creates an "intimidating, hostile or offensive work or study environment" that affects individual performance. A professor's use of "jokes," sexual allusions, and pornographic "anatomy" pictures[15] in the classroom often constitutes this type of abuse. The damage of such group-directed harassment must not be underestimated.[16] While this form of harassment is not a one-on-one personal assault or affront to a student, it serves to undermine her intellectual integrity just as effectively.

The question of whether "sexist remarks" are sexual harassment has generated great controversy. In order to resolve the controversy it is necessary to focus proper attention on the twisted logic underlying the common charge, "she can't take a joke." The perniciousness of the requirement that women at least tolerate public degrading remarks by professors is particularly evident in Tulane University's requirement that "conduct be grossly objectionable to most students and faculty" before it can qualify as sexual harassment.[17] This provision both discredits and belittles the experience of every woman who must endure an offensive remark and the laughter that follows. It is also another instance in which the standard of offense is determined not by the victim but by the majority of nonvictims. The challenge of addressing the full ramifications of the problem of sexual harassment requires not only a perspective based on the victim's point of view but, more fundamentally, a perspective that questions why the "joke" is funny and why a woman should have to "take it" in the first place.

Whenever the issue of sexual harassment is raised, fears are voiced that the university is attempting to legislate morality, to prohibit mutu-

15. Melinda Chateauvert, "A Study of Sexual Harassment and Students: An Analysis of Status, Conditions, and Effects" (Iowa City: University of Iowa, 1981, Mimeographed).

16. Tentative hypotheses about this are found in Wilson and Kraus; Till; and Debbie Lewis, Anna DiStefano, and Jane Levin, "A Report on Sexual Harassment at Washington University" (St. Louis, Mo.: Washington University, 1981, Mimeographed).

17. This is even more outrageous if one considers the mere percentage of male and female students and faculty—particularly in specific courses or departments.

ally satisfying relationships, or even to restrict legitimate student-mentor relationships. However, the underlying criterion in all definitions is that the sexual behavior, conduct, or verbal advances in question be *unwanted*. Occasionally universities address these fears in a forthright and instructive manner as in this statement by the University of California, Santa Cruz: "This code expressly prohibits only unreciprocated and unwelcome relationships, but persons in positions of power/authority/ control over others should be aware of and sensitive to problems which may arise from those relationships which are apparently mutual. Given the pervasiveness and depth of sexism in both men and women, such relationships often involve dynamics which extend far beyond simple mutual attraction. Thus, individuals are urged to examine such relationships before engaging in them especially in terms of emotional health, self-esteem, and respect for the independence of the persons involved."

It is important for more college communities to confront the complexities of the issue of consenting relationships between professors and students. University officials must recognize the fact that these relationships occur, as well as the fact that there is the potential for reprisals when a relationship ends. A related, equally valid consideration is the effect on and perception of other students who believe that favors may be wrongly granted because of such a relationship.

* * *

All the definitions presented in this analysis have limitations and dangerous implications, which is not especially surprising given the current level of knowledge about sexual harassment and the brief period in which universities have been constructively addressing the problem. This section will focus on three central concerns: the use of specific terminology in the definitions, the interpretations of the "most serious" type of harassment, and the concern for protecting academic freedom of speech and action.

The terminology used in a definition to describe the victim's experience and the perpetrator's behavior in an incident of sexual harassment influences the effectiveness of that definition in educating the community and punishing offenders. A number of catch words are often used to describe the victim's response to or view of the acts: "inappropriate," "unwanted," and "unwelcome." In one sense this is the terminology that defines harassment as such—actions and words that are not expected, appreciated, desired, or wanted. On the other hand, its use raises a question: Can there be freely wanted, welcome, or appropriate leers, requests for sexual favors, kisses, or pinches, given a student's dependence on a professor for everything from grades to psychological and professional support? This is first a question of propriety: "It is, for instance, seen as wrong . . . for an athlete to be living with the referee of the events in which the athlete competes, a litigant to be romantically involved with a judge trying the case."[18] Why then is it possibly appropriate in the field of education? Second, it is a question that forces us to consider the society we live in, one in which women are taught that they are valued and judged foremost by their looks and sexuality, in which women are told that they should want (and need) to be sexually desirable to men, and in which men are taught to view women sexually and to be sexually aggressive. What then is the meaning of the word "unwanted" when social roles essentially dictate the behavior as normal, standard, and to be expected? The inclusion of the qualifying words "unwelcome," "unwanted," and "inappropriate" suggests that there are "appropriate" sexual advances, or "wanted" sexual advances that do not constitute harassment and will not be acted upon by university officials.[19] In certain respects, the use of these words betrays the seriousness of the offense because, in a significant way, any verbal or physical advance places the student in a high-risk, treacherous position.

The seriousness of the offense is also minimized by the use of words such as "coercion," "force," and "submission" to characterize the form or style of harassment. While they clearly and accurately convey the lack of reciprocity involved in sexual harassment, there is an underlying suggestion that, without these characteristics, the behavior could possibly be acceptable. Yet if one fully considers the dependence of the student on the professor, it becomes clear that little or no overt force is necessary in order for the implications to be accurately felt.

Similarly, the words "deliberate," "intentional," and "repeated" as used in the American Psychological Association, Duke, and Stanford definitions potentially allow for extreme laxity in preventing, correcting, or punishing sexual harassment. These words imply that there could be a nondeliberate sexual suggestion or an unintentional kiss which would not constitute sexual harassment. Furthermore, how many times must an ass be grabbed, breasts stared at, or invitations to discuss a paper over drinks be made before a student is within her definitional rights to claim and seek redress for sexual harassment?

All of these qualifying and descriptive words allow for excuses and

18. Kenneth S. Pope, Leslie R. Schover, and Hanna Levenson, "Sexual Behavior between Clinical Supervisors and Trainees: Implications for Professional Standards," *Professional Psychology* 11 (February 1980): 157–62, esp. 159.

19. Perhaps a more informative approach is to ask whether any act of sexual harassment is truly ignorable. It should be quite obvious that a student's complaint about a professor's behavior indicates that it was not wanted. The view that the student's "consent" at the time of the sexual advance means that she was not then, and is not now, sexually harassed essentially substitutes the judgment of the perpetrator for the judgment of the student in defining the injury. A related question is, Who defines how a student must say no or indicate refusal or discomfort? Or, why must a student make an explicit refusal for the aggressor to believe that she does not consent?

loopholes—"I didn't think it was sexual harassment," or "I didn't mean anything by it." Given historical and present conditions, it might be understandable that an individual professor would maintain these practices and attitudes. But how long should this behavior be allowed and condoned by university policy? Sexual harassment is not simply committing an act on a list of proscribed behavior, it is the expression of an absence of decency, integrity, and professionalism and the substitution of attitudes of sexism instead. To encourage greater understanding of the problem of sexual harassment, a definition should aid, not obscure, the identification of the attitudinal dimensions behind offensive behavior.

A second area of concern is the implication of labeling as "most serious" those situations involving a threat of, or an actual form of, retaliation or punishment for sexual refusal. There are two major problems with this conception of "serious" sexual harassment: either it suggests that the "fuck or flunk" model is more coercive and damaging than the "A for a lay" model, or it places a requirement that a verbal suggestion be made (regardless of whether it promises reward or punishment). In either case rape is again excluded from the "most serious" category, either because it is clearly more severe, or because institutions do not want to admit that it happens. Both alternatives minimize and potentially deny the seriousness and destructiveness of propositions or advances made without express articulation of threats or punishments or without actual acts of punishment. Underlying this thinking is an assumption that the true offense is punishing or threatening to punish a student who refuses a sexual advance—that suggesting a reward is either not the same or not at issue. This sentiment is expressed by Richard Taylor: "Of course the feeling would be different if any professor offered, not a favor but a threat. . . . This any student would plainly see as coercion, and any professor who attempted it would surely risk losing his tenure."[20]

This attitude suggests that an offer of rewards for sexual "favors" is not so harmful, that no one gains or loses if the offer is declined. This ignores that every "promise of reward" can easily turn into a "punishment for refusal" after a sexual advance is made. Once a student is propositioned, all her future interactions with, and evaluations by, the professor are tainted and suspect, whether a promise or threat was ever made or carried out. Furthermore, by minimizing or trivializing the impact of reward—as opposed to punishment—a definition creates a distinction that has little or no relationship to the effect on a student. Yet note that the National Advisory Council observed, "Where grades are the currency of barter, the attempt to engage a student in an act of what

20. Richard Taylor, "Within the Halls of Ivy—The Sexual Revolution on Campus," *Change* 4 (May/June 1981): 23–29, esp. 28.

may be viewed as prostitution is perhaps less raw than an approach on the street involving money, but it is often all the more harmful for its setting."[21]

By insisting on a verbal articulation of a threat or actual punishment, a definitional structure leaves a vast area of harassment potentially uncovered. Whether the bargain is spelled out or not, the student can never freely choose to say yes or no; the fear of reprisal is inherent in the sexual advance. This becomes particularly troublesome when, as in the Rutgers definition, different standards are applied to instances of sexual harassment concerning "employment or admission to academic programs" and to those concerning "decisions affecting academic standing." In the first category, submission must be "explicitly or implicitly" a term or condition for employment or admission if an advance is to be judged sexual harassment; in the second category, submission or rejection must actually be used as the basis for decision making. The problem here is twofold. First, threats, punishments, and myriad other forms of reprisals are present and feared whether they are explicit or implicit. The harm is done to the student in either case. This is less of a problem, however, than the additional requirement that the student's response to an act of harassment actually or directly affect a decision concerning her academic standing. The implication is that without the external additional harm, sexual harassment either did not occur or is not "serious." Yet, whether a threat is ever carried out is frequently irrelevant in regard to the damage done to the student. The injury to her remains, even if she does not experience inappropriate grades or lose the opportunity to participate in a select seminar.[22] The loss of confidence, the fear of pursuing one's studies with the only person in the department in one's field, are no less real or destructive if the threat is not actualized.

Another matter of concern is the great heed given to claims that prohibitions of sexual harassment infringe on academic freedom of speech. Two universities discuss this issue. Tulane University warns that caution is necessary "in order to set a general standard for judging complaints or sexual harassment without infringing upon freedom of speech or imposing individual standards of propriety upon the community." The University of Minnesota elaborates: "Just as the university is committed to securing for its students and staff a safe environment, one free of sexual harassment, it is equally committed to maintaining academic freedom, to protecting the personal beliefs of students and

21. Till (n. 8 above), p. 16.
22. This issue is particularly relevant since most grievance procedures emphasize that a student's situation can be remedied without sanctioning the professor. These procedures erroneously assume that, if there is no changeable, tangible damage, there is no appropriate relief. They also appear to assume that, if there is no tangible damage, there is no injury (see n. 11 above).

staff and to protecting the expression of those beliefs. Conduct that falls within the protection of academic freedom does not constitute sexual harassment."

The argument that punishing sexual harassment inhibits professors' freedom of speech is most often raised to defend established practice or to rebuff the seriousness of victims' claims. Certainly, the matter needs careful thought and appreciation, but it should not be allowed to function as a means of silencing legitimate discussion of and claims about sexual harassment. One approach to this topic is "to view this problem as one that involves a potential conflict of rights. . . . It seems reasonable and indeed may be necessary for faculty and administrators to ask *which group is hurt more if its right is denied?*" (my emphasis).[23] The key questions are, Who defines sexual harassment and from what point of view? Who is really threatened and hurt by sexual harassment? Who has the most to lose? Whose rights are more protected when administrators staunchly defend "freedom of speech"? These questions become especially acute when coupled with the inescapable fact that university administrations have a strong scholarly and financial investment in their professors—particularly well respected and tenured ones. This issue of academic freedom of speech is not merely theoretical; the interplay between protection of faculty rights and the protection of vested interests is not lost on students who deserve and are entitled to an education free of sexual harassment.

* * *

Given the inadequacies, limitations, and dangers of the existing university definitions of sexual harassment analyzed here, the crucial questions are: How can these definitions be improved? What areas need more attention? What issues need recognition?

A definition must be flexible and it must be designed from the victim's perspective. The National Advisory Council definition is an example of a broadly conceived statement. The most significant aspect of this approach is the clear sense that the victim's experience of harassment must inform the university's attitude. Since the purpose of identifying the issue at all (aside from the question of legal liability) is to assist students who are sexually harassed, it only adds insult to their injury to ignore or deny their perceptions, their feelings about the incident, and all subsequent academic and emotional consequences. Again, the National Advisory Council's work is instructive. In their "Call for Information," in order to develop a more accurate victim-based definition from

23. Phyllis Franklin et al., *Sexual and Gender Harassment in the Academy: A Guide for Faculty, Students, and Administrators* (New York: Modern Language Association of America, 1981), p. 24.

the responses, they did not offer a definition of sexual harassment. "This approach permitted the problem to define itself and avoid limited responses to fit any particular bias or ideology." They found that "respondents described a wider range of incidents as sexual harassment than most existing definitions permit."[24] If university administrators are indeed serious about eradicating sexual harassment, they cannot afford to ignore this lesson.

Consideration of an area not covered by any existing definition clarifies the need for expanded and victim-based definitions. A particularly invidious manifestation of sexual harassment is the requirement that certain "select" students read and/or translate pornographic and/or extremely graphic and embarrassing materials as part of their classroom assignments. Is this verbal or physical harassment? Where is, and who draws, the line on academic freedom to decide literature assignments? Who will judge how "grossly objectionable" the material is?

Women Organized against Sexual Harassment (WOASH) at the University of California at Berkeley has proposed four basic requirements that can serve as a useful guide in further development of definitions. All guidelines must: (1) acknowledge sexual harassment as sex discrimination, not as isolated misconduct; (2) refer to a full range of harassment from subtle innuendos to assault; (3) refer to ways in which the context of open and mutual academic exchange is polluted by sexual harassment; and (4) refer to sexual harassment as the imposition of sexual advances by a person in a position of authority.[25] These categories cover the vital components of a definition. To be effective it should (1) recognize the legal basis for university action and reflect an analytic perspective that places the problem in social context and does not isolate the individuals involved; (2) recognize the need for and value of specific examples that suggest, but do not limit, the range of behaviors and experiences to be considered; (3) recognize the importance of this issue for the integrity of the academic community; and (4) recognize the central fact that sexual harassment occurs between people who have unequal power.

By bearing in mind these four areas, we can devise and incorporate into the fabric of academic life definitions that better serve the entire community. Of course, the effectiveness of any definition will depend not only on the grievance procedure that enforces it but also on the commitment of the university administration and faculty to creating a truly nondiscriminatory environment for all students.

Northeastern University Law School

24. Till (n. 8 above), p. 6.
25. Women Organized against Sexual Harassment, "Conditions for a Title IX Grievance Procedure" (Berkeley: University of California, 1981).

CHANGING THE CURRICULUM IN HIGHER EDUCATION

MARGARET L. ANDERSEN

In Susan Glaspell's short story, "A Jury of Her Peers," a man is murdered, strangled in his bed with a rope. The victim's wife, Mrs. Wright, formerly Minnie Foster, has been arrested for the crime. The men investigating—the sheriff, the county attorney, and a friend—think she is guilty but cannot imagine her motive. "It's all perfectly clear, except the reason for doing it. But you know juries when it comes to women. If there was some definite thing—something to make a story about. A thing that would connect up with this clumsy way of doing it," the county attorney says.[1]

This essay has been developed through the many discussions I have had with people working in women's studies curriculum projects around the country. I am particularly grateful for having been able to participate in the Mellon seminars at the Wellesley College Center for Research on Women. Although I cannot name all of the participants in these seminars, their collective work and thought continuously enriches my thinking and teaching; I thank them all. I especially thank Peggy McIntosh, director of these seminars, for her inspiration and ongoing support for this work. She, Valerie Hans, Sandra Harding, and the anonymous *Signs* reviewers provided very helpful reviews of the earlier drafts of this essay. And I appreciate the support of the Provost's Office of the University of Delaware for providing the funds for a curriculum revision project in women's studies at the University of Delaware; working with the participants in this project contributed much to the development of this essay.
[1] Susan Glaspell, "A Jury of Her Peers," in *The Best American Short Stories*, ed. Edward J. O'Brien (Boston: Houghton Mifflin Co., 1916), 371–83.

This essay originally appeared in *Signs*, vol. 12, no. 2, Winter 1987.

When the three men go to the Foster house to search for evidence, two of their wives go along to collect some things for the jailed Minnie Foster. In the house the men laugh at the women's attention to Minnie's kitchen and tease them for wondering about the quilt she was making. While the women speculate about whether she was going to quilt it or knot it, the men, considering this subject trivial, belittle the women for their interest in Minnie's handwork. "Nothing here but kitchen things," the sheriff says. "But would the women know a clue if they did come upon it?" the other man scoffs.[2] The three men leave the women in the kitchen while they search the rest of the house for important evidence.

While in the kitchen, the women discover several things amiss. The kitchen table is wiped half-clean, left half messy. The cover is left off a bucket of sugar, while beside it sits a paper bag only half filled with sugar. Mrs. Hale and Mrs. Peters see that one block of the quilt Minnie Foster was making is sewn very badly, while the other blocks have fine and even stitches. They wonder, "What was she so nervous about?" When they find an empty bird cage, its door hinge torn apart, they try to imagine how such anger could have erupted in an otherwise bleak and passionless house. Remembering Minnie Foster, Mrs. Hale recalls, "She—come to think of it, she was kind of like a bird herself. Real sweet and pretty, but kind of timid and—fluttery. How—she—did—change."[3] When the women pick up her sewing basket, they find in it Minnie's dead canary wrapped in a piece of silk, its neck snapped and broken. They realize they have discovered the reason Minnie Foster murdered her husband. Imagining the pain in Minnie Foster's marriage to Mr. Wright, Mrs. Hale says, "No, Wright wouldn't like the bird, a thing that sang. She used to sing. He killed that too."[4]

Soon the men return to the kitchen, but the women have tacitly agreed to say nothing of what they have found. Still mocking the women's attentiveness to kitchen details, the men tease them. The county attorney asks, "She was going to—what is it you call it, Ladies?" "We call it, knot it, Mr. Henderson."[5]

"Knot it," also alluding to the method of murder, is a punning commentary on the relative weights of men's and women's knowledge in the search for facts and evidence. Women's culture—"not it" to the men—is invisible, silenced, trivialized, and wholly ignored in men's construction of reality. At the same time, men's culture is assumed to present the entire and only truth.[6]

[2] Ibid., 376.
[3] Ibid., 381.
[4] Ibid., 383.
[5] Ibid., 385.
[6] Building from Simone de Beauvoir's work, Catherine MacKinnon discusses this point. De Beauvoir writes, "Representation of the world, like the world itself, is the work of men;

Glaspell's story suggests the social construction of knowledge in a gender-segregated world. In her story, women's understandings and observations are devalued and women are excluded from the search for truth. How might the truth look different, we are asked, were women's perspectives included in the making of facts and evidence? What worlds do women inhabit and how do their worlds affect what they know and what is known about them?

The themes of Glaspell's story are at the heart of women's studies, since women's studies rests on the premise that knowledge in the traditional academic disciplines is partial, incomplete, and distorted because it has excluded women. In the words of Adrienne Rich, "As the hitherto 'invisible' and marginal agent in culture, whose native culture has been effectively denied, women need a reorganization of knowledge, of perspectives and analytical tools that can help us know our foremothers, evaluate our present historical, political, and personal situation, and take ourselves seriously as agents in the creation of a more balanced culture."[7] Women's studies was born from this understanding and over the past two decades has evolved with two goals: to build knowledge and a curriculum in which women are agents of knowledge and in which knowledge of women transforms the male-centered curriculum of traditional institutions.[8] Curriculum change through women's studies is, as Florence Howe has said, both developmental and transformative: it is developmental in generating new scholarship about women and transformative in its potential to make the traditional curriculum truly coeducational.[9]

Since women have been excluded from the creation of formalized knowledge, to include women means more than just adding women into existing knowledge or making them new objects of knowledge. Throughout this essay, including women refers to the complex process of redefining knowledge by making women's experiences a primary subject for knowledge, conceptualizing women as active agents in the creation of knowledge, including women's perspectives on knowledge, looking at gender as

---

they describe it from their own point of view which they confuse with the absolute truth" (cited in MacKinnon, 537). MacKinnon continues the point by saying that "men create the world from their own point of view which then becomes the truth to be described." As a result, the male epistemological stance is one that is ostensibly objective and uninvolved and does not comprehend its own perspective; it does not take itself as subject but makes an object of all else it looks at. See Catherine MacKinnon, "Feminism, Marxism, Method, and the State: An Agenda for Theory," *Signs: Journal of Women in Culture and Society* 7, no. 3 (Spring 1982): 515–44, esp. 537.

[7] Adrienne Rich, "Toward a Woman-centered University," in *On Lies, Secrets, and Silence* (New York: W. W. Norton & Co., 1979), 141.

[8] Betty Schmitz, *Integrating Women's Studies into the Curriculum* (Old Westbury, N.Y.: Feminist Press, 1985).

[9] Florence Howe, *Myths of Coeducation* (Bloomington: Indiana University Press, 1984).

fundamental to the articulation of knowledge in Western thought, and seeing women's and men's experiences in relation to the sex/gender system. Because this multifaceted understanding of "including women in the curriculum" is an integral part of the new scholarship on women and because we have not developed language sufficient to reflect these assumptions, readers should be alert to the fact that phrases like "scholarship on women," "including women," and "learning about women" are incomplete but are meant to refer to the multidimensional reconstruction of knowledge.

Women's studies has developed from feminists' radical critique of the content and form of the academic disciplines, the patriarchal structure of education, the consciousness education reproduces, and the relation of education to dominant cultural, economic, political, and social institutions. Women's studies seeks to make radical transformations in the systems and processes of knowledge creation and rests on the belief that changing what we study and know about women will change women's and men's lives.[10] Hence, curriculum change is understood as part of the political transformation of women's role in society because all teaching includes political values. As Florence Howe has written,

> In the broadest context of that word, teaching is a political act: some person is choosing, for whatever reasons, to teach a set of values, ideas, assumptions, and pieces of information, and in so doing, to omit other values, ideas, assumptions, and pieces of information. If all those choices form a pattern excluding half the human race, that is a political act one can hardly help noticing. To omit women entirely makes one kind of political statement; to include women as a target for humor makes another. To include women with seriousness and vision, and with some attention to the perspective of women as a hitherto subordinate group is simply another kind of political act. Education is the kind of political act that controls destinies, gives some persons hope for a particular kind of future, and deprives others even of ordinary expectations for work and achievement.[11]

This discussion raises important questions about how we define women's studies in the future and how, especially in this conservative political period,[12] the radicalism of women's studies can be realized within

    [10] Marilyn J. Boxer, "For and About Women: The Theory and Practice of Women's Studies in the United States," *Signs* 7, no. 3 (Spring 1982): 661–95.

    [11] Howe, 282–83.

    [12] Deborah Rosenfelt, "What Women's Studies Programs Do That Mainstreaming Can't," in "Special Issue: Strategies for Women's Studies in the 80s," ed. Gloria Bowles, *Women's Studies International Forum* 7, no. 4 (1984): 167–75.

institutions that remain racist and sexist and integrally tied to the values and structures of a patriarchal society. But, as Susan Kirschner and Elizabeth Arch put it, women's studies and inclusive curriculum projects are "two important pieces of one work."[13] Feminists in educational institutions will likely continue working for both women's studies and curriculum change, since both projects seek to change the content and form of the traditional curriculum[14] and to contribute to social change through curriculum transformation. It is simply impossible, as Howe has put it, "to move directly from the male-centered curriculum to what I have described as 'transformation' of that curriculum into a changed and co-educational one—without passing through some form of women's studies."[15]

Building an inclusive curriculum

Peggy McIntosh estimates that since 1975 there have been at least eighty projects that, in various ways, examine how the disciplines can be redefined and reconstructed to include us all.[16] This estimate gives some idea of the magnitude of the movement to create new curricula that include women. Moreover, according to McIntosh, although fewer projects are now being funded through sources external to the institutions that house them, internal funding for such projects seems to be increasing.

Curriculum-change projects in women's studies have varied widely in their purposes, scope, institutional contexts, and sources of funding. For example, projects at Wheaton College and Towson State University (both funded through the Fund for the Improvement of Post Secondary Education [FIPSE]) are university-wide projects engaging faculty in the revision of courses across the curriculum. Other projects involve consortia of several campuses, such as those at Montana State University, the Southwest

[13] Susan Kirschner and Elizabeth C. Arch, " 'Transformation' of the Curriculum: Problems of Conception and Deception," in Bowles, ed. 149–51.

[14] Florence Howe, "Feminist Scholarship: The Extent of the Revolution," in *Liberal Education and the New Scholarship on Women: Issues and Constraints in Institutional Change: A Report of the Wingspread Conference*, ed. Anne Fuller (Washington, D.C.: Association of American Colleges, 1981), 5–21.

[15] Howe, *Myths of Coeducation*, 280.

[16] The 1985 directory of such projects from the Wellesley College Center for Research on Women is reprinted in Schmitz. Although such a directory is quickly outdated, it is useful for seeing the diversity of projects that have been undertaken on different campuses across the country, as well as by professional associations. *Women's Studies Quarterly* periodically publishes reports from various projects; see vol. 11 (Summer 1983) and vol. 13 (Summer 1985). See also Peggy McIntosh, "The Study of Women: Processes of Personal and Curriculum Re-vision," *Forum* 6 (April 1984): 2–4; this issue of *Forum* and the vol. 4 (October 1981) issue of *Forum* also contain descriptions of curriculum-change projects on twenty-six campuses. *Forum* is available from the Association of American Colleges, 1818 R Street N.W., Washington D.C. 20009.

Institute for Research on Women (SIROW) at the University of Arizona, and the University of Massachusetts—Amherst.

The SIROW project has several dimensions, including course development and revision at the University of Arizona and a three-year project for integrating women into international studies and foreign language courses at several universities in Arizona and Colorado. Funded by the Women's Educational Equity Act program (WEEA), the Montana State project began as a two-year faculty development project intended to reduce bias in the curriculum; it was later renamed the Northern Rockies Program on Women and was expanded to develop curriculum resources in a twenty-five school consortium in Montana, Utah, Wyoming, and Idaho. The project "Black Studies/Women's Studies: An Overdue Partnership," funded by FIPSE, includes faculty from the University of Massachusetts, Smith College, Hampshire College, Mount Holyoke College, and Amherst College; twenty-nine faculty from this project met to create new courses and build theoretical and curricular connections between black studies and women's studies. The Mellon seminars at the Wellesley College Center for Research on Women, funded through the Andrew W. Mellon Foundation, have drawn together faculty from the New England area to apply feminist scholarship to curriculum transformation.

At the University of Delaware, the university provided funds for a development project for faculty in the social sciences who were revising introductory and core courses to make them inclusive of gender and race; faculty in the project met in an interdisciplinary faculty seminar on feminist scholarship, followed by a day-long conference on curriculum change and a one-year program for visiting consultants who gave public lectures and advised faculty on the reconstruction of their courses. The Women's Research and Resource Center at Spelman College, funded by the Ford Foundation, has emphasized curriculum revision in freshmen courses in English, world literature, and world civilization with the purpose of building a cross-cultural perspective that would illuminate both the contributions and experiences of Afro-American women and women in the Third World. Still other projects are designed primarily for resource development, such as the project of the Organization of American Historians that produced curriculum packets designed to integrate material on women in the United States and Europe into survey courses at both the college and secondary school level. The Geraldine R. Dodge seminars also focus on the secondary school level. Involving teachers from public and private secondary schools in three regions of the country, these seminars are intended to help teachers become better acquainted with feminist scholarship and to develop high-school curricula that reflect women's history, experiences, and perceptions.

There are so many of these projects that it is impossible to describe all of them here. These few examples do, however, give an idea of the range of activities and the different institutional contexts of inclusive curriculum projects. All of them rest on the concept of faculty develop- ent since building faculty knowledge of new interdisciplinary scholar- ship from feminist studies is an integral and critical part of curriculum transformation.

Directors of these projects typically begin with the recognition that women's studies scholarship has not fully made its way into the "main" curriculum of colleges and universities and that, without programs de- signed to bring the new scholarship into the whole curriculum, most students—male and female—will remain untouched by scholarship on women and therefore unprepared to understand the world. Elizabeth Minnich suggests that, though liberal arts advocates claim that a liberal arts education instills in students the perspectives and faculties to understand a complex world, instead, students learn about a detached and alienating world outside their own experiences. Were we honest about traditional education, she says, we would teach them the irony of the gap between stated educational missions and actual educational practices. Schools do not typically teach a critical view of the liberal arts we have inherited; we seem to have forgotten that, historically, liberal arts education was an entrée into ruling positions for privileged males. Liberal arts education taught privileged men the language of their culture, its skills, graces, principles, and intellectual challenges, modeled on one normative charac- ter. It thus emphasized sameness over difference, even in a world marked by vast differences of culture, race, class, ethnicity, religion, and gender.[17] Consequently, there is now entrenched in the liberal arts a curriculum claiming general validity that is, however, based on the experience, values, and activities of a few.

Curriculum-change projects designed to bring the scholarship on women into the whole curriculum have been variously labeled "main- streaming," "integrating women's studies into the curriculum," and "gen- der-balancing the curriculum." There are problems with each of these labels, since they may imply that curriculum change through women's studies follows some simple programmatic scheme when women's studies cannot be merely assimilated into the dominant curriculum. McIntosh says the label "mainstreaming" trivializes women by implying that we have been out of, and are only now entering, the mainstream. The term implies that there is only one mainstream and that, by entering it, women will be indistinguishable from men. It makes the reconstructive work of curricu- lum change seem like a quick and simple process, whereas women's studies builds its understanding on the assumption that there are diverse and plural streams of women's and men's experience.[18]

[17] Elizabeth Kamarck Minnich, "A Feminist Criticism of the Liberal Arts," in Fuller, ed., 22–38.

[18] Peggy McIntosh, "A Note on Terminology," *Women's Studies Quarterly* 11 (Summer 1983): 29–30.

The use of the terms "integration" and "balance" to describe these projects is also problematic. Feminist scholarship has rested on the assumption that the exclusion of women leads to distorted, partial, and false claims to truth, yet "balancing" may imply that all perspectives are equally accurate or significant. Certainly, women's studies instructors do not want room in the curriculum for all perspectives, thereby including those that are racist, anti-Semitic, ethnocentric, class-biased, and sexist. Furthermore, liberal calls for balance often cloak an underlying appeal for analyses that are detached and dispassionate, as if those who are passionately committed to what they study cannot be objective. Gloria Bowles and Renate Duelli-Klein, among others, argue that it is unrealistic to seek a balanced curriculum in a world that is unbalanced.[19] Their concern reflects the understanding that most educational curricula mirror the values and structure of the dominant culture, yet they may underestimate the power of education to generate change.

Similarly, "integration" implies that women's studies can be assimilated into the dominant curriculum, when women's studies scholarship demonstrates that women cannot be simply included in a curriculum already structured, organized, and conceived through the experience of men. Critics of curriculum-integration projects, including Bowles and Duelli-Klein, caution that these projects might dilute the more radical goals of the women's studies movement by trying to make women's studies more palatable to those who control higher education. Integration is inadequate if it means only including traditionally excluded groups in a dominant system of thinking. So, if integration is interpreted as assimilation, these critics are right, but the history of the black protest movement in America indicates that the concept of integration cannot be dismissed merely as assimilation. Advocates of integration in the black protest movement understood that integration required a major transformation of American culture and values, as well as radical transformation of political and economic institutions. In the development of black studies, integration and separatism have not been either/or strategies, though they do reflect different emphases in black political philosophy and have been used strategically for different, yet complementary, purposes. If we take its meaning from black culture and politics, integration is a more complex idea and goal than assimilation; movements for integration in black history reflect a broad tolerance for diverse efforts to make radical transformations of educational institutions and the society at large.[20]

This controversy is more than a semantic one because the debate about

[19] Gloria Bowles and Renate Duelli-Klein, eds., *Theories of Women's Studies* (Boston: Routledge & Kegan Paul, 1983).

[20] Margaret Andersen, "Black Studies/Women's Studies: Learning from Our Common Pasts/Forging a Common Future," in *Women's Place in the Academy: Transforming the Liberal Arts Curriculum*, ed. Marilyn Schuster and Susan Van Dyne (Totowa, N.J.: Rowman & Allanheld, 1985), 62–72.

terminology reflects political discussion among feminists who sometimes disagree about the possibilities and desirability of including women's studies in the curriculum. Because women's studies rejects the assumptions of the dominant culture and finds the traditional compartmentalization of knowledge inadequate for the questions women's studies asks, both the language and the work of curriculum change by necessity must maintain that what is wrong with the dominant curriculum cannot be fixed by simple addition, inclusion, and minor revision.[21] Feminist critics of curriculum-integration projects fear that these projects change the primary audience of women's studies to "academics who wish to reform the disciplines but see no need to challenge the existing structure of knowledge based on the dominant androcentric culture."[22] Other feminist criticisms reflect a concern that the political radicalism of feminism will be sacrificed in order to make women's studies scholarship more acceptable to nonfeminists.[23] As Mary Childers, former associate director at the University of Maine at Orono project, states it, curriculum-integration projects may transform feminist work more than they transform the people at whom the projects are directed.[24]

The debate about women's studies and curriculum-change projects has been described as a debate between autonomy and integration,[25] and it reflects the origins of women's studies as both an educational project and as a part of broader societal efforts for emancipatory change. Those who argue for autonomy worry that integration projects compromise women's studies by molding it to fit into patriarchal systems of knowledge. Developing women's studies as an autonomous field is more likely, they argue, to generate the new knowledge we need because it creates a sustained dialogue among feminists working on common questions and themes.[26] Integrationists see a dialectical relationship between women's studies and inclusive curriculum projects and recognize that curriculum-revision projects are not a substitute for women's studies.[27] They see curriculum projects as both growing out of women's studies and fostering its continued development (pointing out that on many campuses where inclusive curriculum projects preceded women's studies, the projects resulted in the

[21] Johnella Butler, "Minority Studies and Women's Studies: Do We Want to Kill a Dream?" in Bowles, ed., 135–38.

[22] Bowles and Duelli-Klein, eds., 9.

[23] Marian Lowe and Margaret Lowe Benston, "The Uneasy Alliance of Feminism and Academia," in Bowles, ed. (n. 12 above), 177–84.

[24] Mary Childers, "Women's Studies: Sinking and Swimming in the Mainstream," in Bowles, ed., 161–66.

[25] This debate can best be reviewed in Bowles, ed. (n. 12 above).

[26] Sandra Coyner, "The Ideas of Mainstreaming: Women's Studies and the Disciplines," *Frontiers* 8, no. 3 (1986): 87–95.

[27] Peggy McIntosh and Elizabeth Kamarck Minnich, "Varieties of Women's Studies," in Bowles, ed., 139–48.

creation of women's studies programs). Developers of inclusive curriculum projects know that the projects cannot replace women's studies programs and, in fact, rest on the continued development of women's studies programs and research. Moreover, the presence of inclusive curriculum projects in institutions has typically strengthened women's studies programs.[28]

Projects to balance the curriculum also raise the question of what it means to have men doing feminist studies, since curriculum-revision projects are typically designed to retrain male faculty. Elaine Showalter discusses this in the context of feminist literary criticism where a number of prominent men have now claimed feminist criticism as part of their own work. She asks if men's entry into feminist studies legitimates feminism as a form of academic discussion because it makes feminism "accessible and subject to correction to authoritative men."[29] And, does it make feminism only another academic perspective without the commitments to change on which feminist studies have been grounded? The radical shift in perspective found in women's studies stems, in large part, from the breach between women's consciousness and experience and that of the patriarchal world.[30] Merely having men study women as new objects of academic discourse does not necessarily represent a feminist transformation in men's thinking. Showalter concludes that, in literature, only when men become fully aware of the way in which they have been constituted as readers and writers by gender systems can they do feminist criticism; otherwise, she says, they are only engaging in a sophisticated form of girl-watching. By further implication, transforming men through feminist studies must mean more than their just becoming aware of new scholarship on women or understanding how their characters and privileges are structured by gender; it must include their active engagement in political change for the liberation of women.

For women and for men, working to transform the curriculum through women's studies requires political, intellectual, and personal change. Those who have worked in curriculum-revision projects testify that these

[28] See Myra Dinnerstein, Sheryl O'Donnell, and Patricia MacCorquodale, *How to Integrate Women's Studies into the Traditional Curriculum* (Tucson: University of Arizona, Southwest Institute for Research on Women [SIROW], n.d.); JoAnn M. Fritsche, ed., *Toward Excellence and Equity* (Orono: University of Maine at Orono Press, 1984); and Schmitz (n. 8 above). See also Betty Schmitz, *Sourcebook for Integrating the Study of Women into the Curriculum* (Bozeman: Montana State University, Northwest Women's Studies Association, 1983); and Bonnie Spanier, Alexander Bloom, and Darlene Boroviak, eds., *Toward a Balanced Curriculum: A Sourcebook for Initiating Gender Integration Projects* (Cambridge, Mass.: Schenckman Publishing Co., 1984).

[29] Elaine Showalter, "Critical Cross-Dressing: Male Feminists and the Woman of the Year," *Raritan* 3 (Fall 1983): 130–49; quotation is from Gayatri Spivak, "Politics of Interpretations," *Critical Inquiry* 9 (September 1982): 259–78, cited in Showalter, 133.

[30] Marcia Westkott, "Feminist Criticism of the Social Sciences," *Harvard Educational Review* 49 (November 1979): 22–30.

are mutually reinforcing changes—all of which accompany the process of curriculum revision through women's studies.[31] Understanding the confluence of personal and intellectual change also appears to help women's studies faculty deal with the resistance and denial—both overt and covert—that faculty colleagues in such projects often exhibit.[32] Women's studies scholarship challenges the authority of traditional scholarship and, as a consequence, also challenges the egos of those who have invested their careers in this work. Revising the curriculum is therefore also a process of revising our personalities since our work and our psyches have been strongly intertwined with our educations.[33]

The reconstruction of the curriculum through women's studies is occurring in a context of significant change in the demographic composition of student populations. Women now represent a majority of the college population, and by the year 1990 it is projected that minorities will constitute 30 percent of the national youth cohort.[34] In a report to the Carnegie Foundation, Ernest Boyer and Fred Hechinger conclude that "from now on almost all young people, at some time in their lives, need some form of post-secondary education if they are to remain economically productive and socially functional in a world whose tasks and tools are becoming increasingly complex."[35]

At the same time, current appeals for educational reform threaten to reinstate educational privilege along lines determined by race, class, and sex. Various national reports conclude that there is a crisis in education defined as the erosion of academic standards and the collapse of traditional values in education. In all of these appeals, the decline of academic standards is clearly linked to the proliferation of scholarship and educational programs in women's studies and black studies.[36] And, though seemingly different in tone and intent, conservative academic arguments about the need to "return to the basics" and to reclaim the legacy of "the classics" are actually attempts to reinstate patriarchal authority.[37] The

[31] Peggy McIntosh, "WARNING: The New Scholarship on Women May Be Hazardous to Your Ego," *Women's Studies Quarterly* 10 (Spring 1982): 29–31; and McIntosh, "The Study of Women," (n. 16 above).

[32] Dinnerstein et al.

[33] Peggy McIntosh, "Interactive Phases of Curricular Re-Vision: A Feminist Perspective," Working Papers Series, no. 124 (Wellesley, Mass.: Wellesley College Center for Research on Women, 1983).

[34] Marilyn Schuster and Susan Van Dyne, "Curricular Change for the Twenty-first Century: Why Women?" in Schuster and Van Dyne, eds. (n. 20 above), 3–12.

[35] Ernest L. Boyer and Fred M. Hechinger, *Higher Learning in the Nation's Service* (Washington, D.C.: Carnegie Foundation for the Advancement of Teaching, 1981), 28.

[36] Michael Levin, "Women's Studies, Ersatz Scholarship," *New Perspectives* 17 (Summer 1985): 7–10. *New Perspectives* is published by the U.S. Commission on Civil Rights.

[37] The Family Protection Act, proposed by the New Right, and introduced to Congress on September 24, 1979, would prohibit "any program which produces or promotes courses of

assumption is that, if we do not reclaim the classical legacy of the liberal arts, we will lose the academic rigor on which such forms of education are seen as resting.[38] By implication, women's studies and black studies are seen as intellectually weak and politically biased, while study of the classics is seen as both academically rigorous and politically neutral.

One of the goals of women's studies is to insure that education becomes democratic. Women's studies practitioners know that the skills acquired through education cannot be merely technical and task-oriented but must also address the facts of a multiracial and multicultural world that includes both women and men. Case studies from universities that have had inclusive curriculum projects show that students do learn through women's studies to enlarge their worldviews and to integrate academic learning into their personal experience even though the process by which this occurs is full of conflict, resistance, and anger.[39] Other research shows that, following women's studies courses, students report increased self-esteem, interpret their own experiences within a larger social context, increase their identification with other women, expand their sense of life options and goals, and state more liberal attitudes about women.[40] Moreover, faculty in inclusive curriculum projects often report that students are most captivated by the material that focuses specifically on women and gender; students in these projects also report that their classmates and their instructors are more engaged in class material where women are included as agents and subjects of knowledge.[41]

---

instruction or curriculum seeking to inculcate values or modes of behavior which contradict the demonstrated beliefs and values of the community" or any program that supports "educational materials or studies . . . which would tend to denigrate, diminish, or deny role differences between the sexes as it has been historically understood in the United States" (Senate Bill 1808, 96th Congress, first session, title 1, sec. 101; cited in Rosalind Petchesky, "Antiabortion, Antifeminism, and the Rise of the New Right," *Feminist Studies* 7 [Summer 1981]: 225). The Family Protection Act would return moral authority to the heterosexual married couple with children and would eliminate women's studies and any other educational programs that suggest homosexuality as an acceptable life-style; it would also severely reduce federal jurisdiction over desegregation in private schools.

[38] Nan Keohane, "Our Mission Should Not Be Merely to 'Reclaim' a Legacy of Scholarship—We Must Expand on It," *Chronicle of Higher Education* 32 (April 2, 1986): 88.

[39] In Fritsche, ed. (n. 28 above): Christina L. Baker, "Through the Eye of the Storm: Feminism in the Classroom," 224–33; Jerome Nadelhaft, "Feminism in the Classroom: Through the Eye of the Storm," 235–45; and Ruth Nadelhaft, "Predictable Storm in the Feminist Classroom," 247–55.

[40] Karen G. Howe, "The Psychological Impact of a Women's Studies Course," *Women's Studies Quarterly* 13 (Spring 1985): 23–24. In addition to a discussion of her own research, Howe includes an excellent review of literature on this topic.

[41] Betty Schmitz, Myra Dinnerstein, and Nancy Mairs, "Initiating a Curriculum Integration Project: Lessons from the Campus and the Region," in Schuster and Van Dyne, eds., 116–29.

However, given the brief history of inclusive curriculum projects and the fact that balanced courses are still a small percentage of students' total education, evaluating student responses to such projects reveals only part of their significance. Equally important are the opportunities for revitalizing faculty when faculty positions are threatened by budget cuts, retrenchment, and narrowed professional opportunities.[42] Faculty in inclusive curriculum projects report new enthusiasm for their work and see new research questions and directions for their teaching as the result of this work.[43] After her review of inclusive curriculum projects around the country, Lois Banner reported to the Ford Foundation that the projects are also particularly impressive in the degree to which participants discuss and share course syllabi, pedagogical problems and successes, attitudes about themselves, and the changes they are experiencing. She finds this especially noteworthy since college faculty do not ordinarily share course materials with ease and regard their teaching as fundamentally private.[44]

The phases of curriculum change

Several feminist scholars have developed theories to describe the *process* of curriculum change. These are useful because they provide a conceptual outline of transformations in our thinking about women and because they organize our understanding of curriculum critique and revision as an ongoing process. These phase theories also help unveil hidden assumptions within the curriculum and therefore help move us forward in the reconceptualization of knowledge.[45]

An important origin for phase theories is Gerda Lerner's description of the development of women's history.[46] Lerner describes the theoretical challenges of women's history as having evolved in five phases. The first phase was the recognition that women have a history, which led to the second phase, conceptualizing women as a group. In the third phase,

[42] Marilyn Schuster and Susan Van Dyne, "Placing Women in the Liberal Arts: Stages of Curriculum Transformation," *Harvard Educational Review* 54 (November 1984): 413–28.

[43] Dinnerstein et al. (n. 28 above).

[44] Lois Banner, "The Women's Studies Curriculum Integration Movement: A Report to the Ford Foundation" (New York: Ford Foundation, March 1985, typescript).

[45] For a discussion of phase theories see Mary Kay Thompson Tetreault, "Women in the Curriculum," 1–2; Peggy McIntosh, "Women in the Curriculum," 3; Peggy McIntosh, "Convergences in Feminist Phase Theory," 4; all in the vol. 15 (February 1986) issue of *Comment. Comment* is available from RCI Communications, 680 West 11th Street, Claremont, Calif. 91711.

[46] Gerda Lerner, "The Rise of Feminist Consciousness," in *All of Us Are Present*, ed. Eleanor Bender, Bobbie Burk, and Nancy Walker (Columbia, Mo.: James Madison Wood Research Institute, 1984), and "Symposium: Politics and Culture in Women's History," *Feminist Studies* 6 (Spring 1980): 49–54.

women asked new questions about history and compiled new information about women. In the fourth phase, women's history challenged the periodization schemes of history that had been developed through the historical experiences of men, leading them, in the final phase, to redefine the categories and values of androcentric history through consideration of women's past and present.

Lerner's description of the evolution of feminist thought in history showed feminist scholars in other disciplines that scholarship on women was evolving from simply adding women into existing schemes of knowledge into more fundamental reconstructions of the concepts, methods, and theories of the disciplines. She was not the first to see this, but her articulation of these phases of change provided a map for the process through which women were traveling.

McIntosh has developed an analysis of phases in curriculum change that is unique in that it relates patterns of thought in the curriculum to human psyches and their relation to the dominant culture.[47] McIntosh calls phase 1 in the curriculum "womanless" (for example, "womanless history," "womanless sociology," or "womanless literature"). Only a select few are studied in this phase of the curriculum, and highly exclusionary standards of excellence are established. Since the select few in a womanless curriculum are men, we come to think of them as examples of the best of human life and thought. In turn, the curriculum reproduces psyches in students that define an exclusive few as winners and all the rest as losers, second-rate, or nonexistent.

Phase 2 of curriculum change maintains the same worldview as phase 1, since women and a few exceptions from other excluded groups are added in, but only on the same terms in which the famous few have been included. McIntosh defines this phase as "women in history," "women in society," or "women in literature," to use examples from the disciplines. In this phase of curriculum change the originally excluded still exist only as exceptions; their experiences and contributions are still measured through white, male-centered images and ideas. This phase can suggest new questions about old materials, such as, What are the images of women in so-called great literature? Also, this phase raises new questions like, Who were the best-selling women novelists of the nineteenth century? However, while this phase leads to some documentation of women's experience, it tends to see a few women as exceptions to their kind and never imagines women and other underclasses as central or fundamental to social change and continuity.

McIntosh calls the third phase of curriculum change "women as a problem, anomaly, or absence." In this phase, we identify the barriers that have excluded so many people and aspects of life from our studies, and we

---

[47] Peggy McIntosh, "Interactive Phases of Curricular Re-vision" (n. 33 above).

recognize that, when judged by androcentric standards, women and other excluded groups look deprived. As a result this phase tends to generate anger, but it is also the phase in which feminist scholars begin to challenge the canons of the disciplines and seek to redefine the terms, paradigms, and methods through which all of human experience is understood. Thus, it leads to more inclusive thinking in which class, race, gender, and sexuality are seen as fundamental to the construction of knowledge and human experience. Moreover, we recognize that inclusive studies cannot be done on the same terms as those preceding, thereby moving us to phase 4—"women on their own terms."

Phase 4, exemplified by "women's lives as history" or "women as society," makes central the claim that women's experiences and perspectives create history, society, and culture as much as do those of men. This phase also departs from the misogyny of the first three phases wherein women are either altogether invisible or are seen only as exceptional, victimized, or problematic relative to dominant groups. Phase 4 investigates cultural functions, especially those involving affiliation; understudied aspects of men's lives, such as their emotional lives and nurturant activities, become visible in this phase. In phase 4, according to McIntosh, boundaries between teachers and students break down as the division between the expert and the learner evaporates and teachers and students have a new adjacent relationship to the subjects of study. This phase also leads to a search for new and plural sources of knowledge.

Phase 5, McIntosh says, is harder to conceive because it is so unrealized—both in the curriculum and in our consciousness. She imagines this as a radical transformation of our minds and our work, centered on what she calls "lateral consciousness"—attachment to others and working for the survival of all.

Marilyn Schuster and Susan Van Dyne see curriculum change evolving from recognizing the invisibility of women and identifying sexism in traditional knowledge, to searching for missing women, then to conceptualizing women as a subordinate group, and, finally, to studying women on their own terms.[48] Through these first steps, women's studies poses a challenge to the disciplines by noting their incompleteness and describing the histories that have shaped their developments. Schuster and Van Dyne add women's studies as a challenge to the disciplines to their phase theory and define the last phase as one that is inclusive of human experience and appropriates women's and men's experience and the experiences generated by race and class as relational. The final phase of curriculum transformation, therefore, would be one based on the differences and diversity of human experience, not sameness and generalization. Schuster and Van Dyne identify the implied questions, incentives for change, pedagogical

[48] Schuster and Van Dyne, eds. (n. 20 above), 27–28.

means, and potential outcomes for each of the six phases they identify, and they ask what implications each phase has for changed courses. They also provide a useful index of the characteristics of transformed courses.

In another analysis of curriculum change, Mary Kay Tetreault defines the phases of feminist scholarship as male scholarship, compensatory scholarship, bifocal scholarship, feminist scholarship, and multifocal or relational scholarship.[49] The first phase she identifies, like the first phases described by McIntosh and by Schuster and Van Dyne, accepts male experience as universal. Phase 2 notices that women are missing but still perceives men as the norm. The third phase, bifocal scholarship, defines human experience in dualist categories; curricula in this phase perceive men and women as generalized groups. This phase still emphasizes the oppression of women. Tetreault calls phase 4 "feminist scholarship"; here women's activities, not men's, are the measure of significance, and more attention is given to the contextual and the personal. Sex and gender are seen within historical, cultural, and ideological contexts, and thinking becomes more interdisciplinary. Tetreault's fifth phase, multifocal scholarship, seeks a holistic view in which the ways men and women relate to and complement each other is a continuum of human experience. In this phase, the experiences of race, class, and ethnicity are taken fully into account.

Tetreault suggests that understanding these different phases of curriculum change can be useful for program and course evaluation since they provide a yardstick for measuring the development of feminist thinking in different disciplines. Nevertheless, none of the authors of phase theories intends them to represent rankings or hierarchies of different kinds of feminist scholarship, and it is important to note that these phases have fluid boundaries and that their development does not necessarily follow a linear progression. Still, organizing women's studies scholarship into phases demonstrates how asking certain kinds of questions leads to similar curricular outcomes. As one example, adding black women into the history of science can reveal patterns of the exclusion of black women scientists and can then recast our definition of what it means to practice science and to be a scientist; this shows the necessity of seeing science in terms other than those posed by the dominant histories of science.[50] Furthermore, Showalter points out that different phases of thinking can coexist in our consciousnesses,[51] so for purposes of faculty development, it is important to

[49] Mary Kay Thompson Tetreault, "Feminist Phase Theory," *Journal of Higher Education* 56 (July/August 1985): 363–84.

[50] Evelyn Hammonds, "Never Meant to Survive: A Black Woman's Journey: An Interview with Evelyn Hammonds by Aimee Sands," *Radical Teacher* 30 (January 1986): 8–15. Evelyn Fox Keller, *Reflections on Gender and Science* (New Haven, Conn.: Yale University Press, 1985).

[51] Elaine Showalter, *A Literature of Their Own* (Princeton, N.J.: Princeton University Press, 1977).

recognize that certain phases are appropriate as faculty awareness progresses in different institutional, disciplinary, and course contexts.

Finally, identifying the phases of curriculum change is helpful in developing feminist pedagogy. Drawing from work by Blythe Clinchy and Claire Zimmerman[52] on cognitive development among undergraduate students, Francis Maher and Kathleen Dunn[53] discuss the implications of different phases of curriculum change for pedagogy. Clinchy and Zimmerman describe the first level of cognitive functioning for college students as dualist, meaning that students posit right and wrong as absolute and opposite. Maher and Dunn say the pedagogical complement to this phase of student development is the lecture format in which students are encouraged to see faculty members as experts who impart truth by identifying right and wrong.

Multiplism is the second phase in Clinchy and Zimmerman's analysis. This phase of cognitive development describes knowledge as stemming from within; in this phase, students discover the validity of their own experience. According to Maher and Dunn, this produces among students a highly relativistic stance—one in which they accept the legitimacy of different worldviews and experiences, thus opening themselves up to experiences that vary by class, race, and gender but seeing all experiences and perspectives as equally valid. Contextualism is the third phase of cognitive development identified by Clinchy and Zimmerman; according to Maher and Dunn, we can encourage this phase of student development through the creation of a pluralistic curriculum in women's studies.

Like those who have articulated phase theories of curriculum change, Maher and Dunn see the ultimate goal of women's studies as developing a curriculum that is inclusive in the fullest sense—taking gender, race, class, and sexuality in their fullest historical and cultural context and developing an understanding of the complexities of these experiences and their relatedness. Such a curriculum would no longer rest on the experiences and judgment of a few. Since phase theories help us move toward this goal, they are an important contribution to faculty and student development through women's studies.

Critique of the disciplines

The new enthusiasm that participants in women's studies faculty development projects report for their work is a sign that the insights of feminist

[52] Blythe Clinchy and Claire Zimmerman, "Epistemology and Agency in the Development of Undergraduate Women," in *The Undergraduate Woman: Issues in Educational Equity*, ed. Pamela Perun (Lexington, Mass.: D. C. Heath & Co., 1982), 161–81.

[53] Frances Maher and Kathleen Dunn, "The Practice of Feminist Teaching: A Case Study of Interactions among Curriculum, Pedagogy, and Female Cognitive Development," Working Papers Series, no. 144 (Wellesley, Mass.: Wellesley College Center for Research on Women, 1984).

scholarship are on the theoretical and methodological cutting edge of the disciplines. Working to build a balanced curriculum has renewed faculty and brought them and their students a new level of awareness about women in society, culture, and history. In fact, the revisions in the disciplines that this literature stimulates are so extensive that it is reasonable to conclude that "whether or not you are in women's studies, its scholarship will affect your discipline."[54]

As Schuster and Van Dyne argue,[55] there are invisible paradigms within the educational curriculum that represent tacit assumptions that govern what and how we teach, even when we are unaware of these ruling principles. The feminist movement exposes these unexamined standards by showing their relation to the ideology, power, and values of dominant groups, who in our culture most often are white, European-American men. Thus, although women's studies is often accused of being ideological, it is the traditional curriculum that is nested within the unacknowledged ideology of the dominant culture. The more coherent and tacitly assumed an ideology is, the less visible are the curricular paradigms that stem from it and the more unconsciously we participate in them.

Feminist criticism is generated by the fact that women are both insiders and outsiders to the disciplines; the contradictions imposed by their status create a breach between their consciousnesses and their activity, generating critical dialogue and producing new sources of knowledge.[56] Feminist criticism across the disciplines reveals that what is taken to be timeless, excellent, representative, or objective is embedded within patriarchal assumptions about culture and society. Consequently, recentering knowledge within the experience of women unmasks the invisible paradigms that guide the curriculum and raises questions that require scholars to take a comprehensive and critical look at their fields.

Creating an inclusive curriculum means more than bringing women's studies into the general curriculum because it also means creating women's studies to be inclusive so that women's studies does not have the racist, class, heterosexist, and cultural bias that is found in the traditional curriculum.[57] Feminist curriculum change, then, must not exclude the voices of women of color in posing the research questions, defining the facts, shaping the concepts, and articulating theories of women's studies. How would the work be enriched, both cognitively and emotionally, by listening to the voices and fully including the experiences of women of color? What kind of knowledge is made by ignoring not only class and gender but also race as origins for and subjects of scholarship? If the curriculum—both inside and outside of women's studies—is focused on

---

[54] F. Howe, *Myths of Coeducation* (n. 9 above), 256.

[55] Schuster and Van Dyne, "Placing Women in the Liberal Arts" (n. 42 above).

[56] Westkott (n. 30 above).

[57] Patricia Bell Scott, "Education for Self-Empowerment: A Priority for Women of Color," in Bender, Burk, and Walker, eds. (n. 46 above), 55–66.

white cultures, it will continue to define women of color as peripheral and to see white experience as the norm and all others as deviant or exceptional. It will, in effect, reproduce the errors of classical education.[58]

Esther Chow[59] suggests three strategies for incorporating the perspectives of women of color into courses: the comparison method, special treatment, and mainstreaming. The comparison strategy brings materials on women of color into courses for purposes of comparison with the dominant group experience, and it exposes students to a wide range of materials by examining women's experiences from different perspectives. Chow suggests, however, that it can perpetuate the marginality of women of color by leaving white women at the center of the major paradigm for analysis. Alternatively, the special-treatment approach makes women of color the topic of general survey courses, special topic courses, or independent reading. The advantage to such courses is that they allow for in-depth understanding of themes in the lives of women of color, although, since these courses tend to be electives, they do not make an impact on a wide range of students. The mainstreaming strategy incorporates materials on women of color into existing courses so that they appear throughout, not just in segregated areas of courses or the curriculum. Chow is careful to point out that the substance of these courses should not be divided along clear racial and gender lines. And she concludes that the effectiveness of these different strategies is dependent on the needs and goals of particular courses, the institutional setting, and interaction between teachers and students of various racial-ethnic backgrounds.

Creating an inclusive curriculum both within women's studies and within traditional disciplines is initiated by asking two questions: What is the present content and scope and methodology of a discipline? and How would the discipline need to change to reflect the fact that women are half the world's population and have had, in one sense, half the world's experience?[60] Those who work in women's studies know that women's studies scholarship cannot be simply added into the existing curriculum, as it challenges the existing assumptions, facts, and theories of the traditional disciplines, as well as challenging the traditional boundaries between the disciplines. The identification of bias in the curriculum is the first step in analyzing the multiple implications of the fact that women have been excluded from creation of formalized knowledge.[61] But as feminist scholarship has developed, more fundamental transformations can be imagined.

[58] Maxine Baca Zinn, Lynn Weber Cannon, Elizabeth Higginbotham, and Bonnie Thornton Dill, "The Costs of Exclusionary Practice in Women's Studies," *Signs* 11, no. 2 (Winter 1986): 290–303.

[59] Esther Ngan-Ling Chow, "Teaching Sex and Gender in Sociology: Incorporating the Perspective of Women of Color," *Teaching Sociology* 12 (April 1985): 299–312.

[60] McIntosh, "Interactive Phases of Curricular Re-vision" (n. 33 above).

[61] Mary Childers, "Working Definition of a Balanced Course," *Women's Studies Quarterly* 11 (Summer 1983): 30 ff.

Several volumes specifically address the impact of feminist scholarship on the disciplines[62] and, were this essay to review fully the impact of feminist scholarship on the disciplines, the whole of women's studies literature would need to be considered. Of course, this essay cannot possibly do this; instead, it addresses the major themes that emerge from consideration of curriculum change effected through women's studies.

The arts and humanities

Feminist criticism shows that the arts and humanities have in the past created and reinforced definitions of life that exclude the experiences of, deny expression to, and negate the creative works of the nonpowerful, even though the humanities claim to take the concerns of all humanity and the human experience as their subject matter.[63] Women have been excluded from literary and artistic canons on the grounds that their work does not meet standards of excellence,[64] though, as Paul Lauter suggests, "standards of literary merit are not absolute but contingent. They depend, among other considerations, upon the relative value we place on form and feeling in literary expression as well as on culturally different conceptions of form and function."[65]

The exclusion of women from literary and artistic canons suggests that the canons themselves are founded on principles embedded in masculine culture, even though many literature teachers and critics will say that great literature and art speak to universal themes and transcend the particularities of sociocultural conditions like race, class, and gender. In tracing the development of the canon of American literature, Lauter has shown that the exclusion of white women, blacks, and working class writers from the

[62] See Ellen Carol DuBois, Gail Paradise Kelly, Elizabeth Lapovsky Kennedy, Carolyn W. Korsmeyer, and Lillian S. Robinson, eds., *Feminist Scholarship: Kindling in the Groves of Academia* (Urbana: University of Illinois Press, 1985); Diane L. Fowlkes and Charlotte S. McClure, eds., *Feminist Visions: Toward a Transformation of the Liberal Arts Curriculum* (University: University of Alabama Press, 1984); Elizabeth Langland and Walter Gove, eds., *A Feminist Perspective in the Academy: The Difference It Makes* (Chicago: University of Chicago Press, 1981); Julia A. Sherman and Evelyn Torton Beck, eds., *The Prism of Sex: Essays in the Sociology of Knowledge* (Madison: University of Wisconsin Press, 1979); Eloise C. Snyder, ed., *The Study of Women: Enlarging Perspectives of Social Reality* (New York: Harper & Row, 1979); Dale Spender, ed., *Men's Studies Modified: The Impact of Feminism on the Academic Disciplines* (New York: Pergamon Press, 1981); Marianne Triplette, ed., *Women's Studies and the Curriculum* (Winston-Salem, N.C.: Salem College, 1983).

[63] Elizabeth Abel, ed., "Writing and Sexual Difference," *Critical Inquiry* 8 (Winter 1981): 173–403.

[64] Lillian Robinson, "Treason Our Text: Feminist Challenges to the Literary Canon," Working Papers Series, no. 104 (Wellesley, Mass.: Wellesley College Center for Research on Women, 1983).

[65] Paul Lauter, ed., *Reconstructing American Literature* (Old Westbury, N.Y.: Feminist Press, 1983), xx.

canon of American literature was consolidated in the 1920s when a small group of white elite men professionalized the teaching of literature and consolidated formal critical traditions and conventions of periodization.[66] Since then, the aesthetic standards of the canon have appeared to be universal because without revealing their history, the learned tastes and common experiences of certain academic men are exaggerated as universal. And, as Annette Kolodny argues, once a canon is established, the prior fact of canonization tends to put works beyond questions of merit.[67]

Other feminist critics in the arts and humanities have identified the chronological presentation of materials as deeply problematic. Natalie Kampen and Elizabeth Grossman, for example, say that the idea that time is fundamentally linear and progressive—fundamental in the study and teaching of art history through chronology—produces accounts of the development of human culture that are more linear than the actual historical evolution of the culture has been. Chronological presentation also assumes competition as a part of human creativity and suggests that hierarchical arrangements are inevitable in all organization of cultural reality.[68]

Including women in the curriculum has been especially difficult in fields like the history of philosophy where the canon is fixed and relatively small. Even in ethics, where it is more difficult to ignore variations in human values, the subject tends to be studied from the vantage point of those in power, lending the impression that only elites can understand cultural norms.[69] In the humanities, when women do appear in texts and as artistic objects, their own experiences are seldom primary. In American literature, for example, women, native Americans, and blacks sometimes "inhabit" texts but are rarely given primary voices within them. This reveals a deep sex, class, and race bias in the teaching of the arts and humanities.

Were we to begin study in the arts and humanities through the experience of traditionally excluded groups, new themes would be revealed. Gloria Hull, for example, in her account of reading literature by North American women of color, identifies several themes that arise from immer-

---

[66] Paul Lauter, "Race and Gender in the Shaping of the American Literary Canon: A Case Study from the Twenties," *Feminist Studies* 9 (Fall 1983): 435–64.

[67] Annette Kolodny, "Dancing through the Minefield: Some Observations on the Theory, Practice, and Politics of a Feminist Literary Criticism," in Spender, ed., 23–42.

[68] Natalie Kampen and Elizabeth Grossman, "Feminism and Methodology: Dynamics of Change in the History of Art and Architecture," Working Papers Series, no. 121 (Wellesley, Mass.: Wellesley College Center for Research on Women, 1983); and Norma Broude and Mary Garrard, *Feminism and Art History: Questioning the Litany* (New York: Harper & Row, 1982).

[69] Linda Gardiner, "Can This Discipline Be Saved? Feminist Theory Challenges Mainstream Philosophy," Working Papers Series, no. 118 (Wellesley, Mass.: Wellesley College Center for Research on Women, 1983).

sion in this literature on its own terms.[70] An acute awareness of racial and sexual oppression pervades this literature, but so do themes of bicultural identity (especially expressed through language), alternative understandings of sexuality, and the importance of preserving cultural tradition in forms of expression.

History, like literature and the arts, has tended to focus on the historical experience of a few. Because historians tend to concentrate on heroes, they ignore the lives of ordinary men and women. Thus, much of the impact of feminist scholarship in history has been to expand the "characters" of historical accounts. But, more than adding in new characters, feminist scholarship in history shows how the traditional periodization of historical accounts is organized through the experience of bourgeois men.[71] From a feminist perspective, including women means not only including those who have been left out but rethinking historical paradigms to generate new frameworks in which women are agents of history and that examine the lives of women in their own terms and bring them into accounts of historical change. Feminist revisions of history do more than expand the subjects of history; they introduce gender relations as a primary category of historical experience. So, although the narrative style of history has tended to produce singular tales of historical reality, feminist scholarship in history produces accounts that reflect the multiple layers of historical experience.[72] As one example, in American studies, scholars have focused on a singular myth of the physical and metaphysical frontier of the new world as a place to be conquered and possessed. In contrast, Kolodny's work on women's consciousness and westward expansion shows that women imagined the frontier as a garden to be cultivated.[73]

Feminist scholars suggest that how excellence is produced and defined by literary and cultural institutions should become part of the study of the arts and humanities. This requires methodological self-consciousness, asking, for example, what social conditions are necessary for certain female images to emerge? Whose interests are served by these images? How do they affect women? And what are the varieties of women's tastes, working methods, ideas, and experiences?[74]

[70] Gloria Hull, "Reading Literature by U.S. Third World Women," Working Papers Series, no. 141 (Wellesley, Mass.: Wellesley College Center for Research on Women, 1984).

[71] Joan Kelly-Gadol, "The Social Relations of the Sexes: Methodological Implications of Women's History," *Signs* 1, no. 4 (Summer 1976): 809–24.

[72] Susan Armitage, "Women and Western American History," Working Papers Series, no. 134 (Wellesley, Mass.: Wellesley College Center for Research on Women, 1984).

[73] Phyllis Cole and Deborah Lambert, "Gender and Race in American Literature: An Exploration of the Discipline and a Proposal for Two New Courses," Working Papers Series, no. 115 (Wellesley, Mass.: Wellesley College Center for Research on Women, 1983); Annette Kolodny, *The Land before Her: Fantasy and Experience of the American Frontiers, 1630–1860* (Chapel Hill: University of North Carolina Press, 1984).

[74] Broude and Garrard.

These questions help us identify bias in the curriculum and ultimately reveal more deeply embedded habits of thought. In her analysis of foreign language textbooks, Barbara Wright shows that the texts ignore most social classes, except for educated, upper middle-class surgeons, professors, and businessmen.[75] She identifies several phases of critique of the curriculum in foreign language instruction by examining the images of women and girls in textbooks, then studying women's place in the culture being presented, and, finally, developing a critical look at language itself. This last phase of questioning helps us see the value judgments that inform decisions to include or exclude certain semantic and syntactic possibilities in the language and, therefore, reveals ways in which gender, class, and race are embedded in the language of a culture and in our language teaching. Feminist criticism understands that the "circumstances in which culture is produced and encountered, the functions of culture, the specific historical and formal traditions which shape and validate culture—these all differ somewhat from social group to social group and among classes. In this respect, the problem of changing curriculum has primarily to do with learning to understand, appreciate and teach about many varied cultural traditions."[76]

Carolyn Heilbrun writes, "The study of literature cannot survive if it cannot . . . illuminate human experience; and human experience cannot today be illuminated without attention to the place of women in literature, in the textuality of all our lives, both in history and in the present."[77] From feminist work in these fields we begin to see past and present cultures as "multi-layered, composites of men's and women's experiences, and rich in complexity and conflict."[78] This vision of cultural multiplicity explored through feminist scholarship would help the humanities to present a full account of human experience.

The social sciences

As in the arts and humanities, the exclusion of women from the social sciences leads to distortion and ignorance of their experience in society and culture.[79] Whereas the social sciences claim to give accurate accounts of

[75] Barbara Drygulski Wright, "Feminist Transformation of Foreign Language Instruction: Progress and Challenges," Working Papers Series, no. 117 (Wellesley, Mass.: Wellesley College Center for Research on Women, 1983).

[76] Lauter, ed., Reconstructing American Literature, xxi.

[77] Carolyn G. Heilbrun, "Feminist Criticism in Departments of Literature," Academe 69 (September–October 1983): 14.

[78] Carroll Smith-Rosenberg, "The Feminist Reconstruction of History," Academe 69 (September–October 1983): 26–37.

[79] Marcia Millman and Rosabeth Moss Kanter, eds., "Editorial Introduction," Another Voice (Garden City, N.Y.: Doubleday & Co., Anchor Press, 1975); Margaret L. Andersen, Thinking about Women: Sociological and Feminist Perspectives (New York: Macmillan Pub-

social reality, the exclusion of women's experiences and perspectives has produced concepts and theories that, while allegedly universal, are, in fact, based on gender-specific experiences, and so these theories often project the assumptions of masculine, Western culture into the social groups under study.[80]

As a result, feminist scholars suggest that core concepts in the social sciences are gender biased. As one example, the assumed split between public and private spheres is reproduced in social science concepts that tend to be grounded in public experience and that ignore private experience and the relation between public and private dimensions of social life. Focus on the public sphere as the primary site for social interaction omits women's experience and much of men's.[81] Economic activity, for example, is defined as taking place only in the public sphere, leading to the total omission of household work as a measurable category of economic activity in economics. Thus, caring for the sick, elderly, or young is productive economic activity when performed for wages but not when performed by persons in the privacy of the household. Moreover, by assuming white Western male experience as the norm, mainstream economists assume that economic activity is based on rational choice and free interaction. A feminist approach, however, would develop economic analyses that identify constraints on choice and the process of choosing.[82]

Likewise, in political science, textbooks describe political activity only as it occurs in formal public political structures. The representation of women and minority groups in elected offices is typically included, as is some recognition of federal legislation on civil rights. But always omitted are such topics as women's and minority groups' participation in community politics, ethnic identity as a dimension of political activity, or sexuality as the basis of organized political movements. Were we to rely on these texts for our understanding of political systems and behavior, as do most faculty and students, the virtual omission of race, sex, gender, class, and ethnicity would lead us to believe that none of these has been significant in the development of political systems and behavior.[83]

The location of social science concepts within the public and masculine realm reflects the dichotomous thinking that prevails in both social science content and method. Dorothy Smith's work in the sociology of knowledge

lishing Co., 1983); Carolyn Sherif, "Bias in Psychology," in Sherman and Beck, eds. (n. 62 above), 93–134.

[80] Rayna Reiter, ed., *Toward an Anthropology of Women* (New York: Monthly Review Press, 1975).

[81] Millman and Kanter, vii–xvi.

[82] Barbara Bergmann, "Feminism and Economics," *Academe* 69 (September–October 1983): 22–25.

[83] James Soles, "Recent Research on Racism" (paper presented at the University of Delaware, 1985 Lecture Series on Racism, Newark, January 1985).

investigates the implications of the fact that men's experience in the public world has been segregated from that of women in the private sphere. She posits that men are able to become absorbed in an abstract conceptual mode because women take care of their everyday, emotional, and bodily needs. As a result, concepts in the social sciences, as they have been developed by men, are abstracted from women's experience and do not reflect their realities or worldviews.[84] Others have also argued that social science research methods polarize human experience by forcing respondents into either/or choices to describe their social experiences and attitudes. This is especially the case in experimental and survey research and in research on sex differences.[85] Furthermore, research methods in the social sciences routinely isolate people from the social contexts in which they are studied. And, in empirical research, race and sex, if mentioned at all, are treated as discrete categories and are reported as if they were separate features of social experience. It is an exceptional study that even presents data by race and by sex, and, when this is done, race and sex are most often reported separately. For example, sociologists comparing income by race and by sex typically report blacks' and whites' incomes and, in another table, compare men's and women's incomes. In reporting race and sex separately, the particular experiences of black women, white women, black men, and white men disappear from view. This practice produces false generalizations, perpetuates the invisibility of women of color, and denies that women of color have unique historical and contemporary experiences.

One of the greatest obstacles to curriculum change in the social sciences is the disciplines' search to establish themselves as sciences. The scientific method, as adopted in the social sciences, generates hierarchical methodologies in which the knower is seen as expert in the lives of others and produces research methodologies that deny that social relationships exist between researchers and those they study. Since the relationship between the knower and the known is part of the knowledge produced through research, denial of this relationship distorts the accounts produced by social science. Judith Stacey and Barrie Thorne conclude that, in sociology, positivist epistemology prohibits the infusion of feminist insights because positivism sees knowledge in abstract and universal terms that are unrelated to the stance of the observer. Feminist transformation has been

[84] Dorothy Smith, "Women's Perspective as a Radical Critique of Sociology," *Sociological Inquiry* 4 (1974): 7–13, and "Toward a Sociology for Women," in Sherman and Beck, eds., 135–88; Sandra Harding and Merrill B. Hintikka, eds., *Discovering Reality: Feminist Perspectives of Epistemology, Metaphysics, Methodology and Philosophy of Science* (Dordrecht: D. Reidel Publishing Co., 1983).

[85] Michelle Hoffnung, "Feminist Transformation: Teaching Experimental Psychology," Working Papers Series, no. 140 (Wellesley, Mass.: Wellesley College Center for Research on Women, 1984); Sherif, 93–134.

more possible, they argue, in disciplines where interpretive methods are used. Interpretive methods are reflexive about the circumstances in which knowledge is produced and see researchers as situated in the action of their research; thus, they are better able to build knowledge in the social sciences that takes full account of social life.[86]

Feminist methodologies in the social sciences begin from the premise that the relationship between the knower and the known is a socially organized practice. The assumed detachment of scientific observers from that which they observe is, as feminists see it, made possible through organized hierarchies of science where, for example, women work as bottle washers, research assistants, or computer operators.[87] Moreover, feminists argue that the assumption of scientific detachment and rationality is a masculine value, one that is made possible only by ignoring the role of women in the practice of science. Additionally, Shulamit Reinharz suggests that feminist research in the social sciences should see the self-discovery of the researcher as integral to the process of doing research; consequently, it is ludicrous in her view to imagine the act of "data gathering" as separate from the act of "data analysis."[88]

In response to the preoccupation with scientific method in the social science disciplines, feminist scholars suggest that critiques of the scientific method should be a primary concern in feminist revisions of social science courses. In developing, for example, a feminist approach for teaching methods of psychology, Michelle Hoffnung suggests including a variety of approaches and methods and investigating in each case their assumptions about scientists' relations to the worlds being investigated.[89] Similarly, in teaching courses like the history of psychological thought, we need to recognize that women are more active in the history of psychology and social science disciplines than texts lead us to believe. When texts focus only on the internal development of a science, histories of the discipline wrongly ignore the external social and historical conditions that create scientific investigations.[90] As in the arts and humanities, putting women into social scientific courses requires this more reflexive approach—one that puts women and men in the full context of their historical and cultural experiences and that does not assume the universality of concepts, theories, and facts.

[86] Judith Stacey and Barrie Thorne, "The Missing Feminist Revolution in Sociology," *Social Problems* 32 (April 1985): 301–16.

[87] Marian Lowe and Ruth Hubbard, eds., *Woman's Nature* (New York: Pergamon Press, 1983).

[88] Shulamit Reinharz, "Experiential Analysis: A Contribution to Feminist Research," in Bowles and Duelli-Klein, eds. (n. 19 above), 162–91.

[89] Michelle Hoffnung.

[90] Laurel Furumoto, "Placing Women in the History of Psychology Courses," Working Papers Series, no. 139 (Wellesley, Mass.: Wellesley College Center for Research on Women, 1984).

Science and technology

Of all the disciplines, the natural and physical sciences have the closest connections to political and economic structures, yet they make the strongest claims to academic neutrality. For feminist scholars in the sciences, seeing how scientific studies reflect cultural values is a good starting point for understanding the interwoven worlds of science, capitalism, and patriarchy.

To begin with, scientific descriptions project cultural values onto the physical and natural world. Ruth Hubbard explains that kingdoms and orders are not intrinsic to the nature of organisms but have evolved in a world that values hierarchy and patrilineage.[91] Though it is often claimed that scientific explanations run counter to the widely shared beliefs of society, it is also true that scientific explanations are often highly congruent with the social and political ideology of the society in which they are produced.[92] Research on brain lateralization, for example, reflects a seeming intent to find a biological explanation for sexual differences in analytical reasoning, visual-spatial ability, and intuitive thought that cannot itself be clearly and consistently demonstrated in scientific investigations.[93] And perhaps nowhere else are culturally sexist values so embedded in scientific description and analysis as in discussions of sexual selection, human sexuality, and human reproduction.[94]

The feminist critique of science, as in the humanities and social sciences, looks at cultural dualisms associated with masculinity and femininity as they permeate scientific thought and discourse.[95] Some question whether the scientific method is even capable of dealing with collective behavior due to the fact that it parcels out behaviors, cells, categories, and events. In science, like the humanities and social sciences, explanations thought to be true often do not stand up when examined through women's

[91] Ruth Hubbard, "Feminist Science: A Meaningful Concept?" (paper presented at the annual meeting of the National Women's Studies Association, Douglass College, New Brunswick, N.J., June 1984).

[92] Ruth Hubbard, "Have Only Men Evolved?" in *Biological Woman: The Convenient Myth*, ed. Ruth Hubbard, Mary Sue Henifin, and Barbara Fried (Cambridge, Mass.: Schenckman Publishing Co., 1982), 17–46; Ethel Tobach and Betty Rosoff, eds., *Genes and Gender*, vol. 1 (New York: Gordian Press, 1979); also see the four subsequent volumes of *Genes and Gender*.

[93] Ruth Bleier, *Science and Gender* (New York: Pergamon Press, 1984).

[94] Mina Davis Caulfield, "Sexuality in Human Evolution: What Is 'Natural' about Sex?" *Feminist Studies* 11 (Summer 1985): 343–63.

[95] Helene Longino and Ruth Doell, "Body, Bias, and Behavior: A Comparative Analysis of Reasoning in Two Areas of Biological Science," *Signs* 9, no. 2 (Winter 1983): 206–27; Nancy Hartsock, "The Feminist Standpoint: Developing the Ground for a Specifically Feminist Historical Materialism," in *Money, Sex and Power*, ed. Nancy Hartsock (New York: Longman, Inc., 1983), 231–51; Elizabeth Fee, "Woman's Nature and Scientific Objectivity," in Lowe and Hubbard, eds., 9–28.

experiences. For example, whereas medical researchers have typically described menopause as associated with a set of disease symptoms, new research by feminist biologists finds that the overwhelming majority of postmenopausal women report no remarkable menopausal symptoms.[96]

The feminist critique of science can be organized into five types of studies: equity studies documenting the resistance to women's participation in science; studies of the uses and abuses of science and their racist, sexist, homophobic, and class-based projects; epistemological studies; studies that, drawing from literary criticism, historical interpretation, and psychoanalysis, see science as a text and, therefore, look to reveal the social meaning embedded in value-neutral claims; and feminist debates about whether feminist science is possible or whether feminists seek simply a better science—undistorted by gender, race, class, and heterosexism.[97]

Building the feminist critique of science can therefore begin from several questions, including, Why are women excluded from science? How is science taught? What are the scientific research questions that, as feminists, we need to ask? How is difference studied in scientific institutions? Or, how is the exclusion of women from science related to the way science is done and thought? Some of these questions are similar to those asked in social studies of science. But feminist discussions of science specifically examine what Evelyn Fox Keller calls the science/gender system—the network of associations and disjunctions between public and private, personal and impersonal, and masculine and feminine as they appear in the basic structure of science and society. Keller argues that asking "how ideologies of gender and science inform each other in their mutual construction, how that construction functions in our social arrangements, and how it affects men and women, science and nature" is to examine the roots, dynamics, and consequences of the science/gender system.[98]

Science bears the imprint of the fact that, historically, scientists have been men. Therefore, asking how and why women have been excluded from the practice of science is one way to reveal deeply embedded gender, race, and class patterns in the structure of scientific professions and, consequently, in the character of scientific thought. As a consequence, while encouraging the participation of women in science is an obvious question of equity, it also reaches deeply into the social construction of science and provides insights about why some concepts gain legitimacy in science while others do not. So, important as it may be, women's experience is excluded from biological theory because it is considered to be

[96] Anne Fausto-Sterling, *Myths of Gender: Biological Theories about Women and Men* (New York: Basic Books, 1985), 117.

[97] Sandra Harding, *The Science Question in Feminism* (Ithaca, N.Y.: Cornell University Press, 1986).

[98] Keller (n. 50 above).

subjective and therefore is considered to be outside the realm of scientific inquiry. Moreover, since it cannot be measured in scientific ways, the topic, not the method, is seen as illegitimate.[99]

Collectively, the work of feminist scientists raises new possibilities for the way science is taught[100] and conceived. By making us more conscious of the interrelatedness of gender and science, this work underscores the connection between science and the sex/gender system. Moreover, a feminist view of science would take it as only one of a number of ways to comprehend and know the world around us so that the hegemony of science as a way of knowing would be replaced with a more pluralistic view.

Resource materials in the disciplines

New scholarship on women does not automatically get translated into new teaching within the disciplines. Therefore, several of the professional organizations have sponsored projects that have produced guidelines for integrating new material on women into courses in the disciplines. These are especially valuable for assisting faculty teaching core courses in the disciplines and teaching new courses about women. The series published by the American Political Science Association[101] is a five-volume set with review essays, sample syllabi, field exercises, and suggested reading. The authors review explanations for the underrepresentation of women as public officials and examine sex discrimination against women as attorneys, judges, offenders, and victims. Moreover, they examine the traditional assumption that women are apolitical by looking at the political activity of women in community organizations and grassroots movements that are organized around such issues as sexual harassment, women's health, and violence against women.

Other professional groups have developed materials that focus particularly on integrating the study of women into the introductory curriculum; such materials are available in sociology, psychology, American history, and microeconomics.[102] These collections typically include a sample sylla-

---

[99] Patsy Schweickart, lecture presented at Mellon Faculty Development Seminar, Wellesley College Center for Research on Women, Fall 1985.

[100] Dorothy Buerk, "An Experience with Some Able Women Who Avoid Mathematics," *For the Learning of Mathematics* 3 (November 1982): 19–24; Anne Fausto-Sterling, "The Myth of Neutrality: Race, Sex, and Class in Science," *Radical Teacher* 19: 21–25, and *Myths of Gender*; see also the special issue, "Women in Science," ed. Pamela Annas, Saul Slapikoff, and Kathleen Weiler, *Radical Teacher*, vol. 30 (1986) for several excellent pieces evolving from the feminist critique of science.

[101] American Political Science Association, *Citizenship and Change: Women and American Politics*, 9 vols. (Washington, D.C.: American Political Science Association, 1983).

[102] Judith M. Gappa and Janice Pearce, "Sex and Gender in the Social Sciences: Reassessing the Introductory Course: Principles of Microeconomics" (San Francisco: San Francisco State University, 1982, mimeographed); Barrie Thorne, ed., *Sex and Gender in the*

bus for introductory courses, with suggestions for new topics, examples, and readings in the different areas usually included in introductory courses. One collection from Feminist Press, *Reconstructing American Literature*, contains sixty-seven syllabi for courses in American literature. The American Sociological Association has recently published an excellent collection that includes syllabi for courses on sex and gender with suggested student assignments and exercises, lists of film resources, and essays on teaching women's studies, dealing with homophobia in the classroom, integrating race, sex, and gender in the classroom, and the experience of black women in higher education.[103]

The appendix of Schuster and Van Dyne's book, *Women's Place in the Academy: Transforming the Liberal Arts Curriculum*, is especially useful because it is organized by disciplines and separates suggested readings into those for classroom use and those more appropriate for teacher preparation. Faculty working to integrate scholarship on women into their courses would be wise to consult the various review essays published in *Signs* that summarize major research and theoretical developments in the academic fields and to consult the papers on curriculum change in the working papers series published by the Wellesley College Center for Research on Women. Newsletters from campuses with inclusive curriculum projects often include essays on revising courses written by faculty who are working to revise their courses.[104] Finally, women's caucuses within the professional associations of the disciplines can typically provide bibliographies and other resources designed to assist in the process of curriculum change.

A wealth of other materials are available to assist faculty specifically in the process of integrating women of color into the curriculum of women's studies and disciplinary courses. Gloria Hull, Patricia Bell Scott, and Barbara Smith's collection, *All the Women Are White, All the Blacks Are Men, But Some of Us Are Brave* is a classic and invaluable source. It includes not only essays on different dimensions of black women's experi-

---

Social Sciences: Reassessing the Introductory Course: Introductory Sociology (Washington, D.C.: American Sociological Association, 1983); Nancy Felipe Russo and Natalie Malovich, *Sex and Gender in the Social Sciences: Reassessing the Introductory Course: Introductory Psychology* (Washington, D.C.: American Psychological Association, 1982); Bonnie Lloyd and Arlene Rengert, "Women in Geographic Curricula," *Journal of Geography* 77 (September–October 1978): 164–91; Organization for American Historians, *Restoring Women to History: Materials for U.S. I and II*, 2 vols. (Bloomington, Ind.: Organization of American Historians, 1983).

[103] Barrie Thorne, Mary McCormack, Virginia Powell, and Delores Wunder, eds., *The Sociology of Sex and Gender: Syllabi and Teaching Materials* (Washington, D.C.: American Sociological Association Teaching Resources Center, 1985).

[104] See especially newsletters from the Center for Research on Women, Memphis State University, and "Re-Visions," the newsletter from the Towson State curriculum project funded by the Fund for the Improvement of Post-Secondary Education.

ences and contributions to knowledge and culture but also a superb selection of syllabi incorporating the study of women of color into courses and bibliographies and bibliographic essays of print and nonprint materials by and about black women.[105]

The Center for Research on Women at Memphis State University publishes a bibliography in the social sciences that is an excellent review of research about women of color;[106] their other projects include summer institutes on women of color and curriculum change, a visiting scholars program, faculty development seminars, and a working papers series. Maxine Baca Zinn's review essay in *Signs* includes an excellent bibliography for including Chicana women in the social sciences,[107] and *Estudios Femeniles de la Chicana* by Marcela Trujillo includes a proposal for Chicana Studies and course proposals and outlines that are useful for curriculum development.[108] Anne Fausto-Sterling and Lydia English have produced a packet of materials on women and minorities in science that is a collaborative project by students enrolled in a course at Brown University on the history of women and minority scientists; their collection includes essays written by the students about their experiences in science. In addition, Fausto-Sterling and English have printed a course materials guide that is an extensive bibliography of books, articles, bibliographies, visual aids, and reference works on the subject of women and minorities in science.[109]

The journal *Sage* is also an invaluable resource for scholars. *Sage* publishes interdisciplinary writing by and about women of color; recent issues have highlighted the topics of education, women writers, and mothers and daughters.[110] Other journals have published special issues devoted to studying women of color.[111] In addition to this growing primary research literature by and about women of color, there are numerous review essays that provide a guide to this important area of research.[112]

[105] Gloria Hull, Barbara Smith, and Patricia Bell Scott, eds., *All the Women Are White, All the Blacks Are Men, But Some of Us Are Brave* (Old Westbury, N.Y.: Feminist Press, 1983).

[106] Memphis State University Center for Research on Women, "Selected Bibliography of Social Science Readings on Women of Color in the U.S." (Memphis, Tenn.: Memphis State University Center for Research on Women, n.d.).

[107] Maxine Baca Zinn, "Mexican-American Women in the Social Sciences," *Signs* 8, no. 2 (Winter 1982): 259–72.

[108] Marcela Trujillo, *Estudios Femeniles de la Chicana* (Los Angeles: University of California Press, 1974).

[109] Anne Fausto-Sterling and Lydia L. English, *Women and Minorities in Science: Course Materials Guide*. Pamphlet and other materials are available from Anne Fausto-Sterling, Department of Biology, Brown University, Providence, R.I. 02921.

[110] *Sage: A Scholarly Journal on Black Women*, Box 42471, Atlanta, Ga. 30311.

[111] See *Journal of Social Issues*, vol. 39 (Fall 1983); *Conditions*, vol. 5 (1979); *Spelman Messenger*, vol. 100 (Spring 1984); *Sinister Wisdom*, vols. 22–23 (1983).

[112] Marilyn Jimenez, "Contrasting Portraits: Integrating Materials about the Afro-Hispanic Woman into the Traditional Curriculum," *Working Papers Series*, no. 120 (Welles-

Such a wealth of material about women of color invalidates teachers' claims that they would include material on and by women of color if it were available. It also underscores the need to reeducate by recentering toward the lives of those who have been excluded from the curriculum and to do so by changing the materials and experiences we use in constructing classroom contents. Including the study of women of color in all aspects of the curriculum is rooted in a fundamental premise of women's studies: that there is great variation in human experiences and that this diversity should be central to educational studies. Although, as Johnella Butler notes, reductionist habits in the classroom make teaching about multiplicity difficult,[113] if the classrooms are more pluralistic both teachers and students will be better able to understand the pluralistic world.

Materials to assist in the process of curriculum change are abundant—so much so that one of the problems in faculty development projects is that faculty who have not followed the development of feminist scholarship over the past two decades must now learn an entirely new field of scholarship. Obviously, this cannot be accomplished quickly and, although we may sometimes feel discouraged by the magnitude of the needed changes, it is useful to remember that we are trying to reconstruct systems of knowledge that have evolved over centuries. Small changes, while obviously incomplete, do introduce larger changes—both in course content and in the political, intellectual, and personal transformations that this process inspires. Although it is also sometimes difficult to imagine what a revised curriculum would look like, Butler reminds us that working to build an inclusive curriculum requires a willingness to be surprised.

All of the materials reviewed above help us assess the climate for change in particular disciplines and devise appropriate strategies for the different fields in which we work and teach. With this information in mind and with the underlying philosophies of different projects specified, we can better analyze the context for curriculum change in various disciplines and imagine multiple ways of accomplishing educational change within them.

Conclusion

Adrienne Rich pointed the way to curriculum change through women's studies when she distinguished between claiming and receiving an education. Receiving an education is only "to come into possession of; to act as receptacle or container for; to accept as authoritative or true," while

---

ley, Mass.: Wellesley College Center for Research on Women, 1983); Baca Zinn (n. 107 above).

[113] Johnella Butler, "Complicating the Question: Black Studies and Women's Studies," in Schuster and Van Dyne, eds. (n. 20 above), 73–86.

claiming an education is "to take as the rightful owner; to assert in the face of possible contradiction."[114] For women, Rich said, this means "refusing to let others do your thinking, talking, and naming for you."[115]

For women's studies to realize Rich's vision means we must develop women's studies itself to be inclusive; building an inclusive curriculum means both working to build women's studies into the curriculum and doing the work and thinking that makes women's studies multicultural and multiracial. These two dimensions will also strengthen women's studies as a field of its own, since they ask us to examine our own assumptions, methods, and relationship to the society in which we live. In this sense, changing the curriculum has three dimensions: changing our selves, changing our work, and changing society.

These are sobering times for women's studies scholars who seek through education an end to the injustices and patterns of exclusion that have characterized our culture. In the current political climate, one in which we are experiencing a serious backlash in educational change, women's studies and the feminist movement will meet new resistance.[116] Current appeals to return to the basics and to stabilize the curriculum threaten once again to exclude women, people of color, and gays and lesbians from the center of our learning, but Howe provides us with hope for change when she writes, "It is essential to revelatory learning to see the opposition clearly. . . . In a period when the opposition will be most visible, we may be able to do our best work."[117]

Department of Sociology
University of Delaware

[114] Adrienne Rich, "Claiming an Education," in *On Lies, Secrets, and Silence* (n. 7 above), 231.

[115] Ibid., 231.

[116] Banner (n. 44 above).

[117] F. Howe (n. 9 above), 28.

FOR AND ABOUT WOMEN: THE THEORY AND PRACTICE OF WOMEN'S STUDIES IN THE UNITED STATES

MARILYN J. BOXER

In 1977, a decade after the first women's studies courses appeared across the United States, the National Women's Studies Association was founded to promote and sustain "the educational strategy of a break-through in consciousness and knowledge" that would "transform" individuals, institutions, relationships, and, ultimately, the whole of society.[1] Insisting that the academic is political and the cognitive is affective, the NWSA's constitution clearly reflected the influence of the women's liberation movement on women's studies. Research and teaching at all educational levels and in all academic and community settings would be not

I would like to thank Holly Smith for assistance in locating materials for this essay and Florence Howe for helpful comments on an earlier draft. My colleagues Pat Huckle, Elyce Rotella, and Bonnie Zimmerman have provided the encouragement and constructive criticism that make a Department of Women's Studies a wonderful place for an academic feminist to work.

1. This definition is taken from the preamble to the constitution of the NWSA, drafted at the Founding Convention in San Francisco, January 13–17, 1977, and published in *Women's Studies Newsletter* 5, nos. 1–2 (Winter/Spring 1977): 6–8.

EDITORS' NOTE: *Because feminist theory finds one of its major expressions in programs of women's studies, this review essay by Marilyn J. Boxer has particular relevance here. Moreover, Boxer's descriptions of the educational methods of women's studies and of the debates among its practitioners illustrate graphically the ways in which feminist theory offers a critique of all ideology, including its own.*

This essay originally appeared in Signs, vol. 7, no. 3, Spring 1982.

only *about* but *for* all women, guided by "a vision of a world free not only from sexism, but also from racism, class-bias, ageism, heterosexual bias—from all the ideologies and institutions that have consciously or unconsciously oppressed and exploited some for the advantage of others."[2] Women's studies, then, challenged its practitioners to think beyond the boundaries of traditional sex roles, of traditional disciplines, and of established institutions. By breaking down the divisions that limit perceptions and deny opportunities, by revising pedagogical processes as well as courses and curricula, this educational reform has itself become a social movement.

Given this mission and momentum, "women's studies is everywhere" today: in more than 300 women's studies programs, in some 30,000 courses in colleges and universities, in a dozen national and international scholarly journals as well as countless newsletters, in community groups and centers, and in conferences and programs all over the world.[3] This review essay cannot attempt to cover this phenomenon completely but will survey the literature about women's studies as a field in American higher education: its history, political issues, theories, and structures. Because of the nature of women's studies itself, these categories often overlap, and some literature will be discussed more than once. My task is complicated by the limited number of available books and monographs; most writing about women's studies has appeared as articles and notes in periodical publications. This review is therefore offered as a first step toward integrating this wealth of literature.

History

Women's studies first appeared in the last half of the 1960s when women faculty in higher education, stronger in number than ever be-

2. Ibid. In a discussion of the psychology of women, Mary Brown Parlee makes a useful distinction concerning research centered on women: "Sexist research on women is of course still being done, but its creators do not identify themselves as being in the field of the psychology of women. Feminist psychologists' power to define and name their own field has evidently prevailed, and the psychology of women denotes and connotes research that is feminist in some very broad (and perhaps arguably so) sense of the term. Psychologists who do not want to be associated with this perspective no longer use the label for their work, even if their research is about women" ("Psychology and Women: Review Essay," *Signs: Journal of Women in Culture and Society* 5, no. 1 [Autumn 1979]: 121–33, esp. 121, n. 1). To a large extent this statement applies generally to women's studies, although in some cases women's studies programs must or choose to allow students credits toward women's studies degrees for any course that deals in substantial measure with women.

3. "Women's Studies Everywhere" was the title of the Second Annual Conference of the Pacific Southwest Regional Women's Studies Association held at the University of Southern California, May 19–21, 1978. A useful guide to the literature which supports research and teaching on women is Esther Stineman, *Women's Studies: A Recommended Core Bibliography* (Littleton, Colo.: Libraries, Inc., 1979).

fore, began to create new courses that would facilitate more reflection on female experience and feminist aspiration.[4] Supported and sometimes led by feminist students, staff, or community women, these innovators were often political activists who sought to understand and to confront the sexism they had experienced in movements for the liberation of other oppressed groups.[5] Their efforts at organization and course development were inspired by both the free-university movement and the civil rights movement, which provided the model of black studies courses and programs.[6] The large number of early courses on women in literature can perhaps be attributed to the relative accessibility of that field to women. At the same time, a "passion for women's history" represented "more than just a desire for a female heritage"; it was also a "search for ways in which a successful female revolution might be constructed."[7]

4. In 1966 Cathy Cade and Peggy Dobbins taught a course on women at the New Orleans Free School, as did Naomi Weisstein at the University of Chicago (Sara Evans, *Personal Politics: The Roots of Women's Liberation in the Civil Rights Movement and the New Left* [New York: Alfred A. Knopf, Inc., 1980], pp. 183, 185–86). The same year Annette Baxter taught women's history at Barnard College (Janice Law Trecker, "Women's Place Is in the Curriculum," *Saturday Review* [October 16, 1971], pp. 83–86, 92). Despite their larger absolute numbers, in some fields the proportion of women had decreased. Between the 1920s and 1960s, the percentage of Ph.D.s awarded to women in the social sciences declined, especially in economics, history, and philosophy (see Victoria Schuck, "Sexism and Scholarship: A Brief Overview of Women, Academia and the Disciplines," *Social Science Quarterly* 55, no. 3 [December 1974]: 563–85; on representation of women between 1960 and 1970, see Helen S. Astin, "Career Profiles of Women Doctorates," in *Academic Women on the Move,* ed. Alice S. Rossi and Ann Calderwood [New York: Russell Sage Foundation, 1973], pp. 139–61).

5. Beginning in 1968 and 1969, faculty women also reacted to the discrimination they experienced by forming caucuses in academic professional organizations (Kay Klotzberger, "Political Action by Academic Women," in Rossi and Calderwood, eds., pp. 359–91).

6. According to Florence Howe, the first "political" women's studies course emerged from the student movement and was taught at the Free University of Seattle in 1965 ("Feminism and Women's Studies: Survival in the Seventies," in *Report on the West Coast Women's Studies Conference,* ed. [Joan Hoff Wilson and] Women's Studies Board at California State University, Sacramento [Pittsburgh: Know, Inc., 1974], pp. 19–20). For an excellent summary of the early development of women's studies, see Florence Howe and Carol Ahlum, "Women's Studies and Social Change," in Rossi and Calderwood, eds., pp. 393–423.

7. Trecker, p. 86. Although Sheila Tobias claimed that the feminist movement began on campuses where "the intellectual content of feminist ideology was very high and the challenge to the assumptions of the behavioral sciences significant" (Sheila Tobias, ed., *Female Studies I* [Pittsburgh: Know, Inc., 1970], p. [ii]), Jo Freeman felt that the university—"the most egalitarian environment most women will ever experience"—was not the source of the movement ("Women's Liberation and Its Impact on the Campus," *Liberal Education* 57, no. 4 [1971]: 468–78). Indeed many important works by popular writers appeared on the first women's studies syllabi, whatever the course title: Simone de Beauvoir, *The Second Sex,* trans. H. M. Parshley (New York: Alfred A. Knopf, Inc., 1953); Caroline Bird, *Born Female: The High Cost of Keeping Women Down* (New York: David McKay Co., 1968); Betty Friedan, *The Feminine Mystique* (New York: W. W. Norton & Co., 1963); and Kate Millett, *Sexual Politics* (New York: Avon Books, 1971).

Among the pioneers, the quest for revolution was clear from the beginning. Women's studies was a necessary part of women's "struggle for self-determination"; its goal was "to understand the world and to change it."[8] The paraphrasing of Marx demonstrates the importance placed on radical change in the early years and the leading role played by veterans of the New Left in launching the new feminism as well as women's studies.

In mid-1970, in one of the first essays to discuss the neglect and distortion of women in university courses and curricula, Sheila Tobias called for a new program of "Female Studies" at Cornell University, justifying her stand with an analogy to black studies. Cornell's community had already witnessed the validity and vitality of this innovative approach at a conference on women in the winter of 1969 and in a multidisciplinary course on "female personality" team-taught to some 400 students in the spring of 1970.[9] At the same time, courses on women appeared at a number of universities, including a program of five at San Diego State College (now University). That autumn, *Female Studies I* was published, the first in a ten-volume series through which practitioners of the new teaching shared their syllabi, reading lists, and experiences. Compiled by Tobias and published by the feminist press Know, Inc., it featured outlines of sixteen courses taught or proposed during 1969 and 1970, as well as a ten-course curriculum from San Diego State, which in September 1970 became the first officially established integrated women's studies program in the nation.[10]

In December, Know published *Female Studies II,* an anthology of sixty-six course outlines and bibliographies collected by the Commission on the Status of Women of the Modern Language Association and edited by its chairperson, Florence Howe. With Howe's leadership the commission had begun to function as a "clearinghouse" for information in the new, mushrooming field she then designated as "feminist studies."[11]

8. Roberta Salper, "The Theory and Practice of Women's Studies," *Edcentric* 3, no. 7 (December 1971): 4–8, esp. 8.

9. Sheila Tobias, "Female Studies—an Immodest Proposal," mimeographed (Ithaca, N.Y.: Cornell University, July 20, 1970); Sheila Tobias et al., eds., *Proceedings of the Cornell Conference on Women* (Pittsburgh: Know, Inc., 1969). An analogy with black studies was also developed in Salper.

10. Tobias, ed. Programs were established early also at Portland State University (Oregon), Richmond City College (New York), Sacramento State University (California), and the University of Washington.

11. Florence G. Howe, ed., *Female Studies II* (Pittsburgh: Know, Inc., 1970). The general acceptance of the name "women's studies" rather than "feminist studies" probably represents an implicit recognition that expediency favors maintenance of a token of traditional academic "objectivity." However, it is clear that women's studies means feminist studies. The presence of male bias in allegedly objective science is a fundamental assumption of women's studies and has been documented repeatedly across a wide spectrum of scholarly fields. Although the title "feminist studies" fell out of currency in the early 1970s,

The rapid growth of women's studies reflected the widely shared perception that changing what and how women (and men) study about women could and would affect the way women live. It offered a new opportunity for students and scholars to redefine themselves and their experiences in the world. Between 1970 and 1975, 150 new women's studies programs were founded, a feat that was repeated between 1975 and 1980.[12] The number of courses grew to some 30,000, offered at most of the colleges and universities in the United States. This phenomenal expansion was documented in—as well as facilitated by—the *Female Studies* series and other publications of Know, established in Pittsburgh in 1969, and of the Feminist Press, founded by Howe and Paul Lauter in Baltimore in 1970 and moved to the State University of New York (SUNY) College at Old Westbury in 1972.[13] That year also saw the birth of three cross-disciplinary journals: *Women's Studies* and *Feminist Studies* to publish scholarly articles, and the *Women's Studies*

---

it was recently adopted for a new degree program at Stanford University; and the question of renaming was reopened by Susan Groag Bell and Mollie Schwartz Rosenhan, who object not only to the ungrammatical construction of "women's studies," but also to its implication that it means "the study of any topic whatever . . . performed by women" (Richard West, "Feminist Program at Stanford a First," *Los Angeles Times* [May 12, 1981], p. 3; Susan Groag Bell and Mollie Schwartz Rosenhan, "A Problem in Naming: Women Studies—Women's Studies?" *Signs: Journal of Women in Culture and Society* 6, no. 3 [Spring 1981]: 540–42, esp. 541). A case for "feminology" is made by Nynne Koch in "The Why, When, How and What of Feminology," in *Feminology*, ed. Ragnhild Silfwerbrand-Ten Cate et al. (Nijmegen, Netherlands: University of Nijmegen, 1975), pp. 18–20. See also Margrit Eichler in "Discussion Forum: The Future Direction of Women's Studies," *Canadian Newsletter of Research on Women* 5, no. 3 (October 1976): 10–12; and Marilyn Webb, "A Radical Perspective on Women's Studies," *Women: A Journal of Liberation* 3, no. 2 (1973): 36–37.

12. "Editorial," *Women's Studies Newsletter* 5, no. 3 (Summer 1977): 2; Florence Howe and Paul Lauter, *The Impact of Women's Studies on the Campus and the Disciplines,* Women's Studies Monograph Series (Washington, D.C.: National Institute of Education, 1980), p. 4. The latest count is 330.

13. The rest of the series includes Florence Howe and Carol Ahlum, eds., *Female Studies III* (Pittsburgh: Know, Inc., 1971); Elaine Showalter and Carol Ohmann, eds., *Female Studies IV* (Pittsburgh: Know, Inc., 1971); Rae Lee Siporin, ed., *Female Studies V* (Pittsburgh: Know, Inc., 1972); Nancy Hoffman, Cynthia Secor, and Adrian Tinsley, eds., *Female Studies VI: Closer to the Ground—Women's Classes, Criticisms, Programs 1972* (Old Westbury, N.Y.: Feminist Press, 1972); Deborah S. Rosenfelt, ed., *Female Studies VII: Going Strong—New Courses, New Programs* (Old Westbury, N.Y.: Feminist Press, 1973); Sarah Slavin Schramm, ed., *Female Studies VIII: Do-It-Yourself Women's Studies* (Pittsburgh: Know, Inc., 1975); Sidonie Cassirer, ed., *Female Studies IX: Teaching about Women in the Foreign Languages—French, Spanish, German, and Russian* (Pittsburgh: Know, Inc., 1976); Deborah S. Rosenfelt, ed., *Female Studies X: Learning to Speak—Student Work* (Old Westbury, N.Y.: Feminist Press, 1976). See also Carol Ahlum and Florence Howe, *The New Guide to Current Female Studies* (Pittsburgh, Know, Inc., 1971), and *The Guide to Current Female Studies II* (Old Westbury, N.Y.: Feminist Press, 1972); Tamar Berkowitz, Jean Mangi, and Jane Williamson, eds., *Who's Who and Where in Women's Studies* (Old Westbury, N.Y.: Feminist Press, 1974); and Betty E. Chmaj and Judith A. Gustafson, *Myth and Beyond: American Women and American Studies* (Pittsburgh: Know, Inc., 1972).

Newsletter to serve as a forum for the women's studies movement in the community as well as in schools at all levels.[14] Florence Howe and Carol Ahlum described this abundance as "an intellectual feast long denied," a "classical instance of a movement without unified organization or direction" whose spread followed the geography of the new women's movement.[15] Its roots, however, lay deep in the history of American feminism and the education of American women.

Introducing a symposium on "masculine blinders in the social sciences," Victoria Schuck perceived three "rounds" in the history of the women's movement, of which only the third and present posed a challenge to the social sciences. Contemporary feminism, through women's studies, "aimed at destroying the sexual stereotypes bequeathed by nineteenth-century male academics."[16] To Howe, women's studies represented a third phase in American women's struggle for education. First, in the early and mid-nineteenth century, proponents of improving female education accepted cultural assumptions about women's nature and demanded a higher education appropriate to woman's role as a moral teacher. Next, in the late nineteenth century, they began to stress the identity of male and female intellectual capacities and to call for access to the standard courses of studies that M. Carey Thomas of Bryn Mawr College labeled the "men's curriculum." Only in the current third phase did they challenge the male hegemony over the content of college courses and the substance of knowledge itself.[17]

14. *Women's Studies'* editor Wendy Martin explained in the inaugural issue her premise that "careful and disciplined research, illuminated by a feminist perspective by both women and men, can contribute to effective social change" (*Women's Studies: An Interdisciplinary Journal* 1, no. 1 [1972]: 2). *Feminist Studies* was founded to "encourage analytic response to feminist issues and analyses that open new areas of feminist research and critique" (*Feminist Studies* 1, no. 1 [1972], inside front cover). In addition to reporting events and promoting dialogue, the *Women's Studies Newsletter* has played an important role in raising critical issues and in suggesting solutions to common problems. In 1977, the *Newsletter* was chosen as the official organ of the NWSA; in spring 1981 it became the *Women's Studies Quarterly,* still published by the Feminist Press.

15. Howe and Ahlum, "Women's Studies and Social Change" (n. 4 above), pp. 413–14.

16. While "Round 1" from Seneca Falls to the Civil War challenged widely accepted images of femininity, "Round 2" from the Civil War to 1920 attempted no "social redefinition" of female identity, so that the new disciplines that arose in the late nineteenth century could develop and sustain a view of women derived from "moral philosophy" (Schuck [n. 4 above], p. 563).

17. Howe has developed this scheme in several essays. See "Feminism and the Education of Women," in *Frontiers of Knowledge,* ed. Judith Stiehm (Los Angeles: University of Southern California Press, 1976), pp. 79–93; "Three Missions of Higher Education for Women: Vocation, Freedom, Knowledge," *Liberal Education* 66, no. 3 (Fall 1980): 285–97; "Myths of Coeducation" (lecture delivered November 2, 1978), and "Women's Studies and Women's Work" (lecture delivered September 26, 1979), both available from Wellesley College Center for Research on Women, Wellesley, Mass. 02181.

But in its early years, women's studies remained essentially a centerless, leaderless movement, marked by diversity in aim, content, and style. As the number of courses and programs multiplied, duly noted in the national press, newcomers could begin to draw on the reflections of the pioneers who, conscious of the historical importance of women's studies and committed to the cooperative principle, continued to publish not only syllabi and reading lists but detailed accounts of their experiences, bad along with the good.[18] Essays by these early practitioners—Florence Howe, Carol Ahlum, Catharine R. Stimpson, Sheila Tobias—all raised questions without easy answers about the tensions between academic and political goals of classroom teaching, the responsibility of women's studies to the women's movement, and the implications of organizational structure and program governance for impact on the university.[19]

The double purpose of women's studies—to expose and redress the oppression of women—was reflected in widespread attempts to restructure the classroom experience of students and faculty. Circular arrangement of chairs, periodic small-group sessions, use of first names for instructors as well as students, assignments that required journal keeping, "reflection papers," cooperative projects, and collective modes of teaching with student participation all sought to transfer to women's studies the contemporary feminist criticism of authority and the validation of every woman's experience. These techniques borrowed from the women's movement also were designed to combat the institutional hierarchy and professional exclusiveness that had been used to shut out women.[20] Indeed, collectivity in teaching and in program governance

18. See "Women's Studies," *Newsweek* (October 26, 1970), p. 61; Trecker (n. 4 above); and Cheryl Fields, "Women's Studies Gain: 2,000 Courses Offered This Year," *Chronicle of Higher Education* (December 17, 1973), p. 6. For a summary of reasons for and against establishment of a women's studies program by Penn Women's Studies Planners, see *1972 Summer Project Report: A Descriptive Analysis of a National Survey* (Philadelphia: New Morning Press, 1972).

19. Howe and Ahlum examined the origins of women's studies, its relationship to educational reform and to women's education, its basic assumptions and goals, and its role as a feminist movement for change ("Women's Studies and Social Change" [n. 6 above], pp. 393–423). In "The New Feminism and Women's Studies," Stimpson analyzed her reasons for teaching a women's studies course, stressing the multicausality of social, educational, and political circumstances that favored the development of women's studies and the resulting diversity of aims, styles, and goals the movement encompassed (*Change* 5 [September 1973]: 43–48). Tobias reviewed her experiences teaching women's studies at three universities and shared her expectations for its expansion ("Women's Studies: Its Origins, Organization, and Prospects," in *The Higher Education of Women*, ed. Helen Astin [New York: Holt, Rinehart, & Winston, 1978], pp. 80–94, also in *Women's Studies International Quarterly* 1, no. 1 [1978]: 85–97).

20. On new dynamics in early women's studies classrooms, see discussions by Florence Howe, Lillian Robinson, Maureen Greenwald, and Gerda Lerner in Howe, ed. pp. 1–4, 42–43, 70–73, and 86–88, respectively. See also descriptions of women's studies programs

has been deemed the most radical and vital contribution of the women's movement to educational innovation.[21]

Yet the adaptation of feminist principles to teaching and governance in women's studies soon led to controversy. In a widely circulated essay on the defects of the feminist ideal of "structurelessness," Jo Freeman demonstrated that the rejection of formal leadership with visible lines of responsibility favored the development of informal networks where power flowed through underground channels based on friendship, thus creating the very evil it sought to suppress: control by elites.[22] Among Freeman's readers, some hoped that women's studies would avoid the doctrinaire allegiance to ideologies that had proved so destructive in the women's liberation movement.[23]

The responsibility of women's studies to the larger feminist community also became a debated issue in the early years. At two major women's studies conferences in the early 1970s, bitter conflict developed between factions who weighed differently the political and academic aims of the campus movement. The first was a small, invitational conference held at the University of Pittsburgh in November 1971, which polarized into a "revolutionary feminist caucus" of students and political activists and a group of established academics who had come to discuss theoretical issues about women's studies.[24] The second was the West Coast Women's Studies Conference held at Sacramento State College (now University) in May 1973 on problems of "survival in the seventies." A deep cleavage developed when a highly organized group diverted

at SUNY/Buffalo, Cambridge-Goddard Graduate School for Social Change, Portland State University, City University of New York (CUNY)/Richmond College, Sacramento State College, and San Diego State College, in Howe and Ahlum, eds., *Female Studies III*, pp. 142–48, 164–73. See also essays in Showalter and Ohmann, eds., esp. Elaine Showalter, "Introduction: Teaching About Women, 1971," pp. i–xii.

21. Christine Grahl, Elizabeth Kennedy, Lillian S. Robinson, and Bonnie Zimmerman, "Women's Studies: A Case in Point," *Feminist Studies* 1, no. 2 (Fall 1972): 109–20; Sarah Slavin Schramm, *Plow Women Rather Than Reapers: An Intellectual History of Feminism in the United States* (Metuchen, N.J.: Scarecrow Press, 1978); Sheila Tobias, "Teaching Women's Studies: Looking Back over Three Years," *Liberal Education* 58, no. 2 (May 1972): 264; Staff, "Teaching Collectively," *Women's Studies Program: Three Years of Struggle* (San Diego: California State University at San Diego, 1973), pp. 42–44. Despite the emphasis on cooperative and group experience, however, women's studies courses made heavy demands on students and teachers. To preclude accusations of "academic anemia," some instructors resorted to "intellectual overkill" (Wendy Martin, "Teaching Women's Studies—Some Problems and Discoveries," in Showalter and Ohmann, eds., p. 9).

22. Jo Freeman, "The Tyranny of Structurelessness," *Berkeley Journal of Sociology* 17 (1972–73): 151–64, reprinted in *Women in Politics*, ed. Jane S. Jaquette (New York: John Wiley & Sons, 1974), pp. 204–14.

23. Mollie Schwartz Rosenhan, "Women's Studies and Feminism: Ideological Conflict in the Academy" (paper presented at the annual meeting of the American Historical Association, San Francisco, December 30, 1973).

24. Rae Lee Siporin, "Introduction: Women and Education: The Conference as Catalyst," in Siporin, ed., pp. iii–xiv.

scheduled sessions from their announced purposes to discuss issues on its own agenda. Exhibiting deep distrust of conference planners and movement leaders, the group attacked "white, middle-class, heterosexual" feminists for attempting to separate women's studies from the radical women's movement. In the face of physical as well as verbal confrontation, some of the 700 participants withdrew.[25]

The *Report on the West Coast Women's Studies Conference* is a remarkable document of a period in women's studies history when difficult lessons about process and pluralism were learned. It includes proceedings as well as postconference statements from both sides. In one interpretive essay, Deborah Rosenfelt characterized "the cleavage in purpose and ideology that ran like a crack in the earth" through conference activities as a manifestation of the division within the women's movement between "socialist feminists" and "cultural feminists" ("Marxists" and "Matriarchs"), who attacked each other for, respectively, employing "male" modes of analysis and confrontation, and enjoying the rewards of apolitical, middle-class academic privilege. Rosenfelt emphasized the creative aspects of the struggle.[26]

More fearful that women's studies would be destroyed by internal conflict if not by external opposition, Catharine Stimpson analyzed the source of the internecine quarrels in a perceptive essay that remains pertinent today. In "What Matter Mind: A Critical Theory about the Practice of Women's Studies," she identified the problems as women's acceptance of cultural stereotypes of femininity and their consequent distrust of women in power, as well as ideological conflict among five categories of women's studies practitioners: "pioneers" who had taught about women before women's studies began, "ideologues" who had come to women's studies through the feminist movement, "radicals" who had been politicized by other movements, "latecomers" who became interested after women's studies began, and "bandwagoneers" who found women's studies fashionable and useful for their careers. The fiercest strife arose between the "ideologues" and "radicals." While somewhat pessimistic about the future, Stimpson saw hope for survival in the "buoyancy that comes from sensing that to work for women's studies is to belong to a historical tide." To strengthen the growing community of scholars and teachers, she suggested the establishment of a national organization.[27]

25. See Ann Forfreedom, "Whither Women's Studies?" in *Report on the West Coast Women's Studies Conference*, pp. 110–113, esp. p. 113.

26. Deborah Rosenfelt, "What Happened at Sacramento?" in Women's Studies Board at California State University, ed., pp. 78–83, also in *Women's Studies Newsletter* 5 (Fall 1973): 1, 6–7. See also Betty Chmaj, "Confrontation in Anger and in Pain," ibid., pp. 140–43, also in Chmaj and Gustafson, pp. 24–39,

27. Catharine R. Stimpson, "What Matter Mind: A Critical Theory about the Practice of Women's Studies," *Women's Studies* 1, no. 3 (1973): 293–314, also available from ERIC

The perspective that the radical feminist goals of women's studies made it incompatible with the university system led to a complete change in faculty at the earliest of programs, San Diego State, in 1974.[28] Adrienne Rich addressed this issue of women's studies' possible co-optation within the university system at another troubled conference at the University of Pennsylvania in the same year, "Women's Studies: Renaissance or Revolution?" She expressed the fear that women's studies, if integrated into male-defined and -dominated universities, might become isolated pockets of academic life where a few women could nourish a "false illusion of power."[29] More recently, in the foreword to a collection of her prose, she finds that, despite its tenuous hold on the university, women's studies continues to be a place where women may "claim" rather than "receive" an education, may demand to be taken seriously and taught what they really need to know to live as women in the world.[30] Even if staffed by "tokenists," women's studies might, Rich felt, serve as a catalyst "toward a woman-centered university."[31]

Rich envisioned a university transformed by feminist principles, with competition replaced by cooperation, fragmentation by wholeness, and even the line between campus and community shaded. It was a goal which depended on women learning to use their power constructively, as "power to change." Academic feminists would have to succeed in re-designing not only the women's studies classroom but also the

---

(ED 068078) 1972 and in condensed form, "A Critical View of Women's Studies," *Women's Studies Newsletter* 2 (Winter 1972): 1–4.

28. The entire faculty resigned, stating, "We have realized that professionalizing Women's Studies and the institutionalizing of this program is part of the strategy of those in power in the university. . . . A collective program like San Diego's either must develop into a traditional elitist approach to education, or the women who have maintained the collective approach will be fired and replaced by women who are not committed to student interests or needs. In either case, Women's Studies as we have known it, is incompatible with the institution and is eliminated" (Women's Studies Board, San Diego State College, *Women's Studies and Socialist Feminism* [San Diego: San Diego State College, April 20, 1974], pp. 5–7). On the early development of this program see Roberta Salper, "Women's Studies," *Ramparts* 10, no. 6 (December 1971): 56–60; later history, Marilyn J. Boxer, "Closeup: Women's Studies Department at San Diego," *Women's Studies Newsletter* 6, no. 2 (Spring 1978): 20–23.

29. Adrienne Rich, "Women's Studies—Renaissance or Revolution?" *Women's Studies* 3, no. 2 (1976): 121–26.

30. Adrienne Rich, "Claiming an Education" (lecture delivered at Douglass College, September 6, 1977), and "Taking Women Students Seriously" (lecture delivered at New Jersey College and University Coalition on Women's Education, May 7, 1978), both in Adrienne Rich, *On Lies, Secrets, and Silence: Selected Prose 1966–1978* (New York: W. W. Norton & Co., 1979), pp. 231–35, 237–45 (hereafter cited as *On Lies*).

31. Adrienne Rich, "Toward a Woman-centered University," in *Women and the Power to Change*, ed. Florence Howe (New York: McGraw-Hill Book Co., 1975), pp. 15–46, reprinted in Rich, *On Lies*, pp. 125–55, and excerpted in *Chronicle of Higher Education* (July 21, 1975).

"clockwork of male careers" and the value structure on which the university and society were based. With the resources available now, however, much could be done, and even an activist skeptical of academic feminism could "find happiness" teaching women's studies.[32]

By mid-decade women's studies entered a "second phase," settling in for the long haul, no longer justifying itself as primarily compensatory and ultimately, if successful, self-liquidating. This new consciousness was manifested in a series of reports from the field that appeared in the *Women's Studies Newsletter* under the title, "The Future of Women's Studies."[33] One coordinator pointed out that "in order to change or add to the traditional perspectives of the disciplines, women's studies has to be of them, in them, and about them." A second considered it essential to make women's studies "part of the fundamental structure of our schools." A third gave an indication of how far the movement had come from the search for forgotten women in the suggestion that women's studies "constitutes a genuine discipline, understood as we now understand English or history or physics."[34]

To assess the state of women's studies after seven years, the National Advisory Council on Women's Educational Programs commissioned a study by Florence Howe of fifteen "mature" programs with line budgets; paid administrators; officially recognized curricula; and accredited majors, minors, or certificate programs. The report, *Seven Years Later: Women's Studies Programs in 1976,* stressed the successes: student interest and enrollment growth, the breadth and depth of course offerings, the vitality of women's studies scholarship, and the impact on university faculty and curricula.[35] While demonstrating how effectively women's studies programs used resources, it pointed to insufficient and unstable staffing and funding as key issues affecting the future. It said little about some problem areas, such as program governance and relations with the feminist community, but called for further study of others, including the involvement of minority women, the effectiveness of women's studies teaching, the impact of women's studies on host institutions. Although

32. Florence Howe, "Women and the Power to Change," and Arlie Russell Hochschild, "Inside the Clockwork of Male Careers," in Howe, ed., *Women and the Power to Change,* pp. 127–71, 47–80; Carol Anne Douglas, "Can A Radical Feminist Find Happiness Teaching Women's Studies?" *off our backs* 7, no. 1 (December 1977): 11, 14–15.

33. Gayle Graham Yates, "Women's Studies in Its Second Phase," *Women's Studies Newsletter* 5, nos. 1–2 (Winter/Spring 1977): 4–5; "The Future of Women's Studies," ibid., vol. 3, no. 2 (Spring 1975), ibid., vol. 3, nos. 3–4 (Summer/Fall 1975), ibid., vol. 4, no. 1 (Winter 1976).

34. Dana V. Hiller, director of Women's Studies, University of Cincinnati, *Women's Studies Newsletter* 3, no. 2 (Spring 1975): 4; Joan Geetter, acting director of Women's Studies, University of Connecticut, ibid.; and Susan Phipps-Sanger, administrative assistant-advisor, and Toni McNaron, coordinator of Women's Studies, University of Minnesota, ibid., 3, nos. 3–4 (Summer/Fall 1975): 26.

35. Florence Howe, *Seven Years Later: Women's Studies Programs in 1976* (Washington, D.C.: National Advisory Council on Women's Educational Programs, 1977).

the report has been seen as "women's studies dressed in her 'Sunday best,'" it captures the essential shape and spirit.[36]

Placed alongside *Female Studies I* (or *II* or *III*), *Seven Years Later* offers dramatic evidence that women's studies was higher education's success story of the decade. Despite a new era of hard times for public education, new programs continued to appear. They were established in technical institutes, Catholic and Mormon universities, anti-ERA states in the South, some high schools, and many community colleges. Women's studies was germinating in the "grass roots."[37]

With the changing cultural environment and increasing integration of women's studies into the educational establishment, a new constituency of students entered the classroom.[38] Unlike the students of the early 1970s, they were less likely to identify themselves as feminists, or sometimes even to understand such basic concepts as sexism and feminism. Susan Sniader Lanser was startled to find her students not only apolitical but still suffering the burden of traditional sex-role expectations.[39] "Consciousness raising," borrowed from women's liberation to become a teaching device in early women's studies classrooms, took place less often but continued to be perceived as a latent function of the formal educational process.[40] Cheri Register identified four stages in

36. Nancy Hoffman, "Seven Years Later: Women's Studies Programs in 1976: A Review," *Radical Teacher* 6 (December 1977): 54–56.

37. For women's studies programs in diverse settings, see, e.g., *Radical Teacher* (Special Issue on Women's Studies in the 70's: Moving Forward), vol. 6 (December 1977). On Catholic colleges, Betty Burnett, "Grass Roots in Women's Studies: Kansas City, Missouri," *Women's Studies Newsletter* 5, no. 3 (Summer 1977): 3–4; and Barbara B. Stern, "How To Establish a Women's Studies Course When the Administration Is Against It, the Students Think It's Too Hard, Your Department Is Out of Money, and You Are Probably Too Old to Be Teaching Anymore," *International Journal of Women's Studies* 2, no. 1 (January/February 1979): 100–101. On a Mormon university, see Judith Gappa and J. Nicholls Eastmond, "Gaining Support for a Women's Studies Program in a Conservative Institution," *Liberal Education* 64, no. 3 (October 1978): 278–92. On women's studies in the South, see Nancy Topping Bazin, "Expanding the Concept of Affirmative Action to Include the Curriculum," *Women's Studies Newsletter* 8, no. 4 (Fall/Winter 1980): 9–11; Mollie C. Davis, "Grass Roots Women's Studies: Piedmont, North Carolina," ibid., 4, no. 2 (Spring 1976): 1–2; and Linda Todd, "Grass Roots Women's Studies: South Carolina," ibid., 4, no. 3 (Summer 1976): 4. On community colleges, see Allana Elovson, *Women's Studies in the Community Colleges*, Women's Studies Monograph Series (Washington, D.C.: National Institute of Education, 1980).

38. From Portland State came the following dialogue, which aptly expresses some of the internal changes. Nancy: "Do you think our 'constituency' has changed? Are there fewer of us now who tend to see women's studies as coextensive with our egos?" Julie: "Not really, and that's not a good way to put it. We're pretty diverse in our needs and uses for the program. Somehow, though, we're all getting older" (Nancy Porter, Julie Allen, and Jean Maxwell, "From Portland State University—in Three Voices," *Women's Studies Newsletter* 3, no. 2 [Spring 1975]: 5).

39. Susan Sniader Lanser, "Beyond *The Bell Jar:* Women Students of the 1970s," *Radical Teacher* 6 (December 1977): 41–44.

40. Ellen Boneparth, "Evaluating Women's Studies: Academic Theory and Practice," *Social Science Journal* 14, no. 2 (April 1977): 23–31. This special issue of *Social Science*

both the classroom process and the development of women's studies and the women's movement. Moving from compensating, to criticizing, to collecting and constructing, and finally to conceptualizing anew, students and teacher would pass through despair to emerge with a new and positive basis for understanding and living with a feminist perspective.[41] However, after a study of the literature evaluating women's studies teaching and their own investigation of the values expressed by teachers, Nancy M. Porter and Margaret T. Eileenchild found no clear evidence of the changes in attitude and perception often reported by students and teachers. They suggested that future evaluations place the women's studies experience in a broad educational context that would encompass such variables as sex of instructor and student, political perspective and goals of the instructor, and classroom structure. Neither the necessary data nor the measurement instrument appropriate to the task are yet available, although the development by Marcia Guttentag of an evaluation method involving participants in setting objectives may prove particularly appropriate to measuring the impact of women's studies.[42]

New perceptions of women's studies were accompanied by new structures. To facilitate communications among practitioners and to enhance the development of scholarship and teaching, the National Women's Studies Association was founded at San Francisco in 1977.[43] After many months of careful preparation, it was designed to express both professional and feminist values. A complicated structure allowing equitable representation to various constituencies—regional groups,

---

Journal (Women's Studies: Awakening Academe) was also published as Kathleen Blumhagen and Walter Johnson, eds., *Women's Studies* (Westport, Conn.: Greenwood Press, 1978). See also Deborah Silverton Rosenfelt, "Introduction," in Rosenfelt, ed. (n. 13 above), p. viii; Barbara A. Schram, "What's the Aim of Women's Studies?" *Journal of Teacher Education* 26, no. 4 (Winter 1975): 352–53; and Schramm (n. 21 above), pp. 345–46. Ellen Morgan worried lest the consciousness-raising experience leave her students alienated from society but lacking an adequate factual and theoretical basis to live as feminists ("On Teaching Women's Studies," *University of Michigan Papers in Women's Studies* [May 1978], pp. 27–34). Blanche Hersh finds Morgan's analysis a useful guide to fulfillment of women's studies' promise to effect change in consciousness (Women's Studies Program, Northeastern Illinois University, "On Teaching Women's Studies," *Program Notes*, vol. 4, no. 1 [January/ February 1979]).

    41. Cheri Register, "Brief, A-mazing Movements: Dealing with Despair in the Women's Studies Classroom," *Women's Studies Newsletter* 7, no. 4 (Fall 1979): 7–10.

    42. Nancy M. Porter and Margaret T. Eileenchild, *The Effectiveness of Women's Studies Teaching*, Women's Studies Monograph Series (Washington, D.C.: National Institute of Education, 1980); Marcia Guttentag, Lorelei R. Brush, Alice Ross Gold, Marnie W. Mueller, Sheila Tobias, and Marni Goldstein White, "Evaluating Women's Studies: A Decision-Theoretic Approach," *Signs: Journal of Women in Culture and Society* 3, no. 4 (Summer 1978): 884–90.

    43. On preparation, see Elsa Greene, "The Case for a National Women's Studies Association," *Women's Studies Newsletter* 4, no. 1 (Winter 1976): 1, 3; Elsa Greene and Elaine Reuben, "Planning a National Women's Studies Association," ibid., 4, no. 2 (Spring 1976): 1, 10–11; Sybil Weir, "Planning Continues for the National Founding Convention," ibid., 4, no. 3 (Summer 1976): 1, 10–11.

students, staff, elementary and secondary teachers, lesbians, Third World women, community women—was designed to counter the tendency toward exclusiveness that characterizes many other professional organizations. Sliding registration fees for conventions would provide funds to equalize transportation costs for residents of nearby and distant places. Widespread participation would be encouraged by eliminating keynote speakers.

The successful outcome of the founding convention and subsequent annual conferences reflected the sensitivity of the planners to the problems that beset earlier gatherings.[44] By the end of the decade, the "room of one's own" for which feminists had fought at the beginning was becoming, in the optimistic words of the NWSA's coordinator Elaine Reuben, a "several-story building."[45] Its future remained, however, contingent on the resolution of fundamental, continuing problems.

Political Issues

In fulfillment of the commitment of women's studies to be inclusive of all women and all women's concerns, programs for the NWSA conferences at the University of Kansas in 1979, Indiana University in 1980, and the University of Connecticut, Storrs, in 1981 included more than 250 sessions. Their titles indicate that the concerns and conflicts manifested in the early 1970s in the *Female Studies* series remain alive, while some new issues have emerged. If women's studies is now established firmly enough to survive a decade that began with the accession to political power of right-wing forces clearly allied with antifeminism, it faces continuing challenges from within.[46] The most extensive debates continue to address the relationship of women's studies to the feminist movement and the integration of activist and academic goals, inside as

44. Florence Howe, "What Happened at the Convention," *Women's Studies Newsletter* 5, 1–2 (Winter/Spring 1977): 3–4; Beverly Watkins, "Feminist Educators Seek to Improve Status of Women's Studies," *Chronicle of Higher Education* (January 31, 1977), p. 8. On the 1979 conference, see *Women's Studies Newsletter* 7, no. 3 (Summer 1979): 15–28 and *Frontiers: A Journal of Women Studies*, vol. 5, no. 1 (Spring 1980): 1–70. On the 1980 conference, see *Women's Studies Newsletter* 8, no. 3 (Summer 1980): 3–24. On the 1981 conference, see *Women's Studies Quarterly* 9, no. 3 (Fall 1981): 4–22, 35–40.

45. Elaine Reuben et al., "Visions and Revisions: Women and the Power to Change," *Women's Studies Newsletter* 7, no. 3 (Summer 1979): 18–22.

46. Phyllis Schlafly considers enrollment in women's studies the worst thing a middle-aged woman can possibly do (*Power of the Positive Woman* [New Rochelle, N.Y.: Arlington House Publishers, 1977], p. 59). See also Linda Gordon and Allen Hunter, "Sex, Family and the New Right: Anti-Feminists as a Political Force," *Radical America* 11, no. 6, and 12, no. 1 (November 1977–February 1978): 9–25. According to Catharine Stimpson, women's studies "now has the maturity to move from a defensive to a stalwart posture" ("The New Scholarship about Women: The State of the Art," *Annals of Scholarship* 1, no. 2 [1980]: 2–14).

well as outside the classroom. Although these debates serve to stimulate and to enrich women's studies, they also provide a source of potential conflict among constituent groups and require that the NWSA perform a delicate "balancing act."[47]

Present from the beginning, the old issue of women's studies' possible co-optation remains unresolved. Over the years numerous observers, pointing to the history of home economics, have expressed a fear that women's studies might be absorbed by the academy, lose its feminist thrust, and become a female ghetto with minimal impact on mainstream education and society.[48] Some programs, however, including those at SUNY/Buffalo and Portland State University in Oregon, have continued to consider the struggle against traditional hierarchical organization, in program governance as well as classroom dynamics, critical to the mission of women's studies.[49] The controversy over an early unsuccessful scheme to integrate academic women's studies into a broad spectrum of educational, social, and community services in Southern California and a current conflict over the location of a women's studies institute in West Germany also reflect this concern within the movement.[50] The Feminist Studies Program at Cambridge-Goddard, dedicated to integrating social research and social action, recently dissolved itself rather than com-

47. Barbara Hillyer Davis and Patricia A. Frech, "Diversity, Fragmentation, Integration: The NWSA Balancing Act," *Women's Studies Quarterly* 9, no. 1 (Spring 1981): 33–35.

48. Ruth Crego Benson, "Women's Studies: Theory and Practice," *AAUP Bulletin* 58, no. 3 (September 1972): 283–86; Ann Snitow and Margaret Mahoney, "Higher Education and Women," *Arts in Society* 11, no. 1 (Spring/Summer 1974): 95–96; Jill K. Conway, "Coeducation and Women's Studies: Two Approaches to the Question of Women's Place in the Contemporary University," *Daedalus* 103, no. 4 (Fall 1974): 239–49; Freeman, "Women's Liberation and Its Impact" (n. 7 above); Greene, "Case for a National Women's Studies Association"; Barbara Sicherman, "The Invisible Woman: The Case for Women's Studies," in *Women in Higher Education,* ed. W. Todd Furniss and Patricia Alberg Graham (Washington, D.C.: American Council on Education, 1974), p. 172; and Tobias, "Teaching Women's Studies" (n. 21 above), p. 263.

49. On Portland State, see Nancy Hoffman, "A Class of Our Own," in Showalter and Ohmann, eds. (n. 13 above), pp. 14–28; "Working Together: The Women's Studies Program at Portland State University," in Hoffman et al., eds. (n. 13 above), pp. 164–228; and Porter et al., p. 5. On SUNY/Buffalo, see Grahl et al. (n. 21 above); also Women's Studies College, SUNY/Buffalo, "Proposal for a College of Women's Studies" (unpublished paper, Fall 1971), "Women's Studies College Charter" (unpublished paper, October 15, 1974), "Women's Studies Struggle Continues . . ." (unpublished paper, Spring 1976); "From SUNY/Buffalo," *Women's Studies Newsletter* 3, nos. 3–4 (Summer/Fall 1975): 5–6; and Abstract 60 in "Selected Abstracts from the First National Conference of the National Women's Studies Association, May 30–June 3, 1979, Lawrence, Kansas," *Frontiers: A Journal of Women Studies* 5, no. 1 (Spring 1980): 12–13.

50. For Southern California, see Salper, "Women's Studies." For West Germany, see Tobe Levin, "Women's Studies in West Germany," *Women's Studies Newsletter* 7, no. 1 (Winter 1979): 21–22; Hanna-Beate Schöpp-Schilling, "Women's Studies Research Centers: Report from West Germany," ibid., 8, no. 2 (Spring 1979): 28–29; Peggy McIntosh, "The Women's Studies Conference in Berlin: Another Chapter in the Controversy," ibid., 8, no. 4 (Fall/Winter 1980): 24–26.

promise its commitment to structural change in the education process. But revolutionary fervor cannot be maintained endlessly, and historical circumstances change. Perhaps in light of the spectacular, and to some extent unforeseen, flowering of feminist scholarship—which has created an increasingly strong foundation and justification for the movement— academic women's studies has become less directly a strategy for institutional change and more specifically an attack on sexist scholarship and teaching.

Yet the conviction remains strong that women's studies must be explicitly political, consciously an academic arm of women's liberation, and actively part of a larger social movement that envisions the transformation of society.[51] Unlike other academic pursuits, it must not separate theory from practice. Since "feminist activity made women's studies possible, women's studies must in turn make feminist activity possible."[52] At the NWSA founding convention, one group charged that university women "have taken much more from the Women's Movement than they have to date returned" and suggested ways in which "academic privilege" might benefit the women's movement.[53] Today women's studies practitioners and programs enter into innumerable community activities in many ways: teachers are taking women's studies to nursing homes and prisons, bringing together mothers and daughters, and transforming academic feminism into grass-roots theater.[54]

51. For a cogent statement of this point of view, see Linda Gordon, "A Socialist View of Women's Studies: A Reply to the Editorial, Volume 1, Number 1," *Signs: Journal of Women in Culture and Society* 1, no. 2 (Winter 1975): 559–66.

52. Melanie Kaye, "Closeup on Women's Studies Courses: Feminist Theory and Practice," *Women's Studies Newsletter* 6, no. 3 (Summer 1978): 20–23.

53. S. Brown, E. Hawkes, F. Klein, M. Lowe, E. B. Makrides, and R. Felberg, "Women's Studies: A Fresh Perspective," *The Longest Revolution* 1, no. 3 (February 1977): 13–14, 16. The opposite perspective was expressed by an academic feminist at the International Women's Year Conference in Houston. Noting that the resolution on education ignored women's studies, Amy Swerdlow asserted that "women's studies has supported the women's movement, now it's time for the movement to support women's studies" (quoted by Elizabeth Baer and Dora Janeway Odarenko, "The IWY Conference at Houston: Implications for Women's Studies," *Women's Studies Newsletter* 6, no. 1 [Winter 1978]: 3–6). Linda Gordon has suggested that "we should take our questions from the movement but not our answers" ("What Should Women's Historians Do: Politics, Social Theory and Women's History," *Marxist Perspectives* 1, no. 3 [Fall 1978]: 128–36).

54. Diane T. Rudnick and Sayre Phillips Sheldon, "Teaching Women's History to Men in Prison," and Dorothy Kilton, "Your Mind—Use It or Lose It: Women's Studies in a Nursing Home," *Women's Studies Newsletter* 8, no. 2 (Spring 1980): 9–12; Cynthia D. Kinnard, "Feminist Teaching in a Women's Prison" (NWSA Session Abstract, NWSA Convention, Indiana University, Bloomington, 1980); Nancy Schniedewind, "Reaching Out to the Community: The Mothers and Daughters Conference at SUNY/New Paltz," *Women's Studies Newsletter* 8, no. 1 (Winter 1980): 28–29; Carol Perkins, "Tricks of the Trade," *Radical Teacher* 14 (December 1979): 23–26. See also Catharine R. Stimpson, "Women's Studies and the Community: Some Models," *Women's Studies Newsletter* 2, no. 3 (Summer 1974): 2–3.

Individuals are experiencing and resolving their personal tensions between academics and activism in various ways. For some, it means leaving the university. Jo Freeman, whose work has contributed to both women's studies and the women's movement, has decided that feminism is compatible with scholarship but not with academic life. Mary Howell, on the other hand, has consciously compromised by applying traditional standards in her professional life and dedicating herself to community feminism and women's culture in her private life. Others seem to temper if not transcend the problem by accepting the emerging consensus that women's studies in the long run implies profound change in the structure of knowledge, the university, and society.[55]

Feminist sensitivity to social process is perhaps manifest most clearly in the ongoing, if not always successful, attempt in women's studies to fight against oppression on the basis of race, class, age, religion, and sexual preference as well as sex. A proposed amendment to the NWSA constitution states that "freedom from sexism by necessity must include a commitment to freedom from racism, national chauvinism, class and ethnic bias, ageism, heterosexual bias." The two most critical current issues involve the integration into women's studies and the NWSA of women of color and lesbians.

The NWSA as an organization has acknowledged widespread neglect of women of color in women's studies courses, materials, programs, and conferences. Although the *Women's Studies Newsletter,* the official journal of the NWSA, has during the past five years published a number of articles on research and resources pertinent to black women, considerably less work has appeared on other women of color.[56] At the found-

---

55. Jo Freeman, "The Feminist Scholar," *Quest* 5, no. 1 (Summer 1979): 26–36. Freeman's anthology, *Women: A Feminist Perspective* (Palo Alto, Calif.: Mayfield Publishing Co., 1975), is one of the most widely adopted texts for introductory courses, while her essays have illuminated important issues on the women's movement. See also Mary Howell, "Can We Be Feminists and Professionals?" *Women's Studies International Quarterly* 2, no. 1 (1979): 1–7, and the proceedings of women's studies conferences sponsored by the Great Lakes Colleges Association (GLCA): Beth Reed, ed., *The Structure of Knowledge: A Feminist Perspective: Proceedings of the Fourth Annual Great Lakes Colleges Association Women's Studies Conference* (Ann Arbor, Mich.: Great Lakes Colleges Association Women's Studies Program, 1978) (hereafter cited as *Structure of Knowledge*), and *Toward a Feminist Transformation of the Academy: Proceedings of the Fifth Annual Great Lakes Colleges Association Women's Studies Conference* (Ann Arbor, Mich.: Great Lakes Colleges Association Women's Studies Program, 1979) (hereafter cited as *Toward a Feminist Transformation*). Both are available from the GLCA Women's Studies Program, 220 Collingwood, Suite 240, Ann Arbor, Michigan 48103.

56. Barbara Smith, "Doing Research on Black Women," *Women's Studies Newsletter* 4, no. 2 (Spring 1976): 4–5, 7; Michele Russell, "Black-Eyed Blues Connections: Teaching Black Women," ibid., 4, no. 4 (Fall 1976): 6–7, and ibid., 5, nos. 1–2 (Winter/Spring 1977): 24–28; Nancy Hoffman, "White Woman, Black Women: Inventing an Adequate Pedagogy," ibid., 5, nos. 1–2 (Winter/Spring 1977): 21–24; Rita B. Dandridge, "On Novels by Black American Women: A Bibliographical Essay," ibid., 6, no. 3 (Summer 1978): 28–30;

ing NWSA conference in 1977, Third World women formed a caucus and presented a series of resolutions aimed at greater inclusion of women of color. Provisions for permanent status for the caucus and special representation on the NWSA Coordinating Council were incorporated into the initial governance plan, while other proposals (including the guarantee that any resolutions to which the caucus objected would not be passed until after review of a Third World women's position paper) were to become part of the finished constitution.[57] Reacting to complaints of inadequate Third World participation in the first and second national conventions, the NWSA selected "Women Respond to Racism" as the theme of the third annual conference in 1981.[58] By scheduling daily consciousness-raising sessions in which participants could focus on the personal as well as societal effects of racism, the association also demonstrated its intention to move beyond tokenism and abstract discussions of the interaction of sexism and racism in society. It was a way of responding to black women's charge that the more or less institutionalized women's studies of recent years has traded its "radical life-changing vision" for "acceptance, respectability and the career advancement of individuals."[59]

Pioneers of black women's studies, such as Barbara Smith, use "black women" as a metaphor for the essential revolutionary message of women's studies. A women's studies committed to research, writing, and teaching that makes the experience of black women immediately accessible to all women would necessarily "require and indicate that fundamental political and social change is taking place."[60] As Gloria T. Hull writes, the experience of working on—and with—a black female subject

---

T. Cross, F. Klein, Barbara Smith, and Beverly Smith, "Face-to-Face, Day-to-Day, Racism CR," ibid., 8, no. 1 (Winter 1980): 27–28; Ann Cathey Carver, "Building Coalitions between Women's Studies and Black Studies: What Are the Realities?" ibid., 8, no. 3 (Summer 1980): 16–19; Betsy Brinson, "Teaching Black Women's Heritage," ibid., 8, no. 4 (Fall/Winter 1980): 19–20. See also Angela Jorge, "Issues of Race and Class: A Puerto Rican Woman's Thoughts," ibid., 8, no. 4 (Fall/Winter 1980): 17–18.

57. *Women's Studies Newsletter* 5, nos. 1–2 (Winter/Spring 1977): 6.

58. For 1979, see Nupur Chaudhuri, "A Third World Woman's View of the Convention," Rayna Green, "American Indian Women Meet in Lawrence," Barbara Smith's comments in "Visions and Revisions: Women and the Power to Change," all in *Women's Studies Newsletter* 7, no. 3 (Summer 1979): 5–6, 6–7, and 19–20. Smith's presentation is also in *Frontiers: A Journal of Women Studies* 5, no. 1 (Spring 1980): 48–49. For 1980, see Catharine R. Stimpson, "Writing It All Down: An Overview of the Second NWSA Convention," *Women's Studies Newsletter* 8, no. 3 (Summer 1980): 5–7; and Nancy Polikoff, "Addressing Racism," *off our backs* 10, no. 7 (July 1980): 17–19.

59. Barbara Smith, comments in opening panel, in *Structure of Knowledge,* p. 14. See also Pat Miller, "Third NWSA Convention to be Held in Connecticut," *Women's Studies Quarterly* 9, no. 1 (Spring 1981): 30, and report on CR sessions at Storrs in *Women's Studies Quarterly* 9, no. 3 (Fall 1981): 13–16.

60. Smith in *Structure of Knowledge,* p. 13.

in feminist scholarship may summon a researcher to explore the tenets of her own life and work.[61]

Another group of women suffering special oppression in contemporary American society are lesbians. The paucity of literature addressing the treatment of lesbians in women's studies parallels feminists' relatively late decision to make elimination of heterosexual privilege and homosexual oppression a central aim. This commitment offers women's studies an opportunity to affirm its radical vision. However, although the NWSA constitution acknowledged the need for specific representation of lesbian women and conference planners have scheduled numerous lesbian-oriented sessions and cultural events, women's studies practitioners have produced very little relevant literature on research or teaching.[62] Toni McNaron's 1977 account of exploring lesbian experience and culture in a drug treatment center and the guidelines suggested very recently for studies of lesbianism by Peg Cruikshank, J. R. Roberts, and Bonnie Zimmerman are rare exceptions to the rule of silence, which confirms Adrienne Rich's observation that, with regard to lesbians, women's studies (and black studies) have "reinforce[d] the very silence out of which they have had to assert themselves."[63] A survey of texts used widely in introductory women's studies classes confirms the impression that "heterosexism is alive and well in the women's studies textbook market."[64] The lesbian perspective that "enforced heterosexuality is the extreme manifestation of male domination and patriarchal rule" remains largely inarticulated.[65]

61. Gloria T. Hull, "Researching Alice Dunbar-Nelson: A Personal and Literary Perspective," *Feminist Studies* 6, no. 1 (Summer 1980): 314–20, to be included in *Black Women's Studies*, ed. Gloria T. Hull, Patricia Bell Scott, and Barbara Smith (Old Westbury, N.Y.: Feminist Press, 1981). Charles P. Henry and Frances Smith Foster similarly call on black studies to include the history of black female activism and of black feminism in black studies, and they call on women's studies to make more than token efforts to include black women ("Black Women's Studies: Threat or Challenge?" *Western Journal of Black Studies*, in press).

62. Toni White, "Lesbian Studies Flourish at National Women's Studies Conference," *off our backs* 10, no. 7 (July 1980): 16–18.

63. Adrienne Rich, "It Is the Lesbian in Us," in *On Lies*, p. 201 (hereafter cited as "Lesbian in Us"). See also Toni McNaron, "Finding and Studying Lesbian Culture," *Women's Studies Newsletter* 5, no. 4 (Fall 1977): 18–20; Peg Cruikshank, "Lesbian Studies: Some Preliminary Notes," J. R. Roberts, "Black Lesbian Literature/Black Lesbian Lives: Materials for Women's Studies," and Bonnie Zimmerman, "Lesbianism 101," all in *Radical Teacher* 17 (November 1980): 11–25. Both Roberts and Cruikshank offer specific suggestions for course building. Cruikshank is editing *Lesbian Studies* (Old Westbury, N.Y.: Feminist Press, in press).

64. Bonnie Zimmerman, "One Out of Thirty: Lesbianism in Women's Studies Textbooks," in Cruikshank, ed. Zimmerman notes that neither the first (1975) nor the second (1979) edition of Freeman's widely used text, *Women: A Feminist Perspective*, includes an article on lesbianism.

65. Barbara Smith, "Racism and Women's Studies," *Frontiers: A Journal of Women Studies* 5, no. 1 (Spring 1980): 48–49.

The assumption of heterosexuality both reflects and reinforces ignorance about lesbians and lesbian perspectives. As Adrienne Rich
points out, even to acknowledge that "heterosexuality may not be a
'preference' at all but something that has had to be imposed, managed,
organized, propagandized, and maintained by force" requires the courage to risk shattering confirmed convictions.[66]

In a recent, provocative essay, Marilyn Frye contends that even in
women's studies the supposition of heterosexuality remains "so complete
and ubiquitous that it cannot be perceived for lack of contrast." Presenting perhaps one pole of contemporary lesbian political thought,
while Rich on the other speaks to "the lesbian in us all," she calls for
lesbians to withdraw support from women's studies unless heterosexual
feminists begin to examine the ground of *their* choice of sexual preference.[67] Whatever their reaction to Frye's proposal, practitioners of wom-
en's studies must by now recognize that any effort to educate about and
for women must include consideration of lesbian experiences and of a
range of lesbian political perspectives. For prior self-scrutiny by women's
studies teachers, the CR guidelines offered by Elly Bulkin are helpful.[68]
The establishment of a clearinghouse for lesbian feminist materials
should also aid in remedying the current neglect.[69]

By the early 1980s, the tension between academics and activists in
women's studies had been largely resolved with the answer "both/and."[70]
A lingering distrust of leadership remained, as well as some resistance to
scrutiny of "congenial truths."[71] Challenges from lesbians and women of
color to make women's studies truly inclusive continue. Recent writings,
however, suggest that the major thrust of the second decade will be
toward directing the movement outward, toward "mainstreaming." Despite a decade of the new scholarship, women's studies has so far made

66. Adrienne Rich, "Compulsory Heterosexuality and Lesbian Existence," *Signs:
Journal of Women in Culture and Society* 5, no. 4 (Summer 1980): 631–60.

67. Marilyn Frye, "Assignment: NWSA—Bloomington 1980: Speak on 'Lesbian Perspectives on Women's Studies,' " *Sinister Wisdom* 14 (Summer 1980): 3–7, and "On Second
Thought . . . ," *Radical Teacher* 17 (November 1980): 37–38. See also Rich, "Lesbian in Us,"
pp. 199–202. I am indebted to my colleague Bonnie Zimmerman for this analysis.

68. Elly Bulkin, "Heterosexism and Women's Studies," *Radical Teacher* 17 (November
1980): 28–30.

69. Sample course outlines, bibliographies, and other materials may be obtained from
Coralyn Fontaine, Lesbian-Feminist Study Clearinghouse, Women's Studies Program,
1012 Cathedral of Learning, University of Pittsburgh, Pittsburgh, Pennsylvania 15260.

70. This term is used by Peggy McIntosh in her discussion of the community/
university conflict in Berlin (n. 50 above), p. 26.

71. Marlene Mackie suggests that because of their ideological sympathies, women's
studies scholars may succumb to the "temptation to demand that science substantiate
[their] values" and fail to challenge work that they find pleasing. She calls on practitioners
of women's studies to "cultivate skepticism of results congruent with [their] value premises"
("On Congenial Truths: A Perspective on Women's Studies," *Canadian Review of Sociology
and Anthropology* 14, no. 1 [February 1977]: 117–28, esp. 122).

little progress toward its "ultimate strategy" of transforming the established male-biased curriculum. The primary impact of women's studies has been the establishment of programs that make feminist scholarship visible and available, but usually only on an elective basis.[72] The failure of affirmative action to add women to existing faculties, the limited prospects for growth expected in the coming decade, and the spreading appeal of "back to basics" all suggest that fundamental change in educational institutions will come only after feminist academics insinuate women's studies into the traditional, and especially the required or general education, curriculum.[73]

In late 1979 the Fifth Annual Great Lakes College Association Women's Studies Conference adopted as its theme "Toward a Feminist Transformation of the Academy." Emphasizing the extent to which the feminist vision challenges the male-centered definition of knowledge, keynote speaker Elizabeth Kamarck Minnich compared the work of women's studies with "Copernicus shattering our geo-centricity, Darwin shattering our species-centricity."[74] While a few male administrators may follow the lead of Louis Brakeman, provost of Denison University, in facilitating the passage of new requirements for courses in women's studies or minority studies, most may be expected to resist change.[75] Feminists must therefore recognize, as Alison Bernstein points out, that "liberal education reform is a women's issue" and find ways to direct the argument.[76]

For example, Florence Howe has prepared an outline of five reasons why women's studies is particularly appropriate to the goals of liberal education: it is interdisciplinary and unifying, it teaches skills in critical analysis, it assumes a problem-solving stance, it clarifies the issue

72. See Florence Howe, "Editorial," *Women's Studies Quarterly* 9, no. 1 (Spring 1981): 2; and Howe and Lauter (n. 12 above), p. vii.

73. At a talk given at the December 1979 meeting of the Modern Language Association in San Francisco, "Writers We Still Don't Read," Howe observed that only women teachers care if women writers are taught. She suggests one strategy for change: accurate labeling of traditional courses, e.g., naming a course on Melville, Whitman, Emerson, and Thoreau "Male Writers of the Nineteenth Century in the United States." For arguments that women's studies has made few inroads into the traditional liberal arts, see Lois Banner, "Women in the College Curriculum: A Preliminary Report," mimeographed (Washington, D.C.: Department of History, George Washington University, 1978); Ann Froines, "Integrating Women into the Liberal Arts Curriculum: Some Results of 'A Modest Survey,'" *Women's Studies Newsletter* 8, no. 4 (Fall/Winter 1980): 11–12.

74. Elizabeth Kamarck Minnich, "Friends and Critics: The Feminist Academy," in *Toward a Feminist Transformation of the Academy* (n. 55 above), p. 7.

75. Louis Brakeman in closing panel, "Curriculum Reform, or What Do You Mean, 'Our College Should Have a Feminist Curriculum?'" in *Toward a Feminist Transformation*, pp. 49–52. On resistance to the elimination of sexism in academia, see remarks of Paul Lauter in closing panel, "The Feminist Critique: Plans and Prospects," in *Structure of Knowledge*, pp. 53–58.

76. Alison Bernstein, comments in closing panel, in *Toward a Feminist Transformation*, pp. 59–61.

of value judgment in education, and it promotes socially useful ends.[77] Nancy Topping Bazin, in describing her successful campaign to convince university administrators that a bias in curriculum is also subject to affirmative action measures, and Carolyn C. Lougee, in her account of general studies revision at Stanford University, agree on another reform strategy: women's studies should be integrated into general education by redefinition and expansion of basic required courses rather than offered as an alternative general education curriculum.[78] Some feminist educators may see this approach as a threat to the survival of separate women's studies courses or question whether content can be abstracted from a feminist framework or taught by faculty at large without sacrificing essential goals. Others may find classroom dynamics transformed by the presence of students seeking mainly to fulfill degree requirements.[79]

Theories

Whatever the possibilities for and implications of integration into the "core" curriculum, it seems certain that the future of women's studies will extend well beyond the five or ten years that some observers once thought its likely life span.[80] Just as many feminists found that the goals of the women's movement could not be fulfilled by the "add-women-and-stir method," so women's studies scholars discovered that academic fields could not be cured of sexism simply by accretion. In one discipline after another, initial "compensatory" scholarship led to the realization that only radical reconstruction would suffice.[81] In terms of a scheme developed by Catharine Stimpson, the deconstruction of error and the reconstruction of (philosophical and scientific) reality from a feminist perspective have now led to a third stage of women's studies

77. Florence Howe, "Toward Women's Studies in the Eighties: Pt. 1," *Women's Studies Newsletter* 8, no. 4 (Fall 1979): 2.

78. Bazin (n. 37 above); and Carolyn C. Lougee, "Women, History and the Humanities: An Argument in Favor of the General Studies Curriculum," *Women's Studies Quarterly* 9, no. 1 (Spring 1980): 4–7.

79. Perhaps feminist educators could press for faculty development programs to accompany general education revision. See Elizabeth Ness and Kathryn H. Brooks, *Women's Studies as a Catalyst for Faculty Development*, Women's Studies Monograph Series (Washington, D.C.: National Institute of Education, 1980); and Boxer (n. 28 above), p. 22.

80. Florence Howe foresees a century of research ("Introduction: The First Decade of Women's Studies," *Harvard Educational Review* 49, no. 4 [November 1979]: 413–21).

81. The expression "add-women-and-stir method" was used by Charlotte Bunch in a panel, "Visions and Revisions: Women and the Power to Change" (NWSA Convention, Lawrence, Kansas, June 1979); excerpts were published in *Women's Studies Newsletter* 7, no. 3 (Summer 1979): 20–21. Bari Watkins summarizes this process of discovery in "Feminism: A Last Chance for the Humanities," in *Theories of Women's Studies*, ed. Gloria Bowles and Renate Duelli-Klein (Berkeley: Women's Studies, University of California, Berkeley, 1980), pp. 41–47.

scholarship, the construction of general theories. Feminist thinkers are now asking a question with far-reaching implications for the future: "Is women's studies a discipline?"[82] Although raised early in the movement, it was pursued little until recently.[83] While the relative lack of theorizing about women's studies may be due to a certain reluctance to engage in what is considered a traditionally male province, it may also reflect the widespread use of the ill-defined term "interdisciplinary" to describe a practice that has been for the most part multidisciplinary and inter-departmental.[84] Given also the history of women's studies; its origins in the women's movement; its dependence on faculty with marginal status in the academy; and its practical, opportunistic, and immensely success-ful method of growth, essential abstract questions have understandably received sustained attention only recently.

Although practice has taken precedence over theory, even those content to define women's studies as "what women's studies' students do" have, with Devra Lee Davis, called for a new perspective from which to develop questions about the "woman in the moon." Women's studies needed a new "unifying framework [to] give it functional integrity within the academy."[85] A relatively simple answer, which received little attention, was Kenneth Boulding's suggestion that women's studies con-stitutes the beginnings of a new science of "dimorphics," which in a hundred years might be able to explain the implications of the human gender system.[86] This seems, however, a way of institutionalizing gender differences that feminists hope to overcome.

Others, beginning with Davis, found considerable powers of expla-nation in Thomas Kuhn's theory of scientific revolutions.[87] Kuhn not

82. Catharine R. Stimpson, "Women's Studies: An Overview," *University of Michigan Papers in Women's Studies* (May 1978), pp. 14–26.

83. See Susan S. Sherwin, "Women's Studies as a Scholarly Discipline: Some Ques-tions for Discussion," in Siporin, ed. (n. 13 above), pp. 114–16. Mollie Schwartz Rosenhan called for recognition of women's studies as a new discipline in "The Quiet Revolution" Xeroxed (Stanford, Calif.: Center for Research on Women, 1978).

84. Gloria Bowles and Renate Duelli-Klein, "Introduction: Creating Women's Studies Theory," in Bowles and Duelli-Klein, eds., pp. i–iv. On feminist reluctance to deal in theories, see also Charlotte Bunch, "Not by Degrees," *Quest: A Feminist Quarterly* 5, no. 1 (Summer 1979): 7–18.

85. Devra Lee Davis, "The Woman in the Moon: Prolegomenon for Women's Studies," in Siporin, ed., pp. 17–28.

86. Kenneth Boulding, "The Social Institutions of Occupational Segregation: Com-ment 1," *Signs: Journal of Women in Culture and Society* 1, no. 3, pt. 2 (Spring 1976): 75–77. Sheila Tobias sees a redefinition of women's studies as dimorphics as a means of attaining academic legitimacy at the possible cost of separation from the women's movement ("Women's Studies: Its Origins, Organization, and Prospects" [n. 19 above], p. 93). Hanna Papanek considers dimorphics useful as a "gender-blind" term to describe a type of re-search on women but inadequate to describe the whole. See her comments in "Discussion Forum: Future Direction of Women's Studies" (n. 11 above), pp. 18–20.

87. Thomas Kuhn, *The Structure of Scientific Revolutions* (Chicago: University of Chicago Press, 1970). Analysts using the Kuhnian model include Sandra Coyner, "Wom-

only presents a model for fundamental change over time that applies even to the allegedly "objective" disciplines of the "hard" sciences, he also describes a process that at several points seems familiar to feminists challenging ideas in the humanities and social sciences. Whenever women seek to apply theories of human behavior based on men's lives to their own experience, they confront what Kuhn terms the "anomalies" that then lead to the challenge to and ultimately the reversal of "paradigms" in "normal science." The fullest feminist analysis of Kuhn, which includes an excellent discussion of the meaning and uses of the concept "discipline," is Sandra Coyner's provocative essay "Women's Studies as an Academic Discipline: Why and How to Do It." Stressing the disadvantages of interdisciplinarity—the denial of autonomy and recognition, the difficulty of transcending disciplinary thinking—Coyner advises women's studies practitioners to abandon the energy-draining and still overwhelmingly unsuccessful effort to transform the established disciplines. Instead they should continue developing the new community of feminist scholars who will eventually discover new paradigms and found a new normative science.

Viewing women's studies in the Kuhnian perspective, Coyner brings a new clarity to the massive resistance against which feminist scholars struggle. Overcoming the sexism of men and institutions is less fundamental a problem than is accomplishing a complete scientific revolution in each discipline women's studies touches. But "scientific revolutions are not simple matters of accumulating or improving the quality of explanation," she points out.[88] They require the passing of a generation. Rather than waste time and effort in battle, feminist scholars should break free and pronounce women's studies a discipline. The new staffing patterns Coyner proposes would perhaps be the most difficult part of her plan to realize; according to this scheme, one faculty member might teach "Women in American History," "Psychology of Women," and "The Family" as well as a women's studies survey or seminar. For Coyner the problem of finding such qualified persons would be solved by future generations of scholar-teachers with Ph.D.s in women's studies based on multidisciplinary graduate training. The appropriate administrative structure for such a program is, of course, a department.

The pole opposite Coyner in this debate over ideal structures is grounded in the feminist philosophy that rejects disciplinarity itself as

---

en's Studies as an Academic Discipline: Why and How to Do It," and Renate Duelli-Klein, "How to Do What We Want to Do: Thoughts about Feminist Methodology," in Bowles and Duelli-Klein, eds., pp. 18–40, 48–64. See also Devra Lee Davis, "Woman in the Moon," in Siporin, ed. (n. 13 above), pp. 17–28; Ginny Foster, "Women as Liberators," in Hoffman et al., eds. (n. 13 above), pp. 6–35; Ann Fitzgerald, "Teaching Interdisciplinary Women's Studies," *Great Lakes Colleges Association Faculty Newsletter* (March 1978), pp. 2–3; Rosenhan, "Quiet Revolution."

88. Coyner, pp. 18–40.

fragmentation of social experience, a male mode of analysis that cannot describe the whole of female—or human—existence. By stressing the indivisible nature of knowledge, women's studies could become a force for liberation from a dehumanizing overspecialization. Co-optation of women into the dominant culture might foreclose humanity's "last chance for radical change leading to survival," says Ginny Foster, who sees women's studies as a means through which women, the majority of the population, might derail a male-driven train to doom.[89] Many analysts have stressed the salutary function of creating totalities from the insights of several disciplines, usually using the term "interdisciplinary" in the sense of "multidisciplinary."[90]

In the first issue of *Signs,* the editors suggested several possible patterns for the new interdisciplinary scholarship: "One person, skilled in several disciplines, explores one subject; several persons, each skilled in one discipline, explore one subject together; or a group, delegates of several disciplines, publish in more or less random conjunction with each other in a single journal."[91] That the interdisciplinary promise proved difficult to fulfill was admitted several years later by Catharine Stimpson. Beyond the "fallacy of misplaced originality," she had encountered unexpected resistance, even within women's studies, to moving outside one field of expertise. She hoped to see women's studies produce "translators," persons equipped to "interpret the languages of one discipline to persons in another."[92]

Taking a middle position, Christine Garside Allen, a scholar trained in philosophy and religious studies, has argued that women's studies should combine introductory and advanced-level "interdisciplinary" courses (for which she suggests "conceptual history" as a method) with intermediate course work in the disciplines.[93] Allen's colleague in English and fine arts, Greta Hoffman Nemiroff, has described their experiences in building and teaching a thematically based introductory course that moves beyond the disciplines. In a very interesting treatment of the meaning and implications of interdisciplinarity, Nemiroff analyzes the difficulties and the value of transdisciplinary work. Because women's

89. Foster.
90. See, e.g., Christine Garside Allen, "Conceptual History as a Methodology for Women's Studies," *McGill Journal of Education* 10 (Spring 1975): 49–58; Annette K. Baxter, "Women's Studies and American Studies: The Uses of the Interdisciplinary," *American Quarterly* 26, no. 4 (October 1974): 433–39; Fitzgerald; Tobias, "Women's Studies: Its Origins, Organization, and Prospects"; Joanna S. Zangrando, "Women's Studies in the U.S.: Approaching Reality," *American Studies International* 14, no. 1 (August 1975): 15–36.
91. Catharine R. Stimpson, Joan N. Burstyn, Domna C. Stanton, and Sandra M. Whisler, "Editorial," *Signs: Journal of Women in Culture and Society* 1, no. 1 (Autumn 1975): v–viii, esp. v.
92. Stimpson, "Women's Studies: An Overview"; also "The Making of *Signs,*" *Radical Teacher* 6 (December 1977): 23–25.
93. Allen, p. 57.

studies challenges the discipline-based categories in which the structure and economy of most universities are grounded, it cannot be easily assimilated within the academy. Despite the disadvantages and even dangers to its faculty, women's studies also offers advantages to all involved: a new inventiveness, an impetus toward fruitful collaboration, a "working model of critical thought." Although present categories of knowledge may limit women's studies in attaining "full 'disciplinehood' within its own interdisciplinarity," practitioners can advance its development by systematic efforts to examine and expand its "interface" with other disciplines.[94]

Dissatisfaction with the limits imposed by the disciplines has led others to speculate on how women's studies might transcend traditional divisions of knowledge. The change might come slowly, through the discovery of questions unanswerable by disciplinary thinking, as Diana Grossman Kahn suggested in her treatment of a hypothetical new science of "grockology." Or after a decade of small changes, the near future might bring the breakdown of currently accepted categories, a possibility foreseen by scientist Anne Fausto-Sterling, whose own interests bridge the biological aspects of development and semiotics. Florence Howe calls for women's studies to concentrate on "breaking the disciplines" so that they release their hold on women and women's studies. According to Howe, the history of the disciplines—from their origins in religious studies through the secularization and professionalization of the nineteenth century—has led to a fragmented contemporary academy that is antithetical to women's studies' holistic view and problem-solving intention. These essential characteristics of the new scholarship, along with a historical perspective, a critical approach, and an empirical practice, might pave the way to the "radical reinvention" of research, teaching, and learning which will characterize the "woman-centered university."[95]

If interdisciplinarity implies transdisciplinarity in a transformed university, what does it mean for the contemporary practice of women's studies? Gloria Bowles has said that "perhaps one day the Renaissance man will be replaced by the interdisciplinary woman," but she admits that this person does not yet exist. Meanwhile, she agrees with Catharine Stimpson that women's studies scholarship "at its best is an act of translation." Although Bowles has pioneered a course on "theories of wom-

94. Greta Hoffman Nemiroff, "Rationale for an Interdisciplinary Approach to Women's Studies," *Canadian Women's Studies* 1, no. 1 (Fall 1978): 60–68.

95. Diana Grossman Kahn, "Interdisciplinary Studies and Women's Studies: Questioning Answers and Creating Questions," in *Structure of Knowledge*, pp. 20–24; Anne Fausto-Sterling, "Women's Studies and Science," *Women's Studies Newsletter* 8, no. 1 (Winter 1980): 4–7; Florence Howe, "Breaking the Disciplines," in *Structure of Knowledge*, pp. 1–10; and Adrienne Rich, "Toward a Woman-centered University," in Howe, ed., *Women and the Power to Change* (n. 31 above), pp. 30–31.

en's studies," she cautions against the potential danger of what Mary Daly calls "methodolatry." Instead of artificially constructing a new system of thought, perhaps women's studies practitioners should find their questions in the women's movement and derive methods appropriate to women's survival needs.[96]

It is precisely this feminist effort to improve women's lives that Renate Duelli-Klein, coeditor with Bowles of the first volume of *Theories of Women's Studies,* considers central to development of women's studies' methodology. The way to avoid sexist methods such as "context stripping"[97] is to ground theory in "feminist action research." Researchers must abandon the pretext of "value-free objectivity" for a "conscious subjectivity" more appropriate to studies explicitly intended to be for as well as about women.[98]

Duelli-Klein's analysis of feminist methodology draws on Marcia Westkott's analysis of how sexist content, method, and purposes affect representations of women in the social sciences. Westkott suggests alternative ways of thinking about social reality that link rather than separate subject and object, forming what she terms an "intersubjectivity" that is expressed in a dialectical relationship of subject and object. Feminist thought characteristically replaces dichotomous with dialectical modes of analyzing self and other, person and society, consciousness and activity, past and future, knowledge and practice. It is "open, contingent and humanly compelling" in contrast to that which is "closed, categorical and human controlling." It also fortifies abstract understanding with active commitment to improve the condition of women.[99] At this stage, Westkott finds, feminist criticisms of content, method, and purpose are "strands" just beginning to emerge; they do not add up to a new discipline. But since the social creation of gender is a basic assumption of women's studies, Westkott's analysis offers more than just a criticism of established social science: it becomes a solid building block for the building of women's studies theory.

Structures

Definitions of women's studies imply relationships to structures. In practice interdisciplinarity within the academic program has led to the

96. Gloria Bowles, "Is Women's Studies an Academic Discipline?" in Bowles and Duelli-Klein, eds., pp. 1–11.

97. See Parlee (n. 2 above).

98. Duelli-Klein provides an example based on a project undertaken by sociologists in Germany who worked with battered women toward analysis of their collective experience.

99. Marcia Westkott, "Feminist Criticism of the Social Sciences," *Harvard Educational Review* 49, no. 4 (November 1979): 422–30.

formation of networks and committees staffed and supported by several disciplines, departments, divisions, or colleges. This is a structure appropriate to the aim of infiltrating the disciplines, professional schools, and other academic units. Since the committee coordinating women's studies usually has limited responsibilities for personnel and budget decisions (which are controlled by departments), it can often include staff, students, and even community women, whose presence highlights and helps to implement the feminist assumption that women's studies is for all women. From the beginning, planners feared that departmental status for women's studies might narrow its focus and limit its impact by reproducing the male model of fragmented knowledge and bureaucratized isolation; it could create a feminist ghetto far from the arena of the women's movement and threaten the implementation of feminist principles.[100]

Given the choice between establishing a separate department that could, like many black studies programs, be forgotten or perhaps eliminated in periods of retrenchment or of creating a decentralized program as a base from which to reach out, most academic feminists might have chosen the latter. The Women's Studies Planners at the University of Pennsylvania recommended against a departmental structure. At San Francisco State, the women's studies governance board opted "to *not* work towards a separate 'Women's Studies' department since our major purpose is the recognition of women's important 'place' at every level in all disciplines rather than its 'special character.' "[101] One study showed that students, who favored the departmentalization of black studies and wanted courses in women's studies, did not favor a department of women's studies.[102] In many cases, however, no deliberate choice was made. Women's studies developed along the lines of least resistance: courses here and there, according to faculty interest and administrative openness; committees composed of whoever was interested and able to participate.

Catharine Stimpson and Florence Howe, from their perspectives as editors of *Signs* and *Women's Studies Newsletter,* respectively, both ob-

100. E.g., Gerda Lerner felt that women's studies "implicitly challenges the basic assumptions underlying all of social science, all of our culture—that man is the measure. Such an all-encompassing challenge cannot be approached by a narrow disciplinary focus" ("On the Teaching and Organization of Feminist Studies," in Siporin, ed., pp. 34–37, esp. p. 34). Nancy M. Porter describes how a "shadow department" at Portland State University maintained its commitment to women's studies as action not subject in "A Nuts and Bolts View of Women's Studies," in Hoffman et al., eds., pp. 167–77.

101. Quoted by Howe and Ahlum, "Women's Studies and Social Change," in Rossi and Calderwood, eds. (n. 4 above), p. 420.

102. Michele H. Herman and William E. Sedlacek, "Student Perceptions of the Need for a Women's Studies Program," *College Student Journal* 7, no. 3 (September–October 1973): 3–6.

served that the opposite sides of segregation and isolation were independence and autonomy. Acknowledging the diversity of circumstances and—perhaps in light of the internal conflicts of 1973—the dangers of establishing a single model for women's studies, Stimpson declared that "each program must work out its destiny . . . that women's studies should be seen as a multiplicity of intersecting activities."[103] Howe, strongly influenced by her experience in the "free-university" movement of the 1960s and the apparent decline of black studies during the 1970s, tended to stress the pitfalls of separation or what she called "stuffing women in a corner." Fearing that "women and minority groups [would] rest content with their piece of turf rather than turn their energetic movements into strategies for changing the university as a whole," she stressed the advantages of programs maintained through non-departmental channels.[104]

By the spring of 1974 when the *Women's Studies Newsletter* raised a series of questions about the viability of various structures, the non-departmental pattern was already established. The following year, while noting the network structure's disadvantages to (especially untenured) faculty in allowing joint appointments and divided responsibilities, Howe still felt that the departmental alternative would render women's studies more vulnerable to excision. In her national survey, she found the fifteen "mature" programs she visited "clear about their strategic mission: not to build an empire in one small corner of the campus, but to change the curriculum throughout."[105]

Advocacy of administrative independence in the early years was rare. Although Sheila Tobias felt that departments might be able to put up a stronger fight for resources than programs would, only San Diego State and SUNY/Buffalo developed rationales that geared separation to essential feminist goals.[106] Both groups considered structure more significant than content and emphasized the need for autonomy. At San Diego State, the original women's studies program was designed as one unit in a proposed ten-part women's center that would include components for research, publication, child care, storefront operations, cultural activities, recruitment and tutorials, community outreach, campus women's liberation, and center staff operations.[107] A coordinating committee representing all components and the community would govern

103. Stimpson, "The New Feminism and Women's Studies" (n. 19 above).

104. Florence Howe, "Structure and Staffing of Programs," *Women's Studies Newsletter* 3, no. 2 (Spring 1975): 1–2, and "Introduction," in Howe, ed., *Women and the Power to Change* (n. 31 above), pp. 1–14, esp. p. 9.

105. See also "Editorial," *Women's Studies Newsletter* 2, no. 2 (Spring 1974): 2; "Structure and Staffing of Programs," p. 2; and *Seven Years Later* (n. 35 above), p. 21.

106. Tobias, "Teaching Women's Studies" (n. 21 above), p. 263.

107. Salper, "Women's Studies" (n. 28 above).

the center collectively, fulfilling the founders' belief that "the actual curriculum of the university is less important than the structure of the education itself. . . . What you learn in school is how to fit into the structure of domination and power hierarchy which is the basis of all institutions of class society. . . . Women's studies, based on collective structure, exists in opposition to the structure of the university."[108] Within the college where it was established, the women's studies program was responsible directly to the dean and, until three members achieved tenure, subject to the supervision of a committee of tenured faculty. Although the program underwent a complete change in faculty in 1974, it retained its original autonomy within the college and was recognized as a full-fledged department.[109]

Autonomy at SUNY/Buffalo meant establishing a separate college within the university system set up in the 1960s to allow students to develop experimental and innovative programs. Although its faculty positions and degree-granting power were located in American studies, the Women's Studies College offered some courses exclusively for credit in women's studies, while others were cross-listed with a variety of departments. Despite a major controversy with the administration during a rechartering process in 1974 and 1975, the college continues committed above all to "organizational struggle," which its separate structure facilitates. As a "center of women's lives," it is apparently less concerned about "ghettoization" than about its ability to maintain collective governance and educational methods "which develop in our students and instructors the capabilities and assertiveness necessary to accept the active responsibility for their own educations."[110]

Given the diversity of existing academic units, the forms of women's studies may be infinite. Noteworthy uncommon types include the Department of Ethnic Studies and Women's Studies at California State University, Chico, and the consortia for women's studies organized by the Five Colleges in Western Massachusetts, the Great Lakes Colleges Association, and the Big Ten.[111] One of the most perceptive statements

108. Women's Studies Board, San Diego State College (n. 28 above), p. 8.
109. See Boxer (n. 28 above). The department now has three tenured as well as three tenure-track faculty and is no longer subject to an external advisory committee.
110. "Women's Studies College Charter," SUNY/Buffalo (n. 49 above). At present the collegiate system is being phased out. The Buffalo program is moving to combine its American studies and women's studies resources into one B.A. program which maintains as many as possible of the innovative and structural aspects of the Women's Studies College.
111. See Gayle Kimball, "From the California State University, Chico," *Women's Studies Newsletter* 3, nos. 3–4 (Summer/Fall 1975): 23; Catharine E. Portugues, "From the University of Massachusetts, Amherst," ibid., pp. 25–26; Beth Reed, "The GLCA Women's Studies Program: A Consortial Approach," ibid., 6, no. 1 (Winter 1978): 17–19; Gayle Graham Yates, "Big Ten Forms Women's Studies Permanent Consortium," ibid., 7, no. 1 (Winter 1979): 31.

on the question of structure came from the director of a women's studies
department, Juanita Williams of the University of South Florida:

> The establishment of a separate program, as contrasted to the of-
> fering of courses about women in existing traditional departments
> . . . is and probably will continue to be an important administrative
> and fateful issue, one that will not be resolved soon, and perhaps
> never. The reason for this, as I see it, is that women's studies, more
> than any other part of the curriculum at the present time, are
> emerging in idiosyncratic ways on campuses; the forms that their
> establishment take are a function of the beliefs, energies, and per-
> sonalities of the women promoting them, and of the character of the
> institution and the supporting community.[112]

Williams provides an excellent summary of the evident advantages of
separation, which she feels outweigh the potential dangers of isolation:
essentially a central structure provides identity, generates research,
exercises relative autonomy in selection of faculty and in curriculum
development, and indicates a substantial institutional commitment.
Noting the many demands on women's studies faculty to sit on university
committees, to present guest lectures, and to participate in public relations activities, Williams finds no evidence of insularity. On the contrary, she suggests that "a little occasional isolation would be welcome at
times."[113]

Reports from the field since the mid-1970s suggest that the commitment to structural innovation declined as the early ties to community
women's liberation weakened and as the practitioners of women's studies
on campus began to seek the security of stable course offerings for
students, tenure-track appointments for faculty, and continuing and
adequate funding for programs. Research revealing both the sexism in
the content, methods, and fundamental assumptions of established disciplines and the potential of women's studies for creating a renaissance
in the liberal arts seems to have encouraged an ethos that emphasizes
obtaining and maintaining resources for the long haul. Programs without a departmental base find this particularly hard. They depend on the
"charity of departments," which they routinely have to convince to offer
the courses they need. They lack the ability to hire their own faculty;
those they borrow from departments often labor under double responsibilities and fear adverse tenure or promotion decisions specifically
because of their work in women's studies.[114] One case of a negative

---

112. Juanita H. Williams, "Administering a Women's Studies Program," *Women's
Studies Newsletter* 2, no. 3 (Summer 1974): 5, 11–12, esp. 11.

113. Ibid., p. 12.

114. See comments by Sybil Weir and Dana V. Hiller, *Women's Studies Newsletter* 3, no.
2 (Spring 1975): 4–6, and Greene (n. 43 above), pp. 4–5. Christa Van Daele, "Women's
Studies: Time for a Grass Roots Revival," *Branching Out* 5, no. 1 (1978): 8–11, presents a

tenure decision allegedly made on this ground gained nationwide notoriety.[115]

Although it is too early to know what models will prove most enduring or effective, increasingly positive perceptions of the departmental model have appeared. Defusing earlier criticism, Dana Hiller points out that women are no more ghettoized in women's studies than in many other fields.[116] Coyner questions the validity of the home economics and black studies analogies, noting that interdisciplinary departments of biochemistry and linguistics have prospered.[117] Sarah Slavin Schramm asserts that "women's studies is worthy of separate status," which, given its collective orientation and community ties, need not produce "isolation and excision."[118]

Comparing the situation of the Women's Studies Program with that of the Department of Ethnic Studies at the University of California, Berkeley, Gloria Bowles clearly feels the latter has the stronger position. Recognizing explicitly a fact generally obscured in the debate over strategies and structures, she notes that "if Women's Studies had begun in 1969, we might be in the same position [as Ethnic Studies]."[119] For Madeleine Goodman, the key to success is the commitment made by a university when it establishes a separate unit with permanent faculty, space, and support, where women's studies can be the "central professional responsibility of a group of individuals hired and evaluated as professors of women's studies." From this secure base, they can also

---

gloomy picture of faculty marginality in two Ontario universities, as does R. J. Smith for the University of Michigan ("Women's Studies on Trial," *Michigan Daily* [April 13, 1980], p. 3). Howe discussed faculty problems in *Seven Years Later,* pp. 63–66. Emily Abel and Deborah Rosenfelt focus on the situation of part-time faculty in women's studies ("Women Part-Time Faculty," *Radical Teacher* 17 [November 1980]: 61).

115. On the case of Maija Blaubergs against the University of Georgia, see Lorenzo Middleton, "Academic Freedom vs. Affirmative Action: Georgia Professor Jailed in Tenure Dispute," *Chronicle of Higher Education* (September 2, 1980), p. 1.

116. Dana V. Hiller, "Women's Studies Emerging," *Journal of National Association for Women Deans and Counselors* 41, no. 1 (Fall 1977): 3–6.

117. "The problem is not just separation but continuing racism and sexism" (Coyner, p. 38). Greta Hoffman Nemiroff, however, attributes the survival of biochemistry and other science and computer-based interdisciplinary fields to infusions of money from government and industry (p. 65).

118. Schramm (n. 21 above), pp. 351–55. This analysis appeared earlier as "Women's Studies: Its Focus, Idea, Power and Promise," *Social Science Journal* 14, no. 2 (April 1977): 5–13.

119. Gloria Bowles, interviewed by Deborah Rosenfelt, "Ethnic Studies and Women's Studies at UC/Berkeley: A Collective Interview," *Radical Teacher* 14 (December 1979): 12–18. The Ethnic Studies Department had a budget of over a $1 million and fourteen ladder positions, compared with $30,000 and no regular faculty in women's studies. The autonomous programs at San Diego State, South Florida, and SUNY/Buffalo all date from the early 1970s.

reach out in many directions. Goodman describes many campus and community activities that demonstrate that the program at the University of Hawaii, though separate, "has hardly been a ghetto."[120]

In the economically troubled early 1980s, however, the opportunity to choose "either/or," department or network, may be unlikely. Some universities indeed still provide no resources beyond departmentally based courses and urge faculty "to develop devices to maintain and nurture communication with each other" on their own time.[121] Perhaps the best option will be evolution into "both/and," that is, a core of faculty devoted only to women's studies, perhaps persons trained in more than one discipline to become the "interdisciplinary women," working with interested teachers in whatever places they may dwell.[122] While it appears that by 1980 a network model had become the most common form of women's studies program, at the present time a data base adequate for assessment over time remains unavailable. In any case, clearly the organization must fit the university's existing structure and ambience.[123]

Conclusion

The greatest promise of women's studies and its most enduring problem are inextricably linked. The "exhilaration beyond exhaustion"[124] that moves women's studies flows out of the combination of personal and professional interests it allows and demands. The integration of scholarship and politics provides academic feminism with an endless supply of questions to research, courses to teach, and missions to accomplish. It affects every major issue considered here: the adaptation of feminist principles to the classroom, the conflict between political and academic aims, the attempt to transform academic structures as well as curricula, the interaction of campus and community feminism, the struggles against racism and homophobia inside and outside of women's

120. Madeleine J. Goodman, "Women's Studies: The Case for a Departmental Model," *Women's Studies Newsletter* 8, no. 4 (Fall/Winter 1980): 7–8.

121. Barrie Thorne, "Closeup: Michigan State University," *Women's Studies Newsletter* 4, no. 2 (Spring 1976): 8.

122. Some programs have developed majors which use a "core plus" model; faculty appointment may or may not follow the same plan. See, e.g., Boneparth (n. 40 above), p. 25; Hester Eisenstein, "Women's Studies at Barnard College: Alive and Well and Living in New York," *Women's Studies Newsletter* 6, no. 3 (Summer 1978): 4; Elaine Hedges, "Women's Studies at a State College," ibid., 2, no. 4 (Fall/Winter 1975): 5; Yates, "Women's Studies in its Second Phase" (n. 33 above), p. 5.

123. Howe and Lauter (n. 12 above), pp. iv, 4. Judith Gappa and J. Nicholls Eastmond describe a carefully contrived and successful campaign to fit women's studies into a most unlikely structure (n. 37 above).

124. This phrase is borrowed from Minnich (n. 74 above), p. 5.

studies, the difficulties of interdisciplinarity in a discipline-based world, the ambivalence of both autonomous and multidepartmental structures, the search for a new unifying framework and appropriate methodology.

These are all facets of the symbiotic relationship between women's studies and women's liberation, a connection that provides strength to both parts but also allows for a potentially counterproductive confusion. This is evident in the difficulties experienced by the NWSA. Committed to the feminist goal of including all oppressed and underrepresented women, it has built a structure that threatens to produce "an elite of officially-recognized caucuses."[125] Although it thereby strives to deal continuously and substantially with the effects of centuries of economic discrimination and social violence against women of color and lesbians, it nevertheless remains vulnerable to charges of racism and homophobia and to countercharges that communication is inhibited and fragmentation encouraged by pressure to pass as a "true feminist."[126] As a result, delegates at national conventions have felt obliged to promise action that the association's meager resources may not be able to sustain.[127] If inflated expectations and narrow politics combine to prevent open presentation of views deemed unacceptable, and controversy is submerged under waves of consensus, the NWSA may become representative of only a part of the women's studies constituency. The survival of the organization, the profession, and the unfulfilled mission itself requires that women's studies practitioners recognize the complexities of the relationship between education and social change, understand the limitations of their present power, and, while continuing to struggle with difficult issues of current concern, address new questions as well. The building of a discipline—and a better world—takes place through the constructive resolution of disparate ideas, interests, and aims.

While multipurpose gatherings such as the annual NWSA conventions serve many needs, the vast majority of participants who completed the evaluation questionnaire in 1979 rated networking and renewing acquaintances more important concerns than curriculum development or administrative and employment needs, which, however, more

---

125. Nanette Bruckner, "Dialectics or Diversity" (position paper prepared for the NWSA Coordinating Council to present to the membership, Storrs, Connecticut, Spring 1981). For a more positive view, see Deborah S. Rosenfelt, "A Time for Confrontation," *Women's Studies Quarterly* 9, no. 3 (Fall 1981): 10–12.

126. Davis and Frech (n. 48 above), pp. 33–35. On fragmentation, see also reports on the conferences in Kansas and Indiana in the *Women's Studies Newsletter* 7, no. 3 (Summer 1979): 5–9, and ibid., 8, no. 3 (Summer 1980): 3–9; and the comments of Alice Chai and Helen Stewart as reported in *off our backs* 11, no. 7 (July 1981): 20–21.

127. On the conflict between feminist goals and "fiscal responsibility," see Barbara Hillyer Davis's report on the finance committee (*Women's Studies Newsletter* 7, no. 3 [Summer 1979]: 25) and Alice Henry's report on the 1981 assembly (*off our backs* 11, no. 7 [July 1981]: 2–6).

than half considered very important.[128] Perhaps other ways to foster contemplation and communication need to be developed: shorter, simpler conferences on single issues such as integrating theory and practice in the classroom; moving students beyond the favored courses in health, psychology, and sexuality to the less popular courses on economic and political systems; finding or creating job markets for graduates; opening general education to women's studies; building a major or graduate program; implementing feminism in hiring practices; developing means to produce more women's studies teachers; pioneering cross-disciplinary Ph.D. programs; and surviving "Reaganomics" and New Right attacks on academic freedom. Published proceedings from such meetings would fulfill needs now barely touched for the most part by brief articles and notes of the type surveyed in this essay. Perhaps it is also time for *Female Studies: Series Two,* for practitioners of the second decade to reach out and share, to deliberate over strategies and contend about tactics, but also to celebrate achievements and join hands for the long struggle to reform education and society in the image and interest of us all.

Department of Women's Studies
San Diego State University

128. Patricia A. Frech and Barbara Hillyer Davis, "The NWSA Constituency: Evaluation of 1979 Conference Participation," *Frontiers: A Journal of Women Studies* 5, no. 1 (Spring 1980): 68–70.

TRYING TRANSFORMATIONS:
CURRICULUM INTEGRATION AND THE PROBLEM OF RESISTANCE

**SUSAN HARDY AIKEN, KAREN ANDERSON,
MYRA DINNERSTEIN, JUDY LENSINK, AND
PATRICIA MACCORQUODALE**

"Out in this desert we are testing bombs"
[ADRIENNE RICH, "Trying to Talk with a Man"]

The persistence of the androcentric academy has led to the initiation of dozens of feminist curriculum integration projects throughout the country during the last several years. Among the earliest and most extensive of these was a four-year cross-disciplinary project that we conducted in the women's studies program at the University of Arizona, sponsored by the National Endowment for the Humanities (NEH).[1] This enterprise had

Like the curriculum project described here, this article is a collaborative effort, the product of many long and fruitful discussions. We would like to thank Lynn Fleischman for reading an earlier draft and contributing many helpful suggestions. A version of this essay will appear in our book on curriculum integration, *Changing Our Minds: Feminist Transformations of Knowledge* (Albany: State University of New York Press, in press).

[1] The University of Arizona is a large (30,000 students, 1,200 faculty) research institution without a history of faculty development focused on teaching improvement; our project was virtually the first one on this campus to stress such development. Subsequently, women's studies at the University of Arizona has continued its curriculum integration work and expanded its scope. The Western States Project on Women in the Curriculum (1983–88), funded by the Ford Foundation through the Southwest Institute for Research on Women

This essay originally appeared in *Signs*, vol. 12, no. 2, Winter 1987.

three distinctive sets of characteristics. First, its sheer size (forty-five participants representing thirteen departments), duration, and the consequent frequency of association between project leaders and participants enabled us to recognize recurrent patterns of interaction. Second, our targeted faculty group was composed almost entirely of white, middle-class, tenured men.[2] Finally, we developed an interdisciplinary format that brought together in weekly seminars faculty from a broad range of fields and emphasized a preliminary grounding in feminist theory before proceeding to course revision.

Now that this project is completed, we can reflect not only on our own local experience but also on the larger implications of the now-widespread feminist endeavor to transform the academy. In this essay, we attempt to interpret one of the many components of that highly complex dynamic between feminists and traditional educators: the problem of resistance to feminist curriculum integration. We have been ambivalent about writing on this subject. We are aware of its political implications and its potential to be misinterpreted and misused by those hostile to curriculum integration. Thus, we want to affirm at the outset that we believe curriculum integration to be absolutely essential to feminist efforts to transform the academy, for women's studies courses alone cannot reach the thousands of students who graduate every year from our universities.[3] Yet in order for curriculum transformation projects to be most effective, their leaders need to be forewarned of the pitfalls they are likely to encounter. While the successes

---

(SIROW), has supported integration projects on twenty-one campuses in the West. Integrating Women into International Studies (1984–87), funded by the Department of Education, involves forty-seven faculty members on seven campuses in Arizona and Colorado. All of these projects included more women, more minorities, and more untenured faculty than did the one described here. (See below for more information on this project.)

[2] Because the conditions of the NEH grant stipulated the local institutionalization of results, and because we sought a permanent impact, we decided to focus only on tenured faculty in the first three years of the project with the assumption that they would be more likely to remain at the university. (During a fourth, extended year, we were able to include nontenured faculty.) Because over 90 percent of tenured faculty in the fields we dealt with were men, most of our project participants were male (forty-two out of forty-five). Also reflective of the academy in general was the fact that most of these men were white and middle-class, with only one black participant and two Mexican-Americans. In this essay, we focus on the male participants in the project because we hesitate to generalize about so small a sample of women. Further, because there were only three women in the project, it is impossible to ensure their anonymity.

[3] The exclusion of feminist frameworks from mainstream courses and scholarship constitutes an overt, if unacknowledged, policy of containment in the face of feminist challenges to traditional disciplines, the academy, and the society at large. We believe it necessary to strike a balance between women's studies programs (which are essential for both intensive and extensive focus on women) and collective efforts to transform the traditional curriculum and contest the masculinist premises on which it is based. Without that transformation, women's studies programs risk continued ghettoization.

of curriculum integration have been widely documented, very little has been said about the resistances such projects may confront. The following analysis seeks to map that underexplored terrain. By detailing the kinds of problems curriculum integration leaders might anticipate, we hope to contribute to the development of strategies to overcome these resistances and ensure the maximum success of future projects.

The curriculum integration strategy

Our project began in the summer of 1981. Each year, a steering committee of women's studies faculty conducted interdisciplinary seminars in feminist theory and pedagogy for approximately ten participants.[4] The participating faculty, who received either a stipend or released time for taking part in the project, were required to revise at least one course to include materials by and about women.[5] At the end of the semester in which participants taught the course targeted for integration, we administered evaluations to measure the degree of change in their classes as a result of their work in the program.

The successes of this project were considerable. A number of the participants, through the quality of their intellectual efforts and the depth of their commitment, discovered in the scholarship on women a basis for a profound reconceptualization of their disciplinary tenets, their course structures and content, and their research agendas. As we had hoped, feminist paradigms gave them a framework for understanding what had seemed like anomalous data, reinterpreting traditional texts, and expanding the canons in their fields to include previously unknown materials. In the best sense they became our colleagues and comrades, enhancing our knowledge and understanding of the feminist project as they developed their own.[6]

---

[4] During the last two years of the project, the steering committee added three men, former participants in the program, to help plan and reorganize the readings of subsequent seminars, but, except for occasional presentations, they were not involved in the seminars themselves. Core readings (to name only a few) included works by Nancy Chodorow, Bonnie Thornton Dill, and Heidi Hartmann; Michelle Zimbalist Rosaldo's theoretical overview to *Woman, Culture, and Society*, ed. Michelle Z. Rosaldo and Louise Lamphere (Stanford, Calif.: Stanford University Press, 1974), and other readings from that collection; literary critical essays by Annette Kolodny and Elaine Showalter; selections from Elaine Marks and Isabelle de Courtivron, eds., *New French Feminisms: An Anthology* (New York: Schocken Books, 1981); and selections from Hester Eisenstein and Alice Jardine, eds., *The Future of Difference* (Boston: G. K. Hall & Co., 1980).

[5] Other project activities included participation in lectures and workshops by a series of visiting scholars, preparation by participants of an annotated bibliography of readings in feminist scholarship, and consultations with women's studies faculty in their disciplines.

[6] For examples of the sorts of scholarship generated and the profound changes experienced by these participants, see our collection of their essays, *Changing Our Minds*.

Even when the changes were less dramatic, our evaluations showed that many participants made measurable alterations in the perspective and content of their courses, alterations that will perhaps be extended and elaborated in years to come.[7] Moreover, the involvement of several strategically placed administrators, who through their participation developed sincere goodwill toward our project, has already meant that the institutional structure itself has been affected in important ways—for example, in the hiring of feminist faculty members in some departments and in positive promotion and tenure decisions for feminist scholars in others.

Despite these successes, however, we came to realize that we had seriously underestimated the magnitude and intractability of the resistances we would confront. These proved hydra-like: no sooner had we sought to deal with one than another would arise. Thus, although the project made significant headway in modifying the liberal arts curriculum on our campus, it also served to reveal in stark detail the nature and depth of opposition to feminist scholarship. By situating large numbers of older, generally powerful men as students of younger, less privileged, feminist women (the majority of them nontenured), our project reflected in microcosm the power structure of the university itself, while enacting a temporary reversal. Each seminar, then, became a theater where the gender politics of the academy operated in a particularly dramatic and revealing fashion. Throughout the project we confronted, sometimes in their most extreme forms, the resistances that may often typify the response of academics to feminist curriculum integration.[8]

---

[7] Evaluation data were collected in the courses that were targeted for change and in a control group of unchanged courses matched according to size, level, and department. The student evaluations indicate that the project was successful on two counts: (1) courses targeted for change included more material on women in assigned readings, topics in the syllabus, lectures by instructors, and class discussions; and (2) generally, students reacted positively to these materials, becoming more aware of women's issues and wanting similar courses to contain more such materials. Looking back over the four years, we judge that the project affected approximately half of the participants positively. Of these, perhaps one-quarter experienced intellectual and/or personal changes that dramatically altered their teaching, research, and/or politics. Another quarter met project goals by incorporating varying amounts of material on women into their courses. The remaining half were relatively unchanged. It is this latter group that we discuss here.

[8] Although it can be argued that our choice of tenured participants—the majority of whom, for reasons noted earlier (see n. 2 above), were white, middle-class men—may have guaranteed high levels of faculty resistance, this group nevertheless represents what feminists face at most American universities. For another perspective on some of the potential hazards of curriculum integration, especially as they pertain to the development and perpetuation of women's studies programs, see Mary Childers's incisive "Women's Studies: Sinking and Swimming in the Mainstream," *Women's Studies International Forum* 7, no. 3 (1984): 161–66. Our situation differed notably from Childers's: she worked in a university with no women's studies program, whereas our university has a strong, well-established one. Nevertheless, we would concur with many of her conclusions.

Patterns of resistance

At the simplest level, our hopes for what the project would accomplish were sometimes incompatible with what we could realistically expect, given the participants' goals and motivations. While a number of participants, as we have suggested, came to the project highly motivated and open to change, others came for a variety of different reasons. For a few, the grant stipend appeared to be the primary motivation. Others joined out of curiosity, intending to assess *whether*—rather than how—scholarship on women was valid or useful. Some of these seemed to decide in the negative and sat out the remainder of the seminars, neither contradicting nor contributing. Other participants engaged in selective reading and hearing, deflecting discussions onto tangents—debating, for example, whether Aristotle or Plato better exemplified the classical tradition, or the exact beginning date of the (male) Renaissance. A variant of this mode occurred when some participants attacked subtly argued articles as diverse (and often even as opposed) as, for instance, Sherry Ortner's "Is Female to Male as Nature Is to Culture?" and Carol MacCormack's "Nature, Culture and Gender: A Critique" as being monolithic repetitions of the same thesis.[9] This confusion not only suggests cursory reading by these participants but also exhibits the degree to which stereotypical expectations about feminist scholarship can obscure the understanding of intelligent academics.

More numerous—and more frustrating—were those who, in the seminars, politely agreed with the readings but limited the changes in their thinking and course designs to an absolute minimum. In certain cases, this resistance appeared related to an unwillingness or inability to perceive the implications of feminist critiques. For example, we had chosen an interdisciplinary format not only to provide a theoretical stimulus for participants' reconceptualizations of their own disciplines but also because the interdisciplinary approach is fundamental to feminist epistemology, which calls into question traditional academic boundary systems. Thus, participants faced a dual task: to rethink the role of gender within their disciplines *and* to interrogate the very structures on which their disciplines were erected. This group, however, had difficulty getting beyond the epistemological constraints of their own fields and theorizing across disciplinary boundaries. Such participants often found the readings irrelevant because they were not discipline specific. One professor, for instance, could not see a connection between our texts on women and society and his efforts to develop statistical information on the gender gap in politics through the use of public opinion polls.

[9] Sherry Ortner, "Is Female to Male as Nature Is to Culture?" in Rosaldo and Lamphere, eds., 67–87; Carol P. MacCormack, "Nature, Culture and Gender: A Critique," in *Nature, Culture, and Gender,* ed. Carol P. MacCormack and Marilyn Strathern (Cambridge: Cambridge University Press, 1980), 1–24.

Some participants resisted theoretical readings in general, requesting instead preassembled "how-to" classroom materials that they might fit into their otherwise unchanged courses. In some ways, this form of resistance is the most understandable because it so straightforwardly requires that others do all of the work. Professors in this group usually objected that including materials on women in their courses would mean sacrificing something *more important*, instead of recognizing that what is needed is precisely the sort of radical reformulation that would obviate such objections. Often, this form of resistance was reflected in rhetoric: one participant spoke repeatedly, for example, of how he planned to "shoehorn" a few women's issues into his otherwise untouched syllabus. His metaphor suggested that, given the small space he planned to allot to women, such "shoehorning" would necessitate the academic equivalent of *footbinding*. This preoccupation with "what to cut," like the other forms of resistance sketched above, illustrates that without genuine commitment to the legitimacy of feminist scholarship and serious consideration of its epistemological implications, academics will probably achieve only the most minimal changes. These difficulties, however, represent only the superficial symptoms of deeper, more complicated forms of resistance.

The problem of translation

Throughout the seminars, many participants seemed to find discourse on gender both alien and profoundly troubling. We tended to forget the extent to which our own years of work on these issues had given us an encoded, almost shorthand, system of linguistic reference with which we were at ease but which the participants could neither translate nor speak. Our challenge, then, was to find a level of discourse simultaneously accessible to those unfamiliar with feminist thinking and sophisticated enough to do justice to the subject. Introducing participants to feminist paradigms, however, was not enough. We spent a great deal of time explaining basic concepts, defining essential terms, and correcting misconceptions born of partial understanding. Unfortunately, in subsequent sessions the same misconceptions and definitional questions sometimes recurred as though never addressed before. As in many teaching situations, we needed to repeat distinctions and definitions many times. One participant, for instance, after six weeks of seminars during which sex and gender had been repeatedly distinguished, asked us to explain how they were different. Several participants, near the end of one set of seminars in which the term *patriarchy* was frequently discussed, appeared to be unfamiliar with the word. What makes this situation different from other kinds of teaching, however, is that, in addition to asking participants to learn to speak and understand feminist discourse, we were also asking them to "unlearn" an enormous amount of the discourse of traditional culture.

The cross-disciplinary scope of our project sometimes created other linguistic difficulties as well. A major problem with any interdisciplinary study in an academy divided along disciplinary boundary lines is that those who venture outside their own areas of specialization will often be regarded with suspicion: at best as neophytes—stereotypical tourists who cannot speak the language of the field they presume to visit and who overlook nuances and complexities apparent to the natives; and at worst as dangerous trespassers, or colonizers seeking to expropriate territory not their own. Thus, for example, in a seminar devoted to exploring the underlying similarities of the perceptions of women articulated in Genesis 2–3, Aristotle's *On the Generation of Animals*, selections from Thomas Aquinas, and the *Malleus Maleficarum*, we were accused by a historian of being ahistorical: there is, he claimed, no common tradition or connection among these texts—an assertion that overlooks the extensive use in *Summa Theologica* of *both* Genesis and the *Generation* and the reliance of the authors of the *Malleus* on the medieval patristic misogyny culminating in the *Summa*. When reminded of these intertextualities, he dismissed them as irrelevant.

This perception of territorial invasion is doubly complicated by the issue of gender. As Carole Pateman has shown, women traditionally have been perceived by masculinist thinkers as figures of what Rousseau termed "disorder," potential disrupters of masculine boundary systems of all sorts, all the more fearsome because situated within the very heart of "civilization."[10] Given the gender ratio of our groups, this paradigm, though unacknowledged, appeared operative on a number of occasions. Under these circumstances, the male academics' appeals to disciplinary boundaries sometimes seemed to serve as a rod for simultaneously measuring our shortcomings and "correcting" us, keeping us in line or in place by, as it were, disciplining us.

What these questions of linguistic competence mask is that the academy speaks, as we know, at least two languages: one the language of scholarship, the other the language of power. In the contested terrain where gender is signified, the question of who owns the discourse becomes inseparable from questions of ownership of all sorts.[11] Hence, it is perhaps

---

[10] Carole Pateman, "The Disorder of Women: Women, Love, and the Sense of Justice," *Ethics* 91 (October 1980): 20–34. See also Natalie Zemon Davis, "Women on Top: Symbolic Sexual Inversions and Political Disorder in Early Modern France," in *Society and Culture in Early Modern France*, ed. Natalie Zemon Davis (Stanford, Calif.: Stanford University Press, 1975), 124–51.

[11] We were continually reminded of the truth of the fundamental feminist insight that the intellectual tradition is and has been used to rationalize male dominance. As Adrienne Rich

not surprising that when we articulated our ideas most forcefully, some participants reacted as if we had unfairly wrested control of academic debate. Confusion at this perceived usurpation was intensified by the fact that it was not easy to dismiss us on intellectual grounds. As scholars, we were respectable according to traditional sets of criteria; yet we were using precisely the same tools of scholarly discourse that compelled their admiration—to undermine the very tradition that had developed and valorized those tools. Other participants—presenting us with a far more difficult situation—tried to contest our scholarly authority altogether, labeling our assertions as "ideologically motivated" while leaving the ideological grounding of their own epistemologies unexplored. It became essential, therefore, to expose the ideology inherent in "neutral" scholarship and to demonstrate that recognizing its presence does not necessarily leave scholars with only a mindless relativism that disregards evidence and logic.

Text and subtext

These reenactments of well-worn cultural gender scripts were related to another form of resistance. Having volunteered to study women, many participants found that they were also forced to think about themselves in disquieting new ways. Because feminist scholarship's insistence on the social construction of gender inequality constitutes an implicit (and sometimes explicit) critique of men, it challenges masculine self-images and involves many men in a curious dilemma. If they assume both their own agency in social processes and the injustice of women's secondary status, then they must acknowledge complicity in gender imbalance. Our curriculum transformation projects ask that they commit themselves not just to lip-service to such attempts but instead to genuinely radical reconceptualizations that would question their inherited bodies of knowledge and some of their most cherished assumptions, procedures, and methodologies. Yet such commitment means relinquishing their positions as self-defined custodians and beneficiaries of a "meritocracy." But refusal or failure to initiate changes creates guilt and dissonance between their actions and

---

has eloquently put it, the university, like other social institutions, is still "man-centered," "a breeding ground not of humanism, but of masculine privilege. As women have gradually and reluctantly been admitted into the mainstream of higher education, they have been made participants in a system that prepares men to take up roles of power in a man-centered society, that asks questions and teaches 'facts' generated by a male intellectual tradition, and that both subtly and openly confirms men as the leaders and shapers of human destiny both within and outside academia" (Adrienne Rich, "Toward a Woman-centered University," in On Lies, Secrets, and Silence: Selected Prose, 1966–1978 [New York: W. W. Norton & Co., 1979], 127).

their self-images as just and thoughtful people. To maintain their self-respect, they have to reconcile such dissonances. For participants who see themselves as liberal and sympathetic toward women, yet who resist the thoroughgoing transformation implicit in the feminist project, the implications of this conundrum are all the more stinging.

The emotionally fraught nature of this situation was revealed in our project at a number of levels. Whenever discussions deal with sexual politics—especially in the context of a feminist analysis of those politics—they are bound to provoke highly charged emotional responses, particularly, perhaps, from those people who think that they have transcended or are liberated about such matters. The provocative and potentially threatening nature of the material made it inevitable that the project seminars functioned simultaneously on at least two levels: an intellectual, consciously rational discourse set in tension with dynamics approaching those of an encounter group. That is, the meetings had both an explicit text and a potentially explosive subtext, a communal unconscious that was often unrecognized or unacknowledged by the participants (and, at least at the outset, by us) but all the more potent for such repression. Not surprisingly, this situation sometimes produced very negative dynamics, absorbing much of the time and energy of the group.[12]

Anxieties within the seminar were further exacerbated by the inverted gender dynamics of the group, in which women occupied the unsettling position of experts. Some participants seemed to experience this as a direct threat to their authority, to feel—even though the program was voluntary—that we constituted a kind of "police force" or, as one of them insisted on characterizing it, a group of "schoolteachers": the stereotypical specter of every schoolboy's nightmares. While attesting to the power of the ideas we sponsored, this defensiveness was one of the major blocks to acceptance of those ideas.

Our experiences made it clear to us that the tools of rationality alone are inadequate to the task of intellectual change when the investments in ideas regarding gender are deep-seated and self-interested for all parties. We had consciously chosen to use primarily a conventional ratiocinative approach, concerned lest systematic recourse to the experiential or affective would alienate participants and reinforce stereotypes about both female academics and feminist studies as emotional and unscholarly. In addition, we wished to maintain a collegial relationship with our participants beyond the project itself. It is obvious to us now, however, that the

---

[12] Interestingly, this effect can go on beyond seminar bounds, establishing a genealogy of negativism from one year of a project to the next. One participant, for example, sat in virtual silence through a whole series of meetings. Unknown to us at the time, he had been concealing a great deal of anger. The following year, a much more verbal man entered the project, bringing not only his own ambivalences but the anger of his quieter colleague as well, who had confided in him the previous year.

tension between text and subtext inevitably arose and that there was no obvious or easy resolution of this dilemma. In no other area of the project did the disparities between academic profession/practice and the gendered double standards they create cause more difficulty for us. Even when discussions operated on a very abstract level, we were often accused of talking about ourselves in a particularistic, subjective, and self-interested way. However, participants often advanced their own particularisms and subjectivities as universal, neutral, truth-seeking rationality. Unless feminist scholars can successfully expose and deal with the subterranean emotional text of this discourse, our academic legitimacy will remain suspect. Yet to do so is, ironically, to risk reconfirming the stereotypical prejudices that have for so long prevented us from being taken seriously within an academy which requires "objectivity" and rewards those whose claims to detachment are most widely acknowledged by their peers.

The nature of things

Although challenges and vigorous debate can promote substantive discussions around central intellectual issues, they can also prevent, minimize, or deflect the consideration of the major premise of feminist scholarship: the sociocultural construction of gender. Denying that crucial premise, some participants were forced to fall back on rationalizations based on easily accessible pieces of our cultural baggage—biological determinism, human capital theory, and functionalism, among others. Participants' readiness to resort to such constructs reveals their continuing strength even among liberal academics and reminds us to take seriously the conventional belief structures that we might otherwise dismiss.

The frequency of recourse to biological interpretations of gender asymmetries, in particular, took us by surprise and posed a challenge to a serious consideration of cultural interpretations. The extent to which the influence of sociobiology and other biological perspectives pervades the academy became clear as participants from across a wide disciplinary range alluded to the premises of these fields, although their familiarity with the actual literature was not necessarily extensive. Some discussants relied on hormonal sex differences to explain human gender asymmetry, while others focused on "man the hunter" as the progenitor of contemporary male dominance. In several cases, ideas centering on women's ostensible inferiority in intellect and assertiveness were favored as explanations for cultural inequality.

These discussions of biology and gender difference often raised with particular acuteness the issues of scholarly neutrality and detachment. References to activities of other animal species as paradigms for human behavior—a common form of intellectual shorthand, if not shortcoming—

often characterized the discussions. One participant, for example, cited the treatment of mares by stallions as proof of the naturalness of traditional gender divisions of power. The man-as-hunter argument was vividly exemplified by another participant's claim that males "of all species" are hunters, proving that men "naturally" have higher achievement motivation. Challenged by a participant who specializes in physical anthropology, he ignored her evidence and accused her of "misrepresenting scientific facts."

On another occasion, during a scheduled session on objectivity, one participant stated that the major problem with feminist research was that it rejected the possibility of the biological inferiority of women. Whereas other fields of inquiry would admit any kind of answer, he said, feminism discounted a priori one major area of research and its interpretive possibilities. (However, when we suggested that he substitute race for gender in this paradigm, the implications of his remarks became evident.) Some proponents of the idea of women's intellectual inferiority tried to distance themselves from this position with disclaimers that they were viewing the possibility only as hypothetical. In this context another professor suggested that one can clarify such issues with students by taking the position that, even if women are inferior, that does not justify enslaving or oppressing them. Such an interpretation allows the men who hold it to retain their sense of superiority, to protect their power and privileges, and to secure their self-images as fair and caring people even while making claims on women's gratitude. Under this construction, rights for women devolve into compassionate policies for the defective. As these examples make clear, the frequent imprecision and misinformation evident in such appeals to nature suggest not only lack of knowledge but also another—possibly unintentional—agenda: to convey and veil the defense of male prerogative that is historically inextricable from arguments about women's "natural" inferiority.

In response to these biological arguments, in the second year of the project we introduced readings on biology and gender asymmetry and on male resistance to feminist change. These strategies yielded mixed results. When, for example, we used Ashton Barfield's "Biological Influences on Sex Differences in Behavior," a lengthy, scrupulous summary of the major research on the biological bases for sex difference, many participants complained that we had devoted too much attention to the issue.[13] Nevertheless, possibly due to the difficulty of refuting Barfield, this group did not charge us with misreading biology for political reasons. But when we chose to focus explicitly on the political nature of all such materials through using articles by E. O. Wilson, Stephen Jay Gould, and Ruth Hubbard, one

---

[13] Ashton Barfield, "Biological Influences on Sex Differences in Behavior," in *Sex Differences: Social and Biological Perspectives*, ed. Michael Teitelbaum (Garden City, N.Y.: Doubleday & Co./Anchor Press, 1976), 62–121.

participant attacked Hubbard, a Harvard biologist whose feminist critique of sexism in science was perceived as an attack on science itself. Because Hubbard contested the idea of absolute scientific objectivity, often regarded (especially by nonscientists) as a foundation for scientific inquiry, her work was characterized as dangerous and thoughtless. It is important to note, however, that Gould, who agreed with Hubbard, did not evoke the same hostility.[14]

Ultimately, whatever strategy we adopted toward biological determinism seemed to meet with some resistance, suggesting the intractabilility of the issue. Those participants less interested in discussions of biology worried that we devoted far too much time to it. For others, however, biology was *the* central issue; our insistence on devoting systematic attention to the social construction of gender left us—and feminist theory—open to charges of political bias. Given the import of this issue for gender scholarship, we propose that biological considerations should be formally included early in curriculum integration projects. Although formal discussion did not enable us to move beyond biology with complete consistency, it did reduce the likelihood that consideration of other topics would be sidetracked.

In contrast, our attempt to deal with male resistance by introducing materials that explicitly analyzed it seemed to elicit profound levels of hostility, for which feminist criticism became the object, seen as the contagion, as it were, that engendered male dis-ease. A discussion of William Goode's sociological analysis of "Why Men Resist," for example, became a model of unacknowledged resistance, epitomizing the dynamics participants sought to deny and allowing some participants to distance themselves from any complicity.[15] To refute Goode's claim that men benefit from traditional sexual arrangements, participants pointed to the liabilities men experience under present arrangements (such as higher heart attack rates) or to the advantages they might gain for supporting feminist changes (such as more leisure time to spend at home). These arguments implicitly minimized both women's oppression and men's role in maintaining it, displacing the problems of prejudice and discrimination to different times, places, or social groups. As one professor put it, prejudicial attitudes might exist in the general society but not among academics, "if they are people for whom ideas matter."

Even when the readings contained only an implicit and indirect criti-

---

[14] E. O. Wilson, "Sex," in *On Human Nature* (Cambridge, Mass.: Harvard University Press, 1978), 121–48; Stephen Jay Gould, "Biological Potential vs. Biological Determinism," *Natural History Magazine* 85, no. 5 (May 1976): 12–22; and Ruth Hubbard, "Have Only Men Evolved?" in *Discovering Reality*, ed. Sandra Harding and Merrill B. Hintikka (Cambridge, Mass.: Schenkman Publishing Co., 1979), 45–69.

[15] William Goode, "Why Men Resist," in *Rethinking the Family*, ed. Barrie Thorne with Marilyn Yalom (New York: Longman, Inc., 1982), 131–50.

que of men, many participants became uncomfortable. In the seminar that included major Western thinkers from Aristotle to Rousseau, for instance, our choice of readings came under attack as biased, designed simply to make men look bad. (A survey of traditional thinking on gender does indeed expose most authors who ordinarily qualify as academia's heroes and mentors to be variously unreflective, derivative, or myopic on the subject of women.) Paralleling these traditional works to contemporary masculinist perspectives exacerbated the resistance. In our workshops, some participants' desire to retain their identification with the tradition while avoiding an *open* endorsement of its gender scripts led to tortured constructions of the texts or to a denial of their centrality in the Western tradition. Their sexism was defined as tangential and anomalous or was interpreted out of existence. For example, several professors dismissed Aristotle's pronouncements on gender in such texts as *The Generation of Animals* and the *Poetics* as peripheral and insignificant, not realizing or not admitting their implications for the conceptual foundations of his philosophy. Another scholar interpreted the myth of the Fall in Genesis 2–3 as an indication that Adam had got the worst of things. *He* was cursed to endless toil while women were only burdened with increased fertility, pain in childbirth, and subjugation to men.

The persistence of difference

The conviction that women had little particular or legitimate basis for grievance, past or present, surfaced frequently. Some participants used discussions of other inequalities as the means to discount the importance of gender. They also suggested that because a few groups of women had held certain forms of power over some men, women in general experienced few problems in gaining access to power and privilege. Indeed, that women had occasionally exercised authority over socially disadvantaged males even became the unacknowledged measure of how profoundly these men had been oppressed.

Several participants used the relative oppression argument, comparing (white) women's status with that of black and poor men (not black or poor women), as a means to label women's concerns trivial. In these discussions, other unintended revelations occurred. One participant remarked that it bothered him in discussing inequality that "we talk about this and then attribute it to the problems of women when to a large extent it can be attributed to the problems of young people or . . . the problems of talentless people or people without access or whatever it might be." (In view of the fact that the women's studies faculty in the workshop included women who were generally younger and had less institutional power than the men, this remark is instructive.) This sort of argument was pushed to its limit by a professor in another seminar who suggested, without ironic intent, that we had neglected the problems of discrimination against "the ugly."

The denial of gender points to another problem, at least as complicated: the ambiguous idea of gender blindness. Some of the participants decided to promote the "exceptional" women—women they often discovered in the seminars—to the status of honorary men, eliding the specificities of gender difference. Some literature professors, for example, sought to assimilate female authors into the tradition of *master*works, without realizing that that tradition, and the critical categories historically used to define it, are themselves put radically into question by women's writing. The underlying assumption of such gender blindness, of course, is that men remain the measure of human significance and signification. Thus they can continue to speak for/as women, in effect rendering women themselves unnecessary, redundant, and mute.[16]

Admittedly, human commonalities do exceed differences—even gender differences. On some level, as John Stuart Mill long ago observed, as long as sex/gender systems operate, we simply cannot know what "humanity" means.[17] Indeed, one of the major debates animating contemporary feminisms concerns the problem of at once adequately distinguishing sex/gender difference and comprehending a human being that transcends gender lines, acknowledging the internal differences within each of us that render problematic all traditional, simplistic categorizations of the self as necessarily male or female. As Hélène Cixous has pointed out, such reductive gender oppositions are dangerous precisely because they have traditionally been used to justify those systems that would keep women in their "proper place."[18] Yet the perils of reading "woman" and "man" as monolithic, universally and eternally opposed categories should not obscure the equally pernicious error of assuming no difference at all, which, as Adrienne Rich observes, leads to a reification of the category "human" as equivalent to "male" and thus subsumes and erases *women* yet again: "The urge to leap across feminism to 'human liberation' is a tragic and dangerous mistake. It . . . recycles us back into old definitions and structures, and continues to serve the purposes of patriarchy."[19]

The ineluctable presence of difference made itself felt in another way as

[16] On men's speaking for/as women, see Elaine Showalter, "Critical Cross-Dressing: Male Feminists and the Woman of the Year," *Raritan* 3 (Fall 1983): 130–49; and Nancy K. Miller, "I's in Drag," *Eighteenth Century: Theory and Interpretation* 22 (Winter 1981): 47–57.

[17] John Stuart Mill, "The Subjection of Women," in *Essays on Sex Equality*, John Stuart Mill and Harriet Taylor Mill, ed. Alice Rossi (Chicago: University of Chicago Press, 1970), 148.

[18] See Hélène Cixous, "Sorties," from *La jeune née* (Paris: Union Générale d'Editions, 1975), 114–245, trans. and reprinted in Marks and Courtivron, eds. (n. 4 above), 90–98.

[19] Rich, 134.

well. We had hoped that eventually, as a result of their work with the project, participants would come to see the human experience—male and female—through the eyes of women: that they would attain what Virginia Woolf calls a "difference of view."[20] Although some participants attained this viewpoint at times, most sought repeatedly to return to the topic of men. Ultimately, many resisted seeing either women or themselves from women's perspective—indeed, some appeared to disbelieve that any such perspective existed. This focus on men could be used in a positive way to highlight the significance of gender as a factor of analysis, leading men to understand women's oppression through developing an understanding of their own. Yet such discourse, we concluded, can also serve as a strategy for evading identification with women and for retaining men as the focal point of inquiry.

Even when the seminar topics and readings focused directly on women, such androcentric diversions occurred. In a discussion of a chapter on women's emotion work from Arlie Hochschild's *The Managed Heart*, several participants immediately shifted their attention to the imposition of emotion work on men in American society.[21] Despite the efforts of the moderator and others to bring the subject back to women, these participants repeatedly returned to a focus on men, who (they argued) are expected to sacrifice authenticity and self-esteem for the "feminine" tools of indirection and manipulation in order to function in a hierarchical world. To demonstrate lost masculine status and the tragic impossibility of male omnipotence, participants cited Lee Iacocca's troubles at Chrysler and Henry Kissinger's subordination to Richard Nixon. At one point, two discussants debated at length about housework, attending entirely to its relevance to men's lives and omitting serious consideration of the implications of the question for women themselves. This androcentric focus was particularly evident in the final presentations on the curricular transformations participants had developed. There, many talked at length about disciplinary canons and paradigms rooted in male experience and then finished with only brief discussions of women, often represented as anomalous.

Unfortunately, participants who transcended masculinist preoccupations and attempted to voice feminist positions frequently found their contributions ignored or discounted by others in the groups or found themselves subtly classed as "female" by their colleagues. Often, under

[20] Virginia Woolf, "George Eliot," in *The Common Reader, First Series* (New York: Harcourt Brace & Co., 1925), 176. See Mary Jacobus's astute remarks on this phrase as it relates to "the nature of women's access to . . . male-dominated culture," in *Women Writing and Writing about Women*, ed. Mary Jacobus (Totowa, N.J.: Barnes & Noble Books, 1979), 10–21.

[21] Arlie Hochschild, *The Managed Heart* (Berkeley and Los Angeles: University of California Press, 1983).

these circumstances, the professors being criticized would disown the very insights they had articulated. One participant, for example, early in the seminar delivered a stinging feminist critique of the idea of the objectivity of knowledge, only to retreat, by the end of the term, into traditional masculinist gender paradigms. Even those men who changed dramatically often, perhaps necessarily, did so with a certain detachment from the insights provided by the materials. Others talked about their feminist sympathies only in private conversations with us, wary of public exposure.

What all these examples demonstrate is that men still enjoy greater freedom to select the terms of their discourse than do women. As Nancy Miller has wittily observed, "Only those who have it can play with not having it."[22] This freedom may be partially illusory: the male peer group—not to mention masculinist culture and tradition—exercises a considerable tyranny over many of its members, in effect acting as a tacit police force over their discourse, hence over thought itself.

Male domination of discourse also revealed itself in the gendered conversational patterns well documented by feminist linguistic scholars. At times even the most important topics and perspectives we introduced would be seriously attended to only when reintroduced later by a male participant. Similarly, we had to deal with hearing women discussed as though none were present. When this pattern became pronounced enough that we pointed it out, the group in question did not perceive it as a significant or systematic problem. (In fact, they had not even noticed.)

To the extent that the most resistant participants heard us at all, however, what they generally heard were our criticisms, which they often assumed to be invalid. After one particularly heated discussion of human reproduction in which women's studies faculty joined with many participants to disagree with the presenter, his reaction included the conclusion that the women had been unreceptive to his point of view, their understanding of his presentation clouded by "emotionality." He failed to notice that many of his male colleagues had objected as strenuously as we. The perception that the seminar dynamics pitted women against men (each perceived to be monolithic in their views) all too frequently shaped and signified the unacknowledged subtext for the discussions.

Seeing (as) the Other

What does this mean for women? Throughout our four-year experience, we were continually reminded that phalloreferential/reverential discourse

[22] Nancy K. Miller, "The Text's Heroine: A Feminist Critic and Her Fictions," *Diacritics* 12 (Summer 1982): 48–53. See also Peggy Kamuf, "Replacing Feminist Criticism," *Diacritics* 12 (Summer 1982): 42–47.

assumes many forms. We also found striking confirmation of Nancy Chodorow's observation that men have used their cultural hegemony to express and institutionalize "their unconscious defenses against repressed
yet strongly experienced developmental conflicts."[23] Curriculum integration asks men to value the female, the very element they had unconsciously
rejected in their formation of gender identity, and to relinquish traditional
culture, the very construct with which they had identified in expressing
and allaying their anxieties about separation, selfhood, and power.

Even when the desire to learn about women is sincere, conceptual/
psychological difficulties sometimes prove formidable. In the face of mutual misunderstanding, both men and women involved in such a project
fear objectification: ultimately, each group on some level perceives the
other as a threat to its autonomy and selfhood. In the highly charged
context of contemporary gender relations, all generalizations about
gender-group attributes and behaviors, however carefully qualified and
explicated, carry the threat of such objectification. Women, however,
having been historically relegated to Otherness far more pervasively than
men, are especially vulnerable to this dynamic. We were particularly
sensitive to its enactment in a variety of ways in the seminars: the implicit
and explicit derogation of women, the silencing tactics, and the trivializa-
tion of feminist scholarship designed to invalidate our perceptions and call
our scholarly integrity into question. We were also attuned to the dangers
of women's erasure through what Catharine MacKinnon calls "aperspectiv-
ity": the contention that the male view is the unbiased view, that the
"neutral observer" is in fact really neutral—as well as neuter.[24]

For some of the men, however, the process functioned as an unsolicited
interrogation of their unexamined assumptions and practices not only as
scholars but also as human beings. The primary threat of the seminars for
them was that, in being objectified by us as the Other, they would become,
in every sense, unmanned. Their attempts to know women entailed the
fearful possibility of being *known by them*, of relinquishing the security
and privilege traditionally enjoyed by man the knower. As Simone de
Beauvoir has observed, "man dreams of an Other not only to possess her
but also to be ratified by her."[25] This dream is profoundly disturbed by
feminist scholars' refusal to accept men's premises uncritically, to ratify
unquestioningly their positive self-images, or, more importantly, to play
out the masculinist scenario described by Beauvoir, where women consent
to their own oppression by first putting up an intelligent resistance to the

[23] Nancy Chodorow, "Gender, Relation, and Difference in Psychoanalytic Perspective,"
in Eisenstein and Jardine, eds. (n. 4 above), 3–19.
[24] Catharine A. MacKinnon, "Feminism, Marxism, Method, and the State: An Agenda for
Theory," *Signs: Journal of Women in Culture and Society* 7, no. 3 (Spring 1982): 515–44.
[25] Simone de Beauvoir, *The Second Sex*, trans. H. M. Parshley (New York: Alfred A.
Knopf, 1970), 170.

idea of their inferiority and then capitulating/deferring to men's opinions of women and of themselves. As Beauvoir remarks, man requires "that this struggle remain a game for him, while for woman it involves her very destiny."[26] That the unwritten rules for this cultural "game" may no longer function was deeply unsettling for many men in our project.

As we seek to become our own translators, then, we must remain alert to the linguistic and conceptual pitfalls inherent in such a project and mindful of its emotional as well as its cognitive implications. As long as many scholars remain rooted in the Western academic tradition of distance, detachment, and denial, retaining the conviction that scholarly neutrality is the necessary condition to promote objective truth seeking, this dilemma will persist. Yet when feminists challenge the very idea of neutrality in scholarship, or question traditional conceptualizations of the "self," they may be—as we were—accused of "rampant relativism" and of replacing academic standards with ideological frameworks. The anxieties of participants stemming from this issue did not derive simply from a desire to evade the political implications of the materials or from a projection of their own fears regarding a loss of control and a sense of separate identity: their anxieties were inseparable from their socialization as academics. This particular form of resistance, it would seem, may well be predicated by the very structure of the institution within which, problematically, we must operate even as we seek its transformation.

What all these examples illustrate is the dynamic at the heart not only of curriculum integration efforts but also of culture itself: the problem of difference. Fundamentally, the issue is one of perspective. Each woman or man reads our culture's gender scripts from where she or he stands. For feminist scholars, the project of changing men's minds is therefore inseparable from inducing them to change the ground—intellectual, emotional, academic—from which they assume their point of view and, in so doing, to redefine "woman's place" as well. The ambiguities inherent in our curriculum project, and its potential for being read in completely opposite, mutually contradictory ways by women and men, became for us a metaphor for the whole cultural process, confirming time and again what we all know only too well: that the scripts that underwrite masculinist culture are well learned and intensely resistant to change.

Changing minds

As we remarked at the outset, we have focused on resistances to curriculum integration because we feel that only by exposing these dynamics can we develop effective strategies to deal with them. The difficulties we

[26] Ibid., 172.

confronted diminish neither our belief in the necessity of such projects nor our sense of the significant successes they achieve. It is imperative to remember that change takes many forms: in addition to the rapid and dramatic conversions and the documentable modifications we witnessed, we would also stress subtler, less easily demonstrable forms of change: the slow, incremental, but nonetheless significant process that only began with our project but will have positive, expanding effects for years to come. By keeping these continually in mind, one can simultaneously maintain high standards and expectations and avoid succumbing to discouragement when these appear unfulfilled.

Curriculum integration is, however, an exceedingly complex undertaking, as we have tried to suggest. Those who direct it should anticipate resistances that will shift—in both kind and intensity—according to the changing chemistry of the groups involved. Because resistance assumes such protean forms, there is no single right way to proceed; nevertheless, from our experience we would offer the following, by no means exhaustive, suggestions for avoiding some of the pitfalls we encountered.

In addition to the obvious needs for the project—administrative support and financial resources to provide stipends and/or released time for project directors and participants—we found that it is extremely helpful to have a strong women's studies program in place before attempting curriculum integration. Such a program offers many useful resources, including a faculty experienced in working together and in maneuvering amid the ever-shifting currents of the gender politics on a given campus. The presence of such a program also emphasizes that curriculum integration is not a replacement for women's studies but an extension of it.

Women's studies faculty should retain control over the project, carefully selecting the participants and dispensing the rewards so as to insure accountability for outcomes. It is important to involve as many *senior* women's studies scholars as possible. While we counted on the authority of the *texts*, it is only realistic to recognize that the power of the individuals presenting the material has much to do with its acceptance. We would also suggest a balance of participants—junior and senior, tenured and non-tenured.[27]

Similarly, the diversity of feminist theory and of women's experiences—especially relative to questions of race, class, ethnicity, and sexual preference—should be emphasized from the beginning. Such a focus not only prevents participants from overgeneralizing about women as a group, it also is essential to adequate analytic understanding of gender issues. The interdisciplinary nature of our project necessitated a highly theoretical

[27] Though the goals of our project limited our selection to tenured participants during the first three years, during the fourth year we included nontenured professors, some of whom were outstanding participants.

approach, the strengths and weaknesses of which we have noted above. Retrospectively, some of us wonder whether providing more disciplinary focus (at least in the beginning) and more immediately usable readings directed at specific courses would have worked better. In either case, project leaders should be explicit from the outset about the feminist assumptions that ground the project and be prepared to explain and discuss these issues a number of times. They should also use caution in deciding whether to offer readings that directly analyze men's roles and behaviors, since such texts may elicit explosive reactions. Should leaders experience these defensive dynamics, we think it useful to draw attention to them as they occur.

Because burnout is a besetting problem in the case of lengthy projects, the larger the pool of feminist scholars you have to draw on, the better. Project leaders should anticipate the enormous time commitment curriculum projects demand and be prepared to deal with their own inevitable frustrations and impatience—humorously, if possible—both in and out of sessions with participants. Above all, do not blame yourself if the changes you have worked for so arduously seem painfully slow.

Having tried—and been tried by—curriculum transformation, our sense of accomplishment is tempered by a more realistic awareness of the formidable challenges of the task. As the foregoing analysis suggests, the process confirmed many of the critiques feminist analysts have made of the androcentric academy's resistance to change. We found that dealing with defensiveness—our own as well as that of some participants—became increasingly stressful as time passed, suggesting the cumulative effects of the psychic costs such projects may exact. We also found, however, new colleagues who were eager to accept the holistic intellectual perspective feminist studies provide, colleagues who demonstrated that totalizing generalizations about the blindness of the academy are unwarranted. Finally, and perhaps most importantly, we found ourselves strengthened both individually and as a group by what, borrowing Monique Wittig's alteration of a masculine metaphor, one might call the camaraderie of the trench shared by all *guérrillères:* in combatting resistances, we discovered a unity of purpose that surpassed anything we could have foreseen or imagined. This crucibled melding made our group into a stronger force for change than would have ever been possible otherwise and will clearly endure far beyond our project, empowering us for future efforts to generate feminist transformation within the university and beyond.

Department of English
University of Arizona (Aiken)

Department of History
University of Arizona (Anderson)

Department of Women's Studies
University of Arizona (Dinnerstein)

Department of American Studies
University of Iowa (Lensink)

Department of Sociology
University of Arizona (MacCorquodale)

THE COSTS OF EXCLUSIONARY PRACTICES IN WOMEN'S STUDIES

MAXINE BACA ZINN, LYNN WEBER CANNON, ELIZABETH HIGGINBOTHAM, AND BONNIE THORNTON DILL

As women who came to maturity during the social upheavals of the late sixties and early seventies, we entered academia to continue—in a different arena—the struggles that our foreparents had begun centuries earlier. We sought to reveal untold tales and unearth hidden images, and we believed (or at least hoped) that, once illuminated, the truths of the lives of our people—Black, brown, and working-class white—would combat the myths and stereotypes that haunted us. We were, in that sense, scholars with a special mission. In the tradition of W. E. B. DuBois, Oliver Cox, Joyce Ladner, and other pioneers, we sought to use the tools of history and social science and the media of literature and the arts to improve our people's future and more accurately portray their past.

We each had developed critical perspectives on society and sought theoretical explanations for the continued poverty and oppression of our people. We had different but related foci for our research: on Chicanos and the impact of outside resources on family structure and ethnicity; on working-class consciousness and class conflict; on Black women achieving a college education; and on the relationship of work and family for Black women private household workers. In the process of conducting it, we became acutely aware of the limitations of traditional social science with

The authors wish to thank Barrie Thorne and an anonymous reviewer for their encouragement and helpful suggestions on this piece.

This essay originally appeared in *Signs*, vol. 11, no. 2, Winter 1986.

regard to working-class women and women of color.[1] More profoundly, however, we realized that the experiences of these groups of women were virtually excluded from consideration as vital building blocks in feminist theory.

In the past, many working-class women and women of color have been critical of women's studies for the lack of attention given "their" women.[2] This "Viewpoint" draws from those arguments and adds our own perspectives. Our effort is not only to voice discontent but also to elaborate on some of the implications of the exclusionary nature of women's studies. There are many issues that must be addressed regarding the need for attention to race and class in women's studies. This "Viewpoint" can only attend to some of them. If dialogue is reopened in these or related areas, our goal will have been realized.

The Institutionalization of Privilege

Many recent studies have documented organizational barriers to women's full and equal participation in society. Institutions are organized to facilitate white middle-class men's smooth entry into and mobility in positions of power. These men establish criteria for the entry of others into similar positions, defining success, the reward system, the distribution of resources, and institutional goals and priorities in a way that perpetuates their power. In higher education, as in other areas, women—even white middle-class women—have been excluded from many of these

1. Maxine Baca Zinn, "Review Essay: Mexican American Women in the Social Sciences," *Signs: Journal of Women in Culture and Society* 8, no. 2 (Winter 1982): 259–72, "Social Research on Chicanos: Its Development and Directions," *Social Science Journal* 19, no. 2 (April 1982): 1–7, "Sociological Theory in Emergent Chicano Perspectives," *Pacific Sociological Review* 24, no. 2 (April 1981): 255–69, and "Field Research in Minority Communities: Ethical, Methodological, and Political Observations by an Insider," *Social Problems* 27, no. 2 (December 1979): 209–19; Lynn Weber Cannon, "Trends in Class Identification among Black Americans from 1952 to 1978," *Social Science Quarterly* 65 (March 1984): 112–26; and Reeve Vanneman and Lynn Weber Cannon, "The American Perception of Class" (Memphis State University, Center for Research on Women, 1985, typescript); Elizabeth Higginbotham, "Race and Class Barriers to Black Women's College Attendance," *Journal of Ethnic Studies* (in press), "Issues in Contemporary Sociological Work on Black Women," *Humanity and Society* 4, no. 3 (November 1980): 226–42, and "Educated Black Women: An Exploration into Life Chance and Choices" (Ph.D. diss., Brandeis University, 1980); Bonnie Thornton Dill, "We Must Redefine Feminism," *Sojourner, the Women's Forum* (September 1984): 10–11, "Race, Class, and Gender: Prospects for an All-inclusive Sisterhood," *Feminist Studies* 9 (Spring 1983): 131–50, and "On the Hem of Life: Race, Class, and the Prospects for Sisterhood," in *Class, Race, and Sex*, ed. Amy Swerdlow and Hanna Lessingler (Boston: G. K. Hall & Co., 1983), pp. 173–88.

2. See, e.g., Audre Lorde, *Sister Outsider* (Trumansburg, N.Y.: Crossing Press, 1984); Angela Y. Davis, *Women, Race and Class* (New York: Random House, 1981).

activities. They continue to struggle to move out of token positions of authority and into the true centers of power as presidents, administrators, trustees, members of state governing boards, officers of professional associations, editors of prestigious journals, and members on policy-making boards and on review panels of granting agencies. Over the past decade, women have made gains in approaching those centers of power, but the institutional barriers have been formidable, and the fight to break them down has left many women scarred.

The obstacles white middle-class women face are compounded many times over for women of color and working-class women. For these two groups, completing college and graduate education itself poses financial, emotional, and intellectual challenges.[3] As students, they are more likely than middle-class white women to attend public institutions—community colleges and state universities—or, in the case of Blacks, traditionally Black institutions. As faculty, they are more likely to be employed in public institutions and in those that do not grant doctorates. A 1970 study estimated that Blacks made up only 0.9 percent of faculty in universities and 5.4 percent in four-year colleges. This number drops to only 2.0 percent when traditionally Black institutions are eliminated.[4] Among these less prestigious schools, few have the financial and other resources necessary to facilitate and encourage research and scholarship. In fact, these settings are characterized by high teaching loads, heavy demand for institutional service, and limited dollars for travel, computer facilities, research libraries, secretarial support, or research assistance.

Most of the scholarly research and writing that take place in the United States are conducted at a relatively small number of institutions. To a large extent, research and other scholarly production in women's studies have also been closely tied to the resources and prestige of these academic centers. Indeed, women's studies, partly because of its marginal position in the academy, has sought to validate the field through association with prestigious institutions of higher education. In these schools, there are very few women of color, and while we cannot know how many of the women faculty at these institutions are from working-class backgrounds, it is safe to assume that their numbers also are relatively small.[5]

The result is that women of color and women from working-class backgrounds have few opportunities to become part of the networks that

3. Higginbotham, "Educated Black Women."

4. William H. Exum, "Climbing the Crystal Stair: Values, Affirmative Action and Minority Faculty," *Social Problems* 30, no. 4 (April 1983): 383–97.

5. For a discussion of the experiences of scholars from working-class backgrounds in the academy, see Jake Ryan and Charles Sackrey, *Strangers in Paradise* (Boston: South End Press, 1984); and Carol Sternhell, "The Women Who Won't Disappear," *Ms.* (October 1984): 94–98.

produce or monitor knowledge in women's studies. In addition, those who have the advantage of being researchers and gatekeepers are primarily located at privileged institutions, where they get little exposure to working-class and ethnically diverse students. As a result, they tend to develop and teach concepts divorced from the realities of women of color and working-class women's lives.

For example, a concept such as the "positive effect of the multiple negative" could not have survived the scrutiny of professional Black women or Black women students. The theory suggests that the negative status of being Black combines with the negative status of being female to give professional Black women an advantage in the labor market.[6] Although this may have appeared to be the case for the researcher isolated from significant numbers of Black women as colleagues or students, Blacks' life experiences would have suggested many alternate interpretations. Such cases clearly illustrate that the current organization of the academy perpetuates the production and distribution of knowledge that is both Anglo and middle-class centered.

To explore further the institutional structures that limit the contributions of women of color and women from working-class backgrounds to the field of women's studies, we engaged in a simple exercise. We looked at the published information about the official gatekeepers of two leading interdisciplinary journals in the field of women's studies: *Signs* and *Feminist Studies*. These groups of editors, associate editors, and consultants make important decisions about which individual pieces of scholarship will be contained in the journals' pages and what special issues will be undertaken, officially sanctioning and defining important concerns and critical scholarship in the field. We asked, "Where are women of color located within these publications generated out of the women's movement and its accompanying scholarship?"

Despite white, middle-class feminists' frequent expressions of interest and concern over the plight of minority and working-class women, those holding the gatekeeping positions at these journals are as white as are those at any mainstream social science or humanities publication. The most important groups within the hierarchies of the two journals—that is, the groups most involved in policy decisions—are the eleven editors of *Feminist Studies* and the editor and eight associate editors of *Signs*. Among those twenty women, in 1983–84, there was not a single Black woman, there were no Hispanic women, no Native American women, and no

6. Cynthia Epstein, "The Positive Effects of the Multiple Negative: Explaining the Success of Black Professional Women," *American Journal of Sociology* 78, no. 4 (January 1973): 912–33. Although this article serves as a useful example of failure in the applicability of a theory to reality, we single it out as one among many that could demonstrate the same phenomenon. See below for further discussion of this point in a related context.

Chinese American women. The only woman of color was a Japanese-American woman, an associate editor of *Signs*.[7]

As reported in table 1, token representation also occurs at positions below those of the editors themselves. The primary function of those in these groups is to review articles and on occasion to give advice to the editors. *Feminist Studies* has fifty-nine whites and five women of color serving as associate editors and consultants, whereas *Signs* has thirty-eight whites and three women of color in those categories. Regardless of position, the total number of editors and consultants for both journals combined shows that there are 119 whites, six Blacks, one Hispanic, and two Asian Americans.

It is much easier to designate the ways that women of color have been excluded than it is to show the ways that white working-class women have been kept out of the mainstream. Furthermore, it is more difficult to delineate the ways that classism excludes both whites and women of color who are from the working class. The information that *Signs* gives about the institutional affiliations of its editors and consultants, however, can be used to illustrate other biases in the gatekeeping positions. None of the fifty women in these positions represents a traditionally Black institution; only about six represent schools whose student bodies are primarily constituted of working-class students (i.e., the first in their families to attend college); and only three are from the South—where the highest concentrations of minorities continue to live.

The major implication of these figures is that women of color are rarely sitting around the table when problems are defined and strategies

Table 1

Representation of Minorities on *Signs* and *Feminist Studies* Editorial Boards, 1983–84

	Editor(s)		Associate Editor(s)		Consultants		Total	
	Minor-ity	White	Minor-ity	White	Minor-ity	White	Minor-ity	White
Feminist Studies	0	11	2	13	3	46	5	70
Signs	1	8	...	...	3	38	4	46
Both journals ...	1	19	2	13	6	84	9	116

NOTE.—*Signs*'s associate editors were included under the heading of "Editors" because their functions match more closely those performed by editors of *Feminist Studies*. The data were obtained from the lists published in recent issues of these journals.

7. The new group of associate editors for *Signs*, when it moves to Duke University, will include three Black women, one of whom is a faculty member at a traditionally Black institution. *Feminist Studies* reports that their current (1985) group of editors and consultants includes two women of color as editors (out of twelve), one woman of color as an associate editor (out of fifteen), and fifteen women of color as consultants (out of a total of sixty-four).

suggested. They are not in positions to engage in the theoretical discourse behind specific decisions on what will be published. Thus, even when white feminists attempt to include women of color, there are often difficulties because women of color reject the dominant paradigms and approach problems from divergent perspectives. Typically, women of color then find their work rejected on the grounds that it does not conform to the established ways of thinking. This clash of paradigms resounds through the following example.

In 1981, the planners of a conference on communities of women asked Elizabeth Higginbotham to submit an abstract for a paper.[8] The expectation communicated in the letter of invitation was that her research would demonstrate the applicability to Black women of a concept of women's communities set forth by white feminists. Instead of attempting to alter her work to fit such a model, Higginbotham wrote to the organizers and challenged their narrow definition of communities of women.

Higginbotham noted that, unlike their white sisters who are often excluded from male-dominated spheres or retreat from them, the majority of Black women are ordinarily full participants in mixed-sex spheres and make unique contributions both to the definitions of problems and to solutions. Typically, Black women's vision of their situation leads them not to seek solace from Black males but to create spheres where men, women, and children are relatively protected from racist cultural and physical assaults. Historically, white people, male and female, have rarely validated the humanness of Black people; therefore, it was and is critical for Black people and other people of color to nurture each other. This is a primary fact about the communities of racially oppressed peoples. Thus, as white feminists defined the focus of the conference, only the research of a few Black scholars seemed appropriate—and that research did not necessarily capture the most typical and common experiences of Black women.

The Limitations of Popular Feminist Theory

Practices that exclude women of color and working-class women from the mainstream of women's studies have important consequences for feminist theory. Ultimately, they prevent a full understanding of gender and society. The failure to explore fully the interplay of race, class, and gender has cost the field the ability to provide a broad and truly complex analysis of women's lives and of social organization. It has rendered feminist theory incomplete and incorrect.

8. This conference was held in February 1982. The proceedings can be found in *Signs*, vol. 10, no. 4 (Summer 1985).

Until the past few years, women of color have been virtually hidden in feminist scholarship, made invisible by the erroneous notion of universal womanhood. In an effort to emphasize the shared experiences of sexism, scholars passed over the differences in women's situations.[9] Knowledge assumed to be "universal" was actually based for the most part on the experiences of women who were white and primarily middle class. Feminist scholarship, a center of a developing critical intellectual tradition, increasingly came under fire for this myopia from other critical scholarships, namely, the scholarship on people of color and on the working class. As a result, there now exists in women's studies an increased awareness of the variability of womanhood. Women's studies journals and classroom texts are more likely at present to contain material about minority women. Still, such work is often tacked on, its significance for feminist knowledge still unrecognized and unregarded.

A close look at feminist social science reveals three common approaches to race and class. The first treats race and class as secondary features in social organization with primacy given to universal female subordination. Such thinking establishes what is taken to be a common feminist ground and labels any divergence from it, in Phyllis Palmer's phrase, a "diversionary special interest."[10] To make gender relations primary is to assume that they create a set of universal experiences more important than those of other inequalities.

A second approach acknowledges that inequalities of race, class, and gender generate different experiences and that women have a race-specific and a class-specific relation to the sex-gender system. However, it then sets race and class inequalities aside on the grounds that, while they are important, we lack information that would allow us to incorporate them in the analysis. As Bonnie Thornton Dill puts it, inequalities other than sex and gender are recognized, but they are not explicated.[11] After a perfunctory acknowledgment of differences, those taking this position make no further attempt to incorporate the insights generated by critical scholarship on race and class into a framework that would deal with women generally.[12]

9. Margaret A. Simons, "Racism and Feminism," *Feminist Studies* 4, no. 2 (1979): 384–401, esp. 388.

10. Phyllis Marynick Palmer, "White Women/Black Women: The Dualism of Female Identity and Experience in the United States," *Feminist Studies* 9 (Spring 1983): 151–70, esp. 152.

11. Dill (n. 1 above), "On the Hem of Life," p. 179.

12. For a recent popular example, see Carol Gilligan, *In a Different Voice: Psychological Theory and Women's Development* (Cambridge: Harvard University Press, 1982). The problem of the exclusion of race and class from this work is discussed in a review by Maxine Baca Zinn in *Newsletter of the Center for Research on Women* (Memphis State University, Tenn.), vol. 2, no. 1 (November 1983).

The third approach, often found in conjunction with the first two, focuses on descriptive aspects of the ways of life, values, customs, and problems of women in subordinate race and class categories. Here differences are detailed with little attempt to explain their source or their broader meaning. Such discussions of women are "confined to a pre-theoretical presentation of concrete problems."[13]

Each of these conceptualizations is inadequate for the development of feminist theory. They create an illusion of comprehensiveness and thereby stifle the development of scholarship about women of color. Moreover, when race and class are set aside, even the analysis of white middle-class women's lives is incomplete. A woman's "place" in society, her opportunities and her experiences, must be understood in relation to the societal placement of men as well as of other classes and races of people.

An approach to the study of women in culture and society should begin at the level of social organization. From this vantage point one can appreciate the complex web of hierarchical social arrangements that generate different experiences for women. For example, Denise Segura has recently documented the ways in which gender and race produce distinctive consequences in the labor force experiences of Chicanas. Using a four-way comparison, she examines the occupational profiles of Chicanas, Chicanos, white women, and white men. Her findings reveal that while Chicanas are triply oppressed, the dynamics of class, race, and gender oppression are different. Racial barriers impede access to professional and managerial occupations, whereas gender produces an earnings gap at all occupational levels.[14]

The integration of race and class into the study of gender creates different questions and new conceptualizations of many problems. For instance, in the last few years, there has been a great deal of attention to the entrance of women into professional and managerial occupations. In fact, the levels of female professional and managerial employment are often the standard used to evaluate women's success. In such conceptualizations, Black women are frequently held up as exemplars because they are more concentrated in professional employment than Black males. White women, in contrast, are less concentrated than white males in such positions and are viewed as less "successful" than their Black sisters.[15]

Black professional women understand such seemingly favorable

13. Simons, p. 388.

14. Denise Segura, "Labor Market Stratification: The Chicana Experience," *Berkeley Journal of Sociology* 29 (Spring 1984): 57–91.

15. Marion Kilson, "Black Women in the Professions," *Monthly Labor Review* 100 (May 1977): 38–41. Relevant also is Epstein (n. 6 above).

comparisons differently. The analysis behind them lacks a sense of Black history and of racial stratification and thus ignores a number of underlying factors: the racial barriers that limit educational attainment for Black men; a history of limited employment options for Black women who have only a high school education; and the high concentration of Black professional and managerial women in the public sector and in traditionally female occupations. Each of these realities suggests that professional or managerial work will have a different meaning to Black women.[16] In short, an analysis of gender and occupation that also incorporates race would have raised a variety of other issues and avoided the narrow focus on Black women's "success."

Classism, Racism, and Privileged Groups of Women

We recognize that there are significant reasons behind the fact that a synthesis of class, race, and gender perspectives into a holistic and inclusive feminist theory and practice has not yet taken place. Some derive from both the short- and long-term costs of struggling to overcome institutionally supported and historically reproduced hierarchies of inequality. Others have to do with the benefits that accrue to those in a group with relative power.

White middle-class women profit in several ways from the exclusion of upwardly mobile women and women of color from the ranks of academic equals in their universities, from the pages of women's studies journals, from positions of power in our professional associations, and from a central place in feminist theories. Foremost among these advantages is the elimination of direct competition for the few "women's jobs" in universities; for the limited number of tenure-track and tenured jobs; for the small number of places for women among the higher professorial ranks; for the meager number of pages devoted to research and writing on women in the mainstream professional journals; and for the precious, limited space in women's studies journals. White women, struggling for acceptance by male peers, a secure job, and a living wage in the academy— especially since many are forced to work part-time or on a series of one-year appointments—may not "feel" that they are in a privileged position. Indeed, in many ways and in many cases there is little privilege. However, their relative disadvantage in comparison with white men should not obscure the advantages of race and class that remain.

16. Sharon M. Collins, "The Making of the Black Middle Class," *Social Problems* 30, no. 4 (April 1983): 369–82; Elizabeth Higginbotham, "Employment for Professional Black Women in the Twentieth Century" (paper delivered at the Ingredients for Women's Employment Policy Conference, State University of New York at Albany, 1985).

Despite the benefits to some that derive from exclusionary practices, there are also costs to feminist theory and to women's lives—even to the lives of privileged groups of women. Scholarship that overlooks the diversity of women's experiences cannot reveal the magnitude, complexity, or interdependence of systems of oppression. Such work underestimates the obstacles to be confronted and helps little in developing practical strategies to overcome the sexist barriers that even privileged women inevitably confront.

As women in academia, we are obliged to compete for rewards individually in a system where we are not among the power brokers. Individual competition in a hierarchical scheme based on "merit" may work well to explain the experiences and structure of the lives of middle- or upper-class white men. As a theoretical perspective or guiding principle, it does not explain the life experiences of groups—including that of white middle-class women—who lack power. In this situation, the merit, motivation, and work of an individual who suffers discrimination are not relevant, since discrimination, like all other forms of oppression, operates against a whole group. Thus, as a group, women find themselves up against barriers to success.

Relatively privileged groups of women are nonetheless shielded from awareness of the institutional barriers that their working-class and minority sisters come to recognize early. Many middle-class white women "buy into" the system and assume that it will work for them. Linda Nielsen's comments on her tenure battle show her recognition that she had made just this error: "During those beginning years I was not seriously worried about my future, since I had been exceptionally successful at publishing and teaching, and I believed that this guaranteed my professional security. It did not." She was denied reappointment even though she met objective university criteria.

The experience, she came to realize, found her unprepared for the reality and consequences of sexism and ready, furthermore, to blame herself for the serious blow she had received. "Women continue to look for the enemy as though it were only in themselves, I was no exception."[17] While Nielsen's generalization may be true of many women, the literature shows that minority women are much more likely to blame the system when things go wrong than are white women.[18]

Nielsen also describes herself as experiencing the need for white male approval so common among white women: "I feel my colleagues'

17. Linda L. Nielsen, "Sexism and Self-Healing in the University," *Harvard Educational Review* 49, no. 4 (November 1979): 467–76, esp. 467. Again this account is singled out as only one among many possible examples, useful because it is so forthright.

18. Patricia Gurin, Arthur Miller, and Gerald Gurin, "Stratum Identification and Consciousness," *Social Psychological Quarterly* 43, no. 1 (1980): 30–47.

lack of support would have been far less painful and less detrimental to my self-esteem had I not learned to define my worth so exclusively by men's judgments." After a brief look at some research and at autobiographical accounts, she draws some conclusions about the special difficulties that women have to overcome as a minority group. The characteristics are "over-reliance on male approval, passivity or non-assertiveness, ambivalence and anxiety over contradictory female roles, inclination toward self-blame and guilt, affiliative needs which interfere with achievement, motivation, and discrimination from other females."[19]

Unfortunately, although Nielsen's courageous account is a useful analysis of a white middle-class woman's experience, there is not a single reference in her bibliography to a work by a woman of color. Familiarity with research on minority groups immediately reveals that the reactions Nielsen lists contain responses that do not apply *uniquely* to women. Some, such as discrimination from members of one's own group, are common among other minorities, and others—such as overreliance on male approval, ambivalence and anxiety over contradictory female roles, and passivity or nonassertiveness—do not apply to many women of color. For example, numerous Black working-class women have not employed passivity as a survival mechanism—indeed, their aggressive actions in comparison with those of white middle-class women are often viewed antagonistically by whites as "unfeminine."

Thus, Nielsen's conclusions, while somewhat instructive to white middle-class women, actually shed little light on the circumstances and experiences of upwardly mobile women and women of color. Because she does not look at the latters' situations to understand the nature of all women's oppression, her observations and conclusions are incorrect. Nielsen rightly identifies some responses to discrimination as they are manifested in her own life and the lives of other middle-class white women. Yet from this narrow perspective she can only partially glimpse even her own plight, and her observations do little to recognize hers as part of a wider struggle shared with women who are different from her.

Some Goals and Strategies for Change

We seek to build a more diverse women's studies and an integrative feminist theory. Achievement of these goals requires many structural changes in the practices and policies of academic communities. In the present political climate, we cannot expect leadership in these areas to come from government or university administrations. Instead, we must ourselves make an effort at every level to build alliances, set priorities, and

19. Nielsen, p. 474.

work in whatever ways we can to create more diverse academic communities and a field of women's studies open to wide participation.

First, we need to establish and maintain heterogeneous college faculties. Frequently, feminists are ready to fight for women colleagues but do not extend such support to minorities and people from working-class backgrounds. We must learn about each other and appreciate our differences in order to form the types of alliances that will transform the composition of faculties at our institutions. Without such alliances, any group can be isolated and eliminated without much controversy on any particular campus. Above all, we must withstand the temptation to secure our individual futures by accommodating to the "principles" of the institution.

Second, we should actively encourage dialogue among academic centers, especially in local areas, by forming close links with faculty in different types of institutions. Faculty in elite schools particularly must reach out beyond their campuses to faculty and students in less prestigious centers of higher education. Faculty with low teaching loads, large research funds, and frequent opportunities to travel are indeed privileged; those without such "perks" are no less worthy of respect. In fact, scholars who are struggling to conduct research in institutions where the primary emphasis is on teaching merit our encouragement. Faculty are not distributed among colleges solely by talent and ability; racism, classism, and sexism all function to shape academic careers. Consequently, we have to reject the elitism so prevalent in academe, visit other campuses and learning centers, make friends with new colleagues, and share resources. There are reasons behind the pattern whereby faculty in research institutions conduct and produce research while faculty in teaching institutions fail to publish. The current structure of academia is indeed designed to produce that outcome, and strategies should be designed to change it.[20] The number of women and minorities hired in second-tier, four-year colleges and community colleges makes it imperative that we do everything possible to pull down the structural barriers that block their careers.

Third, efforts should continue to open up the gatekeeping positions in women's studies to include a broad representation of women. Editorial boards need to reject the tokenism that has characterized them so far, and

20. The Center for Research on Women, Memphis State University; the Women's Studies Research Center, Duke University—University of North Carolina; and the Women's Research and Resource Center, Spelman College, are developing a series of working papers on Southern women. To achieve this goal, we are identifying scholars of Southern women outside our institutions, bringing them into a network, providing feedback on their work, and publishing their articles as working papers. We also encourage them to submit their products to journals for publication. We are helping a small but isolated group of researchers to produce work and to participate in the growth of this new area of scholarship.

they must strive to solicit and publish feminist scholarship from all corners. Committees and organizations that plan conferences need diverse membership—members who will seriously address issues of age, race, class, and sexual preference in the definition and formation of programs and in the means used to recruit participants. Dill's comments on the "Common Differences" conference cosponsored by Duke University, the University of North Carolina, and North Carolina Central Universities are illustrative of this point and the positive consequences of such planning: "The most outstanding thing about this conference was . . . the commitment to an honest, frank, and equal exchange among black and white women. . . . It pervaded the entire organization of the conference from the planning committee through the workshops, films, lectures, and presentations. Workshops were led by a team consisting of one black and one white woman. The leaders played an important role in facilitating discussions of the commonalities in black and white womens' lives, and presented approaches to the teaching of women's experiences that initiated the process of transforming curriculum to be more inclusive of racial differences."[21]

In everything we attempt, we must strive to welcome diversity rather than gather around us what is comforting and familiar. Without serious structural efforts to combat the racism and classism so prevalent in our society, women's studies will continue to replicate its biases and thus contribute to the persistence of inequality. We must commit ourselves to learning about each other so that we may accomplish our goals without paternalism, maternalism, or guilt. This requires a willingness to explore histories, novels, biographies, and other readings that will help us grasp the realities of class, race, and other dimensions of inequality.[22] At the same time, we must take the personal and professional risks involved in building alliances, listening to and respecting people who have firsthand knowledge of how to cope with oppression, and overcoming the institutionalized barriers that divide us. Within this context, our efforts to

21. Bonnie Thornton Dill, "Director's Comments," *Newsletter of the Center for Research on Women* (Memphis State University, Tenn.), vol. 2, no. 2 (May 1984).

22. It is important that reading and learning about the diversity of women's experiences is integrated into our lives. You cannot take one week and learn this field, nor does it come from reading one novel. To assist people in this endeavor, the Center for Research on Women at Memphis State University has developed an extensive bibliography on women of color. It has also developed a research clearinghouse on women of color and Southern women. The clearinghouse is a computer-based resource containing up-to-date information on researchers working in these fields and their latest projects, as well as bibliographic references to relevant social science works published in the last ten years on these groups of women. For more information, write to: Research Clearinghouse, Center for Research on Women, Memphis State University, Memphis, Tenn. 38152.

develop common goals have the potential to produce a truly diverse community of people who study women and who understand their scholarship as part of the broader quest to arrest all forms of social inequality.

University of Michigan—Flint (Baca Zinn)
Memphis State University (Cannon, Higginbotham, and Dill)

ALLIANCES BETWEEN WOMEN:
OVERCOMING INTERNALIZED OPPRESSION AND INTERNALIZED DOMINATION

GAIL PHETERSON

The "Feminist Alliance Project" was organized in the Netherlands[1] in order to study and interrupt psychological processes that divide women from one another. Social divisions between women have been a primary focus of feminist scholarship, politics, and therapy for the last decade. This report does not attempt to review those developments; rather, it is a description and analysis of one project that was designed to nurture personal change, political strength, and theoretical understanding of divisions between women.[2]

I want to thank the group organizers and facilitators with whom I worked: Nurith de Vries, Lex Jacott, Eloise Sewell, Flora Kleynjan, Lya Djadoenath, Julia da Lima, Joke Hermsen, Anja Meulenbelt, Anneke van Wijk, Christien Quispel, Tineke Sjenitzer, Bernie de Bie, and Ellen van Aggelen. I am grateful to both the women's team of IVABO and the women's project of the Institute of Clinical Psychology, University of Utrecht, for integrating this project in their study programs. I am also grateful to Bertha van Amstel for her consultations during the first year of the project and to Gosina Mandersloot for her constant emotional and intellectual support. Most essentially, I give credit for what I have learned about alliance to the group participants; it was their openness and earnestness and their solidarity as women that made this project possible.

[1] The project was sponsored by the Institute of Clinical Psychology at the University of Utrecht and the Institute of Advanced Social Studies (called IVABO) in Amsterdam, the Netherlands.

[2] The project framework was influenced by Paulo Freire, *Pedagogy of the Oppressed* (New York: Continuum, 1970); Erving Goffman, *Stigma, Notes on the Management of Spoiled*

This essay originally appeared in *Signs*, vol. 12, no. 1, Autumn 1986.

Parallel groups were formed to address the racism, anti-Semitism, and heterosexism that divide women.[3] One group had seven black[4] and five white women, one had seven Jewish and five non-Jewish women, and one had seven lesbian and five heterosexual women. The balance between oppressed and dominant categories of participants was considered important to counteract the assumption of "normalcy" that white, non-Jewish, and heterosexual women were assumed to have internalized, and to counteract the self-concealment and isolation that black, Jewish, and lesbian women were assumed to have internalized. An attempt was also made to balance the participants across dimensions other than the one upon which the group was focused (such as class, age, or motherhood) in order to emphasize common experiences and also to avoid perpetuating common misconceptions; such as, that all heterosexual women are mothers, all lesbians are nonmothers, all white women are middle-class, and all black women are working-class. Two women, one from each subgroup, acted as facilitators. Class differences between women were addressed within each group and also in a full-day workshop every few months in which all groups met together.

The groups were organized within one project in order to raise consciousness about the interactions between issues and to encourage sharing between groups. Each group met every two weeks for five months, at which time new groups were formed. The present report is based upon four cycles, roughly two years, of parallel groups.

Identity (New York: Prentice-Hall, Inc., 1963); Albert Memmi, *The Colonizer and the Colonized* (Boston: Beacon Press, 1965); Gail Pheterson, "Love in Freedom," *Journal of Humanistic Psychology* 21, no. 3 (Summer 1981): 35–50; Hogie Wyckoff, *Solving Problems Together* (New York: Grove Press, 1980). Parallel work of particular relevance includes Elly Bulkin, Minnie Bruce Pratt, and Barbara Smith, *Yours in Struggle* (Brooklyn, N.Y.: Long Haul Press, 1985); Louise Derman-Sparks and Carol Brunson Phillips, *The Teaching/Learning Dimension of Anti-Racism Education* (Pasadena, Calif.: Pacific Oakes College, 1985); Ricky Sherover-Marcuse, "Toward a Perspective on Unlearning Racism: Twelve Working Assumptions," *Issues in Cooperation and Power*, no. 7 (Fall 1981), 14–15.

[3] An initial report including an elaboration of group methods is published in Dutch: Gail Pheterson, "Bondgenootschap tussen vrouwen: Een theoretiese en empiriese analyse van onderdrukking en bevrijding," *Psychologie en maatschappij*, no. 20 (September 1982), 399–424. The present report is based on two years of continuous simultaneous participation in (and facilitation/organization of) black and white, Jewish and non-Jewish, and lesbian and heterosexual groups. As of 1984, groups have also been run to explore divisions between disabled and able-bodied women, between women in the presence of men, and between prostitute, exprostitute, and nonprostitute women.

[4] After much discussion, the women whose personal or ancestral origins were in (formerly) colonized nations decided to identify themselves uniformly as black—rather than specifically by nationality or culture and rather than Third World, colored, or non-white. The cultural heritages represented were Surinamese, Antillian, Molluccan, and Indonesian. The decision to unite under one strong color identification was an act of solidarity for the purpose of exposing and resisting common racist oppression.

Conceptual framework

The following concepts were used throughout the project to inform the analysis and structure.

Internalized oppression is the incorporation and acceptance by individuals within an oppressed group of the prejudices against them within the dominant society.[5] Internalized oppression is likely to consist of self-hatred, self-concealment, fear of violence and feelings of inferiority, resignation, isolation, powerlessness, and gratefulness for being allowed to survive. Internalized oppression is the mechanism within an oppressive system for perpetuating domination not only by external control but also by building subservience into the minds of the oppressed groups.

Internalized domination is the incorporation and acceptance by individuals within a dominant group of prejudices against others.[6] Internalized domination is likely to consist of feelings of superiority, normalcy, and self-righteousness, together with guilt, fear, projection, denial of reality, and alienation from one's body and from nature. Internalized domination perpetuates oppression of others and alienation from oneself by either denying or degrading all but a narrow range of human possibilities. One's own humanity is thus internally restricted and one's qualities of empathy, trust, love, and openness to others and to life-enhancing work become rigid and repressed.

Visibility is being oneself fully, openly, undefensively, and expressively. Visibility of the oppressed group contradicts self-concealment, isolation, subservience, and dominant denial or avoidance of oppressed persons. Visibility of the dominant group contradicts guilt, fear of exposure, projection, alienation from one's body, and detachment from others.

Pride is self-acceptance and self-respect, in particular, respect for one's identity, one's heritage, and one's right to self-determination. Pride carries with it an indignation against the abuse of any human being, including oneself, and a vast resource for perseverence and righteous struggle. Most fundamentally, pride derives from deep love for oneself and for life. Pride contradicts both internalized oppression and internalized domination.

[5] See Freire; Suzanne Lipsky, "Internalized Oppression," *Black Re-Emergence*, no. 2 (Winter 1977), 5–10; Albert Memmi, *Portrait of a Jew* (New York: Viking Press, 1971); Richard Sennett and Jonathon Cobb, *The Hidden Injuries of Class* (New York: Vintage Books, 1972).

[6] Although the author coined the expression "internalized domination," the basic concept can be found in Alice Miller *For Your Own Good: Hidden Cruelty in Child-Rearing and the Roots of Violence*, trans. Hildegarde Hannum and Hunter Hannum (New York: Farrar, Straus, & Giroux, 1983); William Ryan, *Blaming the Victim* (New York: Random House, 1971); Jean-Paul Sartre, *Anti-Semite and Jew* (New York: Schocken Books, 1965); Ricky Sherover-Marcuse, *Emancipation and Consciousness: Dogmatic and Dialectical Perspectives in Early Marx* (Oxford: Basil Blackwell, 1986); Lillian Smith, *Killers of the Dream* (New York: W. W. Norton & Co., 1949).

Solidarity is knowledge of, respect for, and unity with persons whose identities are in certain essential ways common with one's own. Constructive solidarity requires pride in oneself. Internalized oppression isolates people from one another, especially from others like themselves, and thereby prevents solidarity. Internalized domination binds people together on the basis of their power to dominate others rather than on the basis of their respect for one another. Solidarity is essential to oppressed groups for liberation and to dominant groups for collective alliance.

Alliance is knowledge of, respect for, and commitment between persons who are in essential ways different but whose interests are in essential ways akin. For dominant groups, alliance is a process of sharing power and resources with others in society in order to create structures equally responsive to the needs and interests of all people. This process requires giving up one's drive to superiority, giving up one's prejudices against others, and embracing a more flexible relation to oneself, to others, and to society as a whole. For oppressed groups, alliance is a readiness to struggle with dominant groups for one's right to an equal share of power and resources. This readiness necessitates recognition of and indignation against oppression and it generates the collective confidence and strength to bring about change. Furthermore, readiness necessitates recognition and acceptance of, never gratitude for, true alliance. Both the readiness to struggle and the sharing of power and resources are suppressed by internalized oppression and internalized domination. Pride and solidarity prepare individuals to become partners in alliance against oppression.

Group structure

A flexible structure was designed including the following stages across the five-month experience: (1) telling, and sometimes writing, life stories (visibility), (2) expressing feelings, both positive and negative, about oneself, one's identity, and one's history (pride), (3) exploring feelings and experiences in relation to other women who share one's group status (solidarity), and (4) exploring feelings and experiences in relation to women with different group status (alliance). Attention in the groups focused both on life experiences outside of the group and also on interactions within the group. During each meeting, subgroups would meet separately for various lengths of time; for example, black and white women would have an opportunity to discuss their feelings toward other blacks and other whites in black-only and white-only groups. The identification and interruption of internalized oppression and internalized domination was seen as a necessary condition for building effective alliances and, therefore, as a primary function of the facilitators. To help build the trust required for that task, participants were asked to meet between group meetings in changing dyadic pairs. Meetings were held either at someone's home or at one of the two sponsoring institutes.

Participants read a proposal including the conceptual framework before beginning the project and they agreed upon the basic approach from self-examination to within-group examination to alliance across differences.[7] During the meetings, reference to conceptual definitions was often made in order to illuminate the political origin of internalized conflicts.

Participants

All participants were Dutch or Dutch (ex-)colonized women except the organizer and one facilitator who were originally from the United States.[8] Each woman determined her own social status and appropriate subgroup. About 85 percent of the women identified as feminists; some joined to support their political work; some joined to gain skills for living or working with significant others; some joined because they felt isolated from women who shared their social position and others because they felt isolated from women with different social positions. All of the participants were strongly commited to the issues and to the project.

In the first five-month cycle of groups, the majority of participants were middle-class, although about half had been raised in working-class families. In following cycles, working-class women composed about a third of the participants. About one-third of the black women were born in the Netherlands; about two-thirds were born in their native (ex-)colonized lands.[9] About 95 percent of the Jewish women had one Jewish parent, the other 5

---

[7] See Gail Pheterson, *Liberation and Alliance: A Proposal for Work Groups to Study and Counteract Racism, Anti-Semitism, and Heterosexism between Women* (Amsterdam: Institute of Advanced Social Studies, 1979).

[8] The Netherlands has a long colonial history in South Africa, Indonesia, Surinam, and the Antilles. Only the Antilles are not now independent, but the Dutch influence remains strong in all its ex-colonies. Although each country had a very different relation to the Netherlands, the Dutch colonialists occupied the highest positions, the Dutch language became the official language, and white skin became the sign of higher status in each country. That power relation carried over into relations within the Netherlands after waves of immigration. Great numbers of Indoeuropeans (people of mixed Indonesian and Dutch heritage) and Moluccans (people from one set of islands who served in the Dutch army) were shipped to Holland in 1949 when Indonesia gained independence. The Surinamese (especially middle-class men) immigrated in small numbers before independence in 1975 and in great numbers as whole families after independence. For a study of immigrants and their descendants from the colonies to the Netherlands, see Jan Lucassen and Rinus Pennix, *Nieuwkomers immigranten en hun nakomelingen in Nederland, 1550–1985* (Amsterdam: Meulenhoff, 1985); and Rinus Pennix, "Research and Policy with Regard to Ethnic Minorities in the Netherlands: A Historical Outline and the State of Affairs," *International Migration* 22, no. 4 (1984): 345–66.

[9] See n. 4 above.

percent had two Jewish parents. About half the lesbians had active het-erosexual pasts and about half identified as lesbian since their teens. Participants ranged in ages from early twenties to late fifties; a majority were in their thirties and forties. About a third of the women were biological mothers; several co-mothered their lover's children. Over one hundred women participated. The numbers are inexact because some women participated consecutively in more than one cycle and a few women participated in more than one alliance group.

As one might expect, the groups themselves were intense and demand-ing. Obviously, every participant experienced the alliance process in a uniquely personal way. The purpose here is to examine those experiences within the framework of group identity as defined by political status in society.

Each group experienced movement from defensiveness to assertion. Within each subgroup this movement was characterized by feelings that can be explained within the context of the specific oppression (i.e., racism, anti-Semitism, and heterosexism). The following discussions focus on the change itself and on the internalized resistance to change; they do not provide a literal transcription of each group process.

A common resistance

It became clear that in every group past experiences with oppression and domination distorted the participants' perceptions of the present and blocked their identification with people in common political situations who did not share their history. Jewish women who had experienced the Nazi war trauma sometimes had difficulty identifying with those Jews who had not; black women who were born in the Netherlands sometimes had difficulty identifying with blacks who were born in an (ex-)colonized country; lesbian women who had "always" been lesbian sometimes had difficulty identifying with those who had formerly been married heterosex-uals. Those who had experienced the oppression most acutely in the past were likely to feel like the true oppressed group, for example, the real lesbians or the real Jews: "You're just a nouveau lesbian" or "What do you American Jews know about being Jewish?" In other words, "You haven't suffered enough."

On the other side, those who shared the same political identity in the present but had not experienced the oppression so personally in the past were likely to reject the oppressed status for themselves: "I don't want to be one of them"; "My lesbianism is only political. Sexually I'm hetero-sexual"; or "My mother is Jewish, not me"; or "I've never felt black." Sometimes, however, it was exactly the person who had suffered the most who rejected the identity the strongest, and sometimes it was exactly the one who had suffered the least who embraced the identity with the least ambivalence.

Differentiations on the basis of past experiences were typical for women in dominant as well as oppressed positions: "I'm not Jewish, but I've never been Christian either"; "I'm white, but I grew up with black people"; "I'm heterosexual, but I make love with women, too." Whether in an effort to relieve guilt or to avoid exclusion, the differentiation was an expression of denial of their dominant status.

Black and white alliance

The feelings that most clearly emerged in the group of black and white women were anger from blacks and guilt from whites. Feelings of guilt were present for some of the white women from the very beginning of the group. For some women, those feelings led to paralysis in the mixed group and to anxious revelations of insecurity in the white subgroup. On the first day, in a subgroup, one white woman said, "I just sit there with the black women and feel nervous and guilty and don't know what to do." Later in the process, when a few black women expressed mistrust toward an initiative of a white woman, that woman asked repeatedly, "Why can't you trust me? I know I have integrity." Rather than call on other whites for support in the subgroup, she rejected them as less racially aware than she. Only black approval would affirm her integrity and exempt her from guilt. Those white women who acknowledged feeling guilty expressed a fear of revenge and a need for reassurance from blacks. Both the need for approval and the need for reassurance eventually outraged black women. White dependency on black women—either to affirm their integrity or relieve their fears—in effect, directed the group more toward white insecurities than toward the struggle against racism that was the group's central concern.

The black women began with commitment and skepticism. The first reaction of some of the black women to the white women's guilty requests for reassurance or approval was patiently to explain why such behavior was not appropriate or helpful; other black women sat in silence; others expressed annoyance. During the first few meetings, they differed among themselves about whether and how much to meet in a separate subgroup. Only after the first emotional black-white clash did they agree unanimously on the need to meet separately. They did not want to express their differing reactions to the conflict in the presence of whites.

If guilt paralyzed the white women in the presence of blacks, anger energized the black women into insisting upon time in their subgroup and into blaming whites for being unaware and passive. As the black women met more in their separate group, they began to feel greater solidarity and their reactions and demands in the mixed group became bolder and more confronting. One black woman said, "This group is getting scary and uncomfortable for you white women. That's the way the world outside is for us"; and another said, "You white women wouldn't be working on racism at all if we weren't here. If we'd never come to Holland you wouldn't work on it and if we weren't with you in a group you wouldn't be working on it!"

The black women became more expressive of their ethnic cultural differences and more committed to their racial political commonalities. They asked white women to struggle with their own insecurities, and at the same time they validated themselves as the experts on racism. The white women, having met in their subgroup each time the black women were meeting in theirs, began to need reassurance less often from blacks, and to acknowledge the unawareness that racism fosters in all whites, focusing on what they could do to combat racism. They began to value the awareness they could gain from one another in their attempt to become less dependent on blacks and to feel less competitive with one another for the place of either "best ally" or "least racist." In other words, they too were moving toward greater solidarity.

All of the group's participants came to make deeper and clearer commitments to racism awareness outside of the group. The three white women in teaching positions changed their jobs to include an emphasis on antiracism work. Another white woman realized through her participation in the group how debilitating guilt was in many aspects of her life; she decided to go into individual therapy and return to the alliance project at a later time. A group of the black women expanded their support networks with new initiatives specific to their needs: A black lesbian group was started, and a few women joined a black women's counseling class. A black and a white woman from the group organized seminars on racism and research on processes of change among black and white participants. Another black woman planned to organize a new alliance group like the original one after a six-month period in her black lesbian group.

Everyone in the group agreed that, although the process was difficult, their lives changed significantly. For some women it was unclear whether the changes resulted from this group or from other simultaneous activities in their lives; some felt that the changes did not occur primarily in the group but definitely *because* the group was there. One black woman said during the last meeting that she had begun to take herself more seriously as a black woman and that she had become more assertive and honest in confronting daily racism. A white woman reported the deep shock the group had given her—the shock of realizing the racial bias in every aspect of her life.

Jewish and non-Jewish alliance

In this group an underlying struggle for identity evolved that was characterized by feelings of isolation on the Jewish side and dullness on the non-Jewish side. At one meeting, when discussing the essence of being Jewish, a Jewish woman and a non-Jewish woman began a critical tug of war about the cost of being special versus being ordinary. The Jewish woman had been saying that the essence of being Jewish was being special. She was expressing both her pride and her isolation. The non-Jewish woman said, "I wish I was special. Nobody ever told me that I was special," to which the Jewish woman replied, "I wish I was ordinary," and the non-Jewish woman responded, "I've always been ordinary. I want to be special."

At another meeting, in subgroups, the non-Jews talked about their own specialness and the Jews talked about the isolation they experienced as Jews. By focusing upon their own specialness, the non-Jews confronted an internal question they often felt in their contact with Jewish women: "What about me?" One woman expressed this as follows to a Jewish woman: "I feel like I have no identity when I am with you. I don't know who I am. It would be easier if I were Jewish." The Jewish woman answered that it would not be easier for *her* if the other was also Jewish, but that she did need for the other to know *who* she was. She further admitted often feeling safest and most protected among non-Jews. Nonetheless, this woman jumped in protest when a non-Jewish woman told how she had hidden a newspaper article reporting anti-Semitic incidents from her Jewish lover to "protect her." A discussion followed wherein the Jewish women distinguished between needs for comfort based upon internalized oppression and needs for alliance. They all saw the sharing of information as alliance.

If the Jews in the group sometimes looked to the non-Jews for protection, the non-Jews sometimes looked to the Jews for specialness by association. As one non-Jewish woman said, "I've met active, struggling women in this group and that inspires me to be like that too!" and, "As a child I always identified with Jewish history." Another woman said, "I find most of the Jewish women in my life difficult, but I do like their force and intelligence." The ambivalence of admiring qualities they associated with Jews and at the same time feeling uncomfortable with them was expressed by the non-Jews more than once: "It turned out to be the wrong group for me," said one woman, "I should have joined the black or the lesbian group"; "I can get along fine with the working-class Jewish women; it's the upper-class women I can't stand."

Differences in class backgrounds caused a clash in this group. Often the lines of solidarity were drawn more on the basis of class background than on the basis of Jewish identity. The Jewish working-class women all had politically active socialist backgrounds: "If it hadn't been for our political tie to the resistance, we never would have made it. Most working class Jews didn't." Even within this small group the historical dynamic emerged of Jews pitted against one another in their search for safety; those whose backgrounds were associated closely with white Gentile society were seen by everyone, Jews and non-Jews, as the oppressors.

One non-Jewish woman said, "Eight Jewish women is just too many. It's taken me all this time to get close to one!" Her reaction reflected a situation between Jews and non-Jews that may be specific to post–World War II Europe, and to other places where there are relatively few Jews. For the non-Jews (and some of the Jews) under thirty-five years old, the group afforded a first opportunity to be with many Jews at once.[10] For the Jews (and non-Jews) over thirty-five years old, the group was seen at the beginning as a place to "work on the war." The main association with Jewishness for them was Hitler. One Jewish woman said on the first evening, "I am not here to become more Jewish. I just want to work through my Jewish pain." She told about feeling uncomfortable talking about being Jewish with her children and about avoiding telling people that she had joined the alliance group. After several months, she began to reclaim parts of her Jewish heritage other than the war (such as Jewish food and culture) and began sharing that heritage with her family and friends.

The move from isolation toward contact was shared by all the Jewish women. Everyone began talking more about her Jewishness at home and at work. One woman said, "This group has been an exercise ground for how I can talk with non-Jews . . . it's safer here than in other places. Lots has changed for me." Another Jewish woman said, "I feel prouder about my Jewish identity now, so I can come out more as who I am everywhere." Another woman said, "I've decided to go after the people I want to have in my life."

The non-Jews experienced a move from inconspicuousness toward self-definition. One evening all of the non-Jews agreed that working toward alliance with Jews had challenged their most chronic feelings of insecurity: "I have to work on myself to be a good ally. I'm here for me." Another woman said, "I used to think it was complimentary to say how intelligent Jews are. Now I realize that it was a prejudice that fed my feeling dull. To be an ally I have to know that I'm smart too!" In the course of the group, the non-Jews moved toward greater acceptance of their religious backgrounds, prouder identification with their own culture, and a clearer definition and expression of their personal and political commitments. One woman

[10] Eighty-five percent of the 140,000 Jews living in the Netherlands before the Second World War were killed in Nazi concentration camps. Undoubtedly, the devastation of that loss is the primary association to anti-Semitism in Dutch society today. As an occupied country during the war, the Dutch were forced into positions of either active resistance against Nazism, passivity, or active collaboration with Nazism. That history left behind an enormity of grief and guilt, both of which are sometimes triggered by the mention or presence of Jews. See J. Presser, *Ashes in the Wind: The Destruction of Dutch Jewry* (London: Souvenir Press, 1968).

wrote, "I've begun to understand how my own isolation works and I realize how important it is to define myself and to find recognition and identity." And further, "One thing has become clear to me for life: my commitment against anti-Semitism, I stand for that, you can count on it."

The group was often chaotic, sometimes aggressive, and usually warm, loud, and confusing. One woman called it an "awful exhilarating experience that changed her life." Nearly everyone began to read a lot about Jews and everyone took risks to initiate or deepen a friendship. Both Jewish and non-Jewish women reported stronger self-presentations in their personal and work lives. Alliance did not require Jews to give up or hide their identity, or non-Jews to melt into the code of dominant conformity. To the contrary, the struggle against anti-Semitism demanded solid identities on both sides.

Lesbian and heterosexual alliance[11]

For the lesbian women, the alliance process was characterized by movement from defiance toward self-assertion. During the first week, everyone wrote a paragraph telling what it meant to her to be a lesbian or a heterosexual. One lesbian wrote, "I often feel illegal. . . . The feeling of being different is very fundamental, it sits real deep. It also means being excluded." Another woman wrote, "I don't feel like always having to explain . . . so I don't bother much with men"; and another said, "I should live as a *black* lesbian woman, but then I couldn't be lesbian anymore, or only in silence, and that I don't want!" And another, "Oi vey, what a

[11] The Netherlands is one of the least heterosexist countries in the world by law. A provisional antidiscrimination law including homosexuals is taken seriously by the Dutch. For example, a foreign homosexual can acquire Dutch residency and work rights on the basis of a stable relationship with a Dutch citizen. Such legal justice flows from the Dutch movement for homosexual rights that began with individual activism at the beginning of the twentieth century. The movement took the form of a private club before the Second World War and organized into a formal association of homosexuals (called COC) in 1946. Lesbians are granted legal rights equal to those of homosexual men, although their position in COC is clearly a subordinate one. During the last fifteen years, a distinct lesbian movement has become politically and culturally visible. Within that movement lesbians of color have begun to organize separately both in response to racism and in order to rediscover and develop a distinct black lesbian culture. Jewish lesbians have also begun to organize on a very small scale. Sexual diversity among lesbians, including S-M, has recently emerged as a topic of discussion. Several lesbian magazines are published with specific focus, such as black lesbians, sexuality, and literature. See Rob Tielman, *Homoseksualiteit in Nederland* (Amsterdam: Boom Meppel, 1982). For a comparison of lesbian oppression in the Netherlands and the United States, see Gail Pheterson and Leny Jansen, "Lesbian Struggle against a Pillow or a Wall: A Dutch-American Dialogue," *Journal of Homosexuality*, nos. 3/4 (1986), in press; also see "Special Issues: Research on Homosexuality in the Netherlands," *Journal of Homosexuality*, nos. 3/4 (1986), in press.

shunde [Yiddish for shame], a Jewish girl, a lesbian?" Like every group, this group was filled with multiple interlocking identities and oppressions.

A bisexual woman who joined the group as a heterosexual because she benefits from heterosexual privileges as a married woman wrote, "I'm in the clouds with my love for women. First feeling out of my element, especially in public, now feeling it almost as a challenge." A heterosexual woman wrote, "I don't literally make love with a woman now, sometimes I do with a man, but I protest being called heterosexual. I feel room to move . . . where I can call myself bisexual." Another woman said, "I seldom tell anyone other than feminist friends that I sometimes make love also with women. I realize the social ease I get from a heterosexual relationship and how I rely on that for acceptance."

The ambiguity between lesbian and heterosexual identities was one recurring theme in this group. Ambiguity in group identity was also a theme for some black, white, Jewish, and non-Jewish women, but unlike women in those groups, the lesbians did not have different roots than the heterosexuals (i.e., everyone's ancestors were heterosexuals, or so they assumed), and many lesbians had heterosexual pasts.

From the beginning, group members discussed the choices and pressures that had shaped their lives. During the second meeting, the lesbian subgroup confronted the contrasting meanings lesbianism held in terms of motherhood. One woman said how pleased she was that she had become a lesbian before "making the whole mistake of motherhood and marriage." Another agreed that she was glad not to have children. A third lesbian woman sat silently for a moment and then began to tell how angry she always felt when she heard lesbians belittle motherhood and how proud she was to be the mother of seven children. Another woman explained the importance in her life of mothering her lover's two sons. When the lesbian and heterosexual subgroups joined one another, the discussion focused on motherhood as an issue for women's solidarity. Participants felt that by assuming all lesbian women are not and do not want to be mothers, and that all heterosexuals are or would like to be mothers, they had denied choice to themselves and to other women.

If the lesbians sometimes took a defiant posture to distinguish themselves from other women, the heterosexuals felt identity confusion and sometimes searched for self-definition through others. Attempts by the heterosexual women to win favor with the lesbians sometimes aroused lesbian frustration and anger: "Don't support me by telling me that you're like me. Support me by telling me that you too are choosing what you want and that you're getting what you need." "Don't think you're being a buddy by complaining about men. Don't assume that I hate men and don't assume that I want you to hate men." "Every time you settle as a woman for less than you want, you insult me as well as yourself."

Movement from defiance toward self-assertion for lesbians and from confusion to choice for heterosexuals was neither easy nor consistent within the group. One woman said, "I like it more and more to be with only lesbian women." Another said, "I feel very ambivalent about being in this group. Before it started I was clear about everything and now, through this group I see how big our differences are, also between us lesbians. I don't know anymore." One heterosexual woman said, "In the beginning I was real excited here, especially about my own background, and then I fell into a big hole of confusion." Another heterosexual woman said, "I was terribly confused at the beginning, but now it gets clearer for me. I realize that I don't suffer from lesbian oppression like you lesbians but I do suffer from it." One lesbian woman wrote in her end evaluation: "I'm more visible as a lesbian than I used to be and I have less of a chip on my shoulder. I used to feel, 'poor me or lucky me, nobody knows what it's like to be me' and now I'm better able to communicate naturally about my life and to expect respect from others. I have also begun to accept heterosexuality as a possible real choice, even for women."

As this last quote suggests, by the end of the group, both the lesbian and the heterosexual choice had gained integrity. One heterosexual woman told about objecting to a heterosexual assumption in a public lecture "without explaining that I was standing up for the rights of other women." Sexual choice had become an issue important for all women, regardless of their social status or personal life style.

Conclusion

The processes that evolved within the groups were determined by the starting point of the participants. The choice to participate in an alliance group already reflected a certain consciousness and readiness. Women joining an oppressed subgroup were assuming a politically targeted identity and acknowledging their oppression. Women joining a dominant subgroup were assuming a politically privileged identity and acknowledging their domination. Once in the project, participants were confronted with the fact that group identities are profoundly historical and symbolic. At one meeting a woman said, "I count twelve women here but I feel the presence of thousands."

This study focused its discussion of each group upon a salient dynamic that emerged from the participants' internalized conflicts. It was assumed by the project design that the issues confronted were shaped by external systems of domination and that strategies for psychological survival are necessary. Often, however, internalized oppression and internalized domination become embedded in personality at the expense of identity and freedom and without regard to external reality. Oppression seems to breed a package of psychological processes that distort reality and weaken personal strength. Feeling angry, isolated, and defiant were identified by participants in this study as reactions to oppression. Feeling guilty, dull, and confused were identified as reactions to social positions of dominance. Those feelings spiraled into blaming, needing (protection, reassurance, or approval), and excluding other women. Building alliances seemed to be an effective counterforce for those dynamics. In addition, alliance building may be transferable so that, for example, visibility as a lesbian would equip one to assert herself more powerfully as a Jew or as a white person fighting racism.

It is important to note that internalized oppression and internalized domination interact not only between different persons but also intrapsychically within one person. Oppression and domination are experienced as a mutually reinforcing web of insecurities and rigidities. Although the political consequences of oppression are opposite to those of domination (e.g., powerlessness vs. power), the psychological consequences are surprisingly alike. The fear of violence one feels as a victim of oppression reinforces the fear of revenge she feels as an agent of oppression. The isolation resulting from feelings of inferiority reinforces the isolation resulting from feelings of superiority. The guilt felt for dominating others likewise reinforces the guilt felt for one's own victimization. Since maintaining a posture of dominance is often tenuously balanced upon denying inferior status, the individual suppresses and conceals characteristics which reveal social powerlessness: "I can make it as a professional if they just never discover that I'm a lesbian"; or "As a white person I can become a member of any club, if I don't let on that I'm Jewish"; or "I can't hide being a woman but I can pretend to be one of the boys." The method of domination becomes collusion with oppressive forces, and the cost becomes rigidity and fear of personal growth. The more guilty the white woman feels about her racism, the less adequate she is likely to feel about effecting change and the more dependent she will be on black women to do the work of changing racist attitudes. The more the non-Jew resists recognition of her own social identity, the more she will resent Jewish identity. The more dependent a heterosexual woman is upon male approval, the more threatened she will be by lesbian autonomy. Every human difference thus becomes a confrontation with self.

The organizational and conceptual framework of this project did provide the confrontations for which it was intended. By focusing upon the norms of dominant status and oppressed status, those norms gained political significance and at the same time, lost personal significance. Variations in sexual preference, appearance, and religion all became more apparent and more accepted once the illusion that there were only two politicized poles dissolved. White, straight, and ordinary images of humanity were transformed into more realistic perceptions of human diversity. The recognition and interruption of internalized forms of domination and oppression supported that transformation and supported movement from antagonism toward alliance between women.

Department of Psychology
University of Amsterdam

EDUCATING WOMEN IN AMERICA

SALLY SCHWAGER

Writing in 1974, historian Jill Conway issued a warning: the trend toward coeducation in institutions of higher education over the previous decade was fraught with dangers for women students, women scholars, and women graduates alike. The historical record (which had lain virtually unexamined during the recent campaigns) provided clear evidence that coeducational institutions had neither met women's intellectual needs nor fostered equality. The growth of coeducation over the previous century had, in fact, resulted in "a declining position for women scholars within the American university."[1]

By the early 1970s, political forces in higher education and the contemporary women's movement had converged on the issue of woman's place in the university. Conway's warning followed in the wake of dramatic developments: new federal amendments outlawing sex discrimination in university policy and procedures, vigorous efforts among women faculty to

I wish to thank Sally Gregory Kohlstedt for her many incisive and helpful comments on an earlier version of this essay. I also thank the editors at *Signs* for their generous suggestions.

[1] Jill K. Conway, "Coeducation and Women's Studies: Two Approaches to the Question of Woman's Place in the Contemporary University," *Daedalus* 103, no. 4 (Fall 1974): 239–49, esp. 244.

This essay originally appeared in *Signs*, vol. 12, no. 2, Winter 1987.

document their condition in the academy and to reassess scholarship on women within their various disciplines,[2] the graduation that spring of the first women to have been admitted as "freshmen" to Princeton and Yale; and of particular significance to Conway's discussion, the emergence of women's studies as a formidable challenge to the traditional undergraduate curriculum. Conway estimated that some one thousand colleges and universities offered women's studies courses and programs.[3] Her forecast, however, was wary. Alluding to the historical experience of women in sex-segregated departments and in the service professions, Conway argued that the development of separate women's studies programs inherently risked the relegation of women to marginal positions within the university.

Taking stock of women's declining status in higher education more generally, Patricia Albjerg Graham argued a few months later that the history of women in academe throughout the twentieth century had been one of increasing marginality, not only by virtue of confinement to gender-linked programs but also in relation to types of institutions and roles within the established disciplines. Graham proposed a new research agenda focused on the experience of women who had occupied the bottom rungs and peripheral positions within the university, and she called for a reexamination of institutions where women traditionally had predominated: nonelite women's colleges and normal schools, teachers' colleges, Catholic women's colleges, small coeducational schools, and university departments such as domestic science and elementary education.[4]

The purpose of this essay is to review the literature that has emerged over the past decade in response to these challenges and to assess its direction and impact. Progressive historian Thomas Woody's monumental two-volume *History of Women's Education in the United States*,[5] published in 1929 in the aftermath of the suffrage movement, ought to have established irrevocably the fact that educational reform for women was one of the most dramatic and complex developments of the nineteenth century. Yet in spite of the political context of Woody's work, neither the traditional saga of schooling in America nor the revisionist scholarship that emerged in

---

[2] For an extended discussion of academic women's political activities during the 1970s and policy recommendations, see Patricia Albjerg Graham, "Women in Higher Education: A Report to the Ford Foundation" (Ford Foundation Archival Report, 1977, typescript).

[3] Conway, 246. For a contemporary analysis of women's studies, see Barbara Sicherman, "The Invisible Woman: The Case for Women's Studies," in *Women in Higher Education*, ed. W. Todd Furniss and Patricia Albjerg Graham (Washington, D.C.: American Council on Education, 1974), 155–77.

[4] Patricia Albjerg Graham, "So Much to Do: Guides for Historical Research on Women in Higher Education," *Teachers College Record* 76, no. 3 (February 1975): 421–29.

[5] Thomas Woody, *A History of Women's Education in the United States*, 2 vols. (New York: Science Press, 1929).

the 1960s analyzed the impact of women's reform efforts, scholarship, or institutions. The debates of the early 1970s over coeducation and women's studies, however, forced the consideration of gender into ongoing analyses of education as a dynamic of social change, and investigations into the current status of women yielded evidence that challenged historical wisdom. Increased access to education had not resulted *as a matter of course* in women's intellectual, political, or social emancipation.[6]

The fact that the new scholarship on women's educational history was rooted in these controversies has also, however, shaped the direction of the research and resulted in the neglect of several important areas of inquiry. First, there has been a preponderance of research on women's higher education—the stage on which the debates of the seventies took place. There has been a relative dearth of research on dame schools, female academies, seminaries, kindergartens, and normal and training schools. Similarly, scant attention has been paid to girls in elementary and secondary schools and in nonformal settings, and this has led to an unevenness in our understanding of women's experience across the broader spectrum of educational history.[7]

Second, the discussions of the early seventies reinforced the dichotomy between single-sex and coeducational settings as a predominant framework for analysis. As a consequence, less attention has been paid to who *controlled* women's education than to the gender composition of student populations. Professional achievement patterns, for example, have been analyzed primarily by comparing graduates from women's colleges with women who attended comparable coeducational institutions. An analysis that considered woman's authority over the educational process, on the other hand, would emphasize the contrast between women who graduated from woman-controlled institutions and those who attended colleges or universities dominated by senior male faculty or male presidents. We might ask, for instance, whether there were differences between the early nineteenth-century subscription schools owned and taught by women (some of which were coeducational) and those controlled by men. Recent

---

[6] See, e.g., Jessie Bernard, *Academic Women* (University Park: Pennsylvania State University Press, 1964); Marion Kilson, "The Status of Women in Higher Education," *Signs: Journal of Women in Culture and Society* 1, no. 4 (Summer 1976): 935–42; M. Elizabeth Tidball, "Of Men and Research: The Dominant Themes in American Higher Education Include neither Teaching nor Women," *Journal of Higher Education* 47, no. 4 (July/August 1976): 373–89; and Helen S. Astin and Werner Z. Hirsch, eds., *The Higher Education of Women: Essays in Honor of Rosemary Park* (New York: Praeger Publishers, 1978).

[7] Two studies of nonformal educational influences on women's lives are notable exceptions: Lois Barber Arnold, *Four Lives in Science: Women's Education in the Nineteenth Century* (New York: Schocken Books, 1984); and Ellen Condliffe Lagemann, *A Generation of Women: Education in the Lives of Progressive Reformers* (Cambridge, Mass.: Harvard University Press, 1979).

research suggests that all-girl academies founded by women differed significantly from those led by male reformers.[8]

A final legacy of the context in which the research of the past decade was accomplished is that, initially at least, studies of professional women, educational leaders, and elite institutions tended to predominate. Studies of women educators and institutions outside New England have been relatively few, and on the collegiate level, attention to the eastern women's colleges still prevails. We know very little, moreover, about the migration of women educated in the East to other parts of the country or what impact their experience in private academies and colleges might have had on the development of public education in other regions.

In spite of these limitations, however, the research that has been accomplished over the past ten years, on topics as seemingly disparate as republican educational ideology, teaching as a profession for women, and the movement for women's higher education, reveals major continuities in the experience of American women. Most fundamentally, societal prescriptions regarding women's domestic roles, especially their responsibilities as mothers, have served to differentiate women's education from the education of men. At the same time, these prescriptions have fueled the campaigns of woman's advocates. Teaching grew over the course of the nineteenth century as the professional manifestation of this ideology and provided paid employment, and sometimes leadership roles, for women across boundaries of race, class, and religion.

A decline in the status of women educators is, however, equally widespread in the larger context of women's educational history. The phenomenon that Conway, Graham, and others described in relation to university scholars at the turn of the twentieth century is evident in the teaching profession as early as 1840. The movement of women teachers from colonial dame and subscription schools and from the early academies into public school teaching by the mid-nineteenth century represented a decline in women's authority over the profession even though women's opportunities increased numerically. This pattern was repeated across regions as urban school systems came to dominate the American landscape, and it appeared again as women moved into the university.[9]

---

[8] I am indebted to Lynne Brickley for this insight into the early academies.

[9] Alison Mackinnon, a historian of Australian education, focuses on this pattern and argues that, far from representing the "feminization of teaching," the movement of women teachers into public schools represented a loss in women's control over their workplace—a process more accurately described as the "proletarianization of teaching." With the notable exception of David Tyack's and Elisabeth Hansot's research on women teachers in urban public schools, few questions concerning the locus and control of women's education have been asked in the American context. See Alison Mackinnon, "A New Point of Departure," *History of Education Review* 13, no. 2 (1984): 1–14, esp. 3; David B. Tyack, *The One Best System: A History of American Urban Education* (Cambridge, Mass.: Harvard University Press, 1974); and David

Republican education

The differential purposes which underlay the education of women and men in America can be seen by looking at women's status in the republican era more generally. Linda Kerber, for instance, argues that a distinctive political purpose led to dramatic improvements in female education following the American Revolution. Kerber demonstrates that gender distinctions were deeply rooted in American educational ideology as a function of postrevolutionary formulations regarding women's relationship to the republic. Though American men had not moved directly to the definition of women as citizens, women were assigned a political role as the educators of sons who would become citizens—a duty for which the Republican Mother required improved education.

The concept of Republican Motherhood, Kerber argues, was a device to integrate the domestic relationships within which women were defined in Western political theory with the political ideology of the new republic. Filling in the gap left by Enlightenment theorists in the colonies as well as those in France and England who had failed to articulate a political role for the republican woman, American thinkers such as Judith Sargent Murray, Susanna Rowson, and Benjamin Rush had begun by 1790 to argue that American women needed to be specially educated so that they might in their personal conduct reflect the political independence of the new nation. Republican women were to be rational, self-reliant, literate, and immune to the vagaries of fashion. The Republican Mother, as Kerber portrays her, "dedicated her life to the service of civic virtue; she educated her sons for it; she condemned and corrected her husband's lapses from it."[10]

We should recognize, of course, that not all groups of early Americans subscribed to the dominant ideology. Joan Jensen, in her study of early Quaker schools for women, argues that the ideology of Republican Motherhood had little efficacy in the Quaker community. Quakers, who for the most part did not actively support the Revolution, responded to the political fervor of the war years by emphasizing "a revival of the inner light

---

Tyack and Elisabeth Hansot, *Managers of Virtue: Public School Leadership in America, 1820–1980* (New York: Basic Books, 1982), esp. 180–201.

[10] Linda Kerber, "The Republican Mother: Women and the Enlightenment—an American Perspective," *American Quarterly* 28, no. 2 (Summer 1976): 187–205, esp. 202; see also Linda K. Kerber, "Daughters of Columbia: Educating Women for the Republic, 1787–1805," in *The Hofstader Aegis: A Memorial*, ed. Stanley Elkins and Eric McKitrick (New York: Alfred A. Knopf, 1974), 36–59, and *Women of the Republic: Intellect and Ideology in Revolutionary America* (Chapel Hill: University of North Carolina Press, 1980). Glenda Riley's pioneering article surveys contemporary advice literature on the education of wives and mothers; see Glenda Riley, "Origins of the Argument for Improved Female Education," *History of Education Quarterly* 9, no. 4 (Winter 1969): 455–70.

and separation from the world." The impetus to improve female education among Quakers, explains Jensen, *preceded* the American Revolution. Education of both boys and girls was emphasized for purposes of religious training rather than for political responsibility.[11]

Practices regarding the education of Quaker women certainly did not conflict, however, with those that emerged in the years following the Revolution; in fact, they influenced them. Quakers had long been pioneers in women's education. As in Massachusetts, dame schools had existed in Pennsylvania as early as the late seventeenth century. By the middle of the eighteenth century, the Philadelphia Yearly Meeting (the Quakers' representative decision-making body) was providing schooling for poor parents who were unable to educate their children adequately. Anthony Benezet, in 1778, opened a grammar school in Philadelphia with the express purpose of educating rural mothers who, like all Quaker mothers, bore the responsibility of providing basic education to their children. After 1790, women ministers took the lead in advocating advanced education and teacher training for women, envisioning a plan in which women would assume responsibility for educating the poor, blacks, and women, even at advanced levels. The period between 1800 and 1840 in Pennsylvania was characterized by a proliferation of boarding schools for young women that were among the earliest and most advanced in the country.

In spite of their distinctive features, however, the purposes for educating both Quaker women and Republican Mothers were grounded in women's domestic responsibilities. Thus Kerber's analysis of the paradox inherent in the prevailing rationale for women's education holds true for the Quaker experience as well. Kerber argues that while the Republican Mother was entitled to new and improved education, her new political role served also to reinforce a subordinant status and to enhance the rationale for educating women differently from men. Thus, this intimate relationship between women's domestic roles and their presumed educational needs actually embodied an anti-intellectualism that conditioned beliefs about women's mental capabilities well into the twentieth century.

Still, in spite of the limitations inherent in the ideology of Republican Motherhood, we should beware of underestimating the positive impact it had on women's education. By placing American reforms in a comparative context with female education in England and Europe, Mary Beth Norton highlights the revolutionary nature of advances in America during the last decades of the eighteenth century. The most forward thinkers in England—Hannah More, Erasmus Darwin, and Thomas Gisborne—continued to emphasize ornamental accomplishments for girls at a time when

---

[11] Joan M. Jensen, "Not Only Ours but Others: The Quaker Teaching Daughters of the Mid-Atlantic, 1790–1850," *History of Education Quarterly* 24, no. 1 (Spring 1984): 3–19, esp. 5.

even conservative American reformers Benjamin Rush and Noah Webster were advocating the cultivation of women's intellectual powers. Norton concludes that the vast expansion of academies for girls and an "upsurge in reformist impulses" was a phenomenon utterly unique to the American experience: foreign educational theorists showed no interest in the creation of independent, rational female adults. American reformers, on the other hand, most notably Judith Sargent Murray, Sarah Pierce, and Susanna Rowson, even went so far as to propose and to execute educational programs that would, in Pierce's words, "vindicate the equality of female intellect."[12]

Female literacy

The dramatic increase in female literacy during the early republican period provides another measure of the advancement in women's education nurtured by the Revolution. Nancy Cott and Linda Kerber both analyze estimates from Kenneth Lockridge's *Literacy in Colonial New England*[13] and conclude that major improvements in female education took place between 1790 and 1830. Cott points to the significant disparity in literacy between colonial men and women which had been alluded to earlier by Thomas Woody and other historians and goes on to confirm this disparity with evidence from numerous literary sources.[14] Kerber shows that even in learned families women's literacy fell far short of men's (aside from a few exceptional couples like John and Abigail Adams). Lockridge's figures seem to demonstrate that this literacy gap actually increased during the colonial period, so that by 1780 New England women's literacy, based on the ability to sign, was half that of men's. Male literacy had risen from about 50 percent during the first generation of New England settlement to 80 percent or more by 1780, while female literacy rates rose from 30 percent to about 40 percent by 1700 and then stagnated for most of the eighteenth century—a phenomenon Lockridge attributes to the public schools' discrimination against girls. By 1850, however, the first federal census to measure basic literacy reported that the number of northeastern women who could read and write was nearly equal to that of northeastern men, though, as Jensen reports, black female literacy seriously lagged. In Penn-

[12] Quoted in Mary Beth Norton, *Liberty's Daughters: The Revolutionary Experiences of American Women, 1750–1800* (Boston: Little, Brown & Co., 1980), 271. For a discussion of developments in England, see Joan N. Burstyn, *Victorian Education and the Ideal of Womanhood* (New York: Barnes & Noble Books, 1980).

[13] Kenneth Lockridge, *Literacy in Colonial New England: An Inquiry into the Social Context in the Early Modern West* (New York: W. W. Norton & Co., 1974).

[14] Nancy F. Cott, *The Bonds of Womanhood: "Woman's Sphere" in New England, 1780–1835* (New Haven, Conn.: Yale University Press, 1977).

sylvania only 50 percent of black women were literate in 1850; percentages for white women in Pennsylvania, even in rural areas, were comparable to those for women in Massachusetts, who were approaching complete literacy. Jensen attributes this differential, in part, to the in-migration of blacks from southern states where teaching blacks to read and write was outlawed.

Kerber argues, moreover, that because literacy served, directly, as a key to the modern world, "no social change in the early Republic affected women more emphatically than the improvement of schooling."[15] To understand the social implications of differential male and female literacy, she points out, we must consider that female culture, in its reliance on the spoken word, was premodern at a time when male culture increasingly depended on written communication—an important measure of modernization in a society. The practical competencies and cosmopolitan outlook that literacy fosters, Kerber suggests, may therefore have lagged for women and reinforced the separateness of women's and men's experience.

The academy experience

Mary Beth Norton argues that we must look at individual institutions, at the actual training girls received in the many academies that were founded after the Revolution, and at the lives of early academy graduates in order to discover "the enduring effects of the revolutionary redefinition of woman's place."[16] The development of the female academies was, she suggests, a major advance, for it suddenly, "within the space of two decades, made higher education available to young American women from middling and well-to-do families."[17] The female academy, Norton claims, put into practice the republican rhetoric about the education of American girls: it stressed academic subjects and thus helped to close the gap that traditionally had separated the education of girls from that of their brothers, it provided a new occupational and intellectual role for women as teachers, and it produced a new cohort of women leaders.

Few other historians have similarly identified the early female academy as a critical turning point in women's education. Ann D. Gordon's article on the Young Ladies Academy of Philadelphia[18] is one of the few published scholarly studies of an individual female academy; Lynne Templeton Brickley's study of Sarah Pierce's Academy in Litchfield, Connecticut, is

---

[15] Kerber, *Women of the Republic*, 193.

[16] Norton, 255.

[17] Ibid., 273.

[18] Ann D. Gordon, "The Young Ladies Academy of Philadelphia," in *Women of America: A History*, ed. Carol Ruth Berkin and Mary Beth Norton (Boston: Houghton Mifflin Co., 1979), 68–91.

still in dissertation form.[19] This lack of secondary source material on early female academies has led even the historians most familiar with women's education of the period to underestimate both the magnitude of female institution building during the eighteenth century and the centrality of the female academy to women's later access to coeducational public high schools, all-male academies, and colleges.

Surveying the level of education achieved by the 222 women born before 1810 whose biographies are included in *Notable American Women*, Norton found a dramatic increase in the availability of advanced schooling for those women, born in the 1770s, who were of school age when the first republican academies were founded in the mid-1780s. The percentage of her sample who received advanced instruction, after remaining constant at roughly 22 percent for those born from the beginning of the eighteenth century to 1769, more than doubled to 46 percent for women born in the 1770s; it climbed to 63 percent for those born between 1780 and 1789; and then reached 74 percent for those born during the first decade of the nineteenth century.[20]

Norton also suggests that the significance of the early academy can be traced through the lives of individual graduates who achieved fame in the nineteenth century—leaders of the abolitionist and woman's rights movements, and educational reformers such as Zilpah Grant, Mary Lyon, Emma Willard, and Catharine Beecher. This evidence leads her to conclude, in fact, that the "egalitarian rhetoric of the Revolution provided the woman's rights movement with its earliest vocabulary and the republican academies produced its first leaders."[21]

The entire discussion about the influence and purpose of the republican girls' academy, however, lacks the important context of contemporary developments in boys' education. Ann Gordon, though still constrained by the lack of scholarship on comparable female institutions, does address this problem in her discussion of the Young Ladies Academy. This academy, which opened in 1787, offered girls an education that was remarkably similar to that available to boys. Gordon suggests, in fact, that the college

---

[19] Lynne Templeton Brickley, "Sarah Pierce's Litchfield Female Academy, 1792–1833, Litchfield, Connecticut" (Ed. D. diss., Harvard University, 1985), and "'Female Academies Are Every Where Establishing'" (special qualifying paper, Harvard Graduate School of Education, 1982). Using an unusual group of sources, including late nineteenth- and early twentieth-century histories of education, state chronicles, town histories, and books on schoolgirl art and needlework, Brickley has identified over 360 secondary-level schools for girls established throughout America prior to 1830. Not only did all of these schools teach academic subjects (some used the texts in use in the male colleges), but many, including those in the South, enjoyed well-established reputations, long histories, and large enrollments— attributes that run counter to the persistent claims that what schools did exist were small and ephemeral.

[20] Norton, 288–89.

[21] Ibid., 299.

graduates who founded the Young Ladies Academy applied the content and method of their own training to the education of girls as an expression of the changing attitudes of republican men toward the education of women. As Gordon summarizes, "The academy provided a miniature platform on which late eighteenth-century sexual politics came to life."[22]

In this context, Gordon makes an important observation which should serve as a warning against confusing rhetoric about female education with actual training and practices. In the case of the Young Ladies Academy, girls were taught the same subjects, with the same books and methods of instruction, as boys. The rationale given, however, differed when the curriculum was applied to the education of girls. For instance, Gordon points out that writing skills, which were emphasized in the education of boys for their utility in public life and business, were said, in the case of girls, to be a mark of social status; arithmetic, which by the eighteenth century had become important to the conduct of business, commerce, and the trades, was justified as a suitable subject for young ladies because as wives they might be called upon to assist their husbands or to watch the family finances. Depending on how we interpret this tension between the public discussion and the new competencies that girls privately were gaining through their studies, we might conclude, as does Cott, that the emphasis placed on utilitarian education during the eighteenth century had different ramifications for men and for women—that "education for men in America had to increase in scope . . . in order to be functional," but utilitarian education for American women "*narrowed* their prospects because it was based on a limited conception of woman's role."[23] Or, we might argue that while the ideology of republican womanhood certainly conditioned the experience of young women students, no amount of rhetoric about limits on women's lives could totally negate the *broadening* effects of rigorous intellectual training and academy attendance.

Gordon's research shows that, for at least some women, academy attendance served to nurture ambitions and skills. The experience of functioning as individuals in the school community led to the discovery of a new social role—one that was very different from the domestic responsibilities of the daughter at home. Girls learned to compete and to be judged by their competence in each subject; prizes and awards reinforced girls' desires to achieve; and the practice of emulation, adopted directly from the boys' schools, taught young women to value public recognition. The culture of the republican girls' academies, then, may have fostered qualities in women that their founders never anticipated—independence, ambition, and public leadership.

This outcome certainly had come to be feared by the 1830s when

[22] Gordon, 69.
[23] Cott (n. 14 above), 109.

educators of young women such as William Woodbridge and George Emerson were waging a campaign against rituals of competition in the education of girls because, as Nancy Green reports, they were believed to "unfit females for the duties of their sex, encourage boldness, vanity and selfishness at the expense of humility, devotion to duty, and the desire to do right for its sake."[24] Green argues that it was this concern with the pernicious effects of competition on the female character in particular which fueled the general debate over the practice of emulation among educational theorists of the antebellum period. The academy experience, then, highlighted the central paradox in women's educational history— that education for women served the conservative function of preserving dominant cultural values of domesticity and subservience, while at the same time it provided women with the skills, the insights, and the desire to advance nontraditional values and, in some cases, even radical change.

Anne Firor Scott, in her study of Emma Willard's school, places educational advances for women at the heart of the nineteenth-century woman's movement. Though the explicit purpose of Troy's founder was "to educate women for responsible motherhood and train some of them to be teachers," in retrospect, Scott argues, "the school can be seen to have been an important source of feminism and the incubator of a new style of female personality."[25]

Emma Willard was a prime example of this new female personality and an important purveyor of new forms of behavior for American women: though she was a woman of her time, rooted in social conventions, she was also a woman of the future. Scott argues, in fact, that Willard and others like her who were able to integrate new values with traditional notions of women's proper role were effective agents of change because of their seeming conservatism. Their public statements, however, have misled historians, as well as the women's peers, into thinking of them simply as exemplars of true womanhood—pious, submissive, and bound to the concept of domesticity.

The same might be said of the Troy Female Seminary, Scott argues. Its attention to the intellectual development of women was subversive; its mission of training women to become teachers, while cloaked in the

[24] Nancy Green, "Female Education and School Competition: 1820–1850," *History of Education Quarterly* 18, no. 2 (Summer 1978): 129–42, esp. 134.

[25] Anne Firor Scott, "The Ever Widening Circle: The Diffusion of Feminist Values from the Troy Female Seminary, 1822–1872," *History of Education Quarterly* 19, no. 1 (Spring 1979): 3–25, esp. 3. On Willard, see Anne Firor Scott, "What, Then, Is the American: This New Woman?" *Journal of American History* 65, no. 3 (December 1978): 679–703. For an interesting contrast, see Louise L. Stevenson, "Sarah Porter Educates Useful Ladies, 1847–1900," *Winterthur Portfolio* 18, no. 1 (Spring 1983): 39–59. See also Kathryn Kish Sklar, *Catherine Beecher: A Study in American Domesticity* (New Haven, Conn.: Yale University Press, 1973).

rhetoric of Republican Motherhood, was a radical reformulation of women's sphere to include professional work; and its championship of women's advancement reached far beyond the private confines of the school to a vast public audience through the influence of Troy alumnae who taught in the common schools and who established a network of some two hundred schools modeled after "the Troy plan" as far away as Ohio, Indiana, South Carolina, Georgia, and Alabama. Scott concludes, therefore, that recent historians have been wrong to dismiss the early seminaries and pre–Civil War colleges as bulwarks of tradition. Moreover, she argues, when we consider the large number of women who, like the Troy women, tended to be traditional in their behavior but were "to some degree affected by the 'woman movement,'" we see that the changing state of women's self-perceptions "was not simply a matter of a few radicals, but rather one of the major phenomena shaping nineteenth century social history."[26] It was through schools founded by such women and schools in which such women served as teachers that these changing roles were disseminated.

Scott derives her conclusions, in part, from biographical data compiled on more than 3,500 of the 12,000 women who attended Troy between 1821 and 1871. These alumnae, as Scott describes them through both statistical portraits and personal documentation, included many examples of the "new woman" of the nineteenth century. One alumna founded normal schools, another ran a farm; Troy graduates went on to become geologists, medical missionaries, translators, and midwives; an unusually large number worked with their fathers or beside their lawyer, minister, or businessman husbands—a phenomenon that suggests the married life of women who received advanced educations may have differed substantially from that of women who did not have the same intellectual training. In fact, Scott's statistical analysis confirms her suggestion that Troy students were quite different from the general population: a rather high proportion (22 percent) remained single; when they did marry, Troy alumnae tended to have small families (an ironic outcome, Scott notes, for women whose education ostensibly was to prepare them for motherhood); an unusually high percentage of married women continued to work after marriage (6 percent); and of those alumnae who became teachers, many (an estimated 40 percent) made teaching a serious career.

What still is unclear, however, is whether this experience was truly unique. Scott claims that Troy was a first in its provision of higher education for women and that Willard's emphasis on training women to become teachers, her organization of an alumnae network, and her curricular and organizational innovations were unprecedented. Brickley contends that

Sarah Pierce and others anticipated many of Willard's achievements a generation before Troy was founded.

It is clear, in any case, that Willard did advance the cause of women's education dramatically; because of her influence on the development of the common schools, Willard's reforms were broadcast nationwide. She was elected supervisor of schools by the male voters of Kensington, Connecticut, in which capacity she established both a demonstration school for training teachers and the Woman's Association for the Common Schools. In her work at Troy, Willard developed a curriculum that was far more innovative in its pedagogy and in the introduction of such courses as science and geography than anything the male academies or colleges of the period had to offer.

In fact, Scott's study illustrates Barbara Miller Solomon's observation that many of the most important curricular innovations of the nineteenth century were the products of women educators who were free to "experiment" in their schools for girls. Solomon's massive and detailed survey of American women's education not only rehabilitates the reputation of the female academies in this regard but also links their leaders to educational reforms more generally. Solomon cites examples of curricular reform and pedagogical innovations emanating from the female academies across a variety of disciplines, especially in the sciences.[27]

Focusing on the sciences, Deborah Jean Warner documents an amazing array of scientific lecture series, courses in girls' schools and academies, and textbooks directed exclusively to female audiences.[28] Many of the leading texts used in boys' schools as well as in female academies were written by women educators, Almira Phelps being perhaps the best known and most successful. Some girls' schools boasted courses, and even scientific apparatus, more advanced than those available at the leading men's colleges. Sharon Female Seminary, one of the Quaker schools studied by Jensen, by 1851 was offering courses in "natural philosophy, chemistry, astronomy, physiology, geology, botany, and other branches of science." Jensen discovered that this so-called ephemeral school (it lasted only twenty years) "boasted over $4,000 worth of astronomical equipment . . . and a large collection of fossils and minerals."[29]

The important point, of course, is that the diffusion of feminist values that Scott identifies in her interpretation of Willard's work may prove to have been even more widespread than the Troy data indicates. Moreover, such educators' belief in women's unlimited intellectual capabilities and

[27] Barbara Miller Solomon, *In the Company of Educated Women: A History of Women and Higher Education in America* (New Haven, Conn.: Yale University Press, 1985).
[28] Deborah Jean Warner, "Science Education for Women in Antebellum America," *Isis* 69, no. 246 (March 1978): 58–67.
[29] Jensen (n. 11 above), 13.

their advocacy of a new public role for women influenced the future of public schooling as their graduates became teachers.

Women and the history of teaching

Who those teachers were, what impact they had on American education, and how the profession of teaching affected nineteenth-century women are questions that recently have led to a reexamination of the teaching profession from several new perspectives. Richard M. Bernard and Maris A. Vinovskis's well-known research on antebellum teachers in Massachusetts provides a reconstruction of patterns of female employment in the schools based on census data, annual school reports, and other historical studies. These data indicate that in Massachusetts (a state whose early commitment to public education was not typical but which, largely through the reform activities of Horace Mann, influenced practices in other states) women teachers outnumbered male teachers throughout the antebellum years. In fact, the absolute number of male teachers actually declined between 1834 and 1860, while the percentage of women in the teaching force "bolted upward" from 56.3 percent to 77.8 percent. This did not mean, of course, that women teachers represented a substantial percentage of all Massachusetts women at any given time: at no point during the antebellum period did teaching provide employment to even 2 percent of white women ages fifteen to sixty; and thus it might seem that the teaching profession could have had only a minor impact on women of the period. In estimating the percentage of antebellum white women who *ever* had taught, however, Barnard and Vinovskis found that approximately one out of five white women (and probably one out of four native-born white women) was a teacher at some time in her life.

Bernard and Vinovskis focus on two aspects of the teaching experience for women—teacher training and the organizational structure of the teaching profession. According to their data, most Massachusetts teachers were poorly prepared, having attended only common schools; they were young (most were between sixteen and twenty-five); they regarded teaching as a temporary career (the average tenure for public school teachers in 1845–1846 was 2.1 years); and vertical mobility for women in public schools was minimal (female principals were few and never were allowed to supervise male teachers; women teachers most often were assigned the younger children). The inferior status of women in the schools was compounded, moreover, by the fact that on the average women earned only 40 percent of the salary paid their male counterparts. This leads the authors to conclude that "self-respect must have been a difficult ideal" for women teachers. On the other hand, the reality of earned income for those women employed for the first time, they argue, "probably outweighed their feelings of resentment over their deprivation relative to male teachers—especially in a society where women were normally subordinated to men outside the home."[30] The limitation of this conclusion, of course, is that it relies on published reports of school officials and schoolmen for information on the conditions under which women taught and learned in antebellum America.

Geraldine Jonçich Clifford argues that a solution to this dilemma exists in the study of diaries, journals, personal correspondence, and autobiographical accounts of anonymous women teachers. Her research provides substantial confirmation that teachers' own perceptions often differed markedly from the perceptions of educational spokesmen (and from the interpretations of recent historians). The common practice in nineteenth-century rural communities of "boarding around" the local teacher in the homes of school families, for example, often was not, from the teacher's perspective, the despised practice that historians have claimed, nor was it disdained by ordinary teachers as it was by spokesmen for the teaching profession. Clifford found that many rural youth relished this "escape from their even-more confining homes and neighbourhoods."[31] Also, in contradistinction to recent historical conceptualizations of nineteenth-century schools as factories, bureaucracies, and the battlefields of home-school conflict, Clifford claims that the letters and diaries of teachers she has read portray countless schools in which individual initiative, local discretion in implementing or ignoring state directives, parent-teacher cooperation, and community support were the salient features of public schooling. On the other hand, Clifford's data confirm Vinovskis and Bernard's portrait of the typical common school teacher as young and ill-prepared. Except for the small minority of teachers who had received normal-school training, Clifford agrees that there is little evidence that the newer pedagogical ideas or educational reform movements concerned nineteenth-century teachers.

Clifford's most important contribution to this discussion, however, is her claim that a teaching career—however brief, and despite the low pay

[30] Richard M. Bernard and Maris A. Vinovskis, "The Female School Teacher in Ante-Bellum Massachusetts," *Journal of Social History* 10, no. 3 (Spring 1977): 332–45, esp. 337–38; see also Maris A. Vinovskis and Richard M. Bernard, "Beyond Catharine Beecher: Female Education in the Antebellum Period," *Signs* 3, no. 4 (Summer 1978): 856–69.

[31] Geraldine Jonçich Clifford, "History as Experience: The Uses of Personal-History Documents in the History of Education," *History of Education* 7, no. 3 (1978): 183–96, esp. 196, "'Marry, Stitch, Die, or Do Worse': Educating Women for Work," in *Work, Youth, and Schooling: Historical Perspectives on Vocationalism in American Education*, ed. Harvey Kantor and David B. Tyack (Stanford, Calif.: Stanford University Press, 1982), 223–349, and "Home and School in 19th-Century America: Some Personal-History Reports from the United States," *History of Education Quarterly* 18, no. 1 (Spring 1978): 3–34. An important collection of personal documents of women teachers is Nancy Hoffman, *Woman's "True" Profession: Voices from the History of Teaching* (Old Westbury, N.Y.: Feminist Press, 1981).

and emotional and physical costs—provided women with "a psychic reward unique to their gender." The woman teacher, unlike most
nineteenth-century women, could choose to postpone or to reject "the
domestic imperative." Clifford describes the "growing self-respect, autonomy, and assertiveness" she discovered in the papers of young country
girls whose teaching often took them to schools far from their homes.[32]

Jensen depicts a similar pattern among the Quaker teachers even
earlier in the century. She argues that Quaker women such as Rachel
Painter, who attended the Westtown School, a boarding school established
in 1799, enjoyed unprecedented independence and intellectual satisfaction during their years at school and, even more important, in their
employment as teachers thereafter. Writing to her cousin in 1817, Painter
described her pleasure in her students' successes, her sense of competence
in executing the "responsibility attach'd to [her] important station," and
her satisfaction in earning a salary by which she could keep herself "gen-
teely and lay up 300 hundred [sic] D. per annum."[33]

Of particular interest is Clifford's observation that teachers' duties also
included business bargaining in the male-dominated world of public officials and school trustees, and that women's public lives as teachers
occasionally propelled them to seek larger audiences as abolitionists, suf-
fragists, or temperance workers. Kathleen Berkeley's research on women
teachers in the Memphis schools in the years following Reconstruction
offers striking evidence of political activism among women teachers (in the
case of Memphis they agitated for equal pay) and suggests that the schools
may even have served as vital training grounds for the suffrage campaign.
Berkeley's study corroborates Clifford's observations that through the
process of teaching women developed political skills. Women teachers, she
argues, felt a collective identity that helped them to organize for other
causes.[34]

New friendships, collegial support, and "sentiments of sisterhood with
other young women teachers" were, according to Clifford, "commonplace
experiences."[35] Women teachers developed networks and assisted one
another in finding schools—a phenomenon, Clifford points out, that is
utterly missing from standard histories of the teaching profession. Clifford
concludes, moreover, that in spite of nineteenth-century rhetoric, and
contrary to historiography that has linked teaching with women's domestic
sphere and defined its growth as a conservative counterforce to women's

[32] Clifford, "History as Experience," 196.
[33] Jensen (n. 11 above), 14.
[34] Kathleen C. Berkeley, "'The Ladies Want to Bring about Reform in the Public Schools':
Public Education and Women's Rights in the Post–Civil War South," *History of Education
Quarterly* 24, no. 1 (Spring 1984): 45–58.
[35] Clifford, "History as Experience," 196.

advancement, teaching made a significant contribution to nineteenth-century feminism.

Women's life-cycle patterns

Inherent in these discussions is the notion that the development of teaching as an occupation for women marked a new phase in the life cycle of nineteenth-century women—a time of relative independence between the domestic duties of the daughter at home and the equally dependent station of the married woman in her husband's home. Clifford highlights the personal freedom that women teachers (even those whose earnings went to support younger siblings) uniquely experienced during this phase of their lives and argues that teaching increasingly provided women with an opportunity to extend that period of education and nonfamilial responsibilities.

Nowhere, however, is this concept more rigorously tested than in David Allmendinger's study of the young women who prepared for teaching at Mary Lyon's Mount Holyoke Female Seminary. Using a variety of sources, including college files, manuscript census data, town records, genealogies, and other biographical materials, Allmendinger was able to reconstruct the family structure and social origin of a large percentage of the 1,400 women who attended Mount Holyoke during its first thirteen years. Allmendinger points out that merely by attending Mount Holyoke, the women who studied there during this period were "taking part in an experience that was altering the female life cycle." Holyoke students and their counterparts at Troy, at the state normal school at Bridgewater, and at similar institutions were adding at least three years of education to their life cycles; they also, Allmendinger explains, were making the female life cycle more complex by adding the option of remaining single and self-supporting.[36]

Though most Holyoke women did marry (81 percent), a significant minority did not (19 percent, as compared to 6–8 percent of the female population as a whole).[37] Moreover, even those women who eventually married did not know at the time they entered Mount Holyoke when or if they would marry. Allmendinger argues that demographic changes had begun to alter parental expectations and the traditional female life cycle of some women in the hill towns of rural New England and New York even as early as 1800. Due to the same forces of population growth and declining land resources which drove the sons of these rural families to seek new land

[36] David F. Allmendinger, Jr., "Mount Holyoke Students Encounter the Need for Life-Planning, 1837–1850," *History of Education Quarterly* 19, no. 1 (Spring 1979): 27–46, esp. 39.

[37] Ibid., 40.

in the West or to train for occupations other than farming, women began to experience a "gap" of about five years between maturity and marriage. Increasingly, then, Allmendinger explains, parents of modest means needed to plan for the support of their daughters during this interval and, perhaps, for their entire adult lives.

Allmendinger, then, describes a very different phenomenon in his economic life-cycle interpretation of the impetus to advanced education for women than traditionally has been attributed to the early academies, seminaries, and women's colleges. Mount Holyoke students were not the daughters of the privileged, and it was neither exemption from economic productivity nor single-daughter status that provided the necessary condition for their advanced education. Instead, like the young male students in the provincial New England colleges whom Allmendinger has described elsewhere,[38] the Holyoke women sought higher education for vocational reasons. They came from what Mary Lyon described as the "country middle classes" and were required by circumstances to contribute to the family economy. Allmendinger calculates that over half of the Holyoke graduates between 1838 and 1850 came from families in the lower economic brackets: over half were farm families whose real estate holdings in 1850 were valued at $3,000 or less—below the average value of estates in mature farming areas. Scattered personal records and an analysis of the attendance patterns of Holyoke students show that economic problems often forced women to interrupt their studies, to interchange years of work and schooling, or to rush through Holyoke at an accelerated pace in order to save money. The structure of Mount Holyoke families, moreover, may have compounded the economic incentive to teach, as half of the families had only one son or none at all, and nearly all boasted a "surplus" of daughters to support—a circumstance that made the investment in a Holyoke education particularly attractive to these families. As teachers, these daughters could help support their families before marriage or remain single and be self-supporting.

Unfortunately, Allmendinger's data on Holyoke, Scott's on Troy, and Bernard and Vinovskis's data on students who attended the four Massachusetts state normal schools are not comparable, and Allmendinger only can suggest possible contrasts between the Holyoke students and young women who attended other institutions. Allmendinger assumes that Mount Holyoke students were more intensely driven by economic considerations than were students at other antebellum academies and seminaries. Mary Lyon introduced cost-cutting measures at Holyoke that held the price of a year's attendance to only one-third the cost of Troy or Ipswich. It is still unclear, however, to what degree tuition differentials

[38] David F. Allmendinger, Jr., *Paupers and Scholars: The Transformation of Student Life in Nineteenth-Century America* (New York: St. Martin's Press, 1975).

reflected distinctive student populations. A substantial number of Troy students, for instance, were given instruction on credit charged against their future earnings as teachers.

Whether Holyoke students were distinctive in their social backgrounds and economic need, then, or whether Allmendinger's portrait might suggest the family attributes of a larger population of women teachers, is difficult to assess in the absence of other detailed analyses at the household level. Sarah Gordon provides evidence, for example, that a small number of similar hill-town families sent their daughters to Smith College to be trained as "teacher specials."[39]

The migration of teachers from New England

Kathryn Kish Sklar in her study of the evangelical and community roots of Mount Holyoke reminds us that it was also the religious commitment of many Holyoke women—a commitment reinforced and nurtured by Mary Lyon—that drove them into the fields of teaching and missionary work initially.[40] Because single women were denied the sponsorship of missionary organizations, many young unmarried women turned to teaching in answer to their "higher calling." After marriage, some of these same women were able to serve alongside their husbands in foreign fields or in the West.

Teaching in the West provided an important opportunity for young women teachers during the antebellum period, and Mount Holyoke graduates and normal-school students from New York and New England were among the number who first left their homes in the East to embrace a new life and calling in the West. Those who migrated west under the sponsorship of the Board of National Popular Education, an evangelical organization in Hartford originally conceived by Catharine Beecher, have been studied by Polly Welts Kaufman, who claims that the experience of religious conversion and a missionary zeal may have been the essential preconditions that helped these teachers gain the courage necessary to leave their homes and go west. The experience of teaching in the West, moreover,

[39] Sarah H. Gordon, "Smith College Students: The First Ten Classes, 1879–1888," *History of Education Quarterly* 15, no. 2 (Summer 1975): 147–67. Tiziana Rota, who has studied the social origins and employment patterns of Mount Holyoke students later in the century, demonstrates that the social composition of the early seminary had shifted by the 1880s and that the majority of students were no longer the daughters of hill-town farmers. See Tiziana Rota, "Between 'True Women' and 'New Women': Mount Holyoke Students, 1837 to 1908" (Ph.D. diss., University of Massachusetts, 1983).

[40] Kathryn Kish Sklar, "The Founding of Mount Holyoke College," in *Women of America: A History*, ed. Carol Ruth Berkin and Mary Beth Norton (Boston: Houghton Mifflin Co., 1979), 177–201.

appears to have reinforced women's sense of psychological power, and for some teaching may even have served as the secular equivalent of the conversion experience. Maria Welch, for instance, a young graduate of Cortland Academy in New York whom Kaufman quotes, wrote in her application to the board that she wished to teach in the West "to try myself alone, and find out who I am."[41]

As with the Holyoke women, it was not spiritual motives alone that attracted these women teachers to the frontier. Kaufman's study of the papers of about half of the six hundred women whom the Board of National Popular Education sponsored during the decade following its establishment in 1846 shows that economic need was at least as prominent a factor in the decision of teachers to go west as was a sense of mission. More than two-thirds of the teachers Kaufman studied already were on their own when they applied to teach in the West; the majority of these had suffered the death of one or both parents. Many of the rest, according to Kaufman, appear to have been older professional teachers who were seeking higher salaries or a change in situation; all were self-supporting out of necessity. Kaufman notes, too, that the median age of those for whom information is available was slightly over twenty-five at the time of their preliminary training with the board; and therefore the option of financial support through marriage may have been less available (or less attractive) to this group of teachers than to a group of younger and less experienced women.

The pioneer teachers provide an interesting case that seems to confirm the broader applicability of Allmendinger's findings concerning changes in the female life cycle and the concomitant attractiveness of teaching to women from rural New England during the antebellum period. Like the women who attended Mount Holyoke, most of the teachers who went west came from northern New England and New York state. The majority already had taught, and most had struggled to obtain their educations, attending an academy or seminary for a few sessions at a time in alternation with teaching or other jobs. Unlike the Holyoke women, however, fewer than one-third of the women Kaufman studied came from families in which both parents were still living.[42] This points to another important aspect of women's lives that may have altered the course of their educational careers: dislocations resulting from the early death of parents or a spouse, sudden financial reversals, or other unexpected changes in family status had a different impact on nineteenth-century women than they did on men to whom a variety of options for self-support were available. For women,

[41] Polly Welts Kaufman, "A Wider Field of Usefulness: Pioneer Women Teachers in the West, 1848–1854," *Journal of the West* 21, no. 2 (April 1982): 16–25, esp. 19, and *Women Teachers on the Frontier* (New Haven, Conn.: Yale University Press, 1984).

[42] Allmendinger claims that the Holyoke students came from intact families, though his data may have reflected the presence of stepparents and thus disguised the orphaned status of some women (see Allmendinger, "Mount Holyoke Students," 36–37).

teaching offered an alternative to the traditional solution of living as a dependent in the homes of willing relatives.

Jacqueline Jones identifies this phenomenon among the northern women who went south to teach freedmen after the Civil War with the American Missionary Association (AMA).[43] Of the nearly three hundred women who taught in Georgia between 1865 and 1874 under the auspices of the AMA, only one-third had two parents living when they left for Georgia—the same proportion found by Kaufman among the teachers who went west through the offices of the Board of National Popular Education. The remaining women in Jones's group were about equally divided between those who had no parent living and those who had only one, most often only a mother.

Jones argues, however, that abolitionist sentiment probably outweighed the need to be self-supporting as the motive for going south among most of the women in her study. AMA teachers could hope to earn only fifteen dollars a month in addition to their lodging and meals in an AMA boarding home, and as a consequence teachers from modest backgrounds, Jones explains, were beset with financial problems and sometimes even had to leave freedmen's work, relinquishing it to those women who could tolerate both the economic and physical hardships of teaching in the South.

Still, the similarities of this group of teachers to those described by Allmendinger and Kaufman are striking (and their low salaries are not far different). The typical AMA teacher was the daughter of a clergyman, farmer, or skilled tradesman in small-town or rural New England. She was white, single, in her late twenties, a member of an evangelical church, and experienced as a common-school teacher. Jones discovered in her detailed biographical research, based on manuscript census data, family genealogies, obituaries, and teachers' applications to the AMA, that most of the northern teachers had received some type of higher education in a normal school or female seminary; a number of them had attended Oberlin; several had attended Mount Holyoke.

The fact that the AMA selected only experienced teachers meant that these women already had chosen teaching as their livelihood, had prepared for teaching during their early twenties, and had worked as teachers before deciding to go south. In this respect, then, they exhibited the same life-cycle pattern as the Mount Holyoke women, and their middle-class background and gentility, therefore, should not be confused with freedom

[43] Jacqueline Jones, "Women Who Were More Than Men: Sex and Status in Freedman's Teaching," *History of Education Quarterly* 19, no. 1 (Spring 1979): 47–59, and *Soldiers of Light and Love: Northern Teachers and Georgia Blacks, 1865–1873* (Chapel Hill: University of North Carolina Press, 1980). See also Sandra E. Small, "The Yankee Schoolmarm in Freedman's Schools: An Analysis of Attitudes," *Journal of Southern History* 14, no. 3 (August 1979): 381–402.

from economic responsibility. The fact that such a disproportionately large number of the AMA teachers came from families that had experienced some kind of crisis should be analyzed further. While the death of a parent may not indicate financial distress, it may tell us something about the attitudes of surviving daughters and about the new forms of independence that by choice or out of necessity they exhibited.

In combination with Clifford's, Allmendinger's, and Kaufman's studies, Jones's biographical data on the teachers who went to Georgia confirm, in fact, an attribute of the teaching profession in general that has been largely ignored by historians. Teaching, unlike factory work, farm labor, or domestic service, was considered throughout the nineteenth century to be a respectable occupation for women, and thus the profession could accommodate women from a wide range of backgrounds, embracing at the same time both well-educated daughters of northern (and southern) families who might be "genteel but impoverished" and New England farm girls who had the benefits of only a common-school education. Furthermore, unlike most nineteenth-century women, whose social status was in large part a function of their father's or husband's status, women teachers occupied a position in their communities that was, to some degree at least, a function of their own occupational role.

The women teachers in both Jones's and Kaufman's studies very clearly conform, in fact, to Anne Firor Scott's definition of the "New American Woman." In Kaufman's words, they "demonstrated a will to direct their own lives to an extent that was unusual for the majority of women of their time [and] were able to attain a higher level of self-sufficiency than practically any other group . . . virtually unnoticed."[44] In the case of the pioneer teachers who went west, this self-sufficiency was manifested in their determination to negotiate favorable living conditions and salaries with sometimes hostile community leaders. Several teachers were charged with the task of opening the first school in a district: primitive schoolhouses, harsh living conditions, and sectarian conflicts were only a few of the problems that these young women confronted. They managed, however, to establish authority in the classroom and to pioneer new teaching techniques and leadership in the community and in regional teachers' institutes; many, moreover, carved out new personal as well as professional lives for themselves on the frontier.

Of the women who went west, nearly two-thirds stayed in their new homes. Kaufman portrays these women as community builders in the larger sense: in addition to starting or continuing as teachers in district or subscription schools, many founded or taught in seminaries where they trained the next generation of teachers. In building new lives for themselves they often achieved positions of considerable influence, and a pat-

---

[44] Kaufman, "A Wider Field of Usefulness," 23.

tern of pioneer teachers marrying prominent men is suggested by Kaufman's sample of former Mount Holyoke and Albany Normal School students who went west. Marriage, furthermore, did not necessarily preclude teaching as a career: husbands sometimes joined in their wives' efforts. Jones tells us that those who went south with the AMA, on the other hand, appear to have returned to their homes in New England or the Midwest, where they resumed teaching or married, and where they continued to support the work of freedmen's aid societies.

Like Scott, who argues that feminist values influenced a broad range of nineteenth-century women, Jones emphasizes that the teachers who went south were ordinary women whose wish for a more active life, whose sense of adventure and sense of mission, and whose desire to escape from family tasks probably were shared by many. Their accomplishments, therefore, are all the more significant as a commentary on nineteenth-century schoolteaching and early Victorian womanhood in general.

Black women teachers

While much of the new research on nineteenth-century women teachers seems to confirm this thesis, we still must qualify the positive findings with a critical acknowledgment that women's advances in education and in the teaching profession took place within the context of a sex-segregated labor market and under the specter of profound discrimination in terms of race, religion, social class, and ethnicity, as well as gender. Bettye Collier-Thomas reminds us in her introduction to a recent collection of biographical scholarship on black women educators that the history of black women teachers differed significantly from the experience of white women in education.[45] Because black women were excluded from opportunities for advanced education for an even longer period of time than were white women, blacks moved into the profession at a different pace.

By 1910, however, U.S. census reports indicated that black women accounted for over two-thirds (22,547) of the nation's 29,772 black teachers (a proportion nearly identical to women's share of teaching jobs nationally). Little is known about these teachers, and it still is unclear what implications can be drawn from the national statistics. Most scholars agree, however, that for black women race augmented sex as a determinant of low pay, low status, and gender segregation within the educational hierarchy.

Linda Perkins argues that in spite of their increasing numbers as teachers, black women suffered a decline in educational and professional opportunities vis-à-vis black men in the years following the Civil War.

[45] Bettye Collier-Thomas, "The Impact of Black Women in Education: An Historical Overview," *Journal of Negro Education* 51, no. 3 (Summer 1982): 173–80.

While coeducational schools for southern blacks had proliferated after the War, and black families placed extremely high value on the education of both sons and daughters, black men began to outnumber black women in higher education. By 1890, Perkins writes, only 30 black women held baccalaureate degrees, compared to over 300 black men and 2,500 white women. Educated black men also increasingly gained greater options in employment; black women were confined almost exclusively to elementary and secondary school teaching.[46]

Perkins attributes this growing inequality in part to the differential power black men achieved in gaining the vote in 1870. The Fourteenth Amendment, Perkins observes, was the first major distinction acknowledged by society toward black men. As they moved into increasingly prominent political positions during Reconstruction, many black men adopted the prevailing posture of white society toward woman's proper place.

This contrasts sharply with the status of black women prior to emancipation, Perkins argues. Black women were among the earliest educators of the race. Katy Ferguson's School for the Poor opened to both black and white pupils in New York City in 1793. That same year, Perkins notes, the Committee for Improving the Condition of Free Blacks in Pennsylvania established a school and recommended a black female teacher. Black women continued to teach, to lecture and write, to run clandestine schools in the South, and to work for abolition throughout the antebellum period.[47]

The experience of the many anonymous black women teachers who carried on the campaign of racial "uplift" after the Civil War has been difficult to retrieve. Oral histories have provided some data. Courtney Ann Vaughn-Roberson's portrait of Oklahoma schoolteachers includes information on twenty-five black women teachers along with data from correspondence and oral interviews of another three hundred white or mixed-blood Indian women.[48] Most of the early black women teachers in Oklahoma, Vaughn-Roberson writes, had been educated elsewhere and had migrated to Oklahoma; they received their training at such institutions as Oberlin, Wilberforce, the University of Chicago, and Fisk University. Later generations of black women born in Oklahoma, mostly the daughters of poor

[46] Linda M. Perkins, "The Impact of the 'Cult of True Womanhood' on the Education of Black Women," *Journal of Social Issues* 39, no. 3 (September 1983): 17–28.

[47] Linda Perkins, "Black Women and Racial 'Uplift' Prior to Emancipation," in *The Black Woman Cross-Culturally*, ed. Filomina Chioma Steady (Cambridge, Mass.: Schenkman Publishing Co., 1981), and "Quaker Beneficence and Black Control: The Institute for Colored Youth, 1852–1903," in *New Perspectives on Black Educational History*, ed. Vincent P. Franklin and James D. Anderson (Boston: G. K. Hall & Co., 1978).

[48] Courtney Ann Vaughn-Roberson, "Sometimes Independent but Never Equal— Women Teachers, 1900–1950: The Oklahoma Example," *Pacific Historical Review* 53, no. 1 (February 1984): 39–58.

farmers, became teachers and stayed in the community. Not surprisingly, they faced severe obstacles. Only one institution within the state accepted black women—the Colored Agricultural and Normal University, founded in 1897. Both Indian and Oklahoma territorial schools were, in practice, segregated from their inception, and separate schools were mandated by the state constitution in 1907.

Vaughn-Roberson points out the irony, though, that many black women in Oklahoma sensed that segregation had created professional opportunities for them. Winnie Franks, one of the black women interviewed by Vaughn-Roberson for this study, recalled the problem for black women teachers when the schools finally were integrated in the 1950s. Previously, black women had assumed almost complete responsibility for the education of black youth, and now they were out of jobs.[49]

The conditions of their employment throughout the period, however, were harsh. Vaughn-Roberson's study (much of which is based on information and memoirs solicited in 1976 by the Oklahoma Retired Teachers Association) does not provide precise data on salaries, years of employment, marital status, or career patterns. But it does give us a unique personal view of teaching conditions and of racism in a state typified by poor, rural, and small-town schools. The personal recollections of these Oklahoma teachers confirm the hardships described by David Tyack, Robert Lowe, and Elisabeth Hansot in their larger and more comprehensive analysis of public schools during the thirties.[50] For many Oklahoma women, the Depression never ended. Jennie Higgins, a white teacher, reported that she had conducted a one-room school of more than a hundred students, only two-thirds of whom had pencils, pens, and other supplies. Ethel McPhaul, a black teacher, wrote that she and other black teachers used their own salaries to provide the same.

Urbanization and feminization

Myra H. Strober and David Tyack allude to the question of race as a variable in the feminization of southern black schools in their study of

[49] Geraldine Clifford compares black women's employment as teachers to that of other minority groups in her study, "'Marry, Stitch, Die, or Do Worse'" (n. 31 above), and concludes that because blacks were barred from the commercial jobs that employed the daughters of many immigrant families, teaching provided an opportunity more rare for educated black women than for women in other groups.

[50] David Tyack, Robert Lowe, and Elisabeth Hansot, *Public Schools in Hard Times: The Great Depression and Recent Years* (Cambridge, Mass.: Harvard University Press, 1984). See also Richard A. Quantz, "The Complex Visions of Female Teachers and the Failure of Unionization in the 1930s: An Oral History," *History of Education Quarterly* 25, no. 4 (Winter 1985): 439–58.

economic and organizational factors that led to women's employment as teachers. Strober and Tyack suggest that one factor in the growth of employment of black women teachers may have been a preference among white (male) officials to employ black women rather than to supervise black men. As they point out, "on the grounds of salary and social prestige one would expect black males to have flocked to get jobs as urban teachers in the South, but they did not."[51]

The domination of southern black rural schools by black women, however, may have been distinctive. Strober and Tyack (in writing without reference to race) conclude that women teachers made their earliest gains, in terms of numerical participation, in the nation's large urban school systems rather than in rural schools, and they present a variety of explanations for this development. The ideological and economic preconditions that made possible the entry of women into the teaching force did not proceed evenly across rural and urban labor markets, in part because daughters' domestic services were more valued by rural families and because men in the countryside had fewer lucrative alternative job opportunities than men in urban areas.

Supply factors alone, however, did not determine the pattern or rate of change toward the employment of women in the schools. Strober and Tyack identify the well-known arguments of educators such as Catharine Beecher, who claimed that teaching was compatible with the presumed future roles of young women as wives and mothers, as the necessary ideological underpinnings of the feminization of schoolteaching. To some degree, sex-role considerations had different consequences in urban schools, where the problem was mitigated by the assignment of men to positions of authority as principals, superintendents, and as teachers in the upper grades. A growing disaffection among male teachers in rural areas led finally to more opportunities for women outside of cities, a pattern that is well documented by Tyack and Strober in a follow-up study. As rural schools became bureaucratized, Strober and Tyack suggest, teaching grew less attractive to men who did not wish to become what one Oregon male teacher called "serfs to be moved about at the will of a state superintendent."[52]

[51] Myra H. Strober and David Tyack, "Why Do Women Teach and Men Manage? A Report on Research on Schools," *Signs* 5, no. 3 (Spring 1980): 494–503, esp. 502.

[52] Strober and Tyack, 499. See also David B. Tyack and Myra H. Strober, "Jobs and Gender: A History of the Structuring of Educational Employment by Sex," in *Educational Policy and Management: Sex Differentials*, ed. Patricia A. Schmuck, W. W. Charters, Jr., and Richard O. Carlson (New York: Academic Press, 1981), 131–52. For a more comprehensive discussion of the demographic and cultural factors that encouraged women to become teachers and to remain in teaching, see Geraldine Jonçich Clifford, "'Daughters into Teachers': Educational and Demographic Influences on the Transformation of Teaching into 'Women's Work' in America," *History of Education Review* 12, no. 1 (1983): 15–28.

According to Margaret Nelson's study of women in Vermont who had taught in both rural and urban or district graded schools, many women teachers also preferred the autonomy that rural schoolteaching afforded. In case after case, women lamented the loss of authority that the transition from the one-room schoolhouse to the graded school involved. Explained one teacher, "For so many years I had been the one who settled everything. . . . That was one of the hardest things for teachers who had always been in a country school to come into a graded school—because you had to follow rules and regulations."[53] Nelson found, however, that women with more advanced educations tended to prefer the climate of the graded schools. Salary considerations, resources within the classroom, and the sociability of colleagues weighed more heavily in their assessments of optimal employment conditions.

According to Strober and Tyack, then, economic preconditions and the structure of economic and status incentives, gender-role ideologies, and the organizational requirements of large urban systems all combined to encourage the feminization of schoolteaching across the country. Marta Danylewycz and Alison Prentice, however, in their discussion of the evolution of school systems in Montreal and Toronto, note that "Nineteenth century city school administrators also had very specific agendas for the men under their jurisdiction."[54] It was often the professional interests of male school heads and other administrators, and not educational considerations, that determined social policy. How such considerations affected school systems in the American context, and especially in the racially segregated South, remains to be studied.

Immigrant women

Similarly, almost nothing is known about the experience of first- and second-generation immigrant women teachers. Clifford cites a 1911 survey that indicated that in 1900, 27 percent of the nation's teachers were native-born daughters of immigrant parentage—a disproportionately large share. Norwegian immigrant women were teaching in Iowa at least as early as 1860; Irish girls trained in Boston's Catholic high school classes later in the century found teaching jobs in the city's public schools; teaching provided some young Jewish women with a ticket out of the ghetto (though there were always costs involved in such departures). Clifford argues that

[53] Margaret K. Nelson, "From the One-Room Schoolhouse to the Graded School: Teaching in Vermont, 1910–1950," *Frontiers* 7, no. 1 (February 1983): 14–20, esp. 15.

[54] Marta Danylewycz and Alison Prentice, "Teachers, Gender, and Bureaucratizing School Systems in Nineteenth Century Montreal and Toronto," *History of Education Quarterly* 24, no. 1 (Spring 1984): 75–100, esp. 91.

teaching provided significant upward social mobility for many immigrant girls at a time when relatively few of their brothers could advance from the working class to the middle class through schooling. By 1920, Clifford reports, teaching ranked fifth among occupations of women with foreign or mixed parentage, employing 7.5 percent (over 153,000) of all such women.[55]

Yet another path to teaching for some groups of immigrant women were the Catholic sisterhoods. Mary J. Oates, in her study of teaching sisters in Boston, documents the dramatic increase in the need for parochial school teachers after the 1884 edict of the Council of Baltimore requiring each parish to maintain a school.[56] According to Oates, efforts to encourage young women to join teaching communities were intense. Sisters were asked to invite high school and normal school pupils to visit them at the convent in hopes of attracting them to the community. Sermons and the Catholic press decried the need for teachers, and women responded in unprecedented numbers—never enough, however, to meet the demand.

The Boston case was unusual in that the church hierarchy for most of the nineteenth century had given little support to parochial schools; however, even in this context of minimal support for the education of teaching sisters, some working-class women received opportunities for higher education that might otherwise have eluded them. Oates's discussion is particularly useful in evaluating the impact of state certification regulations that came to govern the preparation of parochial as well as public school teachers by the 1920s. Novices who previously received little training before entering the classroom suddenly were required to study for college degrees. The demand for qualified Catholic teachers for the Boston parochial schools led eventually to the founding of two women's colleges and the admission of sisters to education courses in Boston College (though only during the summer months). It was not unusual, Oates notes, for sisters to spend some ten years in part-time study toward the baccalaureate.

Maxine Seller's work on the education of immigrant women during the early twentieth century suggests that much of the support for American-born daughters to advance in school came from immigrant mothers whose own struggles to obtain new skills and intellectual opportunities informed their ambitions for their daughters.[57] Seller documents the sexism that

[55] Clifford, "'Marry, Stitch, Die, or Do Worse'" (n. 31 above), 253.

[56] Mary J. Oates, "The Professional Preparation of Parochial School Teachers, 1870–1940," *Historical Journal of Massachusetts* 12, no. 1 (January 1984): 60–72.

[57] Maxine Seller, "The Education of the Immigrant Woman, 1900–1935," *Journal of Urban History* 4, no. 3 (May 1978): 307–30. See also Barbara Brenzel, *Daughters of the State: A Social Portrait of the First Reform School for Girls in North America, 1856–1905* (Cambridge, Mass.: MIT Press, 1983). Brenzel's history of the Lancaster Industrial School is the only major analysis to date of the interrelationships among class, ethnicity, and gender biases

accompanied nativist thinking in the Progressive Era and shows that, except for the narrowly defined Americanization programs taught in night schools, American public education largely neglected the wives of the new immigration. Immigrant women, however, sought opportunities to educate themselves, and the story of their determination and ingenuity lies, therefore, outside the public system in community programs such as the bilingual Hungarian Free Lyceum in New York City, the Bohemian settlement house women's group in Chicago, and the Finnish Lutheran churches.[58] Though some organizations concentrated, like the Americanization programs, on teaching English and traditional homemaking skills, others acknowledged immigrant women's intellectual ambition. In many cases this ambition was displaced onto the academic careers of daughters who might become teachers in America's public schools.

Women's higher education

Gender discrimination in teaching and the development of other "women's occupations" has served as a backdrop for much of the recent historical scholarship on women's higher education. Whether such new career opportunities led to greater equality for women or whether they served merely to reinforce the traditional assignment of women to secondary roles in society has been the subject of much debate. Similarly, the condition of women as students and as faculty in colleges and universities during the nineteenth and twentieth centuries has been reevaluated by several historians whose interpretations have influenced contemporary thinking about the differences between coeducational and single-sex institutions, the experience of women in different academic disciplines, and the rela-

---

that influenced the goals of nineteenth-century educational institutions. In this work and in an earlier article, "Domestication as Reform: A Study of the Socialization of Wayward Girls, 1856–1905," *Harvard Educational Review* 50, no. 2 (May 1980): 196–213, Brenzel shows how assumptions about women's "inherently domestic nature" informed both the criteria used by nineteenth-century reformers to define deviancy in young women and the programs that they designed to rehabilitate "wayward" girls. Brenzel's work provides dramatic evidence that social class and ethnicity cannot be divorced from the context of gender, and her work should serve to point the way to further investigations of the educational history of America's female underclass. With the notable exception of Geraldine Clifford, no other scholar has studied girls' vocational education, either within or outside the public schools. These topics have been so central to recent revisions of American educational history that their absence from the scholarship on women's education is all the more glaring.

[58] Seller also identifies ethnic parishes and women's organizations, Jewish mothers' clubs, the ethnic press, women's literary and singing societies, ethnic labor organizations, the socialist-sponsored Polish University of Chicago, and the Work People's College in Duluth as important educational agencies for immigrant women.

tionship of collegiate and professional training to women's subsequent employment.

The broad outlines for this debate, as I discussed in the introduction to this essay, were set by Jill Conway in her pioneering work on the first generation of American college women.[59] Conway argued that neither the early coeducational colleges (beginning with Oberlin in the 1830s, the first college to admit women) nor the midwestern state universities that began to admit women during the mid-nineteenth century encouraged women to transcend their expected secondary roles in society. The early colleges aimed to train women only as the "help-mates of the men who were to evangelise the frontier"; and the arguments in favor of coeducation that won women admission to state-supported universities and high schools, Conway claims, were "strictly economic"—male and female intellectual equality was not seriously discussed.[60]

It was not until the founding of women's colleges on the model of the elite eastern men's colleges after the Civil War, Conway argues, that women were able to obtain intellectual training that did not assume a compensatory role for women scholars. These institutions produced an exceptional generation of women during the 1890s who, nurtured by the collective female life of the women's college, emerged with aspirations to use their educations outside the confines of women's domestic sphere as it was narrowly defined in marriage. But while this pioneering generation rejected conventional marriage (some 60–70 percent remained single), the professional roles they developed for themselves perpetuated and, in fact, institutionalized the ideology of gender difference. Conway interprets the development of the women's service professions as a conservative trend in which the potential for change in status remained unrealized.

Students at coeducational colleges and universities

Out of Conway's analysis several themes emerged which have been central to recent historical discussions. Her argument that women's access to higher education did not result in equal intellectual or social opportunity has, perhaps, received the most abundant confirmation. Ronald Hogeland's study of coeducation at Oberlin reinforces Conway's own observations about the social attitudes that informed practices at Oberlin to confine women to a subordinate, domestic role within the college.[61]

[59] Jill K. Conway, "The First Generation of American College Women" (Ph.D. diss., Harvard University, 1968).

[60] Jill K. Conway, "Perspectives on the History of Women's Education in the United States," *History of Education Quarterly* 14, no. 1 (Spring 1974): 1–12, esp. 5–7.

[61] Ronald W. Hogeland, "Coeducation of the Sexes at Oberlin College: A Study of Social Ideas in Mid-Nineteenth-Century America," *Journal of Social History* 6 (Winter 1972): 160–76.

Similar attitudes underlay the program at Grinnell, another midwestern liberal arts college that admitted women from its founding. Joan Zimmerman's study traces a pattern at Grinnell that was typical of many institutions: women students initially enjoyed access to all academic courses available to men, but progressively as their numbers increased and the feminization of the college came to be feared by the male leadership and outside observers, women were segregated into separate academic programs, separate housing units, separate social organizations, and were directed toward the women's professions.[62]

Amy Hague's research on student life at Wisconsin shows that discriminatory attitudes and practices were actually exacerbated by successive moves toward increased integration of men and women after 1875. The segregation at Wisconsin, Hague argues, "encouraged women to have traditional goals, just as it discouraged them from believing in their own capabilities."[63] Florence Howe's comparative study of Wellesley and Stanford provides dramatic evidence that Stanford, in spite of its much heralded mandate to give equal advantages to both sexes, maintained as its real mission the production of educated wives and mothers. Howe argues that women as a group were "invisible" and "ignored" throughout Stanford's history; her portrayal of the efforts of women students to be regarded as intelligent, independent human beings is poignant. One anonymous woman, whose appeal Howe describes, wrote an article in 1909 in which she vigorously opposed a university proposal to introduce courses for women in home economics and child-care, arguing that "the first prerequisite for successful wifehood is freedom. The second is liberty, and the third is independence."[64]

Like Stanford, Cornell, which admitted women in 1872, promised to serve as a new model of educational equality between men and women but failed to meet this challenge. Patricia Foster Haines documents the decline of women's status and the differentiation of women and men students at Cornell in her discussion of the controversy surrounding women's confinement to Sage College.[65] Charlotte Williams Conable's history of women at

[62] Joan Zimmerman, "Daughters of Main Street: Culture and the Female Community at Grinnell, 1884–1912," in *Woman's Being, Woman's Place: Female Identity and Vocation in American History*, ed. Mary Kelley (Boston: G. K. Hall & Co., 1979), 171–93.

[63] Amy Hague, "'What If the Power Does Lie within Me?' Women Students at the University of Wisconsin, 1875–1900," *History of Higher Education Annual* (1984), 78–100, esp. 91. For a more comprehensive study of discrimination at one of the first midwestern universities to admit women, see Dorothy Gies McGuigan, *A Dangerous Experiment: 100 Years of Women at the University of Michigan* (Ann Arbor, Mich.: Center for Continuing Education of Women, 1970).

[64] Florence Howe, "Why Educate Women? The Responses of Wellesley and Stanford," in *Myths of Coeducation—Selected Essays, 1964–1983* (Bloomington: Indiana University Press, 1984), 259–69, esp. 267.

[65] Patricia Foster Haines, "For Honor and Alma Mater: Perspectives on Coeducation at Cornell University, 1868–1885," *Journal of Education* 159, no. 3 (August 1977): 25–37, and

Cornell depicts militant students who asserted their right to equal treatment and actively protested against successive new limitations imposed on them by the university. Still, the Cornell women alone could not alter centuries of tradition that secured the university as a preserve of male privilege, and social equality remained as elusive a goal at Cornell as elsewhere.[66]

Lynn D. Gordon's comparative study of Berkeley and Chicago suggests that women's ability to organize around issues central to their advancement was affected by a variety of external conditions.[67] At Berkeley a tremendous student hostility against women resulted in the wholesale exclusion of women from campus life. Efforts after 1890 to provide separate, compensatory facilities and organizations for women did little to change women's limited expectations about their future social and professional roles, and both women students and faculty remained marginal figures at Berkeley throughout the Progressive Era.

The University of Chicago, on the other hand, was relatively hospitable to women scholars during the first decade after its founding in 1892. Gordon attributes this difference to several distinctive features of the University of Chicago: the university's mission to promote advanced research; the strong and experienced leadership of Deans Alice Freeman Palmer and Marion Talbot, who were both graduates of coeducational universities and former Wellesley colleagues; the presence of a large number of women instructors and graduate scholars (354 in 1900); the support of a group of men faculty; and linkages among academic women, students, and the Hull House reformers in Chicago. Women at Chicago were able to develop a strong and coherent community that reflected patterns already established by the eastern women's colleges and the social settlement movement and that supported both their intellectual accomplishments and distinctive social goals.

Gordon concludes, however, that the social separatism promoted by Talbot at Chicago failed to increase women's influence and to secure a legitimate place for women in the intellectual life of the university. Like Conway and other scholars who observe a decline in feminist activity generally by 1920, Gordon argues that the notions of woman's natural distinctiveness and moral superiority that underlay the separatist strategy at Chicago ultimately undermined women's progress. Chicago women,

---

"Coeducation and the Development of Leadership Skills in Women: Historical Perspectives from Cornell University, 1868–1900," in *Women and Educational Leadership*, ed. Sari Knopp Biklen and Marilyn Brannigan (Lexington, Mass.: D. C. Heath & Co., 1980), 113–28.

[66] Charlotte Williams Conable, *Women at Cornell: The Myth of Equal Education* (Ithaca, N.Y.: Cornell University Press, 1977).

[67] Lynn D. Gordon, "Co-Education on Two Campuses: Berkeley and Chicago, 1890–1912," in Kelley, ed., 171–93.

though more respected than their counterparts at Berkeley, still were vulnerable to the attacks of turn-of-the-century male critics who adopted women's own assertions of their innate differences as the rationale for further discrimination. In spite of the efforts of Talbot and her faculty and alumnae allies to counter the growing antagonism toward coeducation at Chicago as female enrollment increased, women were segregated into a separate junior college in 1902. This program gradually was abandoned, but women lost ground in all fields except education and continued to be excluded from the center of academic life. Gordon concludes that the outcome at Chicago was not in the end significantly different from that at Berkeley: separatism, regardless of its type, reinforced inequality.

Women's research gains

The traditional argument that access to higher education led directly to the intellectual liberation of American women seems, then, to have been put to rest. Nevertheless, the substance and consequences of the gains women did win through their access to higher education have not been thoroughly documented. Rosalind Rosenberg's work represents a turning point in this regard.[68] Rosenberg looks beyond the famous "special generation" of college-trained social reformers and identifies a group of women academics working primarily in the emerging social sciences who in both their professional research and personal lives challenged prevailing notions about sex differences and gender roles.

The University of Chicago around 1900 provided the necessary conditions for this revolution in thinking about woman's nature: a creative research environment, coeducation, and the leadership of women who were committed to the advancement of women's scholarship. Marion Talbot, according to Rosenberg, "represented the cutting edge of a new kind of feminism."[69] Her own field of sanitary science as Talbot conceived it was not, Rosenberg insists, intended to teach girls how to run a home; it was designed to equip social science experts with training in chemistry, physics, physiology, political economy, and modern languages in order that they might successfully address the problems of urbanization. Talbot made it clear in her political activities against the "segregationists" at Chicago that she did not believe that women had different interests or capacities from men. And while she lost a battle when the university established a separate program for women in 1902, the fight over coeduca-

---

[68] Rosalind Rosenberg, *Beyond Separate Spheres: Intellectual Roots of Modern Feminism* (New Haven, Conn.: Yale University Press, 1982).

[69] Rosalind Rosenberg, "The Academic Prism: The New View of American Women," in Berkin and Norton, eds., 318–41, esp. 328.

tion "fueled a movement at Chicago that would, within the next decade, challenge the most basic assumptions about personality formation and sex roles."[70]

According to Rosenberg, the work on gender roles and sex differences of researchers such as Helen Thompson and Jesse Taft at Chicago, and Leta Hollingworth and Elsie Clews Parsons at Columbia and Barnard, signaled a triumph for women in higher education and had a major impact on feminism. However, Rosenberg is quick to point out the losses that women suffered as the disciplines matured. The achievements of the first generation were difficult to build on. Male-centered values of science and professionalism undercut the values of the female culture and political climate that had united nineteenth-century women, leaving twentieth-century women scholars isolated in an alien and often hostile world.

Furthermore, as Margaret Rossiter argues, the laboratory findings of this group of women social scientists may have influenced the research of some of their colleagues, but their research on sex differences did not have a significant impact on the behavior of male academics generally or on the policies and practices of institutions.[71] Even those universities that trained large numbers of women doctoral students usually refused to hire them as faculty. As old barriers against women's participation in academe were lowered, Rossiter points out, new hurdles such as antinepotism rules and the tenure track appeared that excluded women or confined them to certain fields, to the lower ranks, and to adjunct positions. By every measure, academic women were paid much less than academic men; their exclusion from professional and social organizations as well as their disproportionate share of teaching duties limited women's opportunities to pursue advanced research; and, not surprisingly, despite their greatly increased numbers and percentages in the 1920s and 1930s, women did not advance "normally" within their disciplines or institutions. Some saw this as evidence of women's lesser ability.

Partially in response to this growing hostility in the male research world, many women retreated to all-female enclaves where they could exercise some authority and strive as individuals for excellence in their chosen work. Rossiter documents a major shift in the tactics of women scientists after 1910 from confrontational politics and overt efforts to achieve full equality with men on university faculties to the more conservative strategy of accepting prevailing inequities and working for limited personal gains. Women scientists, as a result of both institutional discrimination and this new strategy, Rossiter explains, became even more invisible—confined to marginal positions in laboratories, or outside the major

[70] Ibid., 328.
[71] Margaret W. Rossiter, *Women Scientists in America: Struggles and Strategies to 1940* (Baltimore: Johns Hopkins University Press, 1982).

research centers in women's colleges, schools of home economics, and in separate women's scientific organizations. Not unlike their nineteenth-century predecessors—the amateur scientists whom Sally Gregory Kohlstedt introduces to us in her study of women working outside the academy—twentieth-century women scientists worked on the periphery.[72]

Women's institutions

The advantages and disadvantages to women of working in such enclaves still are unclear. Joyce Antler's portrait of the life and work of Lucy Sprague Mitchell, Radcliffe alumna, Berkeley Dean of Women, and founder of the Bank Street School, illuminates the positive, feminist goals of self-determination and autonomy that Mitchell was able to achieve within the "woman's world" of early childhood education—a field she helped to pioneer. Antler shows that within this realm, Mitchell and others were able to advance their work as scientific professionals and at the same time perpetuate the humanistic values of the female world in their professional lives. Antler argues that Bank Street as an institution exemplified "a mediation of public and private spheres," and as such it reflected Mitchell's personal effort to merge her own marriage, motherhood, and scientific training into a profession that could support her multiple ambitions.[73]

For others, the women's colleges provided a superior professional environment where similar community supports and the attributes of the female culture that had been so critical to women's initial successes in academe were still intact. Patricia Palmieri's work on the Wellesley faculty reveals a community of senior women professors whose careers flourished in the supportive setting of Wellesley College.[74] Wellesley, unlike Harvard or Johns Hopkins where the isolated, specialized researcher increasingly was becoming the faculty norm, provided a home as well as an intellectual haven. Palmieri's portrait reveals a world in which family, friendship, and professional activity overlapped. Collaboration was standard, and scholars such as Katharine Lee Bates, Vida Scudder, Emily Greene Balch, and Katharine Coman wrote books together, traveled and built homes together, and jointly sponsored political and social reform efforts such as

---

[72] Sally Gregory Kohlstedt, "In from the Periphery: American Women in Science, 1830–1880," *Signs* 4, no. 1 (Autumn 1978): 81–96.

[73] Joyce Antler, "Feminism as Life-Process: The Life and Career of Lucy Sprague Mitchell," *Feminist Studies* 7, no. 1 (Spring 1981): 134–57, esp. 150.

[74] Patricia A. Palmieri, "Here Was Fellowship: A Social Portrait of Academic Women at Wellesley College, 1895–1920," *History of Education Quarterly* 23, no. 2 (Summer 1983): 195–214, "Patterns of Achievement of Single Academic Women at Wellesley College, 1880–1920," *Frontiers* 5, no. 1 (Spring 1980): 63–67, and "*Incipit Vita Nuova*: Founding Ideals of the Wellesley College Community," *History of Higher Education Annual* (1983), 59–78.

the founding of Denison House, a social settlement in Boston. A virtual colony of devoted mothers and sisters settled at Wellesley and provided the further domestic and psychological support that served as a critical precondition for these women's extraordinary achievements.[75]

Palmieri acknowledges, however, that many of these women academics were not at Wellesley by choice alone—they were locked out of the research universities. Though most Wellesley professors were highly productive scholars, they might have accomplished even more had heavy teaching loads and administrative duties not forced them often to set aside important research projects. A commitment to Wellesley and a desire to remain within its close community, moreover, discouraged some professors from accepting offers for advancement elsewhere. To others, however, it was clear that Wellesley offered the best professional environment available. Palmieri tells us, for instance, that senior philosopher Mary Calkins rejected an offer from Columbia not only because she wanted to remain close to her family and friends at Wellesley, but also because she feared being "trapped" teaching elementary courses at the male-dominated university. Whether women's colleges other than Wellesley served faculty in the same way will remain difficult to evaluate until comparable research on other educational institutions is accomplished.[76]

[75] Joyce Antler, "'After College, What?': New Graduates and the Family Claim," *American Quarterly* 32 (Fall 1980): 409–34. For documentation and extended discussions of this theme, see Solomon (n. 27 above), 115–40; and Pamela J. Perun and Janet Z. Giele, "Life after College: Historical Links between Women's Education and Women's Work," in *The Undergraduate Woman: Issues in Educational Equity*, ed. Pamela J. Perun (Lexington, Mass.: D. C. Heath & Co., 1982), 375–98.

[76] Very little research, for instance, has been done on male faculties other than those at prominent research universities or on the differences between men's and women's liberal arts colleges. For a further examination of this problem, see Patricia A. Palmieri, "Paths and Pitfalls: Illuminating Woman's Educational History," *Harvard Educational Review* 49, no. 4 (November 1979): 447–541; and Geraldine Jonçich Clifford, "'Shaking Dangerous Questions from the Crease': Gender and American Higher Education," *Feminist Issues* 3, no. 2 (Fall 1983): 3–61. Two studies that would figure importantly into new research are Helen Lefkowitz Horowitz's recent work, *Alma Mater: Design and Experience in the Women's Colleges from Their Nineteenth-Century Beginnings to the 1930s* (New York: Alfred A. Knopf, 1984), and Sally Gregory Kohlstedt's study of Simmons College, "Single-Sex Education and Leadership: The Early Years of Simmons College," in Biklen and Brannigan, eds., 93–112, esp. 98. Horowitz argues that the differing architectural styles and campus plans of the women's colleges (domestic cottages at Smith, Gothic halls at Bryn Mawr) reflect opposing concepts of women's education and link women's colleges to the larger universe of nineteenth-century institution building and utopian thought. This relationship of material culture to collegiate life is a provocative subject, heretofore little studied. Kohlstedt's study of Simmons reveals a community in which women students were expected to pursue careers and graduated to become leaders in the new public service fields of library science, social work, institutional management, and public health nursing. Kohlstedt's data on the high percentage of graduates who combined marriage and careers in the early part of the twentieth century is particularly striking and points to the importance of studying institutions and programs for women outside the liberal arts.

According to several recent studies, the so-called Seven Sister Colleges (Barnard, Bryn Mawr, Mount Holyoke, Radcliffe, Smith, Vassar, and Wellesley) all seem to have been more successful historically at producing career-oriented graduates than have coeducational colleges and universities (though debate continues over the reasons for this apparent success). Mary J. Oates and Susan Williamson argue that the relatively high socioeconomic levels of the families who sent their daughters to these colleges may have been an important factor in their subsequent success.[77] Elizabeth Tidball, whose pioneering study of the baccalaureate origins of women cited in *Who's Who of American Women* started this debate, argues that her conclusions regarding the higher achievement of women's college graduates hold true for both elite women's colleges and less selective institutions when they are measured against comparable coeducational schools.[78] Tidball's statistics show that women who attended women's colleges between 1910 and 1959 were approximately twice as likely as those who attended coeducational colleges or universities to be cited in any of several registries, including *Who's Who in America*, the source analyzed by Oates and Williamson. Tidball further correlates women's success after graduation with the presence of large numbers of women faculty and with small numbers of men students on campus.

The successful women who appear in the *Who's Who* series upon which these studies are based, however, represent only a limited range of careers: scientists, for instance, typically do not show up in the standard compendia. This leads Rossiter and others to challenge some of the conclusions that have been drawn about the women's colleges. It may be that obstacles inherent in the various disciplines and professions have conditioned women's ability to achieve recognition more significantly than the variables associated with the women's colleges.[79]

[77] Mary J. Oates and Susan Williamson, "Women's Colleges and Women Achievers," *Signs* 3, no. 4 (Summer 1978): 795–806.

[78] M. Elizabeth Tidball, "Perspective on Academic Women and Affirmative Action," *Educational Record* 54, no. 2 (Spring 1973): 130–35, and "Women's Colleges and Women Achievers Revisited," *Signs* 5, no. 3 (Spring 1980): 504–17.

[79] Margaret W. Rossiter, "Women Scientists in America before 1920," *American Scientist* 62, no. 3 (May/June 1974): 312–23, and "'Women's Work' in Science, 1880–1910," *Isis* 71, no. 258 (September 1980): 381–98. Rossiter argues further in "Sexual Segregation in the Sciences: Some Data and a Model," *Signs* 4, no. 1 (Autumn 1978): 146–51, that the growth rate of a science, which has a strong effect on the careers of scientists in that field, historically has had a different impact on women scientists than on men. Contrary to expectations, women did not necessarily do well in the fastest growing fields between 1921 and 1938; women had a comparative advantage in stagnant or shrinking fields because they were more willing than men to endure the bleak employment prospects. Rossiter concludes that many of the new exclusionary practices associated with the professionalization of science and technology in America developed in direct relation to the growing numbers of women who were available and qualified to enter the new and growing fields.

Women academics and the research university

Patricia Albjerg Graham has shown that such obstacles increased throughout academe as the new value system of the research university, with its emphasis on scholarship, became the standard for assessing prestige in American higher education generally. The coeducational liberal arts colleges, state universities, normal schools, and single-sex colleges which had provided new opportunities for the first generations of college and university-trained women after 1875, Graham argues, by 1925 were faced with the choice of either transforming their programs and standards to come into closer alignment with the model of the research university, or of retaining their traditional standards and thus losing relative acclaim and public support. Women suffered as a result of this growing influence of research: historically women were excluded as participants from the universities now setting the standard; the behaviors required of the professional scholar grew increasingly more at odds with society's prescriptions of the feminine ideal; and the academic roles and institutions to which women had gained access declined in number and prestige.[80]

In fact, according to Graham, women's participation in academic life relative to men was actually higher in 1930 than in 1970. Women undergraduates, for instance, represented 47 percent of the national total in 1920 but then declined to an average of 38 percent over the next five decades and had not fully recouped by 1976 when women accounted for 45 percent of the undergraduate population. Women college presidents, professors, and instructors represented a record 32.5 percent of the total in 1930, but thereafter women's share of such academic positions declined steadily until 1960.[81] Susan Boslego Carter offers persuasive evidence that this last decline did not begin until World War II—an important refinement that is consistent with Frank Stricker's findings on women in the professions.[82] Graham's analysis, nevertheless, makes it clear that whatever their numerical gains or personal successes in higher education, women as a class suffered during the middle decades of this century relative to men.

Rossiter agrees. She concludes that the period from 1920 to 1940 was one of social and psychological containment for academic women despite their overall numerical expansion. Furthermore, in Rossiter's analysis the "sociopolitical concept of prestige" was even more at the heart of discrim-

[80] Patricia Albjerg Graham, "Expansion and Exclusion: A History of Women in American Higher Education," *Signs* 3, no. 4 (Summer 1978): 759–73.

[81] Graham, "Expansion and Exclusion," 764 and table 1, 766.

[82] Susan Boslego Carter, "Academic Women Revisited: An Empirical Study of Changing Patterns in Women's Employment as College and University Faculty, 1890–1963," *Journal of Social History* 14 (Summer 1981): 675–700; Frank Stricker, "Cookbooks and Law Books: The Hidden History of Career Women in Twentieth-Century America," *Journal of Social History* 10 (Fall 1976): 1–19. Stricker also points out that women maintained career aspirations and entered the professional ranks in impressive numbers even after their percentages declined.

ination against women academics than even Graham's discussion would lead us to conclude.[83] Even while prestige differences among institutions was a factor that put women at a disadvantage over time, Rossiter argues that gender became so overriding a consideration in assessing the prestige of one's work that scholarship produced by women was by definition deemed inferior. The concept of prestige thus "guaranteed that whatever the quality of [women's] work, its value would be diminished and their share in a career's normal recognition and glory withheld."[84]

New directions

Over the past decade since Conway, Graham, and others first outlined a new research agenda for the study of women's educational history, significant efforts have been made to redeem that recognition. It remains to be seen, however, at what pace and to what degree this scholarship will change standard thinking about youth and education in America. To date, there has been little evidence that scholars working outside the field of women's history have seriously reconsidered the impact of women's culture on American education. With the exception of an occasional section on leaders such as Catharine Beecher and Mary Lyon, even the most ambitious recent histories have neglected gender as a category of analysis.

The potential for reformulating the history of American education, however, is great. Recent and ongoing studies by Brickley, Scott, Solomon, and others on the female academy and women's seminaries suggest that we no longer can think of the beginnings of secondary education in America exclusively as a utilitarian response to new economic roles for men. The very definition of adolescence in discussions of nineteenth-century youth is challenged by the work of Allmendinger and Clifford on the relationship of the female life cycle to work and education. Antler and Rosenberg have shown that the Progressive movement was not only the effort to tame private enterprise, as it long has been characterized, but was also an effort to redefine women's relationship to the public sphere. The research of Kohlstedt, Rossiter, and others confirms that gender was a more salient feature than any of the other social factors associated with the "culture of professionalism." It is now clear that the standard account of the rise of the American university and professional training is a partial truth at best.

This list is not meant to be exhaustive, nor are the studies cited more than a representation of a larger and impressive body of work now being pursued, much of which is yet unpublished. Critical gaps still exist; the

---

[83] Rossiter, *Women Scientists in America*, 216.
[84] Ibid.

research on normal schools, vocational programs, and nonelite institutions outlined a decade ago is not much advanced, and only a few subgroups of women and geographic regions have been investigated with any thoroughness. Moreover, topics such as curricular and pedagogical reform, which have been a traditional concern in the history of American education, have not yet been addressed from a feminist perspective. Nevertheless, a vigorous assessment of the contributions of women scholars, educational reformers, and the profession of teaching to American feminism clearly is underway, and the story that Thomas Woody began to tell in the 1920s has found its voice in a new generation of women's studies scholars.

Graduate School of Education
Harvard University

WOMEN'S COLLEGES AND WOMEN ACHIEVERS

MARY J. OATES AND SUSAN WILLIAMSON

In recent years, a number of studies have analyzed successful women and attempted to determine those factors which aided or impeded the development of their leadership qualities. These studies generally fall into one of two categories: (1) studies which focus mainly on the characteristics of women working in specific fields over limited chronological periods[1] or (2) surveys of successful college graduates which examine significant features such as educational background but which do not differentiate the women by occupation in much detail.[2] While the importance of higher education to future success has long been accepted, there is need for more knowledge about the relationships between the type of college education received and subsequent educational decisions, the field of work chosen, and the degree of career success.[3] This paper aims to extend our knowledge in this area.

American women seeking a college education have had a choice

---

1. See e. g., Margaret W. Rossiter, "Women Scientists in America before 1920," *American Scientist* 62 (May–June 1974): 312–23; and Margaret Hennig, "Career Development for Women Executives" (Ph.D. diss., Harvard University, 1971).

2. Most notable here is the work of M. Elizabeth Tidball: "Some Undergraduate Institutional Factors Associated with the Probability of Career Success" (paper presented at the annual meeting of the American Association for the Advancement of Science, Washington, D.C., December 27, 1972); "Perspective on Academic Women and Affirmative Action," *Educational Record* 54 (Spring 1973): 130–35; "The Search for Talented Women," *Change* 6 (May 1974): 51; and "Women on Campus—and You," *Liberal Education* 61 (May 1975): 285–92.

3. This need is emphasized by Hilda Kahne, "Employment Prospects and Academic Politics," in *Women and Success*, ed. Ruth B. Kundsin (New York: William Morrow & Co., 1974), p. 167. Of course many women achieve success without a college education. Their experience certainly merits study.

This essay originally appeared in *Signs*, vol. 3, no. 4, Summer 1978.

between a women's college and a coeducational college. If the education and opportunities received in these two types of institutions are identical, then the continued existence of women's colleges would be more a function of tradition than need, a reminder that they were initially established because women were not admitted or, if admitted, only tolerated in many of the nation's leading academic institutions. In recent years, as men's colleges have opened their doors to women, the role of the women's college in higher education has been increasingly questioned. However, a number of studies defending the women's college have appeared, the best known a series of papers by Tidball and a 1973 report by the Carnegie Commission.[4] Such studies argue that women's colleges have produced a disproportionate share of women leaders in American society, and for two major reasons: first, they provide women with more opportunities than coeducational institutions for academic and campus leadership at a critical point in life; and second, they seem to encourage women to concentrate in more unconventional areas of study than do coeducational schools, thus expanding later career horizons. Although the Tidball and Carnegie studies have been frequently cited by nationally recognized leaders in women's education,[5] there has been little serious critical analysis of their major claims. In this paper, we focus on some of these interrelated claims by comparing the occupational choices of leading graduates of women's colleges with those of leading graduates among coeducational-college women. For if such claims can be supported, then stronger arguments than tradition and diversity of option can be made for the retention of existing colleges for women and, indeed, for their expansion within the framework of American higher education.

I. The Data

The basic data source used for our study is *Who's Who in America, 38th Edition, 1974–1975*.[6] Despite some drawbacks, this is the most comprehensive and selective compilation of eminent living Americans available, and it is not restricted by sex. Since we were interested in the occupational choices of society's leading women, we chose to define "suc-

4. Tidball (n. 2 above); and Carnegie Commission on Higher Education, *Opportunities for Women in Higher Education* (New York: McGraw-Hill Book Co., 1973).
5. E.g., see David Truman, "The Women's Movement and the Women's College," in *Women in Higher Education*, ed. W. Todd Furniss and Patricia A. Graham (Washington, D.C.: American Council on Education, 1974), p. 59; Jill K. Conway, "Coeducation and Women's Studies: Two Approaches to the Question of Woman's Place in the Contemporary University," *Daedalus* 103 (Fall 1974): 240; and Barbara W. Newell, "Statement to Department of Health, Education and Welfare regarding the Proposed Title IX Regulations," mimeographed (Wellesley, Mass.: Wellesley College, October 8, 1974).
6. Chicago: Marquis Who's Who, Inc., 1974.

cess" in accordance with the criteria applied in determining society's successful men.[7] More than 3,000 women appeared in *Who's Who, 1974–1975*, but the following were excluded from our consideration: (1) all women who had not received a bachelor's degree, which accounted for the largest number of exclusions; (2) graduates of colleges outside the United States; (3) graduates of several obscure institutions not included in conventional listings of American colleges and universities; and (4) women whose entry data were either incomplete or ambiguous regarding college, type of degree, year of graduation, or occupation.[8] This left us with 1,735 college graduates, more than half of all female entries. Ninety percent of these women graduated from college between 1920 and 1959. Mortality and youth, respectively, contribute to the low representation of the first two decades and the post-1959 years (see table 1, col. 1). In the period 1920–59, the earlier decades show a higher percentage of the total graduating from women's colleges, because coeducational opportunities for women were more limited in those years (table 1, col. 2). Overall, we found that of the 1,735 achievers 61 percent were graduates of coeducational colleges and 39 percent of women's colleges.

Table 1

Distribution of Achievers by Decade of Graduation: All
Achievers and Women's-College Achievers
(%)

Decade	(1)*	(2)†	(3)‡	(4)§
1900–1909	1.0	70.6	83.3	58.8
1910–19	4.8	51.8	72.1	37.4
1920–29	23.5	41.5	69.2	28.7
1930–39	32.2	36.6	50.5	18.5
1940–49	23.6	39.0	45.6	17.8
1950–59	10.6	32.6	51.7	16.9
1960–69	4.3	35.1	50.0	17.6
1970+	.1	. . .	. . .	. . .
1900–1970	. . .	38.8	56.1	21.8

*Total number of achievers in decade/all achievers (N = 1,735).
†Women's-college (WC) achievers/all achievers.
‡SS achievers/WC achievers.
§SS achievers/all achievers.

7. Many of the qualifications noted by Carolyn S. Bell in her examination of *American Men in Science* may be applied to the directory used in this study; see her "Definitions and Data for Economic Analysis," in Kundsin, pp. 151–59.

8. In the case of the woman who attended more than one college, the college considered was the one from which she received her degree. Similarly, although some women had more than one occupation over the years, the latest one reported is identified as her occupation. The occupation of the retired woman is considered to be her last position before retirement.

II. Comparative Rates of Achiever Production: 1930–39

In her study Tidball used *Who's Who of American Women* and found the rate of achiever production of women's colleges to be approximately twice that of coeducational colleges over the five-decade period from 1910 to 1959.[9] In order to determine whether or not women's colleges maintain their higher rate of achiever production in the more selective listing of *Who's Who in America,* we examined the colleges of those achievers listed who graduated during the 1930s, because it is the single decade with the highest representation of achievers (nearly one-third of the total number of achievers graduated during those years) and because those women are still active in their professions. We found that the overall rate of achiever production[10] for this decade was twenty-six achievers per 10,000 graduates for the women's colleges[11] and fourteen per 10,000 women graduates for the coeducational institutions (table 2, col. 3). Thus the women's colleges produced achievers at 1.9 times the rate of the coeducational institutions, a result consistent with Tidball's study. When women's colleges, which are almost exclusively institutions of smaller size, are compared with the small coeducational institutions—defined as having fewer than 500 graduates per year—they still maintain their higher rate of achiever production.[12] Specifically, the rate is twenty-nine achievers per 10,000 graduates for women's colleges and eighteen per 10,000 women graduates for the coeducational colleges. Therefore the small women's colleges produce achievers at 1.6 times the rate of the small coeducational schools, a figure only slightly less than the result for the entire group.

This remarkable difference between the rates for the two types of institution calls for a closer investigation of the women's colleges which actually produced achievers in the 1930s. The absolute number of achievers is of interest in this context. Columns 1 and 2 of table 2 report that during the 1930s fifty-five of the fifty-six achiever-producing women's colleges had fewer than 500 graduates per year and produced, collectively, 187 achievers. The contribution of individual colleges to the

9. Tidball, "Perspective on Academic Women," p. 132.

10. The rate of achiever production of a college (or a collection of colleges) over a given period of time refers to the ratio of the total number of achievers produced by the college(s) during that period to the total number of women graduates produced during the same period. Aggregate data for colleges are taken from U.S. Office of Education, *Biennial Surveys of Education in the United States* (Washington, D.C.: Government Printing Office, 1928–38).

11. The coordinate college is classified as a women's college. This is a "separate but parallel" college for women such as Radcliffe (Harvard) and Newcomb (Tulane). Such colleges produced 22 percent of the women's-college graduates investigated in this study.

12. Hunter College produced an average of over 1,000 graduates per year during the decade of the 1930s, while the largest achiever-producing coeducational colleges graduated approximately 3,000 persons (men and women) per year over the same period.

total varied widely, with the number of achievers ranging between one and twenty-seven. (The corresponding range for small coeducational colleges is one to seven women achievers.)[13] For seven of these small women's colleges, the range is eleven to twenty-seven, while the other forty-eight show a range of one to five achievers. The seven colleges are Barnard, Bryn Mawr, Mount Holyoke, Radcliffe, Smith, Vassar, and Wellesley, the so-called Seven Sisters. This difference of range separates the small women's colleges into two relatively homogeneous classes and justifies the consideration of three rather than two types of institutions of higher learning: the Seven Sisters (SS), the non–Seven Sisters Women's colleges (NSS), and the coeducational colleges (CC). The SS produced achievers at the rate of sixty-one per 10,000 graduates during the decade of the 1930s. In sharp contrast, the small NSS and small CC each pro-

Table 2

Achievers in *Who's Who* Graduating from 1930 to 1939, by Type and Size of Institution

Size*	Number of Institutions (1)	Total Number of Achievers (2)	Rate of Achiever Production (per 10,000 Women Graduates) (3)
Women's colleges:			
1–499	55	187	29
500 +	1	13	11
Total	56	200	26
Seven Sisters:			
1–499	7	103	61
Non–Seven Sisters Women's Colleges:			
1–499	48	84	18
500 +	1	13	11
Total	49	97	16
Coeducational institutions:			
1–499	115	155	18
500 +	43	190	12
Total	158	345	14

*The size of a college is measured by its average number of graduates per year over the 1930–39 period.

13. It is inappropriate to make absolute comparisons of numbers of women achievers graduating from women's colleges and coeducational colleges, since the latter may also have produced male achievers. The maximum number of women achievers produced by a single coeducational college of any size during the 1930s is fifteen.

duced at a rate of eighteen achievers per 10,000 women graduates. The SS rate was 3.4 times that of all other small colleges and four times that of all other institutions, regardless of size. With the exception of the 1940s, at no time do they account for fewer than half of women's-college achievers. Overall, 21.8 percent of the 1,735 achievers graduated from these seven schools (see table 1). The results of this analysis of the 1930s data lead us to believe that comparisons between women's colleges and coeducational colleges with regard to achievers in all decades should include separate and detailed consideration of the two subgroups of women's colleges.

III. Occupational Choices and College Type: 1900–1970

If we accept the notion that women's-college students have tended to choose a wider range of majors, including the sciences, than have coeducational-college women,[14] we should expect, other things being equal, that these colleges in the aggregate would show a pattern of occupational distribution of their eminent alumnae which differs significantly from the pattern of successful coeducational-college graduates. To test this hypothesis, we identified five major occupational categories—arts, business/management, government service, professions, and other work—and classified the 1,735 women in these broad areas.[15] The largest number of women reported their occupation to be one of the professions, with academic professions accounting for 37.5 percent of achievers and nonacademic professions for 25.9 percent.[16] The arts and business occupied 15.2 and 10.6 percent, respectively. The smallest representations were found in "other work" (6.0 percent) and government service (4.7 percent).

In order to determine whether or not the women's-college graduates differed from coeducational-college graduates in occupational choice, we first compared the distribution of achievers within their own respective groups. For example, we analyzed the proportion of the

14. A recent analysis of 137 institutions granting the baccalaureate degree supports Newcomer's finding that students in the single-sex college are more likely to concentrate in areas atypical for their sex than are coeducational college students. Her study of fourteen selected schools reported that in the coeducational colleges 10 percent of the women students majored in the natural sciences, while 19 percent of women's-college students chose those fields. See M. Elizabeth Tidball and Vera Kistiakowsky, "Baccalaureate Origins of American Scientists and Scholars," *Science* 193 (August 20, 1976): 651, citing M. Newcomer, *A Century of Higher Education for Women* (New York: Harper Bros., 1959), p. 95.

15. See Appendix. These categories correspond, with slight modifications, to the "Titles or Functions" listed in the *Who's Who of American Women* questionnaire for the eighth edition.

16. Of academic professionals, 98 percent are engaged in college and university teaching and administration.

674 achievers that the women's colleges produced in each of the major occupational groupings and examined whether these proportions differ from the distribution of the 1,061 coeducational-college achievers over the same categories. Columns 1 and 2 of table 3 show that the basic distributional patterns are not significantly different from each other.[17] Despite this absence of significant differences in the patterns of achiever distribution over the five major occupational categories, it is still possible that differences may exist in achiever patterns over individual occupations within these broad categories. A more disaggregated analysis which focused on the heterogeneity among individual occupations concealed by the broader classification was required. Thus we considered each occupation listed in the Appendix with at least twenty-five achievers. Table 4 indicates that there are no significant differences in the proportional representation of coeducational-college and women's-college achievers in the individual occupations within the arts. But differences do occur within certain occupations in the other four major categories. The coeducational-college achievers are more highly represented than the women's-college achievers as government officials, deans of professional schools,[18] teachers of professional subjects,[19] and librarians. Women's-college achievers, on the other hand, are more highly represented among curators, college presidents, editors, and civic workers. In general, the difference between the positions of the coeducational-college achievers and those of the women's-college achievers seems to be

Table 3

1,735 Achievers Classified by Occupational Group and College Type: Women's Colleges and Coeducational Colleges
(%)

Occupational Group	(1)*	(2)†	Significance Test‡
Arts	16.3	14.4	N.S.
Business/management	12.3	9.5	N.S.
Government service	3.6	5.5	N.S.
Professions	60.8	65.2	N.S.
Academic	35.6	38.7	N.S.
Nonacademic	25.2	26.5	N.S.
Other work	7.0	5.4	N.S.

*WC achievers in occupational group/all WC achievers ($N = 674$).
†Coeducational-college (CC) achievers in occupational group/all CC achievers ($N = 1,061$).
‡Cols. 1 and 2 are nonsignificantly different at $P < .05$.

17. The differences are nonsignificant at $P < .05$. Significance levels are determined by χ^2, using a two-tailed test in all cases.

18. Most coeducational-college achievers in this category are deans of schools of home economics, library science, and nursing.

19. Over three-fourths of all coeducational-college achievers in this category are engaged in teaching home economics/nutrition, nursing, and medicine.

Table 4

1,735 Achievers by Occupation and College Type: Women's Colleges and
Coeducational Colleges
(%)

Occupations with at Least 25 Achievers	(1)[a]	(2)[b]	Significance Test
Author	10.8	8.4	N.S.
Artist (performing)	2.7	2.4	N.S.
Artist (applied)	1.9	2.5	N.S.
Administrator	1.2	2.0	N.S.
Business executive	5.5	4.5	N.S.
Curator/museum official	2.7	.9	*
Association executive	2.5	1.8	N.S.
Government official	3.0	4.9	*
College/university administration:			
President	4.0	.8	*
Dean	4.0	3.4	N.S.
Dean of professional school	1.9	4.4	*
College/university teaching:			
Humanities	8.6	9.0	N.S.
Social sciences	6.5	8.3	N.S.
Natural sciences	6.2	5.2	N.S.
Professional subjects	2.4	5.7	*
Editor	7.0	2.6	*
Attorney	1.3	2.6	N.S.
Physician	3.1	2.6	N.S.
Librarian	5.0	8.5	*
Journalist	2.1	2.9	N.S.
Civic worker	3.4	1.5	*
Consultant/lecturer	1.2	1.8	N.S.
Other	13.0	13.3	N.S.

[a]WC achievers in occupation/all WC achievers (N = 674).
[b]CC achievers in occupation/all CC achievers (N = 1,061).
*Cols. 1 and 2 are significantly different at $P < .05$.

that the former require certifiable skills for entry and the latter liberal arts and sometimes graduate education, but not specific skills. The fact that fourteen of the twenty-seven college presidents who graduated from women's colleges could be identified as members of religious orders at the time of their appointment helps to account for the relative strength of women's colleges in this area, since membership in an associated order has traditionally been a prerequisite for the presidency of many Catholic women's colleges. (This clustering of women in religious orders does not occur among academic administrators other than presidents.)

After investigating the differences between women's colleges and coeducational institutions, we proceeded to determine whether SS achievers show a different occupational pattern from NSS achievers. The distributions of SS and NSS women over the five major occupational categories are given in table 5. Within the arts and the professions, we

Table 5

674 Women's-College Achievers Classified by Occupational Group and
College Type: SS and NSS Colleges
(%)

Occupational Group	(1)[a]	(2)[b]	Significance Test
Arts	20.4	11.1	*
Business/management	11.9	12.8	N.S.
Government service	4.0	3.0	N.S.
Professions	55.3	67.9	*
Academic	28.8	44.3	*
Nonacademic	26.5	23.6	N.S.
Other work	8.5	5.1	N.S.

[a] SS achievers in occupational group/all SS achievers (N = 378).
[b] NSS achievers in occupational group/all NSS achievers (N = 296).
*Cols. 1 and 2 are significantly different at P < .05.

find significant differences in the proportions of SS and NSS achievers. If we examine next the individual occupations with at least twenty-five achievers, we note that SS achievers are more highly represented among authors, physicians, and civic workers than are NSS achievers. The NSS colleges show greater strength among college presidents, deans, deans of professional schools, and librarians (see table 6). The earlier observation about college presidents pertains here also, since religious sisters account for fourteen of the twenty presidents who graduated from NSS colleges. With the exception of physicians, it does not appear that SS graduates are more likely to be found in atypical areas than are NSS graduates.

IV. Conclusions

This analysis of the occupational distribution of a large number of eminent college graduates suggests that explanations for the different impact of women's colleges and coeducational colleges in producing leaders may need further qualification and study. First, although women's colleges have graduated notable women at a higher rate than have coeducational colleges, a large number of these achievers come from a small group of seven colleges. It is not sufficient to observe that these colleges were more selective in admissions than the other women's colleges. Rather, it is our contention that the average socioeconomic level of the student body in these seven colleges may be even more critical in accounting for the differences, although selectivity does remain a factor. The SS have long been considered the female analogue of the most prestigious and selective men's colleges. Had Ivy League colleges been open to women during the period under study, it is likely that some SS graduates would have chosen to attend them instead. The question that

Table 6

674 Women's-College Achievers by Occupation and College Type: SS
Colleges and NSS Colleges
(%)

Occupations with at Least 25 Achievers	(1)[a]	(2)[b]	Significance Test
Author	15.1	5.4	*
Artist (performing)	2.1	3.4	N.S.
Artist (applied)	1.9	2.0	N.S.
Administrator	.5	2.0	...[c]
Business executive	5.8	5.1	N.S.
Curator/museum official	3.2	2.0	N.S.
Association executive	1.9	3.4	N.S.
Government official	4.0	1.7	N.S.
College/university administration:			
President	1.9	6.8	*
Dean	2.4	6.1	*
Dean of professional school	.3	4.1	*
College/university teaching:			
Humanities	9.3	7.8	N.S.
Social sciences	7.1	5.7	N.S.
Natural sciences	4.8	8.1	N.S.
Professional subjects	1.9	3.0	N.S.
Editor	8.5	5.1	N.S.
Attorney	1.1	1.7	...[c]
Physician	5.0	.7	*
Librarian	2.4	8.4	*
Journalist	2.4	1.7	N.S.
Civic worker	4.8	1.7	*
Consultant/lecturer	.8	1.7	...[c]
Other	12.8	12.4	N.S.

[a]SS achievers in occupation/all SS achievers (N = 378).
[b]NSS achievers in occupation/all NSS achievers (N = 296).
[c]χ^2 test inapplicable.
*Cols. 1 and 2 are significantly different at $P < .05$.

remains to be answered is whether these women would have achieved as much had they been graduates of coeducational Ivy League colleges. As the first women graduates of the Ivy League colleges select careers, we will have the data to examine such questions.

Second, the claim that women's colleges prepare their students for a wider range of challenging careers by encouraging study in nontraditional fields is not supported by our investigation of their leading graduates. We have found that women's-college achievers were distributed among five basic occupational categories in proportions similar to those of their coeducational counterparts and that, even within occupational areas, there were few significant differences between the two types of college. It is not traditional compared with nontraditional occupations that differentiate the choices of achievers from coeducational institutions and women's colleges but, rather, that the occupations in which the former show strength require, unlike the latter, specific skills for job entry. Differences between the two types of women's college within individual occupations have been noted in the body of this paper and could provide the basis for a more detailed study of women's colleges.[20] Indeed, our study gives rise to several interesting topics for future research. (1) A decadal analysis of the occupational choices of achievers may reveal new differences among college types and assist in explaining the differences noted here. It may be that changing admissions patterns in recent years have affected occupational patterns among the three college types. (2) Consideration of additional factors such as external control (e.g., public, private, or religious) and institutional size may shed light on questions of occupational choice. (3) A more detailed occupational analysis may suggest that women tend to achieve success in settings in which their clients, coworkers, subordinates, or superiors are women. (4) An examination of the socioeconomic backgrounds of students attracted to various institutional types may provide additional insights into the issues raised in this paper, since wealth and family status have long been recognized as aids to career success. Investigation of these and related questions will add significantly to what is known about the career consequences of higher education of women.

American institutions of higher education, regardless of their sex composition, have produced women leaders who are more heavily concentrated in the arts and the professions, both academic and nonacademic, than in such areas as business/management and government work. The concentration of achievers from both women's colleges and coeducational colleges is low in many of the traditionally male occupations such as photographer and producer in the arts, broker in the area of business/management, and dentist and engineer in the nonacademic professions. In those traditionally male occupations in which women have achieved in sufficient numbers to be considered in our tables, such as business executive and physician, we find no significant differences between the two types of school. American higher education has produced women leaders, but the pattern of their occupational choices seems to conform to society's expectations of women at work.

Appendix

Occupational Categories by Title or Function

Arts

Author	Director (performing arts)
Artist (performing)	Producer (performing arts)

20. E.g., socioeconomic differences between SS and NSS graduates may account for the relatively higher proportion of SS achievers found in the civic-worker category, where volunteer workers are not uncommon.

Artist (applied)
Designer
Composer

Interior decorator
Photographer

Business/Management

Accountant/auditor
Administrator
Business executive
Broker
Contractor
Curator/museum official

Data processor
Corporate director
Statistician/actuary
Association executive
Owner/proprietor/partner
Realtor

Government

Government official

Military Officer

Professions: Academic

Educational administrator,
  college/university:
  President
  Dean[21]
  Dean of professional school
  Other
Educational administrator,
  elementary/secondary

Educator, college/university:
  Humanities
  Social sciences
  Natural sciences
  Professional subjects
Educator, elementary/secondary

Professions: Nonacademic

Architect
Athlete
Editor
Attorney
Chiropractor
Engineer
Clergy/religious worker
Dentist
Home economist/dietician
Physician
Librarian

Scientist (life sciences)
Scientist (mathematics)
Scientist (physical sciences)
Social scientist
Journalist
Social worker
Veterinarian
Physical therapist
Psychologist
Optometrist
Judge

Other Work

Civic worker
Clubwoman
Political party official

Association official
Consultant/lecturer
Other

Department of Mathematics
Regis College (Williamson)

Department of Economics
Regis College (Oates)

21. Other than deans of professional schools.

WOMEN'S COLLEGES AND WOMEN ACHIEVERS REVISITED

M. ELIZABETH TIDBALL

Identifying the baccalaureate origins of achieving women might seem a relatively straightforward task. It is not. Difficulties arise because many standard information sources are inadequate or incomplete, because the definition of achievement not only is open to interpretation but also is limited by the resources available, and because the number of achieving women by any measure is small and rendered smaller when only those achievers who have graduated from college are selected. If achieving graduates are then to be compared on the basis of the type of institution from which they received the baccalaureate degree, this again reduces the number of women in each group. Further subdivisions of sets of achievers or institutions may yield such small groups of subjects that reliability of findings and their interpretations may suffer. Yet researchers still try to delineate the parameters that influence subsequent achievement of women college graduates, or that distinguish among the kinds of accomplishment attained by women graduates relative to their baccalaureate origins. The following report reviews what we have learned about the baccalaureate origins of women achievers and highlights ambiguities inherent in this kind of research and the difficulties of interpreting the data.

I am especially grateful to the editors of *Signs: Journal of Women in Culture and Society* for publishing the figures accompanying this communication, none of which has been published previously.

This essay originally appeared in *Signs*, vol. 5, no. 3, Spring 1980.

Choosing Resource Materials

The choice of how to define achievement and simultaneously indicate baccalaureate origins presents the first set of constraints. Biographical reference works, such as the *Who's Who* series, can be used to determine the baccalaureate origins of women who have achieved a certain professional status or degree of accomplishment. Some professional organizations also have developed registries which can be used for the same purpose. But the number of women listed in virtually all such registries is so small as to make hazardous the subdivision of data into more restricted groups, as would be necessary in the use of a single source for multiple purposes. Such procedures must therefore be approached with caution and the data thus derived interpreted with considerable care.

Who's Who in America, while not technically restricted by sex, nonetheless favors inclusion on the basis of certain high-level occupational positions (fourteen categories listed) or individual achievement—which, however, is less likely and "must be decided by a judicious process of evaluating qualitative factors."[1] *Who's Who in America*'s "stringent selection criteria" have resulted, in the most recent and liberalized editions, in the listing of approximately 3,000 women among the total of 72,000 biographies, that is, about 4 percent. Certainly these women must be deserving; however, the long exclusion of women from professional hierarchies and the failure to acknowledge women's accomplishment as regularly as men's are reflected in this low listing rate. This small sample of women is more representative of the openness to women of certain career hierarchies than of the achievements of women in all the career fields they have entered. It has been well documented, for example, that women natural scientists have traditionally been excluded from a number of prestigious awards and leadership positions, and that even today their achievements are poorly rewarded—if at all.[2]

Some of these difficulties may be ameliorated by choosing a source less restrictive to women, such as *Who's Who of American Women* (founded 1958), which in the sixth edition, for example, listed some 24,000 women in thirty-four broad fields who were included more by virtue of their

1. *Who's Who in America* (Chicago: Marquis Who's Who, Inc., 1976), pp. vi–xi, quotation from p. ix.
2. See, e.g., Harriet Zuckerman and Jonathan R. Cole, "Women in American Science," *Minerva* 13 (1975): 83–102; Evelyn Fox Keller, "Women in Science: An Analysis of a Social Problem," *Harvard Magazine* (October 1974), pp. 14–19; *Research Issues in the Employment of Women: Proceedings of a Workshop* (Washington, D.C.: Commission on Human Resources. Assembly of Behavioral and Social Sciences, National Research Council, National Academy of Sciences, 1975); and Barbara F. Reskin, "Sex Differences in Status Attainment in Science: The Case of the Postdoctoral Fellowship," *American Sociological Review* 41 (1976): 597–612.

achievements than of their titles.[3] Although some deserving women may have been missed by the editors (and some successful women consider it beneath their dignity to be listed other than in *Who's Who in America*), there are eight times more women listed in *Who's Who of American Women* than are listed in *Who's Who in America*. As a research instrument, this wider range of listings minimizes bias in terms of career-field accomplishments: a properly constructed random sample of this population of achieving women would be expected to yield more reliable career information than would the entirety of women listed in any single volume of *Who's Who in America,* although societal biases vis-à-vis career participation for women may still emerge as a limit to reliability for certain fields.

If one is primarily interested in investigating the participation of women college graduates in various careers, obvious sources would include the registries of professional organizations. However, many such organizations have not developed data on their membership by sex; even less have they noted the baccalaureate origins of their participants. An exception is the Doctorate Records File of the National Research Council/National Academy of Sciences, where, starting in 1920, every person who has received a research doctorate is listed by sex, institution of baccalaureate origin, year of baccalaureate, field of doctorate, and a number of other variables.[4] The attainment of a research doctorate, as a measure of accomplishment, is more specifically career achievement related, as opposed to position related, than a citation in *Who's Who in America.* It should be clear, however, that there is no single source available for identifying women's baccalaureate origins, high-level accomplishments, and career patterns simultaneously.

Baccalaureate Origins and Achievement

One common finding has consistently emerged with respect to the baccalaureate origins of women listed in all registries analyzed: graduates of women's colleges are approximately twice as likely to be

3. *Who's Who of American Women* (Chicago: Marquis Who's Who, Inc., 1969), pp. vii–xi.

4. The Doctorate Records File (DRF), maintained by the Commission on Human Resources of the National Research Council, National Academy of Sciences, is a data base containing information on over half a million doctorate recipients from 1920 to the present time in a computer-searchable form. Because the data have been supplied by virtually all doctorate holders who have obtained degrees from U.S. universities, they describe the entire population, so that use of these data involves no problems of sampling error. The following calculations from DRF data, 1920–73, reveal the differential participation in doctoral fields by women and men: in the natural sciences, men have received fourteen times more doctorates than women (i.e., 93 percent of all natural science doctorates are held by men); in the social sciences, men have received 5.5 times more doctorates than women; in arts and humanities, 3.7 times more; and in education, 4.0 times more.

listed as are women graduates of coeducational institutions.[5] The degree of concurrence across several sources and by independent researchers attests to the durability of this finding and generates a number of questions for further investigation.

One explanation for this basic finding offered by some is the suggestion that women's colleges were the only baccalaureate institutions open to the majority of women in the study samples. This is simply not the case. Coeducational opportunities for women were not unduly limited in the early decades of the twentieth century. In 1910, 790 or 73 percent of all baccalaureate institutions were open to women (85 percent were open to men), while, in 1918, coeducational institutions graduated some 11,100 women as compared with 4,500 graduates from the women's colleges. By 1930, 1,123 or 85 percent of all baccalaureate institutions were open to women (84 percent were open to men); and in 1932, coeducational institutions graduated approximately 36,000 women compared with 7,300 graduates of the women's colleges.[6] Indeed, not since before the turn of the century have women's colleges granted more than half of the baccalaureate degrees awarded to women. Today some 95 percent of baccalaureate institutions are open to women and a similar proportion to men.

Other explanations are proffered which might be valid if applied to men but become irrelevant when applied to women. Since most researchers, including women, have been trained in male-dominated environments, it is frequently difficult even to be aware of the male bias of many "basic" assumptions. Assumptions relating to the interplay of socioeconomic background, college choice, and success are an example. Stated briefly, researchers should be aware that, as recently as 1957, only 28 percent of women from the lowest socioeconomic but the highest ability quartiles even *entered* any college, compared with 52 percent of men from this group who did so.[7] On the average, women who have graduated from college have not only had higher test scores than men,

5. M. Elizabeth Tidball, "Perspective on Academic Women and Affirmative Action," *Educational Record* 54 (1973): 130–35, and "The Search for Talented Women," *Change* 6 (1974): 51–52, 64; Mary J. Oates and Susan Williamson, "Women's Colleges and Women Achievers," *Signs: Journal of Women in Culture and Society* 3, no. 4 (1978): 795–806; and M. Elizabeth Tidball, "Wellesley Women in Science," *Wellesley Alumnae Magazine* 59 (1976): 1–3.

6. U.S. Department of the Interior, *Annual Report of the Commissioner of Education* (Washington, D.C.: Government Printing Office, 1900–1918), was published 1899–1900 through 1915–16 but contains limited baccalaureate information by institution and sex. U.S. Department of the Interior, *Biennial Survey of Education* (Washington, D.C.: Government Printing Office, 1918–1947), gives information on the combined number of baccalaureate and first professional degrees by sex, broad field, and institution for every second academic year, 1917–18 through 1930–31. For 1930–31 through 1937–38 this information is available only by sex and institution.

7. Carnegie Commission on Higher Education, *Priorities for Action: Final Report of the Carnegie Commission on Higher Education* (New York: McGraw-Hill Book Co., 1973), p. 97.

they have also come from families of higher socioeconomic status. Furthermore, success for a woman has traditionally been assessed, not primarily on the basis of her career achievements, but on the basis of her husband's or children's success. To what extent a high school senior's selection of a college has been based on her perception that the college's women graduates are likely to be successful in careers has not been investigated. Until careful studies of these variables and their interaction have been accomplished, it is unwise to speculate on their outcome by making analogies to the situations that obtain for boys and men.

Some research, however, has analyzed the differential productivities of women's and coeducational colleges.[8] For these studies, 1,500 women were randomly selected from three editions of *Who's Who of American Women,* and the baccalaureate origins of the 1,116 who were college graduates were identified. Fifty-nine women's colleges and 289 coeducational institutions were represented by the women of achievement, some 60 percent of whom received their degrees between 1910 and 1940. For each decade between these years for each of the 348 institutions, the following items were tabulated: number of women faculty, number of men faculty, number of women students enrolled, number of men students enrolled, number of women graduates, and number of women graduates subsequently cited for their career achievement. The number of women achievers/women graduates or women enrolled was plotted against the number of women faculty/women graduates or women enrolled and a correlation coefficient calculated which was found to be positive and highly significant statistically ($r = +.953, P < .005$). This regression line, along with the standard error of the estimate, is depicted graphically in figure 1. Data from the women's colleges, which are twice as productive of achievers and have a women faculty/women student ratio twice as large as the coeducational colleges, tended to cluster toward the upper portion of the line, and coeducational colleges toward the lower. The high statistically significant dependence between the two variables indicates that this relationship is very unlikely to occur on a chance basis; rather, the substantial importance of women faculty to achiever production can be inferred with considerable confidence. This is not to say that an abundance of adult women role models is the only predictor of subsequent achievement by women students; but it does reinforce the relative importance of this relationship in comparison with other institutional variables. A correlation coefficient was also calculated for the relationship between women achievers and men faculty. The value obtained indicates no statistically significant correlation between these two variables, that is, the number of men faculty neither enhanced nor detracted from the output of women achievers. Additionally, from these data, it was shown that the percentage of men students enrolled

8. Tidball, "Perspective on Academic Women," and "Search for Talented Women."

was negatively correlated with the number of women achievers and that the correlation was also highly significant statistically ($r = -.937, P < .005$). This means that the larger the proportion of men students on a campus, the less likely are the women students subsequently to be cited for career achievement; this is consistent with the fact of greater achiever production on the part of the women's colleges.

The preceding findings on the positive relationship between women faculty and women achievers, the lack of relationship between men faculty and women achievers, and the negative relationship between men students and women achievers emerged from analyses of the population of women achievers as a whole. Further analyses were undertaken upon subgroups of data for women receiving their baccalaureate degrees during the fifty years between 1910 and 1960.[9]

One way of disaggregating these data permits the comparison of women's and coeducational colleges with respect to achiever production on the basis of institutional size. For these studies, women's and coeducational colleges were matched both according to the number of women graduates and according to the total number of graduates (women + men), and categorized according to one of seven size groupings in a logarithmic progression (< 100, 100–199, 200–399, 400–799, 800–1,599, 1,600–3,199, and $\geq 3,200$). The probabilities of becoming an achiever, which had previously been calculated for graduates of each institution, were then plotted against the appropriate institution in each of the size groupings. For both the women's and the coeducational colleges, there appeared the same optimal size vis-à-vis achiever production, a size neither extremely small nor extremely large. However, small colleges were associated with a greater probability of producing achievers than were large ones, and there were no coeducational institutions as small as the smallest women's colleges.

The relationship between college size and achiever production is shown in figure 2. It is apparent that, while college size does bear a relationship to the probability of achievement of its women graduates, analysis of this variable does not explain the twofold or greater difference in achiever production between women's and coeducational colleges *of the same size*. This does demonstrate that smaller colleges in general are more productive of women achievers, and it is noteworthy that virtually all women's colleges are relatively small.

In a continuing search for objective measures by which to differentiate women's and coeducational colleges in order to clarify reasons for their differences in achiever production, a second means of disaggregation of data was undertaken. The women's and coeducational colleges were separated from each other (as for the size study), and then each of these groups was subdivided according to its members' admis-

9. Tidball, "Search for Talented Women."

sions selectivity. The resulting four groups were: highly selective women's colleges (the Seven Sisters), a group of ten highly selective coeducational colleges, the fifty-two other women's colleges in the study population, and the 279 other coeducational colleges in the study population. It was found that the highly selective women's colleges were twice as productive of achievers as were the highly selective coeducational colleges. Similarly, all other women's colleges were twice as likely to have produced achievers as were all other coeducational colleges. These findings demonstrate that when women's and coeducational colleges of similar selectivity are compared, women's colleges are more productive of achievers at both levels of institutional selectivity. They also show that, within both the women's and the coeducational colleges, higher selectivity is associated with greater achiever production. But this analysis does not explain the twofold difference in achiever production between women's and coeducational colleges *of comparable selectivity.*

In their recent report in *Signs* on women achievers, Oates and Williamson selected three groups of colleges for comparison.[10] Their achiever sample consisted of 342 women listed in the thirty-eighth edition of *Who's Who in America* who had graduated from college during the 1930s from institutions with fewer than 500 graduates a year. One group of colleges was identified by virtue of having relatively large numbers of achievers; these were highly selective women's colleges. The other two groups of colleges were identified by virtue of having relatively small numbers of achievers, one group comprising less selective women's colleges and the other group consisting of coeducational colleges of all levels of selectivity. Thus, while the calculations of achievers per 10,000 graduates may be used as a standardized means for reporting data, they do not derive from methodology that permits a comparison of achiever production by women's and coeducational colleges of similar selectivity. The authors used their findings to conclude that only highly selective women's colleges were remarkable for their productivity vis-à-vis women achievers. However, one can deduce from the data presented that the less selective women's colleges were more productive of achievers than were the less selective coeducational colleges, inasmuch as the former graduated as many achievers as did the mixture of both less and highly selective coeducational colleges. If the authors had used groupings of institutions which were truly comparable for comparison, the contributions of non–Seven Sisters women's colleges would have emerged more clearly; and the perspective thus obtained would have prevented the perpetuation of the false view that only the Seven Sisters colleges are importantly involved in the development of women achievers.

The possibility that faculty compensation might influence the rate of achiever production was also considered in my earlier work. Since no

10. Oates and Williamson.

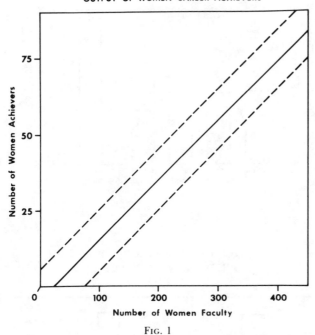

RELATIONSHIP BETWEEN NUMBER OF WOMEN
FACULTY AND UNDERGRADUATE COLLEGE
OUTPUT OF WOMEN CAREER ACHIEVERS

FIG. 1

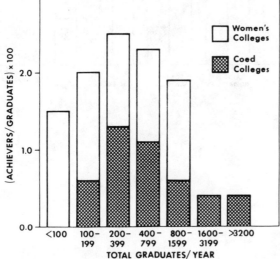

RELATIONSHIP BETWEEN COLLEGE SIZE
AND OUTPUT OF WOMEN ACHIEVERS

FIG. 2

RELATIONSHIP BETWEEN ACADEMIC EXPENDITURES
AND OUTPUT OF WOMEN ACHIEVERS BY COLLEGE TYPE

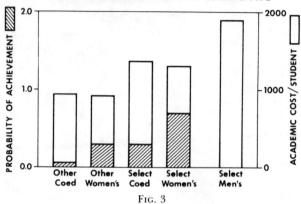

FIG. 3

SOURCE OF WOMEN DOCTORATES IN
SIX FIELDS BY COLLEGE TYPE
1920-1972

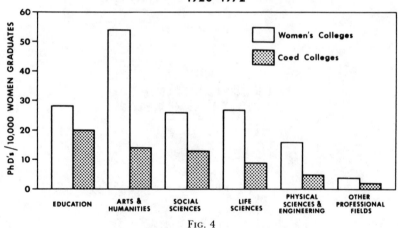

FIG. 4

uniform or reliable fiscal data exist for each institution separately throughout the fifty years encompassed by the study, it was necessary to devise an approximation. Therefore, the following analysis should be appreciated in relative rather than absolute terms with respect to actual dollar amounts. The fiscal data were obtained from the AAUP listing of "Full-Time Faculty Compensation/Student Equivalent" and are referred to as academic expenses.[11]

Four groups of colleges were compared in this portion of the study: six of the Seven Sisters (Radcliffe did not report separately to the AAUP); all other women's colleges in the study that reported to the AAUP (this excluded all of the Roman Catholic colleges); ten highly selective coeducational colleges; and a balanced sample comprising thirty-two other, less selective coeducational institutions from the study population. In addition, academic expenses from seven highly selective men's colleges were included for comparison with the other highly selective groups. The results of these calculations are shown in figure 3.[12] It can be seen that the highly selective women's colleges (six of the Seven Sisters) produced more than twice as many achievers as the highly selective coeducational colleges for the same academic expenditure. The other women's colleges produced approximately three times the number of achievers as the other coeducational colleges for the same academic expenditure. Correlation coefficients calculated to assess the extent of relationship between achiever production and academic expenses indicated that achiever production in coeducational colleges, but not in women's colleges, is closely linked to academic expenses.[13] These data may be interpreted generally to indicate that, in the women's colleges, there is a disproportionately large number of achievers produced/

11. *AAUP Bulletin* 56 (1970): 204–38. The table illustrates the similarities in academic expenses between the two types of highly selective colleges, and between the two types of other, less selective colleges. It also shows the differences in academic expenses between highly selective colleges and other colleges. Appropriate statistical tests validated the lack and presence of the differences noted above.

Institutional Type and Selectivity	Academic Expenses (Mean ± SE)
Highly selective women's colleges	$1,352±111
Highly selective coeducational colleges	1,369±114
Other women's colleges	951± 61
Other coeducational colleges	942± 63
Highly selective men's colleges	1,892±171

12. Tidball, "Search for Talented Women."
13. For the highly selective women's colleges ($r_{exptl} = .444$; $r_{(.95)} = .729$); for the other women's colleges ($r_{exptl} = .253$; $r_{(.95)} = .352$); for the highly selective coeducation institutions ($r_{exptl} = .787$; $r_{(.995)} = .765$).

academic dollars expended, if the relationship between achiever production and academic expenses in the coeducational colleges is taken as the norm. Alternatively, one might infer, using the women's colleges as the norm, that women students in coeducational institutions are not receiving their appropriate proportional share of the dollars expended for academic purposes.

It can also be seen from figure 3 that the other women's colleges produced as high a proportion of achievers as the highly selective coeducational colleges, and that this was accomplished for about one-third less academic expenditure. A χ^2 test performed using the achiever data from these two groups of colleges permitted the statistical conclusion that the two groups do differ with respect to achiever production ($\chi^2_{exptl} = 12.25$; $\chi^2_{(.995)} = 7.88$). That is, the other women's colleges produce proportionately more achievers than would be expected on the basis of the performance of coeducational colleges of high selectivity whose faculties enjoy greater monetary compensation. Neither the greater selectivity nor the larger academic budgets of highly selective coeducational colleges did more than counterbalance the positive environmental factors present in the other women's colleges, even though greater selectivity and larger academic budgets are both associated with greater achiever production when comparisons are made between groups of coeducational colleges and between groups of women's colleges.

From the studies relating academic expenses and selectivity to achiever production according to institutional type, it may therefore be concluded that women's colleges have produced achievers disproportionate to their academic expenses and disproportionate to their selectivity. Women's colleges have thus been not only highly cost effective in economic terms, but also highly efficient in terms of developing human potential qua woman potential.

Baccalaureate Origins and Career Patterns

The preceding section detailed some of the baccalaureate institutional characteristics associated with the likelihood of subsequent career achievement by women graduates. Such studies use the number of women achievers, or the proportion of women achievers, from a given type of institution as a measure of the effect on achievement of various institutional characteristics.

In a somewhat analogous manner, one can study the interrelationships among baccalaureate origins, achievement, and career patterns. One approach is to define achievement on the basis of participation in a career or the attainment of a high-level career credential, and then to determine the baccalaureate origins of these achievers. Again, the number or proportion of women achievers is used as a measure of the effect on achievement of type of baccalaureate institution of origin. Baccalaureate origin and career-field participation are directly related by virtue of using career-field participation as the criterion for achievement. Alternatively, one can define achievement on the basis of inclusion in *Who's Who in America* and then determine both the career fields and the baccalaureate origins of these achievers. In this approach, relationships between baccalaureate origin and career-field participation are indirect and dependent upon a third variable, namely, the selection criteria of the registry.

In my work on the relationship between baccalaureate origins and career patterns, I used inclusion in the Doctorate Record File as the indicator of achievement, since this registry is large, complete, and subcategorized according to six broad fields of career-related accomplishment. From fifty-three years of data, the ratio of the number of women receiving the doctorate to the number of women graduates for each of the six fields was calculated separately for graduates of women's and coeducational colleges.[14] Graduates of women's colleges were more than twice as likely to have received research doctorates in all fields combined as were women graduates of coeducational institutions. Further, certain differences in career-field preferences were observed and are represented graphically in figure 4. Most striking are the very large difference (3.5 times) in the arts and humanities and the relatively small difference (1.2 times) in education, although the productivity of the women's colleges is greater than that of the coeducational institutions in all fields. These distinctions are consistent with the general suggestion of Oates and Williamson that coeducational college achievers were more likely to have entered fields that require "certifiable skills" (e.g., education), while women's college achievers were more likely to have entered fields that require a liberal arts background (e.g., arts and humanities). Studies of baccalaureate institutions that have been the most productive sources of students who subsequently earned doctorates reinforce these findings.[15] The most productive women's colleges were heavily represented by their graduates in four or five major doctoral fields, while the most productive coeducational institutions were heavily represented by their women

14. Tidball, "Wellesley Women in Science." This paper cites the findings that approximately one-third of all science doctorates held by women belong to graduates of women's colleges, even though those colleges have granted only about 15 percent of the baccalaureate degrees during the comparable time span. Calculations of doctoral attainment were made from a 5 percent random sample of the approximately 50,000 women who received the doctorate between 1920 and 1973, from data supplied by the Commission on Human Resources from the DRF. The baccalaureate institutional data required for the calculations were obtained from the *Biennial Survey of Education* and from the Office of Education, Department of Health, Education, and Welfare, *Earned Degrees Conferred* (Washington, D.C.: Government Printing Office, 1948–70).

15. M. Elizabeth Tidball and Vera Kistiakowsky, "Baccalaureate Origins of American Scientists and Scholars," *Science* 193 (1976): 646–52.

graduates in only one or two major doctoral fields, particularly education. This report also revealed the considerable productivity of women's colleges: they were the only type of institution (among public, private, college, university, coeducational, and single sex) that consistently and extensively graduated students of either sex who subsequently earned the doctorate in terms of both the total number and the percentage of graduates who did so.

The attempt by Oates and Williamson, using *Who's Who in America* as the basis for identifying achievers, to assess differences in career-field participation by graduates of women's and coeducational colleges was only marginally successful. Their methodology precluded the realization of their expectation that "other things being equal . . . these [women's] colleges . . . would show a pattern of occupational distribution of their eminent alumnae which differs significantly from the pattern of successful coeducational-college graduates."[16] The problem with their expectation is that other things are decidedly not equal. As suggested herein, recognition for women bears a relationship to the nature of the career. Additionally, these researchers' disaggregation of a highly restricted and very small sample of achieving women has produced serious constraints upon statistical reliability and restricted the extent to which inferences are applicable.

Summary

The research recently reported by Oates and Williamson verifies the outstanding record of the women's colleges in graduating women of accomplishment. With several measures of achievement attesting to this fact, it gains the strength provided through the application of alternate approaches and by different investigators.

The questions "Why?" and "To what end?" have not yet been fully established or explored. Although women students in women's colleges have extensive opportunities for leadership experiences and are encouraged to study fields not traditionally entered by women, these advantages may be derivatives of the fact that high expectations are held for these students by large numbers of adult women who themselves exemplify achievement. Further, while women faculty are more supportive of issues that concern women than are men faculty, the proportion of women faculty in all types of institutions except the women's colleges is so small that their impact on women students is severely constrained. Thus the importance of the number of women faculty, in relation to the total faculty population and to the number of women students, emerges and reemerges as a major influence in the development

16. Oates and Williamson, p. 800.

of women students who subsequently become achievers. Assessment of other institutional variables has revealed that small institutional size, high selectivity, and a high level of faculty compensation may each exert a positive influence on the extent of achiever production in both women's and coeducational colleges. The results of such studies suggest, however, that deficiencies in these conditions may be offset by other attributes of women's colleges not reviewed in this report or not yet investigated. For example, although the *number* of men faculty is not related to the production of women achievers, as is true for the number of women faculty, *attitudes* of men faculty who teach in women's colleges are more facilitating to women than attitudes of men faculty who teach in all other kinds of institutions.[17] Still other attitudes and opinions of faculty and students, such as those reported by Anderson in his study of single-sex and church-related colleges,[18] have been identified as having positive or negative effects upon the total climate of baccalaureate institutions and may thus be related to student outcomes.

Most would agree that more work is needed if we are to gain an understanding of what constitutes an optimal environment for the undergraduate education of women that they may become achievers. The overwhelming majority of women students are to be found in coeducational settings, but we know they have not flourished there in the past in numbers commensurate with their presence. Studying various aspects of the women's colleges and their graduates has provided a glimpse of what women can become when certain environmental conditions obtain, most particularly a high women faculty/women student ratio. Beyond this we are still searching. It is hoped that this paper, with its concerns for reexamining traditional assumptions and its review of earlier work, will stimulate further research in this vital area. Surely all women stand to benefit thereby.

Department of Physiology
George Washington University Medical Center

17. M. Elizabeth Tidball, "Of Men and Research: The Dominant Themes in American Higher Education Include Neither Teaching nor Women," *Journal of Higher Education* 47 (1976): 373–89.

18. Richard E. Anderson, *Strategic Policy Changes at Private Colleges* (New York: Teachers College Press, 1977).

WOMEN'S COLLEGES AND WOMEN ACHIEVERS: AN UPDATE

JOY K. RICE AND ANNETTE HEMMINGS

Over a decade has passed since the publication of Elizabeth Tidball's influential study of the relation between where women received their baccalaureate degrees and their later career accomplishments.[1] Tidball found that in the half century from 1910 to 1960, graduates of women's colleges were twice as likely as women graduates of coeducational institutions to be cited for career achievements in *Who's Who of American Women*. In a later study designed to identify the baccalaureate origins of American scientists and scholars[2] and in other, more recent, similar work on the baccalaureate backgrounds of men and women entering medical school and men and women natural science doctorates,[3] Tidball found that a significantly high proportion of the women had graduated from women's colleges (in particular, the Seven Sisters colleges of Bar-

[1] M. Elizabeth Tidball, "Perspective on Academic Women and Affirmative Action," *Educational Record* 54 (Spring 1973): 130–35.

[2] Elizabeth Tidball and Vera Kistiakowsky, "Baccalaureate Origins of American Scientists and Scholars," *Science* 193 (August 20, 1976): 646–52.

[3] M. Elizabeth Tidball, "Baccalaureate Origins of Entrants into American Medical Schools," *Journal of Higher Education* 56, no. 4 (July–August 1985): 385–402, and "Baccalaureate Origins of Recent Natural Science Doctorates," *Journal of Higher Education* 57, no. 6 (November–December 1986): 606–20.

This essay originally appeared in *Signs*, vol. 13, no. 3, Spring 1988.

nard, Bryn Mawr, Radcliffe, Mount Holyoke, Smith, Vassar, and Wellesley). Tidball attributed the higher career achievement among women's college graduates to the abundance of women faculty at these colleges, based on her finding of a positive relation between these variables in her sample. As support for her claim, she cited results from three items on a lengthy and detailed 1972–73 national survey of college faculty by the American Council on Education. (One item, e.g., asked survey respondents to reply to the statement "Institutional anti-nepotism rules should be abolished.") Women faculty at all types of institutions were more likely to respond affirmatively to these items than were men faculty.[4] Tidball's assertions have been cited widely in the literature deploring the closing of many women's colleges in the mid-sixties and seventies and applauding their renaissance today.[5]

Women's colleges flourished before the turn of the century, offering women who wanted to obtain a higher education the choice of a single-sex environment. Many of these early colleges justified their mission to educate women with the social rationale that educated women would become teachers, reformers, and culture bearers, as well as "better" mothers and wives. Although in the first half of this century elite women's colleges were largely accessible only to the wealthy, they often provided a rigorous curriculum for women that was comparable to that received by men at coeducational institutions.[6] By the late 1960s, however, federal cutbacks and economic constraints on higher education prompted many small colleges to close and universities and colleges to reduce their budgets. Educational equity and the integration of minorities and women was publically debated, and women's colleges increasingly were

[4] In her 1973 sample Tidball noted that there were almost twice as many women faculty per thousand women students in women's colleges as in coed institutions. A more recent survey indicated women constitute 55 percent of the total full-time faculty at four-year women's colleges, more than twice their representation at other four-year colleges and universities (*A Second Profile of Women's Colleges* [Washington, D.C.: Women's College Coalition, 1981], 1). See also M. Elizabeth Tidball, "Of Men and Research: The Dominant Themes in American Higher Education Include neither Teaching nor Women," *Journal of Higher Education* 47, no. 4 (July–August 1976): 373–89.

[5] Pauline Tompkins, "What Future for Women's Colleges?" *Liberal Education* 58, no. 2 (May 1972): 298–303; Carnegie Commission on Higher Education, *Opportunities for Women in Higher Education* (New York: McGraw-Hill, 1973); *A Study of the Learning Environment at Women's Colleges* (Washington, D.C.: Women's College Coalition, 1981); and *A Profile of Recent Women's College Graduates* (Washington, D.C.: Women's College Coalition, 1985).

[6] See Helen Lefkowitz Horowitz's *Alma Mater* (Boston: Beacon Press, 1984) for an excellent analysis of the design of and experience in women's colleges from their nineteenth-century beginnings to the 1930s.

seen by professionals in educational policy studies as an elitist anachronism.[7] In 1960 there were about three hundred colleges for women; by 1970 only half of those colleges remained single-sex institutions. The majority of these were church-related schools, primarily Roman Catholic. As financial pressures grew and coeducation attracted many women to previously all-male schools, many women's colleges began admitting men. The six-month period between June and December 1968, when an astounding sixty-four women's colleges either became coeducational institutions or closed their doors, was a watermark in higher education.[8] Today, 116 women's colleges educate about 125,000 students, roughly 1 percent of all college students and 2 percent of all women college students.[9]

The popularity of coeducation proved to have unanticipated deleterious effects on the ability of women's colleges to provide equal educational opportunity for women students. Vassar's example is instructive.

Instead of merging with Yale, Vassar opened its own campus to men. In an attempt to alter its ladylike image, the college imported male administrators. A man was appointed to the new position of vice president for student affairs, and another man became admissions director. Men were added to the full-time faculty, which was expanded 30 percent to accommodate the hoped-for increased enrollment. The percentage of full-time women faculty dropped from 42.9 percent in 1967–68, a year before coeducation, to 38.2 percent in 1973–74. The percentage of women department chairpersons dropped from 38 percent to 19 percent in this period. However, the percentage of women instructors, lecturers, and non-ladder appointments increased from 50 percent in 1967–68 to 70 percent in 1973–74. Today classes are dominated by men students, who have also taken over the leadership of student government and publications.[10]

The variable that Tidball felt was an important factor in women's postcollege achievement, the prevalence of women role models, seemed seriously jeopardized by the move to coeducation. Some

[7] Christopher Jencks and David Riesman, *The Academic Revolution* (New York: Doubleday & Co., 1968), 310.

[8] Tompkins, 298.

[9] *A Second Profile of Women's Colleges*, 1.

[10] Susan Romer Kaplan, "Women's Education: The Case for the Single-Sex College," in *The Higher Education of Women*, ed. Helen Astin and William Hirsch (New York: Praeger, 1978), 60.

recent data substantiate this concern: women's colleges that stayed single-sex awarded proportionately more baccalaureate degrees to women who subsequently were medical school entrants (in 1975–78) and science doctorates (in 1970–79) than did women's colleges that became coeducational.[11]

In the late 1970s and the early 1980s, women's colleges enjoyed a 25 percent overall increase in enrollment.[12] Many studies of classroom climate, faculty attitudes and expectations, teacher-student interaction and gender, and the declining aspirations of women students indicated that coeducation was a second-class education for women college students.[13] This data buttressed the resolve of leaders at women's colleges to provide a single-sex sanctuary for women in higher education.

Today's proponents of women's institutions claim the colleges provide a uniquely supportive environment in which women can fully develop their potential, free from competing either *with* men for leadership or *for* men for sexual status, and, further, in which women have the advantage of associating with many women leaders, teachers, and mentors.[14] Linda P. Lentz perhaps oversimplifies when she states that with the publication of Tidball's research, the women's colleges found a "raison d'etre."[15] Nonetheless, the preliminary documentation of women's colleges' effectiveness in preparing young women for career accomplishments did raise compelling questions for researchers who followed in Tidball's footsteps.

Follow-up studies

Mary J. Oates and Susan Williamson essentially replicated Tidball's major finding for the single decade of the 1930s (the decade with the highest representation of women achievers in Tidball's study) using *Who's Who in America (WW)* instead of *Who's Who of Amer-*

[11] Tidball, "Baccalaureate Origins of Entrants into American Medical Schools," and "Baccalaureate Origins of Recent Natural Science Doctorates."

[12] *A Second Profile of Women's Colleges*, 1.

[13] A comprehensive bibliography is given in *The Classroom Climate: A Chilly One for Women?* (Washington, D.C.: Project on the Status and Education of Women, Association of American Colleges, 1982).

[14] C. C. Cole, "Review Readers Forum: A Case for the Women's College," *College Board Review* 83 (Spring 1972): 17–21; Marcia K. Sharp, "Women's Colleges: Equity and Optimum,"*College Board Review* 111 (Spring 1979): 18–21; Kaplan; and Jill Conway, "Why Women's Colleges?" *Change* 10, no. 3 (March 1978): 8–9.

[15] Linda P. Lentz, "The College Choice of Career Salient Women: Coed or Women's?" *Journal of Educational Equity and Leadership* 1, no. 1 (Fall 1980): 28–35.

ican Women (WWAW).[16] The number of achievers per 10,000 graduates of women's colleges in the decade of the 1930s was nearly
twice the number of women achievers per 10,000 graduates of coeducational small colleges in the same decade. Oates and Williamson also documented what many casual observers of the women's
college scene have suspected for some time—that overall a larger
proportion (21.8 percent) of all achievers were graduates of the
Seven Sisters colleges than of other women's colleges (17.2 percent). The Seven Sisters colleges awarded degrees to women who
became achievers at the rate of 61 per 10,000 graduates for the
decade of the thirties, as compared to 18 per 10,000 graduates for
the other small women's and coed colleges. Admissions selectivity,
recruitment, and the socioeconomic advantage of students who can
afford the Seven Sisters thus could be proposed as a partial explanation for Tidball's and Oates and Williamson's results.

Other data lend credence to this argument: first-year women
enrolling in "competitive" to "highly competitive" women's colleges were significantly more motivated toward and oriented to
preparing themselves for careers than were first-year women enrolling in comparable small private coed colleges. Moreover, the
higher the competition for admission, the greater was the difference
in the importance-of-career ratings given by first-year women applying to the women's and the coed colleges.[17] Another study compared first-year women at thirty women's colleges with first-year
women at all institutions for fall 1979. The researchers found that
first-year women at women's colleges had achieved a high school
average of B+ or better, planned to achieve an advanced degree,
were accepted by three or more colleges, and chose a college because of good academic reputation more often than did first-year
women at all institutions. Women's college students also had more
highly educated parents.[18] These findings suggest that college admissions selectivity and prior student academic achievement are
more important factors in predicting later career achievement than
the influence of the college environment.[19]

[16] Mary J. Oates and Susan Williamson, "Women's Colleges and Women Achievers," *Signs: Journal of Women in Culture and Society* 3, no. 4 (Summer 1978): 795–
806.

[17] Lentz, 32. The designations of "competitive" and "highly competitive" are
Lentz's.

[18] *A Second Profile of Women's Colleges* (n. 4 above). 6–7.

[19] In general, the literature on the impact of the college on student interests,
attitudes, and level of aspirations frequently concludes that the percentage of profes-
sionally successful graduates a college has is more a function of the type of student
body that enrolls than of the college experience itself. See Alexander W. Astin,
"Productivity of Undergraduate Institutions," *Science* 136, no. 3510 (April 6, 1962):

In response to these conclusions, Tidball noted that Oates and Williamson had compared the Seven Sisters data to all coed colleges and not to a comparable subsample of highly selective coed colleges. Reanalyzing her own data, she found that in proportion to the total number of women graduates, highly selective women's colleges had twice as many graduates who were achievers as did highly selective coeducational colleges. Similarly, all other women's colleges were twice as likely to have high achieving women alumnae as were all other coeducational colleges.[20]

The selectivity of the college, based on admission criteria or the reputation of the college, however, does not take into account the student's socioeconomic status, a variable that is probably a key factor in the student's choice of college and, later, in her occupational achievement. Attending a private college, women's or coed, implicitly suggests a financial status that most students do not have. Thus it seems simplistic to infer a cause and effect relation between women students' career accomplishments and their exposure to women faculty at women's colleges, as has been done in much of the literature that has appeared since the 1973 publication of Tidball's original study.

Another obvious concern of those who question the above findings is whether being listed in *Who's Who in America* or *Who's Who of American Women* is an adequate or even useful measure of career success. Tidball argued that *Who's Who in America*, the directory used by Oates and Williamson, gives the researcher a very narrow band of outstanding women, as it lists only 4 percent of

---

129–35; and G. Stern, "Self-actualization Environments for Students," *School Review* 80, no. 1 (November 1971): 1–25. In his more recent *Four Critical Years, Effects of College on Beliefs, Attitudes, and Knowledge* (San Francisco: Jossey-Bass, 1977), Astin found that attendance at a women's college was a more ambiguous indicator of later career development than was attendance at a men's college. Marvin Bressler, however, extended Astin's work by analyzing the responses to questions about career preferences and educational plans and concluded that aside from initial selection effects, coed colleges had no significant influence on the occupational ambitions of either sex. In contrast, however, among women's college graduates, the ambitions of students frequently shifted during their college years from traditional women's careers to fields traditionally dominated by men (Bressler, "The Sex Composition of Selective Colleges and Gender Difference in Career Aspiration," *Journal of Higher Education* 51, no. 6 [November–December 1980]: 650–63). This latter finding lends credence to the common claim that women's colleges broaden the aspirations and participation of their students in nontraditional areas of study such as math and science.

[20] M. Elizabeth Tidball, "Women's Colleges and Women Achievers Revisited," *Signs* 5, no. 3 (Spring 1980): 504–17. Tidball also noted, "This small sample of women [WW] is more representative of the openness to women of certain career hierarchies than of the achievements of women in all the career fields they have entered" (505).

American women achievers. Oates and Williamson rejoined that
WW avoids the double standard that may be employed by those
who compile a separate directory for women using lower criteria
for women's success.[21] Both recognize that WWAW, or any register
for that matter, may or may not be the most reliable or valid source
of "successful" women. Nonetheless, because WWAW provides a
readily available compilation of women who have achieved career
accomplishments in a broad range of fields and, more important,
because we intended to update Tidball's original study, we also
used WWAW to define a sample of high-achieving American women.

   In addition to possible bias introduced by the criteria used to
select women for WWAW, Tidball's own procedure of attempting to
point randomly to a name on every given number of pages for
inclusion in her sample may have skewed the sample.

   In the present study, we attempted to replicate Tidball's prior
findings with a random sample of recent women achievers who
appear in the 1979–80, 1980–81, and 1983–84 editions of WWAW[22]
and to discover whether the tumultous decade of women's college
closings has had an effect on the number of women achievers who
have graduated from women's colleges, as compared to coeducational institutions. Finally we hoped our study covering the period
from 1901 to 1981 would update Tidball's findings for women
achievers who earned their baccalaureate degrees from 1910 to
1960. We expected to replicate Tidball's earlier findings but hy-
pothesized that, in proportion to the total number of women graduates, the relative number of women achievers who graduated from
women's colleges and coed institutions in more recent years would
be about the same for several reasons. As more and more women's
colleges closed and began to admit men, leaving fewer women's
colleges in existence, academically ambitious women would more
likely have attended selective coed schools as well as selective,
formerly all-male, Ivy League schools. Also in contrast to their early,
fairly homogenous, white, upper-class populations, the student bodies of women's colleges have become more ethnically diverse than
the female populations of colleges and universities in general.[23]

[21] Mary J. Oates and Susan Williamson, "Comment on Tidball's 'Women's Colleges and Women Achievers Revisited,' " Signs 6, no. 2 (Winter 1980): 342–45.

[22] Random numbers were generated and assigned to each of the three volumes
of Who's Who of American Women (Chicago: Marquis, 1979–80; 1981–82; 1983–84)
used in this study, by the University of Wisconsin Survey Research Laboratory.

[23] In 1976 blacks constituted the largest racial/ethnic minority group attending
women's colleges, accounting for 8 percent of the total enrollment. By 1979 there
were slightly more black students (11.2 percent) at women's colleges than at all
other institutions (9 percent), twice the percentages of Asians (2.2 percent vs. 1.1
percent), and significantly more Hispanics (1.8 percent vs. 1.0 percent) (A Profile of
Women's Colleges [Washington, D.C.: Women's College Coalition, 1980]).

Assuming that socioeconomic background is related to access to certain prestigious occupations, as well as to career achievement, we suspected that the growing diversity of socioeconomic status among today's women's college students might be reflected in more balanced proportions of women achievers from women's colleges and coeducational colleges.

New data

Our study of 1,307 women achievers did not include women who had not earned a bachelor or first professional degree, had graduated from institutions outside of the United States, had graduated from one of several obscure institutions not included in conventional listings of American colleges and universities, or whose entry data in WWAW was incomplete or ambiguous regarding college, type of degree, or year of graduation. The sample represented approximately 2 percent of the 61,600 names appearing in the three editions of WWAW. On a per decade basis, the sample was then divided into two groups, those graduating from women's colleges and those graduating from coeducational institutions.[24] Seventy-two women's colleges and 438 coeducational colleges were represented by the women in our study, a broader sample than in Tidball's original study (59 and 289, respectively).

Seventy-seven percent of the sample graduated during the years 1940–79. In contrast, more than 60 percent of Tidball's sample graduated between 1910 and 1940. Graduates of the coeducational and women's colleges during the last four decades (1940–79) were compared on a per decade basis, and the number of achievers were compared to the number of students graduating during the same decade.[25] Overall, we found that of the 1,144 women who graduated between 1940 and 1979, 86 percent were graduates of coeducational

[24] Information about the coed and women's colleges represented in the sample was taken from *The College Blue Book: Narrative Descriptions* (New York: Macmillan Publishing Co., 1983) and from The American Council on Education's *American Universities and Colleges* (New York: Walter de Gruyter, 1983). In the cases of the numerous colleges that became coeducational in the late 1960s and early 1970s, an achiever was considered a graduate of a women's college if the college turned coeducational during her senior year, as she would have experienced the majority of her college life in a women's college environment. If she attended more than one college, the college considered was the one from which she received her degree.

[25] Data on earned degrees for the coeducational institutions came from the *Biennial Survey of Education* and *Earned Degrees Conferred* (Washington, D.C.: Government Printing Office). Data on earned degrees for the women's colleges had to be obtained on a per institution basis as no aggregate figures are available for graduates of women's colleges.

colleges and 14 percent of women's colleges. In comparison, in the Oates and Williamson study of the 1930s, 61 percent of the successful women achievers had graduated from coed schools, and 39 percent from women's colleges.

In her 1973 study, Tidball found that, in proportion to the total number of women graduates, a significantly greater number of women achievers had graduated from women's colleges than from coed colleges in each of the five decades between 1910 and 1960 ($p < .005$). In the current study, comparisons of the number of achievers to number of graduates per decade for women's versus coed colleges also indicated that a significantly greater number of achievers had graduated from women's colleges in the decades 1940–49 ($t = 1.9$, $p < .05$) and 1950–59 ($t = 2.14$, $p < .01$). This result confirms our expectation and Tidball's results of the proportionately higher number of women achievers graduating from women's colleges for these early decades. The relative number of women's college graduates of the 1940s who were cited for high career accomplishment in WWAW was about 1.4 times that of coed college graduates for the same decade. For the 1950s, the relative number of achievers from women's colleges was about 1.25 times that of coeducational institutions. The favorable differences are somewhat lower than those Tidball found, possibly the result of using a more standard methodology to generate a random sample for our study.

In the more recent decades, 1960–69 and 1970–79, however, the difference between the number of women achievers to number of women graduates for women's colleges and for coed colleges was not statistically significant. These are the decades untested by Tidball's original study. According to our data, from 1960–69 the relative proportions of women achievers who graduated from women's and coed colleges were very similar: 97 per 10,000 graduates of women's colleges compared to 93 per 10,000 graduates of coed colleges. For the decade 1970–79, although the difference was not statistically significant, it was somewhat greater: 48 achievers per 10,000 graduates for women's colleges compared to 32 per 10,000 graduates for the coed institutions. In other words, the relative number of women achievers who graduated from women's colleges was about 1.5 times that of coeducational schools. This is approximately the same comparative advantage found by Tidball for women's college graduates in the 1940s. Youth, and thus less time to accomplish career achievement, largely accounts for the small number of achievers who graduated in the 1970s, and another study of this group ten years hence may yield somewhat different results. Overall, across the decades 1940–79, our new data indicated that the relative number of women achievers who graduated from women's colleges was 1.55 times that of coeducational institutions.

The present study thus offers partial support for Tidball's finding of a positive relation between graduating from a women's college and high career accomplishment. Our results, however, also confirm Oates and Williamson's data concerning the prevalence of Seven Sisters graduates among achievers who graduated from women's colleges (over 50 percent in their study), as well as Tidball's finding of the remarkable number of women doctorates with baccalaureate degrees from one of the Seven Sisters.[26] In our study from 1940 to 1979, a consistent 30 to 40 percent per decade of women's college achievers graduated from Seven Sisters colleges and 60 to 70 percent from non–Seven Sisters women's colleges. The percentage of women achievers who graduated from women's colleges declined over the four-decade period, as did the percentage of Seven Sisters graduates. In the 1940s, graduates of the Seven Sisters colleges constituted 7.7 percent of all women achievers in our sample; in the 1970s they constituted 3.0 percent (see table 1).

Summary and reflections

In our study we sought to elucidate the often-repeated assertion in the professional literature on women and higher education, that women's colleges have proportionately more women graduates who later become high achievers than do coeducational schools, by replicating and updating Elizabeth Tidball's pioneer study.[27]

TABLE 1 **DISTRIBUTION OF WOMEN'S COLLEGE (WC) AND SEVEN SISTERS (SS) ACHIEVERS BY DECADE OF GRADUATION (%)**

Decade	(1)	(2)	(3)	(4)
1940–49	3.6	18.5	41.4	7.7
1950–59	3.9	16.8	31.1	5.2
1960–69	4.3	12.6	38.7	4.9
1970–79	2.0	8.5	34.7	3.0

NOTE.—(1) = WC achievers in decade/all achievers across decades (N = 1,144); (2) = WC achievers in decade/total achievers in decade; (3) = SS achievers in decade/WC achievers in decade; (4) = SS achievers in decade/total achievers in decade.

[26] Tidball and Kistiakowsky (n. 2 above), 193. Men's colleges have also graduated a large share of high achievers. In one study, the percentage of graduates from five Ivy League colleges and three other elite colleges who won Nobel prizes was five times the percentage of graduates who won Nobel prizes from colleges and universities generally (Harriet Zuckerman, *Scientific Elite: Nobel Laureates in the United States* [New York: Free Press, 1977], 83).

[27] Tidball, "Perspective on Academic Women and Affirmative Action" (n. 1 above).

The results of our study provide partial support for Tidball's thesis. During the decades of the forties and the fifties, in proportion to the total number of graduates, significantly more women achievers graduated from women's colleges than from coeducational institutions at a ratio of about 3:2 and 4:3, respectively, for the two decades. However, there were no significant differences in the proportion of women achievers who graduated from the two types of colleges for the decades of the sixties and seventies. This result was not unexpected as during this period more than half of all women's colleges in the United States became coeducational or closed their doors in response to financial pressures and women students' declining interest in single-sex education. Our data also partially support the selectivity hypothesis since many of the colleges that could be considered the most selective of all women's colleges became coeducational in this period, and thus their graduates would now be counted among the coeducational achievers.[28] Furthermore, during the past two decades, women's colleges have increased their ethnic and socioeconomic diversity by attracting and providing support for ethnic and racial minorities and disadvantaged women, a trend that could decrease the influence of socioeconomic status as a determinant of career achievement for women's college graduates.

Interestingly enough, despite the lack of statistical significance for the most recent decade, 1970–79, women's colleges had one and one-half times the number of achievers to number of graduates as did coeducational colleges in this period—the same comparative advantage enjoyed by the women's college graduates of the earlier decades. This increase from the 1960s may reflect the recent renaissance and stabilization of the women's college movement. The current increase in enrollment at these schools may also signal that bright women students who in the late 1960s opted for the selective, men's college-gone-coed are now choosing women's colleges. This increase mirrors the growth of the women's movement in the seventies, which undoubtedly influenced the choices many women made about their educations. Those choices reflect an awareness of the importance of an environment of support and challenge rather than one of neglect and discrimination. It will be interesting to see if this trend continues in the future and if it is promoted by the emergence of strong women's studies programs at many women's colleges. Indeed, if Tidball's claim that the prevalence of women role models is what makes women's colleges so advantageous for

---

[28] Radcliffe, Barnard, Vassar, Sarah Lawrence, and Bennington are included in this category.

women students is valid, then the increasing visibility of senior women faculty at coeducational institutions should also contribute to the success of coeducational college women alumnae.

While Tidball has argued that all women's colleges offer women students more women role models and mentors and thus a special environment of support that later gives them a competitive edge in their careers, it is simplistic to consider women's colleges equally beneficial or even comparable. Oates and Williamson's data led them to argue for a separate consideration of the Seven Sisters colleges. One could argue, however, that comparing the Seven Sisters colleges with other women's colleges—southern colleges or Catholic colleges, for example—is misleading since these institutions have developed with very different pedagogic missions, traditions, curricula, and ethos. Historically, the original Seven Sisters were the only women's colleges that were founded on a specific and coherent philosophy of education for women. The colleges for women that were established later often developed in response to geographic and economic demand, which makes categorizing them in subgroups of their own difficult.[29]

The Seven Sisters have fostered and nurtured a long tradition of "specialness," of "quality," of "place." Mary Lyon, the famous American educator and founder of Mount Holyoke, imagined the woman graduate as a pathfinder, a pioneer, and a contributor to society; such a person embodied the mission of these colleges.[30] No one has yet devised a way to measure the impact of the particular experience, the sense of "specialness" conferred by attending one of the Seven Sisters or, for that matter, of attending a Catholic women's college or a southern women's college. College-ranking surveys have singled out some Catholic women's colleges for their strong emphasis on a quality liberal arts education and high academic standards,[31] and one study has found that other women's colleges (primarily southern schools) spend less on education per student and have fewer faculty members with doctorates,[32] but a true picture of what the student gains from attending such colleges will only emerge from research that disentangles the components of the "experience" of attending a particular kind of women's college.

[29] Horowitz (n. 6 above).

[30] Ibid.

[31] In a nationwide survey, several small Catholic affiliated women's colleges were named by 1,308 four-year college presidents as among the nation's highest quality undergraduate schools (*U.S. News and World Report* 95, no. 22 [November 28, 1983]).

[32] Alan L. Sorkin, "Women's Colleges and Universities," *College and University* 48, no. 2 (Winter 1973): 92–99.

There seems little question that an environment in which many women teachers and mentors provide traditional and nontraditional examples of achievement is an advantage to young women. But can the greater visibility of women faculty insure a quality experience for women students? Can it compensate for fewer resources, library holdings, course offerings, smaller endowments, and the lack of specialized training? Moreover, one cannot assume that women faculty, simply because they are women (and, thus, according to Tidball, more concerned with issues related to women than are male faculty), will actively mentor their students or be regarded by their students as role models. In the 1920s, women faculty of women's colleges chafed at the burden of residential life among their student charges and quickly took advantage of the opportunity to live off campus.[33] Indeed, students socialized within a society that discourages women from scholarly and professional pursuits may regard the dedicated woman scholar as odd, rather than as someone to emulate. The character of an individual teacher, rather than her gender, may be the key factor in her influence on students, their overall experience of college, and their career achievement.

Whether the disproportionately high number of women achievers from women's colleges versus coeducational colleges is due to the influence of the environment and the presence of same-sex role models or to the admissions selectivity of the college needs further study. Probably both factors interact and have an influence. The student who applies to the women's college is already a self-selected quantity; probably brighter and more advantaged, she may pick a special environment that in turn nurtures and reinforces her later success. More important, since women's college students represent only 2 percent of their college sisters, the promotion of women's colleges as seedbeds of achievement misses the boat by not focusing on the broader implications of increasing the number of women faculty in coeducational schools. If having a woman mentor and a supportive environment is beneficial to women students in a women's college, then it is likely to be so in a coeducational school as well.

Finally, not only do we need to ask ourselves where and how we can best focus our time and energy, we also need to continue to challenge the definitions and measures of success and achievement. Although Who's Who of American Women provides a convenient and accessible way to tabulate women nationally and across disciplines, it may not be the best or most adequate way to sample women who have made contributions to our culture in less con-

[33] Horowitz, 185.

ventional ways and/or by nonmale standards of success. Women
without advanced degrees or access to professional endorsement
and affiliation could well be unrepresented or underrepresented in
conventional directories. Paradoxically, women's colleges perhaps
are buying into a male standard of success by attempting to justify
their existence by pointing to measures of so-called achiever production. Do women's colleges need such a raison d'etre? We think
not. Women's colleges offer "a room of one's own," a supportive
garden in which to grow and be nurtured, and as such they provide
a singular experience for women students and a unique alternative
to women seeking higher education.

Department of Education Policy Studies
University of Wisconsin—Madison

WANDERING IN THE WILDERNESS:
THE SEARCH FOR WOMEN ROLE MODELS

BERENICE FISHER

The first time I heard the claim that we, as women, needed female role models to make our way through the world, I felt angry. This was the early nineteen seventies, and I had struggled long and hard to make myself an independent woman. That effort had been a lonely one, in a period that offered little support. Now, with a burgeoning movement demanding justice and equality for women, many people, including some feminists, argued the need for role models as well. Secretly, I felt a certain contempt: what we need is guts, not role models! Did these new feminists not know how lucky they were to have so many people on their side? Did they not know what a high price women of my generation had paid to fight these

This essay is dedicated to Barbara Rosenblum—wise, brave, and beautiful friend. In addition to Barbara, I would like to thank Alison Jaggar and members of her 1985 seminar, "Feminist Ways of Knowing," Douglass College, Rutgers University, especially Ruth Berman, Timothy Diamond, Muriel Dimen, Joan Griscom, Heather Karjane, Elinor Lerner, Suzanne Lebsock, Rhoda Linton, Adele McCollum, Uma Narayan, Ferris Olin, Donna Perry, Midge Quandt, Lillian Robbins, Debra Schultz, Joan Tronto, Guida West, and Donna Wilshire; and New York University colleagues Judie Alpert, Pat Carey, Vivian Clarke, Nancy Esibill, Rosalie Miller, Carla Mariano, Mary Sue Richardson, and Emily Wughalter. Finally, I owe a deep debt of thanks to Linda Marks and Lila Braine, Patricia Brown-Height, Suzanne Carothers, Marilyn Coppinger, Roberta Galler, Miriam John, Susan O'Malley, Hanna Pitkin, Harilyn Rousso, May Stevens, and Constance Sutton.

This essay originally appeared in *Signs* Vol. 13, No. 2, Winter 1988.

battles alone? In fact, they did not. Worse still, when some younger feminists accused older professional women of having sold out to the patriarchal establishment, my contempt turned to hurt. There seemed no point in trying to explain my experience of lonely striving. Since I was gradually identifying with the feminist cause myself, my responses could only stand in the way of their acceptance of me. So, I put my awkward feelings aside and joined the movement; but, being an unregenerate intellectual, I did not abandon my critical thoughts. Instead, I took to feminist theorizing and eventually began to write about the ideas that disturbed me—about role models and the related notion of female heroes.[1]

My basic criticism of the feminist enthusiasm for role models and female heroes stemmed from the strongly idealistic way in which such imagery often is used—as though our most important task in achieving feminist goals is to acquire role models and heroes. The notion of role models, in particular, seemed to me little more than a psychological version of the American dream: if women merely follow the lead of so-called role models, we all, every one of us, can succeed. This assumption, I suggested, fosters a dangerous delusion. Capitalist and patriarchal structures prevent us all from succeeding, no matter how many role models or heroes we acquire. Success cannot be attained by everyone: it depends on access to social, economic, and political resources. This applies not only to women striving to succeed in the corporate liberal world but to political activists as well. Reforms and radical change require certain social conditions. Role models and heroes do not guarantee our success and in some instances may undermine our effort. The liberal emphasis on such models sets women up for cooptation when the powers-that-be offer us role models instead of justice. The radical focus on female heroes primes us for moral burnout when we discover that we cannot necessarily live up to the figures we so admire.

My other major criticism concerned the hierarchical implications that the praise of models or heroes often entails. In subtle and not-so-subtle ways, such advocacy perpetuates the logic of domination, by encouraging us to look *up* to "special women" rather than to look around us for the women with whom we might act.[2] The notion of role modeling in particular

---

[1] Amanda Cross offers a witty, though rather broadly painted, picture of academic women dealing with the second feminist wave in *Death in a Tenured Position* (New York: Ballantine Books, 1978). The earlier essays to which I refer are Berenice Fisher, "Who Needs Woman Heroes?" *Heresies* 3, no. 1, issue 9 (1980): 10–13, and "The Models among Us: Social Authority and Political Activism," *Feminist Studies* 7, no. 1 (Spring 1981): 100–112.

[2] One of Barbara Nessim's wonderful line drawings, which accompany the article in *Heresies* cited above, shows a woman looking up to see the outline of a face in the air, while she does not see another woman, who is right in front of her. The theme of the hierarchical or authoritarian nature of heroism has been followed up in many ways. See, e.g., Eric Russell Bentley, *A Century of Hero Worship: A Study of the Idea of Heroism in Carlyle and Nietzsche*

implies an unarticulated theory of leadership in which social leaders—role models—are exempt from the kind of criticism feminists have directed toward political leadership. While feminists indict political authority as leading to domination, we accept the social authority of role models and heroes as naturally benevolent.[3] To me it seemed that we must make room for the criticism of social authority—to see that we do not have to accept automatically the assumptions implied by valuing someone as a role model or hero. Without such criticism, we would have no way of knowing the importance of role models and heroes to our lives or to our work as activists, or teachers, or writers. We could not be fully responsible for promoting such models and heroes in the development of other women before we had undertaken a critique of their importance.

All these arguments and questions about the meaning of role models and heroes seemed, and still seem, perfectly clear to me, but they drew mixed responses from my friends and acquaintances. Some women rejoiced: the term "role model" and the emphasis on heroism long had bothered them, and they were glad that I had unmasked these terms. Others, however, spoke to me with hurt voices. Role models or heroic women had played an important part in these women's liberation. Why was I trying to invalidate their experiences? Their pained responses took me aback. The Marxist in me wondered whether this lack of interest in the material conditions of success grew from false consciousness—from the ideology of individual success with which we have all been raised. But that answer seemed only partly adequate. The women who responded in this way were, in other respects, not so different from myself, and some of them had had to deal much more directly with everyday manifestations of oppression than I. Moreover, it seemed evasive for me to end the matter with this judgment—and it felt unsisterly. So, I sensed there must be something more to this problem, and I kept on thinking.

My present discussion concentrates on the meaning of role models as personal heroes because of what seems to be a special relation between the search for female role models and contemporary feminist sensibility.[4] Since

---

with Notes on Other Hero Worshippers in Modern Times (Philadelphia: J. B. Lippincott Co., 1944). Bentley argues that, historically, the reverence for heroes has both democratic and fascist aspects.

[3] The negative implications of separating social ideals from political realities in feminist practice were pointed out in the early essay by Joreen, "The Tyranny of Structurelessness," reprinted in Radical Feminism, ed. Anne Koedt, Ellen Levine, and Anita Rapone (New York: Quadrangle Press, 1973).

[4] The term "role model" has been used very widely, but it seems to me that the intensity of its meaning for women is not matched elsewhere. My guess is that the very strong influence of psychological thought on the consciousness of feminists and middle-class women in general has played into the appeal of this term. In the research arena, the fields of psychology and education have made use of this term more than any others. Jeanne Speizer reviews the

that sensibility has many variations, I no longer expect to produce a neat and comprehensive analysis of the role model notion. Rather, I seek to convey my own uneven exploration of the topic in order to describe the contradictions I encountered. In the course of this exploration, I have come to appreciate what the search for role models tells us about ourselves: about the differences that divide women, about the conflicts that arise inside each of us, and about the deep connections that often lie beneath these divisions.

*   *   *

Two particular incidents helped me to understand more fully the possibilities of role models for the lives of contemporary women. One was the discovery (through a student who recommended it) of Alice Walker's essay, "Saving the Life that Is Your Own: The Importance of Models in the Artist's Life." It is Walker's essay that also gave me the wonderful phrase, "wandering in the wilderness," with which I named this article.[5] The second was a gathering at which artist May Stevens discussed her recent work.[6]

Walker's discussion of role models comes out of her experience as an artist and the struggle of artists to make their way in the world. The essay begins with a quote from singer Bernice Reagon, pointing out how women "with big legs and big hips and black skin" served as "models" for the community in which she was raised. Then Walker describes a letter that painter Vincent Van Gogh wrote to a friend about the tortured loneliness of the artist rejected by society: "I am suffering," wrote Van Gogh, "under an absolute lack of models." Such models, Walker argues, "enrich and enlarge one's view of existence." They counter the "curse of ridicule" from which artists so often suffer, and they help us find "the common thread, the unifying theme through immense diversity, a fearlessness of growth, of search, of looking that enlarges the private and public world."[7]

Yet, Walker's own efforts to survive as an artist taught her that artists must sometimes persevere without the help of models. She points to Toni

---

psychological literature on role models in "Role Models, Mentors, and Sponsors: The Elusive Concepts," *Signs* 6, no. 4 (Summer 1981): 692–712. This overview reveals the totally contradictory nature of much empirical research on this topic and, to me, indicates the almost complete lack of theoretical, let alone political, criticism of the basic concepts.

[5] Alice Walker's essay was brought to my attention by Patricia Brown-Height. See Alice Walker, "Saving the Life that Is Your Own: The Importance of Models in the Artist's Life," in her *In Search of Our Mothers' Gardens* (San Diego: Harcourt Brace Jovanovich, 1983), 3–14, esp. 12–13.

[6] May Stevens's presentation was sponsored by the New York–based feminist organization, The Crystal Quilt, in March 1985.

[7] Walker, 5.

Morrison's reflections on creativity without the benefit of a model—how Morrison sees art as flowing from the artist's interest, that is, what the artist seeks to put into the world because she does not find it there. Following that vision, "she must be her own model, which is to say herself." This image of the self-made artist appeals to Walker, but she does not rest with it. She goes on to describe her pain as a black woman writer in a world that ignored women like herself, the difficulty of attending courses that ex-cluded black women writers and barely mentioned them in bibliographies. She describes the moment at which she came across the work of Zora Neale Hurston: "What I had discovered, of course, was a model. . . . She had provided, as if she knew someday I would come along wandering in the wilderness, a nearly complete record of her life." Inspired by Hurston, Walker finished a story she had been writing based on her mother's life. This tale "gathered up the historical and psychological threads of the life my ancestors lived, and in the writing of it I felt joy and strength and my own continuity." She felt, she writes, as though "*with* a great many people, ancient spirits, all very happy to see me consulting and acknowledging them, and eager to let me know, through the joy of their presence, that, indeed, I am not alone."[8]

Walker's words went to my core. Perhaps the women who found role models so attractive were wrestling, as I had, with the problem of loneli-ness. Walker's focus on artists seemed especially significant: artists, people trying to make something new. The newer the creation, the more intense the loneliness for, by definition, fewer people can understand or give support and more will find this newness frightening or threatening to their views of the world. Some artists, as Walker's reading of Morrison suggests, tough it out, accepting the need for self-validation and self-support as the price of creativity. For others, that price becomes too high: they abandon their work or, like Van Gogh, pursue it to self-destruction. Still another group, like Walker herself, accept neither loneliness nor tragedy and persist in finding someone to help them. They seek out validation and support from the lives of others, from the awareness that others have done comparable work, from the knowledge that others have survived and that, where they did not, their work lived after them.

Walker's discussion of artistic loneliness reflects not only the realities of creativity but the realities of a social system that systematically isolates artists and many of the rest of us from potential sources of support and validation. This isolation, in turn, affects not only the ways in which we seek to make art but also the ways in which we try to make our lives—to create viable selves in a historical context characterized by deep contradic-tions.

The historical dimension of the search for women role models became

[8] Ibid., 12, 13.

clearer to me through an event at which May Stevens talked about her monumental series of paintings and drawings, "Ordinary. Extraordinary."[9] This series of works concerns two lives: that of the socialist martyr Rosa Luxemburg and that of Stevens's own mother, Alice Stevens. In the course of her presentation, the artist talked about the strange evolution through which her work had gone. Her paintings had begun with a strong image of Luxemburg, whose courage and brilliance Stevens deeply admired, and a weak image of her own mother, an aging working-class woman, whose life had consisted of much suffering and little reward. As the series progressed, Stevens found her mother's portrait becoming stronger and the portrayals of Luxemburg becoming pale and indistinct. As I listened to Stevens talk and looked at the huge oil paintings of Alice Stevens, I sensed the dilemma of being pulled between two poles—the biological and psychological nurturing of the mothers who bore us and the moral and political nurturing of the women we, so often, hope to be. As I thought about this tension in my own life, I began to have a feeling of loss; and, as though we had been thinking with one mind, the women who had gathered around Stevens's paintings began to talk about loss: the loss of mothers who had ended their days in mental institutions, of grandmothers who had comforted us as children, of women whose love and support we never received or now sorely missed. For these women and myself, it seemed clear how much pain had been involved in the necessity of "going it alone" and how much we had struggled to find images of support and validation that did not feel like betrayals of that original nurturance.[10]

This tension between where we had come from and where, hopefully, we were going, brought to my mind the similar strain that so many immigrant mothers and daughters had experienced in the earlier history of the United States. I thought especially of a story by Anzia Yezierska in which the daughter of Jewish immigrants rejects her parents because of their old country ways, yet also rejects the support of a Gentile suitor because he does not really understand what it means to both live in and betray her ghetto culture.[11] I thought also of Jane Addams's work with immigrant women—her recognition of the parallel alienation between

[9] Stevens's ongoing project, "Ordinary. Extraordinary," has been exhibited at numerous galleries. See her "artist's book," *Ordinary. Extraordinary* (n.p., n.d.); and Donald Kuspit et al., *May Stevens: Ordinary-Extraordinary, a Summation, 1977–1984* (Boston: Boston University Art Gallery, 1985).

[10] Compare my account here to Bell Gale Chevigny, "Daughters Writing: Toward a Theory of Women's Biography," in *Between Women: Biographers, Novelists, Critics, Teachers and Artists Write about Their Work on Women*, ed. Carol Ascher, Louise De Salvo, and Sara Ruddick (Boston: Beacon Press, 1984). This book is a treasure trove of essays relevant to the meaning of role models for women.

[11] Anzia Yezierska, "Children of Loneliness" (1923), in *The Open Cage: An Anzia Yezierska Collection*, ed. Alice Kessler-Harris (New York: Persea, 1979).

immigrants and their children and between middle-class mothers and their college-educated daughters. In both instances, Addams saw that the daughters failed to understand what they themselves had lost by rejecting their mothers' values and that such rejection, while perhaps inevitable, also kept them from learning lessons from their mothers' lives.[12]

In a way, Stevens, Yezierska, and Addams all seemed to be addressing the same issue as Walker but each with a slightly different twist. The larger question for all of them was how to make a life that is different from that of our mothers, perhaps also at odds with that of many of our contemporaries; how to make a life that has no clear precedent and that, seemingly, would rob us of the support that traditional ways of living might offer. In Jane Addams's period, as much as our own, this tension between tradition and progress—whether in the form of individuals seeking social mobility or seeking to make a social revolution—places a special burden on women. Since patriarchy assigns us the job of sustaining traditional culture, through rearing children and taking care of many other people, any changes that strain this social web—including even our own rebellion against it—threaten to tear us apart. This rending of not only the social fabric but our very selves as well provides the context for our quest for role models and heroes: images of women who have survived and therefore in some sense negate such contradictions. In this respect, role models and heroes imply a kind of healing, a reconciliation of values that the world presents as contradictory. That reconciliation may, as with Walker and Stevens, lead us back to an appreciation of our mothers, or it may make us feel that we have finally found another kind of mothering, which we also need. But in the end, the search for women role models cannot be reduced to the problem of finding a "good enough mother" of either kind; for the difficulty of finding support, validation, and guidance in changing historical circumstances does not flow only from the inadequacies of individual mothers or mother-substitutes. It also flows from the fact that no authority figures can provide definitive answers or solutions to the problems that such change poses. If historical change has any real meaning, we find ourselves on a constant moral frontier in which neither our or anyone else's experience or knowledge of the world guarantees our transition from the present to the future. Thus, the loneliness of women trying to create new kinds of lives or a new kind of society is not merely psychological or even sociological. It is historical and ultimately, perhaps, existential. It is the loneliness

---

[12] See esp. Jane Addams, "The Subjective Necessity of the Settlement House," in her *Twenty Years at Hull House* (New York: Macmillan, 1912); the discussions of the relationships between women in the Progressive Era in Ellen Condliffe Lagemann, *A Generation of Women: Education in the Lives of Progressive Reformers* (Cambridge, Mass.: Harvard University Press, 1979); and Meredith Tax, *The Rising of the Women: Feminist Solidarity and Class Conflict, 1880–1917* (New York: Monthly Review Press, 1980).

of not knowing where our efforts to change social relationships will take us and whether, in the end, the struggle will be worth the cost.[13]

*   *   *

Although the term "role model" is used in many diverse and even contradictory ways, I have been struck by how often role models are equated with actual people—concrete, publicly identifiable individuals, who play a necessary part in our lives. Women say "she is my role model" in much the same spirit as "she is my mother," while feminist professionals of many sorts recommend a female role model as easily as they might recommend a woman physician or psychotherapist. This equation between role models and people makes intuitive sense for many reasons. One is the tendency to blur the notion of role model with certain social roles, like teacher, and to take the individuals who occupy those roles as such models. (I will come back to this later.) The second reason concerns our very powerful longing for some *one* to guide us through the historical contradictions we face. With all our hearts, we want our role model to be out there. But, even though we may find a variety of people to help us in this struggle, and even though we may adopt some of them as role models, these people and the models we make of them are not the same.[14]

---

[13] The expression "good enough mother" comes from the work of W. D. Winnicott, whose contribution to the psychoanalytic tradition has had considerable impact on feminist work in that area. See, e.g., W. D. Winnicott, "The Theory of the Parent-Infant Relationship," in his *The Maturation Processes and the Facilitating Environment* (New York: International University Press, 1965), 37–55. With respect to integrating the psychological and historical dimensions of role modeling, Erik H. Erikson's essay on "Ego Development and Historical Change," in his *Identity and the Life Cycle* (1959; reprint, New York: W. W. Norton & Co., 1980), suggests the contradictory nature of the realities on which our ego models (to use his term) are based. In the current feminist literature, Jessica Benjamin's discussion of "ideal love" in "A Desire of One's Own: Psychoanalytic Feminism and Intersubjective Space," in *Feminist Studies, Critical Studies*, ed. Teresa de Lauretis (Bloomington: Indiana University Press, 1986) leads to many questions about the childhood origins of the search for role models by women, while her fine essay, "Shame and Sexual Politics," *New German Critique*, no. 27 (Fall 1982), 151–59, points to the historical context in which the problem of women's ideal love may arise. See also Esther Menaker, "Some Inner Conflicts of Women in a Changing Society," in *Career and Motherhood: Struggles for a New Identity*, ed. Alan Roland and Barbara Harris (New York: Human Sciences Press, 1979).

[14] For an example of one broad definition of "role model," as used in the field of psychology, see the scope note on "role model" in *The Thesaurus of Psychological Index Terms*, 3d ed. (Washington, D.C.: American Psychological Association, 1982), namely, "Real or theoretical persons perceived as being ideal standards for emulation in one or a selected number of roles" (150). I have not in any way attempted to survey the wide-ranging use of the term "role model." Some striking examples appear in the special issue "Eminent Women in Psychology: Models of Achievement," ed. Agnes N. O'Connell and Nancy Felipe Rousso, *Psychology of Women Quarterly*, vol. 5, no. 1 (Fall 1980). Nor have I tried to elucidate the far less commonly used expression "negative role model." I sense that this term more often tends to be

To begin with, a role model comes into existence when we choose another person as a model. No matter how deeply rooted or subconscious this process of choosing may be, it implies a certain degree of judgment and consent. Obviously, such decision making does not happen in a vacuum: from birth we are surrounded by external and eventually internal pressures to adopt what our intimates and those with wider power deem the proper models for action. And we do, by and large, adopt them. But regardless of the pressures on us, we know that people are capable of a certain degree of dissent from and resistance to these models because of the frequency with which people refuse to follow them. Moreover, even when we follow conventionally established roles—or ways of acting in the world—we do not automatically perform them in the recommended manner. Our desire to follow a role or perform it in a certain way depends, broadly speaking, on our interest in it. That interest may lie in pursuing the conventional action in the usual manner, and then again, it may not.[15]

Adopting a role model also involves conceptualizing an activity through selecting out certain of its features. That is, we not only choose but also create our role models. We create them by selecting out those features that best suit our interests from our current points of view. Again, this selection does not occur in a social or historical vacuum. When the activity at issue has a long or very well-established tradition behind it, the process of model making approaches copying or imitation. Thus, the *t'ai chi* student learns this ancient martial art by following her teacher's movements as best she can. Try as the student may, she can never copy these movements exactly, nor is that the purpose of the discipline. Nevertheless, she must begin by using her teacher as a literal model in order to acquire this particular way of acting.[16]

When the activity at issue has no clearly recognized tradition or when the role in question has been contested in any significant fashion, the process of making models acquires a different character. Now, we must

---

associated with the ideas of learning as imitation (monkey see, monkey do) than with the spiritual corruption of others (as in the charges against Socrates).

[15] For a review of the vast literature concerning roles, see Theodore Sarbin and Ralph Turner, "Role," in *International Encyclopedia of the Social Sciences*, ed. David L. Sills, 18 vols. (New York: Macmillan Publishing Co., 1968), 13:546–57. My argument concerning roles draws on long-standing critiques of "role theory" by ethnomethodologists and other dissidents in the field of sociology, as well as on the work of philosophers like Charles D. Kaplan and Karl Weiglus, "Beneath Role Theory: Reformulating a Theory of Nietzsche's Philosophy," *Philosophy and Social Criticism* 6, no. 3 (Fall 1979): 289–308.

[16] My interpretation of copying or imitation draws on the historical critique of automatic (biologically determined) learning that was developed by figures like George Herbert Mead, Paul Guillaume, and, after him, Jean Piaget (see Jean Piaget, *Play, Dreams and Imitation in Childhood* [New York: W. W. Norton & Co., 1951]), as well as my own experience studying *t'ai chi ch'uan*.

make our models without "knowing" the features of the activity on which to focus, without having a teacher, so to speak, to correct our movements. Now we must try to imagine which movement will get us to where we are trying to go, when the goal itself has a somewhat hazy and shimmering quality. In effect, we try to construct a model for a way of acting that we can only barely envision and that "society" in its various forms has not validated for us. In this sense, then, model making becomes an instrument of discovery, the creation of an ideal way of acting that is not yet embodied in our experience.[17]

Because model taking and model making speak to ways of acting not yet embodied in our social realities, these efforts do not require the consent of others. One person's desire can bring a role model into being. In this respect, the process of taking and making role models is like falling in love. We do not need the consent of the role model any more than that of the beloved. This is why we can take as our role models not only people we know in our daily lives but also people who have died, or who we have never met (famous or heroic figures), or who never really existed (like characters in a novel). The comparison with falling in love is also apt because taking and making role models entails passion. That passion comes from longing not only for what has not been given but also for what can be—the kind of passion we need to carry us over into the future, to the realization of only vaguely perceived ideals.[18]

One more feature of the development of role models is the extent to which they come into being as either individual or collective creations. I stress the individual as maker of role models in order to counter the narrow view of human nature implied in many political or educational prescriptions that, if people are given role models, they automatically will follow them. But it seems clear that the emergence and maintaining of role models is rarely, if ever, a solely individual or completely social matter. We

[17] For a discussion of how the scientific use of models gets translated into applied settings, see Stephenie G. Edgerton, "What Is a Model? Modeling and the Professions," in *Modeling Mathematical Cognitive Development*, ed. Sigrid E. Wagner (Columbus, Ohio: ERIC Clearinghouse for Science, Mathematics and Environmental Education, 1981), 1–10. See also Ryan D. Tweney, Michael E. Doherty, and Clifford R. Mynatt, eds., *On Scientific Thinking* (New York: Columbia University Press, 1981), esp. Thomas Kuhn, "Unanswered Questions about Science," 45–47; Ian I. Metroff, "Scientists and Confirmation Bias," 170–75; and Mary B. Hesse, "The Function of Analogies in Science," 345–48.

[18] On the emotive dimension of scientific theorizing, see both Evelyn Fox Keller, *Reflections on Gender and Science* (New Haven, Conn.: Yale University Press, 1985); and Elizabeth Sewell, *The Orphic Voice: Poetry and Natural History* (New Haven, Conn.: Yale University Press, 1960). The comparison between choosing role models and falling in love harks back to a type of argument—extending from classical Greece to twentieth-century Europe—in which human growth or learning is interpreted as the reincarnation or re-creation of certain ideals or essential forms. Appealing as I find some of this thought on the metaphorical level, my own argument stresses the socially and historically contingent character of our ideal making.

can, I think, view the construction of role models on a spectrum: on one end are the isolated creative acts in which we, as individuals, struggle to find a new vocabulary that expresses our desires (the situations in which an individual woman makes her own role model), and on the other end are those collective efforts of whole societies to project an ideal of action that embodies wider moral strivings (as when someone becomes our hero). On the individual end of the spectrum, the role model may never become public knowledge, remaining a secret ideal that we hug to our breasts at especially lonely moments. On the collective end of the spectrum, role models as heroes are publicly acknowledged and often ritually celebrated images of what everyone, in some sense, hopes to be. In between these two extremes lie many possible variations, reflecting the historical and social features of a given society. Isolated individuals may come together to discover that they share certain role models in common. Conflicting social groups may glorify particular models or heroic figures who represent competing visions of the future. Ruling elites, with tremendous power at their disposal, can create or reinforce ideals of individual behavior that subvert or distort beyond recognition the legitimate impulse to find and refine heroes of our own. This potential for manipulation, however, does not negate the meaning or importance of role models. It only warns us that what seems to be a deeply personal act takes place in a profoundly political environment in which discovering and holding on to our hopes for the future may involve an ongoing struggle.[19]

*   *   *

Like making works of art, the creation of role models that guide us into the future requires imagination. As in art making, we do not create our work out of whole cloth. History, biography, and chance all provide material from which to shape our role models. We, in effect, sift these materials and select out (often on a relatively unconscious level) those features of a life or way of acting that seem to help us on our path. In the process of selection, we necessarily neglect other aspects of a life or way of acting. This neglect has a positive function to play: no process of model

[19] My image of the interplay between social and individual factors in the creation of role models and heroes has strong affinities to Kathy E. Ferguson's feminist revision of George Herbert Mead's theory of self (see *Self, Society and Womanhood: The Dialectic of Liberation* [Westport, Conn.: Greenwood Press, 1980]). Although I have chosen to focus my own critique on role models, I hope it will help to uncover a part of the complex dynamic underlying the creation of heroes as well. Some of the more interesting treatments of heroism include Philip Rosenberg, *The Seventh Hero: Thomas Carlyle and the Theory of Radical Action* (Cambridge, Mass.: Harvard University Press, 1974); Orin E. Klapp, *Symbolic Leaders: Public Dramas and Public Men* (Chicago: Aldine Publishing Co., 1964); and Hanna Fenichel Pitkin's subtle study of Machiavelli, *Fortune Is a Woman: Gender and Politics in the Thought of Machiavelli* (Berkeley and Los Angeles: University of California Press, 1984).

making, thinking, or even perceiving can take place without selective attention and inattention to various features of the situation. The neglected realities do not disappear. They merely remain out of sight, constituting a potential threat to the choices, truth claims, and passions that the creation of role models entails. Although we can sometimes avoid looking at these suppressed elements for long periods of time, conflict and change tend to bring them to light, to expose in one way or another the limits of the individual and socially created ideals we have held. The experience of recognizing this contradiction between the ideal we have constructed and the realities it fails to embrace holds the promise of furthering our feminist politics. It also carries the potential for self-alienation and the destruction of the often fragile bonds we build with other women.

I would like to tell three stories in exploring these points. One concerns my own role model making, long before the term or even the idea would have had much meaning for me. My university career in the 1950s and early 1960s turned out to be rather long for a woman at that time because I did not marry, because I rather liked the sort of conceptual work they fostered at my school, and because I did not know what to do when I grew up. Somewhere along the line—I think it was when I had trouble finishing my bachelor's paper—a distant cousin who happened to be teaching at the same school began to act as my teacher. He continued then, on and off, to guide my intellectual work through my doctoral degree. I was lucky to come from a family with an academic member, to be in the place where he taught at a time in which I needed guidance, to have encountered someone generous and tolerant enough to help a young woman student. A combination of good luck and social privilege gave me a teacher, but I myself made him into a role model.[20]

In adopting my teacher as a role model, it never occurred to me to discount him because of his gender. There were relatively few women teaching at the universities I attended in that period. I was intimidated by prominent women intellectuals—Who would have thought of going to study with them?—and I was skeptical of the less famous women academics whom I sometimes encountered. Could they really be as good as the men? Were these women still appealing to men? I feared they were not, and for that reason I feared even more being identified with them. Moreover, I did not need to take such women as role models to assure myself that women could think. For a variety of reasons, I had long before acquired an image of

---

[20] Anselm L. Strauss's teaching and writing has continued to influence my thought, despite some important differences in the path I have taken. Some of his most enduring lessons for me concern the interaction between biography and history, the complex ways in which we make and try to make our lives (see Anselm L. Strauss, *Mirrors and Masks: The Search for Identity* [Glencoe, Ill.: Free Press, 1959], and *The Contexts of Social Mobility: Ideology and Theory* [Chicago: Aldine Publishing Co., 1971]).

myself as a thinking woman—not through role models at all but through a childhood passion for reading and philosophizing. By adulthood, I had fully accepted the prevailing idea (prevailing even with so advanced a thinker as Simone de Beauvoir, whose *Second Sex* I had read with wide eyes) that mothering and thinking did not fit together. Since I was not on my way to motherhood, I could go on thinking.[21]

Finding a way to pursue the life of the mind still posed a problem, however. The male academics whom I encountered suggested, through their styles of work, that intellectual activity and caring did not fit together. Attracted as I was to thinking, I still wanted to be a caring person—an element of my acquired femininity I did not want to relinquish. For me, my teacher reconciled this apparent contradiction between thinking and caring. He taught in a caring way. He saw research and writing as human activities, involving relationships between people. His caring intellect gave me the material out of which to build my ideal.

When I became a feminist, I had a hard time dealing with this phase of my life. My earlier career struggle seemed male identified. I knew that some of the attention I enjoyed, in both senses of the word, stemmed from my status as a "special woman" and that if many women had pursued the same path I would not have been so special. I was ashamed, too, of the now obvious self-hatred involved in my rejection of other academic women. Yet, I could not disown these years. Perhaps I had become a feminist too late in my life with too much personal history behind me, or perhaps I liked thinking too much to disavow a relationship in which my intellectual capacity had been so fully supported. For a long time, I could not assimilate this period into my new self, and I could not let it go.

My second story is somewhat fictionalized. A woman I know has become a very successful scientist. She herself came of age with the women's movement, and it has affected her life profoundly. She publishes and speaks widely. By white Anglo-Saxon Protestant standards, she is very attractive. She has four children; her husband has done well in business. When she gives lectures encouraging young women to follow careers in science, they respond with enthusiasm. More often than not, a member of the audience will approach her afterward crying: "I'm so glad to meet you at last. You're my role model!" After one such talk, the scientist and I met for tea. She came in smiling with the glow of success. Then she started talking to me about her life, about the overload of family and professional responsibilities, about the pressure of young women wanting to work with her. As she spoke, the anger finally began to flow. "If one more person calls me her role model," she said, "I'm going to scream."

Being a peer rather than a student, I know the side of her story the

[21] Simone de Beauvoir, *The Second Sex*, trans. and ed. H. M. Parshley (1952; reprint, New York: Alfred A. Knopf, 1968).

younger women fail to see. Despite or perhaps because of her success, the scientist's husband never quite values her work as much as his own. Because both of them fundamentally accept the notion that work at home is her responsibility, she ends up paying the costs of child care. She can hardly talk with the Hispanic woman she has hired to clean the house because of the profound shame that she, the scientist, feels at paying such low wages. She remains furious with the very competent English nanny who takes care of the youngest child because the nanny never attends to her, the scientist's, emotional needs. In short, my acquaintance is filled with feelings of rage and deprivation because of the high costs attached to her considerable accomplishment.

Although I nod with understanding as she speaks, her frustration raises in me mixed emotions. On the one hand, my heart goes out to her because of her pain. On the other, I feel enraged myself: "What kind of feminist are you, anyway?" I want to shout. "Don't you realize that women's success in our society is built on a confluence of class, race, and gender privilege? Why don't you listen to what we radical-socialist-lesbian feminists are saying instead of staying so cooped up in your own precious world?" But in the end I say nothing and just take another sip of tea.

My last story is about a collective rather than an individual effort. Several years ago I reviewed a fine volume on the lives of women activists, based on a set of oral histories.[22] I was deeply impressed by the lives of these women, and I learned a good deal from them. Yet, in a way, they discouraged as much as they encouraged my own activist efforts. I could not understand how these women managed to sustain such morally and politically demanding lives. Their activism seemed almost magical, a mission or gift given to some women and not to others. It was hard to conceive of them having moments of self-doubt or defeat, to imagine how they dealt with loneliness or family obligations, how they obtained comfort, sexual gratification, political counsel—if, indeed, they needed or sought any of these things. I could not imagine how they managed their activism when their resources were drained, when their health failed, or when they began to feel the effects of aging. Did some secret lie behind the projected lives of these women, behind the models and heroes they were intended to be? Perhaps, in truth, they were simply stronger and more courageous than I was, and, therefore, I should not expect such efforts of myself.

Now, what lessons can be drawn from my stories? In each case, some factor—becoming a feminist, adhering to a political vision different from that of the feminist scientist, dealing with loneliness and lack of support— gave me a perspective that called into question a given role model or heroic

---

[22] See Fisher, "The Models among Us" (n. 1 above). The book in question was Ellen Cantarow with Susan Gushee O'Malley and Sharon Hartman Strom, *Moving the Mountain: Women Working for Social Change* (Old Westbury, N.Y.: Feminist Press, 1980).

image. My perspective not only revealed elements that had been omitted or neglected in the creation of these particular ideals: it also evoked painful feelings. I was ashamed of my youthful compliance with patriarchal values. I was enraged when the scientist ignored the realities of so many other women (including myself). I was afraid that the images conveyed in the book on women activists would reveal my own weaknesses. In each instance, my responses assumed that if only those role models had been based on reality, if only they showed the whole truth, I myself could stand in a more comfortable relation to them. As it was, these ideals seemed suspect, if not downright fraudulent.

Although it may have come from the heart, this formulation had several serious problems. It implied that truth is static, uniperspectival, and objectivist, that it is something we can pin down forever, regardless of the contradictions that history and biography create. But equally important, my criticism ignored the choosing and feeling elements in our projection of role models. Role models, as I have suggested, cannot be evaluated solely as truth claims. The process of constructing a moral or political ideal only makes sense in the context of what we choose and feel. This is not to say that truth has no relevance for the creation of role models but that the truth of role modeling needs to be assessed in the context of the commitments it entails and the passion it expresses. Otherwise, this truth cannot be understood at all.[23]

*   *   *

One day, mulling over the story of the feminist scientist, I realized that I had been, in effect, accusing her of bad faith—the bad faith of denying certain evident realities. Then I realized that, at this moment in her life, her choice lay between bad faith and no faith at all. That is, it took a great deal of faith in even a moderate amount of social change for her to resist the class, race, and heterosexual pressures and rewards with which she was surrounded. In focusing on how much her liberal beliefs limited her understanding of herself and other women, I had failed to recognize the faith that sustained her.

This neglect on my part was far from accidental. Rationalism had dominated my upbringing and education. For most of my life, I have viewed religious belief with suspicion and discomfort. In this respect, I think that the faith dimension that I sensed in the praise of role models disturbed me far more deeply than the selectivity and denial involved in creating these ideals. When feminists spoke warmly of their role models,

[23] Feminist critiques of epistemology have raised many leading questions about women's stake in how "the truth" is defined. See, e.g., Sandra Harding and Merrill B. Hintikka, eds., *Discovering Reality: Feminist Perspectives on Epistemology, Metaphysics, Methodology and Philosophy of Science* (Dordrecht: D. Reidel Publishing Co., 1983).

something inside me whispered "graven images," "opiates of the people," while a screen in some distant corner of my mind flashed on an image of painted idols. During my years of work on this paper, my discomfort with the topic of faith has decreased, partly through knowing and reading the work of religiously and spiritually based feminists and partly through dealing directly with the problem of moral burnout in activism. Still, I approach the topic of faith gingerly, unsure of its meaning for myself or for my idea of feminist politics.[24]

With some reservations, then, I would like to use "moral faith" to describe the kind of faith involved in choosing, creating, and admiring role models.[25] In this context, moral faith has three especially important features. The first is that such faith originates in its practice: we create an ideal and at the same time testify to it or witness it by trying out (sometimes first in our imagination) the actions to which it directs us. The second feature of moral faith flows directly from the first: that the practice of such faith has its own truth. It is a dynamic truth, concerned more with discovery than with what is already known. In the case of role models the discovery process expresses itself in the form of a narrative, a story. The role model acts like the central figure in a myth, whose adventures direct our attention to parts of the world and parts of our selves that we can explore. The third feature of moral faith is that it fosters loyalty to an ideal and therefore to others who are willing to work for that ideal. Thus, our choice of a female role model implies a connection to other women who are drawn to the ideal this model represents. It implies the expectation that their faith will echo and support our own.

Without the foundation created by such moral faith, I suspect, a given role model would be nothing but an interesting idea about how to live or

---

[24] See, e.g., Sharon D. Welch, *Communities of Resistance and Solidarity: A Feminist Liberation Theology* (Maryknoll, N.Y.: Orbis Books, 1985); Charlene Spretnak, ed., *The Politics of Spirituality: Essays on the Rise of Spiritual Power within the Feminist Movement* (New York: Anchor Books, 1982); and Berenice Fisher, "Over the Long Haul: Burnout and Hope in a Conservative Era," *Frontiers: A Journal of Women Studies* 8, no. 3 (1986): 1–7. My understanding of this point has grown through conversations with Sister Pat Berliner about her work with Catholic women, Sister Magdalena Kobayashi about her remarkable commitment to social justice, and Lee Zevi about the meaning of faith in my own life. Thinking about my own Reform Jewish background, I sense that our relation to particular kinds of religious belief, or lack thereof, may play a significant part in how we view the process of role modeling.

[25] I am using the term "moral faith" in a way that neither confines it to nor precludes it from a religious or spiritual interpretation. See Welch; Paul Kurtz, "Moral Faith and Ethical Skepticism Reconsidered," *Journal of Value Inquiry* 19, no. 1 (1985): 55–65; and Dallas High's excellent treatment of belief in *Language, Persons and Belief: Studies in Wittgenstein's Philosophical Investigation and Religious Uses of Language* (New York: Oxford University Press, 1967). I am, like so many writers on this topic, also indebted to the classic work of William James (see "The Will to Believe," in *The Will to Believe* [New York: Longmans, Green, 1908]).

how to manage a somewhat difficult activity. In this sense, moral faith constitutes the core of a role model's meaning. Yet finding moral faith at the core of role modeling also raises serious problems. One problem lies in determining the extent to which we can be ethically (and here I also include politically) critical of the values a role model represents. If we were simply talking about adequate descriptions of reality—the social and material conditions it takes to achieve a certain goal—this would pose less difficulty. But the critical assessment of moral faith, our own or anyone else's, cannot be so blithely undertaken. The second problem relates to the notion of truth as discovery. Can our faith really embrace an open-ended image of where this discovery might lead? Can we remain open to unpalatable and contradictory truths about the world and ourselves? Finally, the third problem requires thinking about the sorts of relationships that might result from choosing and creating various kinds of role models, what values this process implies, and what sorts of feminist politics we would be shaping.

I cannot, of course, pretend to solve these problems in the final pages of this essay, but I would like to sketch out a provisional argument that provides at least a base for my recommendations in the final section. To begin with, I would like to argue for not only the possibility but also the importance of criticizing the role-modeling process, not despite, but because of, our role models' base in our faith, because they are so powerful and meaningful. This will not be easy. We may hesitate to criticize another's creation and choice of role models because matters of faith are "personal" and, therefore, off-bounds to criticism. Even if we do not recognize the faith element, we may seem to be intruding on private territory or to be undermining the trust we want to foster in people as part of their emotional maturity. Yet, to abandon the topic of role models as not subject to political discussion is to reinstitute in another form the public-private split, to say, in effect, that our personal ideals are not political. The question seems less one of whether we should make such ideals part of political discussion and more one of how to do so in a way that respects the deep roots of faith no less than the importance of community building.

Second, I think we need to be very wary of the assumption that the faith we express through the projection of role models smooths our way into the future. Because of the very tenuous path we tread through history—the lack of guarantees that our efforts will succeed and the often deeply frustrating character of the contradictions we face—we experience tremendous internal and external pressures to know what to do as well as to know what the results of our actions will be. Fixed, universal images of achievement—be they role models, heroes, foremothers, or goddesses—may seem to offer the possibility of such knowledge. But regardless of the ways in which such figures may embody faith in our capacity to act in one way or another, they give us neither knowledge of the future nor knowledge of how to overcome the differences that divide us. They cannot give us neat, noncontradictory selves or a nonproblematic relation to the world.

Finally, I think that we need to take a careful look at the kinds of relationships implied by the choosing and creating of role models. Although rarely articulated, I think that many women who are attracted to the notion of role models envision a historical progression in which women who have themselves found role models then act as role models for women who come after them.[26] Such a progression, combining both nurturance and justice, feels particularly right. But, as I have argued earlier, this feeling of rightness cannot flow from the process of choosing and creating role models itself because the process does not require consent. No matter how ardently we offer ourselves as role models, we have no guarantee that younger or less experienced women will view this as part of a loving or just interchange. To discover whether bonds of loyalty, trust, and shared political ideals can be fostered in the process of creating role models requires us to talk about how that process functions in a given political context and about the responsibilities to each other that our choice of a given role model implies.

*   *   *

When I first discovered that some women *wanted* to be taken as role models, I was amazed. When I myself was called a role model, I winced. Then I panicked. Would I have to be perfect in her eyes? What would happen when she found out my various failings? Would she expect me to help her become the perfect creature she imagined me to be? I did not want the burden of such an expectation, as a woman or as a teacher.

Many things lay beneath my fears, including an upbringing that valued autonomy more than nurturance; that cautioned me to be very, very good; and that taught me the high price of taking care of others. But interwoven with these fears was a genuine confusion about responsibility. Could I be a teacher without being a role model? If someone took me as her role model, what sort of responsibilities did that imply?

My explorations have suggested some answers to me. In this essay, my treatment of role models assumes that we choose our own political ideals. We do not choose them "freely," of course, because we do not live freely, and we do not choose them in isolation because we live in the world. But, given these limits, responsibility for our political ideals remains our own.

---

[26] This anticipated relation between past, present, and future role models is evident in Carol Pearson and Katherine Pope, *The Female Hero in American and British Literature* (New York: R. R. Bowker, 1981): "No matter how alienated she [the female hero] is from the larger society, the hope present in the description of her experience is that if one woman has made that particular journey beyond convention, so can others. Each is a role model to another, and so on, until eventually the myths and institutions of the entire society are altered" (260).

The responsibility for choosing and creating role models entails nothing more or less than taking responsibility for ourselves. In the terms of Alice Walker's essay, we are the artists who make our own lives, using the materials available to us. These materials vary greatly, reflecting, among other things, the various forms of social injustice to which we are subject. Even in the face of such differences, we can hold each other accountable— for the directions we have taken and the ways we have used or failed to use the materials at hand.

What we cannot do for another person is to take responsibility for the path she has chosen. Nor, by the same logic, can we make her choose a certain path or use a certain vehicle, like a role model, in order to traverse it. Whether or not we believe that a woman needs a role model for the sake of her politics, her career, her mental health, her education, or her immortal soul the choice is hers: to adopt one role model rather than another or to avoid adopting role models of any sort. She may, in fact, find an entirely different way to express her moral faith and its place, if any, in her life.

Now, my argument here does not imply that we can or should avoid offering role models to others whose struggles we wish to support. But it does imply the need to look more closely at our responsibilities in this area. In order to do so, however, we need to make a clear conceptual distinction between three processes: the choosing and creating of role models, activities such as teaching (or counseling or political organizing) in which more experienced women seek to guide less experienced women, and the giving of emotional, social, or material support to others to facilitate their efforts. It is not at all easy to separate these processes in practice, as the example of teaching shows. Students often take their teachers as role models, and teachers often offer themselves as such models. Teachers also often give students emotional and institutional support to help them make it through the system. However, neither acting as a role model nor giving such forms of support is intrinsic to teaching as an activity.[27] A teacher may convey highly valued skills or share important resources without touching the moral core that makes a given student choose her as a role model. For any particular student, one teacher may embody a way of getting through life's contradictions and another teacher may not.

[27] Compare F. N. J. Hibberd, "Must an Educator Be a Model?" *Journal of Moral Education* 12, no. 3 (October 1983): 182–86. Now and then, feminists discussing their own pedagogy complain of the burden of being a role model. See Nancy K. Miller, "Mastery, Identity and the Politics of Work: A Feminist Teacher in the Graduate Classroom," in *The Dynamics of Feminist Teaching*, ed. Margo Culley and Catherine Portuges (Boston: Routledge & Kegan Paul, 1985), 195–99. I would also add that the equation of teachers with role models often implies that we only learn or learn best from those we resemble or with whom we can identify. This formulation totally ignores the many ways in which we learn by thinking against a set of ideas or a prevailing logic (see Herbert Marcuse, *One Dimensional Man: Studies in the Ideology of Advanced Industrial Society* [Boston: Beacon Press, 1968]).

Teaching, in its most authentic form, involves a consensual relationship in which both teacher and student take responsibilities of certain kinds. When someone agrees to be a teacher, or counselor, or mentor, she undertakes to do certain things for her student(s). Thus, teachers can be held accountable for what they do. Role models cannot. When we blur the distinction between role model and teacher, we tend to imply that teachers (or others like them) should embody a moral faith that certain social and historical contradictions can be resolved. This is too great a responsibility to place on anyone's shoulders. Moreover, we have no reason to think that teachers, or any other similar social group, have a particular facility for assuming such responsibility. Indeed, virtually anyone can provide material for creating a role model, just as virtually anyone can teach us lessons crucial to our making our way through the world. (Some of the most important lessons I have learned came from strangers who made just the right point or raised just the right question to me when I was wrestling with an important life decision.) What distinguishes our interactions with strangers or people we have chosen as role models from our relationship with teachers (and others like them) is not teachers' unique abilities to guide our lives but the fact that we engage with them in regularized, consensual relationships that *can* involve mutual obligations and responsibilities.

Along these same lines, I think it is also important to differentiate activities of giving support or sponsorship from the process of becoming someone's role model. As in the case of teachers, counselors, organizers, and so forth, sponsors and supporters who are older, or more powerful, or more experienced than ourselves become likely material out of which to create our role models. Such people, of course, are often pleased to be viewed in this way; but, again, blurring the distinction between people and role models makes it difficult to assess the responsibilities involved in the given relationship and tends to obscure the social and material base that sponsors or supporters provide. The difference between being a model and providing the sponsorship or support for another's efforts becomes perfectly apparent when such support has not been dignified through idealization. The wife who puts her husband through medical school by working as a secretary and ministering to all his physical and emotional needs does not, thereby, become his role model—although she may enable him to sustain his own ideal of achievement, embodied, say, in the figure of a prominent physician who combines qualities the husband hopes to realize. Thus, women, as this example suggests, have a special stake in developing a clear distinction between ideals of action and the conditions that make action possible. This is because we ourselves so often provide the conditions for men's acting without being admitted into the world of action ourselves—without being seen as capable of achieving the same ideals.

By arguing in this way, I have, in a sense, come full circle to the more critical position I described at the beginning of this essay—with a difference. I no longer view the highly selective character of role models or the fact that the conditions of their realization often remain invisible as reasons, in themselves, for discounting their value. Rather, like any other ideals we project, they need to be evaluated in terms of both what they mean to us and what consequences they have for us—and whether any of those meanings or consequences conflicts with other values we hold.

Moreover, that evaluation needs to be done in the context of our own lives and hopes. For the search for our political truth is ultimately a search for ourselves, a search that requires, as Barbara Deming said, "listening to everything we have to say to ourselves (and also to one another) and trusting that we'll come to see how it all fits together. Not being afraid to seem untidy in the process."[28] Ideal versions of other women's lives can help us in this search, but, in the end, the ways in which we present our own lives in talking and working with each other have an even greater impact on its outcome. When we reveal to each other not only our successes in making our way but also the conditions that have made it possible and the contradictions we have failed to overcome, we lay the groundwork for more authentic connection to each other—despite our differences. By sharing these home truths, we neither prevent nor undermine the possibility of finding in each other the embodiment of some ideal of action, though we do reveal aspects of ourselves with which we may be uncomfortable. We make ourselves vulnerable. We allow ourselves and others to question the process by which we have done what we have done, not merely to accept it as a final truth but to open it up to reinterpretation and re-creation as well. This sort of interaction with other women requires self-revelation in the best sense: not random confession but a selective uncovering of those aspects of our lives that help ourselves and others to raise new questions about ourselves, the world, and our relation to it. Such self-revelation does not always come easily, of course, but, as the experience of consciousness-raising shows, the sense that we are searching together for a new sort of truth can give us the moral faith necessary to undertake the search. Faith here refers not solely to our faith in a political ideal but also to our faith in each other, our faith in ourselves, and our faith in the community we are building.

This brings me to my final point concerning responsibility. I have been focusing on the individual as the chooser of role models and role models as an idealized image of individual action. I have done this purposefully, not to laud individualism but to acknowledge its importance in the meaning of role models to most women. Moreover, this perspective stresses our capacity to choose and shape our own political values, even when—in the

---

[28] Mab Segrest, ed., "Feminism and Disobedience: Conversations with Barbara Deming," *Feminary* 11, nos. 1–2 (1980): 71–85, esp. 75.

eyes of others whom we encounter or in our retrospective judgment of ourselves—these values may not appear sufficiently broad or deep. But I would not want the exploration of role models to stop at this point. My own ideal and, I think, any feminist ideal of community requires us to look for a more collectively based and relationally oriented notion of what role models *might be*. I do not know what such models would look like exactly, but it seems to me that many feminist activists and thinkers have been looking in this direction. Most important, perhaps, is the work of black feminists like Gloria Joseph and Suzanne Carothers who, in exploring the relationships between mothers and daughters, suggest that we can both embody an ideal and remain vitally connected to each other in a real and truthful way. The heart of these accounts, as I read them, lies in the fact that the admiration of black daughters for their mothers grows out of understanding the conditions and contradictions that both mothers and daughters must face in a racist society. Thus, when daughters claim their mothers as role models, that claim requires neither denial (it can include the acknowledgment of failure and of the high costs of making a life for black people) nor isolation (it is not necessary to see one's mother as an exceptional woman in order to admire her). Rather, the meaning of being a role model grows out of discovering shared struggles and shared vulnerabilities in relation to the world.[29]

Feminists have been looking toward other arenas, as well, for models of how we can relate to each other—toward friendship, education, psychotherapy, political protest, and the building of feminist organizations.[30] As in the search for individual role models, this attempt to find

[29] See Gloria I. Joseph, "Black Mothers and Daughters: Their Roles and Functions in American Society," in *Common Differences: Conflicts in Black and White Feminist Perspectives*, ed. Gloria I. Joseph and Jill Lewis (New York: Anchor Books, 1981), 75–126; and Suzanne Carothers, "Generation to Generation: The Transmission of Knowledge, Skills and Role Models from Black Working Mothers to Their Daughters in a Southern Community" (Ph.D. diss., New York University, 1987). It is equally important to note that, for some black women, mothers make highly problematic role models: see Gloria Naylor, "Kiswana Browne," in her *Women of Brewster Street* (London: Penguin Books, 1982). Again, I am indebted to Patricia Brown-Height for the reference.

[30] See, e.g., Berenice Fisher and Roberta Galler, "Friendship and Fairness: How Disability Affects Friendships between Women," in *Women with Disabilities: Essays in Psychology, Politics and Policy*," ed. Adrienne Asch and Michelle Fine (Philadelphia: Temple University Press, 1988); Louise Eichenbaum and Susie Orbach, *Understanding Women: A Feminist Psychoanalytic Approach* (New York: Basic Books, 1982); and Charlotte Bunch and Sandra Pollack, eds., *Learning Our Way: Essays in Feminist Education* (Trumansburg, N.Y.: Crossing Press, 1983). For a thoughtful account of women's relationships as a part of organization building, see Susan L. Koen, "Feminist Workplaces: Alternative Models for the Organization of Work" (Ph.D. diss., Union Graduate School, 1984). Jane Rule's essay, "With All Due Respect," offers a valuable glimpse into the relation between feminist group process and the adopting of role models (see *Outlander: Short Stories and Essays* [Tallahassee, Fla.: Naiad Press, 1981], 173–79).

and create relational ideals speaks to our deepest hopes and touches on disturbing contradictions. The hopes concern our desire for rich and loving interaction. The contradictions surface as we try to embody values like equality, justice, compassion, and freedom in our ongoing relationships. Because our social order systematically undermines these relationships by destroying the connections necessary to realize them, experience often teaches the same lesson as the official culture: we must go it alone. Paradoxically, many of the traditional patterns that seem to promote women's connectedness to others—family obligations, economic dependency, our socially shaped capacity to foster relationships—still leave women isolated and angry. That was one of the earliest truths that consciousness-raising uncovered, together with the recognition that an oppressive reality divides us from one another. Thus, the creation of any new ideal of how we can relate to each other requires careful attention to the world in which we actually live. Looking at the social and material realities in which our relationships grow or falter should not destroy our moral faith or our political ideals. Rather, it should keep them, and us, grounded: firmly planted on the earth, reaching out to embrace, and searching an open sky.

Department of Cultural Foundations
New York University

CULTURAL FEMINISM VERSUS POST-STRUCTURALISM: THE IDENTITY CRISIS IN FEMINIST THEORY

LINDA ALCOFF

For many contemporary feminist theorists, the concept of woman is a problem. It is a problem of primary significance because the concept of woman is the central concept for feminist theory and yet it is a concept that is impossible to formulate precisely for feminists. It is the central concept for feminists because the concept and category of woman is the necessary point of departure for any feminist theory and feminist politics, predicated as these are on the transformation of women's lived experience in contemporary culture and the reevaluation of social theory and practice from women's point of view. But as a concept it is radically problematic precisely for feminists because it is crowded with the overdeterminations of male supremacy, invoking in every formulation the limit, contrasting Other, or mediated self-reflection of a culture built on the control of females. In attempting to speak for women, feminism often seems to presuppose that it knows what women truly are, but such an assumption is foolhardy given that every source of knowledge about

In writing this essay I have benefited immeasurably as a participant of the 1984–85 Pembroke Center Seminar on the Cultural Construction of Gender at Brown University. I would also like to thank Lynne Joyrich, Richard Schmitt, Denise Riley, Sandra Bartky, Naomi Scheman, and four anonymous reviewers for their helpful comments on an earlier draft of this paper.

This essay originally appeared in *Signs*, vol. 13, no. 3, Spring 1988.

women has been contaminated with misogyny and sexism. No matter where we turn—to historical documents, philosophical constructions, social scientific statistics, introspection, or daily practices—
the mediation of female bodies into constructions of woman is dominated by misogynist discourse. For feminists, who must transcend
this discourse, it appears we have nowhere to turn.[1]

Thus the dilemma facing feminist theorists today is that our very
self-definition is grounded in a concept that we must deconstruct
and de-essentialize in all of its aspects. Man has said that woman
can be defined, delineated, captured—understood, explained, and
diagnosed—to a level of determination never accorded to man himself, who is conceived as a rational animal with free will. Where
man's behavior is underdetermined, free to construct its own future
along the course of its rational choice, woman's nature has overdetermined her behavior, the limits of her intellectual endeavors,
and the inevitabilities of her emotional journey through life. Whether
she is construed as essentially immoral and irrational (à la Schopenhauer) or essentially kind and benevolent (à la Kant), she is
always construed as an essential *something* inevitably accessible
to direct intuited apprehension by males.[2] Despite the variety of
ways in which man has construed her essential characteristics, she
is always the Object, a conglomeration of attributes to be predicted
and controlled along with other natural phenomena. The place of
the free-willed subject who can transcend nature's mandates is reserved exclusively for men.[3]

Feminist thinkers have articulated two major responses to this
situation over the last ten years. The first response is to claim that
feminists have the exclusive right to describe and evaluate woman.
Thus cultural feminists argue that the problem of male supremacist

[1] It may seem that we can solve this dilemma easily enough by simply defining
woman as those with female anatomies, but the question remains, What is the significance, if any, of those anatomies? What is the connection between female anatomy
and the concept of woman? It should be remembered that the dominant discourse
does not include in the category woman everyone with a female anatomy: it is often
said that aggressive, self-serving, or powerful women are not "true" or "real" women.
Moreover, the problem cannot be avoided by simply rejecting the concept of "woman"
while retaining the category of "women." If there are women, then there must exist
a basis for the category and a criterion for inclusion within it. This criterion need
not posit a universal, homogeneous essence, but there must be a criterion nonetheless.

[2] For Schopenhauer's, Kant's, and nearly every other major Western philosopher's
conception of woman, and for an insight into just how contradictory and incoherent
these are, see Linda Bell's excellent anthology, *Visions of Women* (Clifton, N.J.:
Humana Press, 1983).

[3] For an interesting discussion of whether feminists should even seek such transcendence, see Genevieve Lloyd, *The Man of Reason* (Minneapolis: University of
Minnesota Press, 1984), 86–102.

culture is the problem of a process in which women are defined by men, that is, by a group who has a contrasting point of view and set of interests from women, not to mention a possible fear and hatred of women. The result of this has been a distortion and devaluation of feminine characteristics, which now can be corrected by a more accurate feminist description and appraisal. Thus the cultural feminist reappraisal construes woman's passivity as her peacefulness, her sentimentality as her proclivity to nurture, her subjectiveness as her advanced self-awareness, and so forth. Cultural feminists have not challenged the defining of woman but only that definition given by men.

The second major response has been to reject the possibility of defining woman as such at all. Feminists who take this tactic go about the business of deconstructing all concepts of woman and argue that both feminist and misogynist attempts to define woman are politically reactionary and ontologically mistaken. Replacing woman-as-housewife with woman-as-supermom (or earth mother or super professional) is no advance. Using French post-structuralist theory these feminists argue that such errors occur because we are in fundamental ways duplicating misogynist strategies when we try to define women, characterize women, or speak for women, even though allowing for a range of differences within the gender. The politics of gender or sexual difference must be replaced with a plurality of difference where gender loses its position of significance.

Briefly put, then, the cultural feminist response to Simone de Beauvoir's question, "Are there women?" is to answer yes and to define women by their activities and attributes in the present culture. The post-structuralist response is to answer no and attack the category and the concept of woman through problematizing subjectivity. Each response has serious limitations, and it is becoming increasingly obvious that transcending these limitations while retaining the theoretical framework from which they emerge is impossible. As a result, a few brave souls are now rejecting these choices and attempting to map out a new course, a course that will avoid the major problems of the earlier responses. In this paper I will discuss some of the pioneer work being done to develop a new concept of woman and offer my own contribution toward it.[4] But first, I must spell out more clearly the inadequacies of the first two

[4] Feminist works I would include in this group but which I won't be able to discuss in this essay are Elizabeth L. Berg, "The Third Woman," *Diacritics* 12 (1982): 11–20; and Lynne Joyrich, "Theory and Practice: The Project of Feminist Criticism," unpublished manuscript (Brown University, 1984). Luce Irigaray's work may come to mind for some readers as another proponent of a third way, but for me Irigaray's emphasis on female anatomy makes her work border too closely on essentialism.

responses to the problem of woman and explain why I believe these inadequacies are inherent.

Cultural feminism

Cultural feminism is the ideology of a female nature or female essence reappropriated by feminists themselves in an effort to re-validate undervalued female attributes. For cultural feminists, the enemy of women is not merely a social system or economic institution or set of backward beliefs but masculinity itself and in some cases male biology. Cultural feminist politics revolve around creating and maintaining a healthy environment—free of masculinist values and all their offshoots such as pornography—for the female principle. Feminist theory, the explanation of sexism, and the justification of feminist demands can all be grounded securely and unambiguously on the concept of the essential female.

Mary Daly and Adrienne Rich have been influential proponents of this position.[5] Breaking from the trend toward androgyny and the minimizing of gender differences that was popular among feminists in the early seventies, both Daly and Rich argue for a returned focus on femaleness.

For Daly, male barrenness leads to parasitism on female energy, which flows from our life-affirming, life-creating biological condition: "Since female energy is essentially biophilic, the female spirit/body is the primary target in this perpetual war of aggression against life. Gyn/Ecology is the re-claiming of life-loving female energy."[6] Despite Daly's warnings against biological reductionism,[7] her own analysis of sexism uses gender-specific biological traits to explain male hatred for women. The childless state of "all males" leads to a dependency on women, which in turn leads men to "deeply identify with 'unwanted fetal tissue.' "[8] Given their state of fear and insecurity it becomes almost understandable, then, that men would desire to dominate and control that which is so vitally necessary to them: the life-energy of women. Female energy, conceived by Daly as a natural essence, needs to be freed from its male parasites, released for creative expression and recharged through bonding

---

[5] Although Rich has recently departed from this position and in fact begun to move in the direction of the concept of woman I will defend in this essay (Adrienne Rich, "Notes toward a Politics of Location," in her *Blood, Bread, and Poetry* [New York: Norton, 1986]).

[6] Mary Daly, *Gyn/Ecology* (Boston: Beacon, 1978), 355.

[7] Ibid., 60.

[8] Ibid., 59.

with other women. In this free space women's "natural" attributes of love, creativity, and the ability to nurture can thrive.

Women's identification as female is their defining essence for Daly, their haecceity, overriding any other way in which they may be defined or may define themselves. Thus Daly states: "Women who accept false inclusion among the fathers and sons are easily polarized against other women on the basis of ethnic, national, class, religious and other *male-defined differences,* applauding the defeat of 'enemy' women."[9] These differences are apparent rather than real, inessential rather than essential. The only real difference, the only difference that can change a person's ontological placement on Daly's dichotomous map, is sex difference. Our essence is defined here, in our sex, from which flow all the facts about us: who are our potential allies, who is our enemy, what are our objective interests, what is our true nature. Thus, Daly defines women again and her definition is strongly linked to female biology.

Many of Rich's writings have exhibited surprising similarities to Daly's position described above, surprising given their difference in style and temperament. Rich defines a "female consciousness"[10] that has a great deal to do with the female body.

> I have come to believe . . . that female biology—the diffuse, intense sensuality radiating out from clitoris, breasts, uterus, vagina; the lunar cycles of menstruation; the gestation and fruition of life which can take place in the female body—has far more radical implications than we have yet come to appreciate. Patriarchal thought has limited female biology to its own narrow specifications. The feminist vision has recoiled from female biology for these reasons; it will, I believe, come to view our physicality as a resource, rather than a destiny. . . . We must touch the unity and resonance of our physicality, our bond with the natural order, the corporeal ground of our intelligence.[11]

Thus Rich argues that we should not reject the importance of female biology simply because patriarchy has used it to subjugate us. Rich believes that "our biological grounding, the miracle and paradox of the female body and its spiritual and political meanings" holds the key to our rejuvenation and our reconnection with our specific female attributes, which she lists as "our great mental capacities . . . ; our highly developed tactile sense; our genius for close

[9] Ibid., 365 (my emphasis).
[10] Adrienne Rich, *On Lies, Secrets, and Silence* (New York: Norton, 1979), 18.
[11] Adrienne Rich, *Of Woman Born* (New York: Bantam, 1977), 21.

observation; our complicated, pain-enduring, multi-pleasured physicality."[12]

Rich further echoes Daly in her explanation of misogyny: "The ancient, continuing envy, awe and dread of the male for the female capacity to create life has repeatedly taken the form of hatred for every other female aspect of creativity."[13] Thus Rich, like Daly, identifies a female essence, defines patriarchy as the subjugation and colonization of this essence out of male envy and need, and then promotes a solution that revolves around rediscovering our essence and bonding with other women. Neither Rich nor Daly espouse biological reductionism, but this is because they reject the oppositional dichotomy of mind and body that such a reductionism presupposes. The female essence for Daly and Rich is not simply spiritual or simply biological—it is both. Yet the key point remains that it is our specifically female anatomy that is the primary constituent of our identity and the source of our female essence. Rich prophesies that "the repossession by women of our bodies will bring far more essential change to human society than the seizing of the means of production by workers. . . . In such a world women will truly create new life, bringing forth not only children (if and as we choose) but the visions, and the thinking, necessary to sustain, console and alter human existence—a new relationship to the universe. Sexuality, politics, intelligence, power, motherhood, work, community, intimacy will develop new meanings; thinking itself will be transformed."[14]

The characterization of Rich's and Daly's views as part of a growing trend within feminism toward essentialism has been developed most extensively by Alice Echols.[15] Echols prefers the name

[12] Ibid., 290.

[13] Ibid., 21.

[14] Ibid., 292. Three pages earlier Rich castigates the view that we need only release on the world women's ability to nurture in order to solve the world's problems, which may seem incongruous given the above passage. The two positions are consistent however: Rich is trying to correct the patriarchal conception of women as essentially nurturers with a view of women that is more complex and multifaceted. Thus, her essentialist conception of women is more comprehensive and complicated than the patriarchal one.

[15] See Alice Echols, "The New Feminism of Yin and Yang," in *Powers of Desire: The Politics of Sexuality,* ed. Ann Snitow, Christine Stansell, and Sharon Thompson (New York: Monthly Review Press, 1983), 439–59, and "The Taming of the Id: Feminist Sexual Politics, 1968–83," in *Pleasure and Danger: Exploring Female Sexuality,* ed. Carole S. Vance (Boston: Routledge & Kegan Paul, 1984), 50–72. Hester Eisenstein paints a similar picture of cultural feminism in her *Contemporary Feminist Thought* (Boston: G. K. Hall, 1983), esp. xvii–xix and 105–45. Josephine Donovan has traced the more recent cultural feminism analyzed by Echols and Eisenstein to the earlier matriarchal vision of feminists like Charlotte Perkins Gilman (Josephine Donovan, *Feminist Theory: The Intellectual Traditions of American Feminism* [New York: Ungar, 1985], esp. chap. 2).

"cultural feminism" for this trend because it equates "women's liberation with the development and preservation of a female counter culture."[16] Echols identifies cultural feminist writings by their denigration of masculinity rather than male roles or practices, by their valorization of female traits, and by their commitment to preserve rather than diminish gender differences. Besides Daly and Rich, Echols names Susan Griffin, Kathleen Barry, Janice Raymond, Florence Rush, Susan Brownmiller, and Robin Morgan as important cultural feminist writers, and she documents her claim persuasively by highlighting key passages of their work. Although Echols finds a prototype of this trend in early radical feminist writings by Valerie Solanis and Joreen, she is careful to distinguish cultural feminism from radical feminism as a whole. The distinguishing marks between the two include their position on the mutability of sexism among men, the connection drawn between biology and misogyny, and the degree of focus on valorized female attributes. As Hester Eisenstein has argued, there is a tendency within many radical feminist works toward setting up an ahistorical and essentialist conception of female nature, but this tendency is developed and consolidated by cultural feminists, thus rendering their work significantly different from radical feminism.

However, although cultural feminist views sharply separate female from male traits, they certainly do not all give explicitly essentialist formulations of what it means to be a woman. So it may seem that Echols's characterization of cultural feminism makes it appear too homogeneous and that the charge of essentialism is on shaky ground. On the issue of essentialism Echols states:

This preoccupation with defining the female sensibility not only leads these feminists to indulge in dangerously erroneous generalizations about women, but to imply that this identity is innate rather than socially constructed. At best, there has been a curiously cavalier disregard for whether these differences are biological or cultural in origin. Thus Janice Raymond argues: "Yet there are differences, and some feminists have come to realize that those differences are important whether they spring from socialization, from biology, or from the total history of existing as a woman in a patriarchal society."[17]

Echols points out that the importance of the differences varies tremendously according to their source. If that source is innate, the cultural feminist focus on building an alternative feminist culture

[16] Echols, "The New Feminism of Yin and Yang," 441.
[17] Ibid., 440.

is politically correct. If the differences are not innate, the focus of our activism should shift considerably. In the absence of a clearly stated position on the ultimate source of gender difference, Echols infers from their emphasis on building a feminist free-space and woman-centered culture that cultural feminists hold some version of essentialism. I share Echols's suspicion. Certainly, it is difficult to render the views of Rich and Daly into a coherent whole without supplying a missing premise that there is an innate female essence.

Interestingly, I have not included any feminist writings from women of oppressed nationalities and races in the category of cultural feminism, nor does Echols. I have heard it argued that the emphasis placed on cultural identity by such writers as Cherríe Moraga and Audre Lorde reveals a tendency toward essentialism also. However, in my view their work has consistently rejected essentialist conceptions of gender. Consider the following passage from Moraga: "When you start to talk about sexism, the world becomes increasingly complex. The power no longer breaks down into neat little hierarchical categories, but becomes a series of starts and detours. Since the categories are not easy to arrive at, the enemy is not easy to name. It is all so difficult to unravel."[18] Moraga goes on to assert that "some men oppress the very women they love," implying that we need new categories and new concepts to describe such complex and contradictory relations of oppression. In this problematic understanding of sexism, Moraga seems to me light-years ahead of Daly's manichean ontology or Rich's romanticized conception of the female. The simultaneity of oppressions experienced by women such as Moraga resists essentialist conclusions. Universalist conceptions of female or male experiences and attributes are not plausible in the context of such a complex network of relations, and without an ability to universalize, the essentialist argument is difficult if not impossible to make. White women cannot be all good or all bad; neither can men from oppressed groups. I have simply not found writings by feminists who are oppressed also by race and/or class that place or position maleness wholly as Other. Reflected in their problematized understanding of masculinity is a richer and likewise problematized concept of woman.[19]

[18] Cherríe Moraga, "From a Long Line of Vendidas: Chicanas and Feminism," in *Feminist Studies/Critical Studies*, ed. Teresa de Lauretis (Bloomington: Indiana University Press, 1986), 180.

[19] See also Moraga, "From a Long Line of Vendidas," 187, and Cherríe Moraga, "La Guera," in *This Bridge Called My Back: Writings by Radical Women of Color*, ed. Cherríe Moraga and Gloria Anzaldúa (New York: Kitchen Table, 1983), 32–33; Barbara Smith, "Introduction," in *Home Girls: A Black Feminist Anthology*, ed. Barbara Smith (New York: Kitchen Table, 1983), xix–lvi; "The Combahee River Collective Statement," in Smith, ed., 272–82; Audre Lorde, "Age, Race, Class, and

   Even if cultural feminism is the product of white feminists, it
is not homogeneous, as Echols herself points out. The biological
accounts of sexism given by Daly and Brownmiller, for example,
are not embraced by Rush or Dworkin. But the key link between
these feminists is their tendency toward invoking universalizing
conceptions of woman and mother in an essentialist way. Therefore,
despite the lack of complete homogeneity within the category, it
seems still justifiable and important to identify (and criticize) within
these sometimes disparate works their tendency to offer an essentialist response to misogyny and sexism through adopting a homogeneous, unproblematized, and ahistorical conception of woman.
   One does not have to be influenced by French post-structuralism
to disagree with essentialism. It is well documented that the in-
nateness of gender differences in personality and character is at
this point factually and philosophically indefensible.[20] There are a
host of divergent ways gender divisions occur in different societies,
and the differences that appear to be universal can be explained in
nonessentialist ways. However, belief in women's innate peacefulness and ability to nurture has been common among feminists
since the nineteenth century and has enjoyed a resurgence in the
last decade, most notably among feminist peace activists. I have
met scores of young feminists drawn to actions like the Women's
Peace Encampment and to groups like Women for a Non-Nuclear
Future by their belief that the maternal love women have for their
children can unlock the gates of imperialist oppression. I have great
respect for the self-affirming pride of these women, but I also share
Echols's fear that their effect is to "reflect and reproduce dominant
cultural assumptions about women," which not only fail to represent
the variety in women's lives but promote unrealistic expectations
about "normal" female behavior that most of us cannot satisfy.[21] Our
gender categories are positively constitutive and not mere hindsight
descriptions of previous activities. There is a self-perpetuating cir-
cularity between defining woman as essentially peaceful and nur-

---

Sex: Women Redefining Difference," in her *Sister Outsider* (Trumansburg, N.Y.:
Crossing, 1984), 114–23; and bell hooks, *Feminist Theory: From Margin to Center*
(Boston: South End, 1984). All of these works resist the universalizing tendency of
cultural feminism and highlight the differences between women, and between men,
in a way that undercuts arguments for the existence of an overarching gendered
essence.
   [20] There is a wealth of literature on this, but two good places to begin are Anne
Fausto-Sterling, *Myths of Gender: Biological Theories about Women and Men* (New
York: Basic, 1986); and Sherrie Ortner and Harriet Whitehead, eds., *Sexual Meanings: The Cultural Construction of Gender and Sexuality* (New York: Cambridge
University Press, 1981).
   [21] Echols, "The New Feminism of Yin and Yang," 440.

turing and the observations and judgments we shall make of future women and the practices we shall engage in as women in the future. Do feminists want to buy another ticket for women of the world on the merry-go-round of feminine constructions? Don't we want rather to get off the merry-go-round and run away?

This should not imply that the political effects of cultural feminism have all been negative.[22] The insistence on viewing traditional feminine characteristics from a different point of view, to use a "looking glass" perspective, as a means of engendering a gestalt switch on the body of data we all currently share about women, has had positive effect. After a decade of hearing liberal feminists advising us to wear business suits and enter the male world, it is a helpful corrective to have cultural feminists argue instead that women's world is full of superior virtues and values, to be credited and learned from rather than despised. Herein lies the positive impact of cultural feminism. And surely much of their point is well taken, that it was our mothers who made our families survive, that women's handiwork is truly artistic, that women's care-giving really is superior in value to male competitiveness.

Unfortunately, however, the cultural feminist championing of a redefined "womanhood" cannot provide a useful long-range program for a feminist movement and, in fact, places obstacles in the way of developing one. Under conditions of oppression and restrictions on freedom of movement, women, like other oppressed groups, have developed strengths and attributes that should be correctly credited, valued, and promoted. What we should not promote, however, are the restrictive conditions that gave rise to those attributes: forced parenting, lack of physical autonomy, dependency for survival on mediation skills, for instance. What conditions for women do we want to promote? A freedom of movement such that we can compete in the capitalist world alongside men? A continued restriction to child-centered activities? To the extent cultural feminism merely valorizes genuinely positive attributes developed under oppression, it cannot map our future long-range course. To the extent that it reinforces essentialist explanations of these attributes, it is in danger of solidifying an important bulwark for sexist oppression: the belief in an innate "womanhood" to which we must all adhere lest we be deemed either inferior or not "true" women.

[22] Hester Eisenstein's treatment of cultural feminism, though critical, is certainly more two-sided than Echols's. While Echols apparently sees only the reactionary results of cultural feminism, Eisenstein sees in it a therapeutic self-affirmation necessary to offset the impact of a misogynist culture (see Eisenstein [n. 15 above]).

Post-structuralism

For many feminists, the problem with the cultural feminist response to sexism is that it does not criticize the fundamental mechanism of oppressive power used to perpetuate sexism and in fact reinvokes that mechanism in its supposed solution. The mechanism of power referred to here is the construction of the subject by a discourse that weaves knowledge and power into a coercive structure that "forces the individual back on himself and ties him to his own identity in a constraining way."[23] On this view, essentialist formulations of womanhood, even when made by feminists, "tie" the individual to her identity as a woman and thus cannot represent a solution to sexism.

This articulation of the problem has been borrowed by feminists from a number of recently influential French thinkers who are sometimes called post-structuralist but who also might be called post-humanist and post-essentialist. Lacan, Derrida, and Foucault are the front-runners in this group. Disparate as these writers are, their (one) common theme is that the self-contained, authentic subject conceived by humanism to be discoverable below a veneer of cultural and ideological overlay is in reality a construct of that very humanist discourse. The subject is not a locus of authorial intentions or natural attributes or even a privileged, separate consciousness. Lacan uses psychoanalysis, Derrida uses grammar, and Foucault uses the history of discourses all to attack and "deconstruct"[24] our concept of the subject as having an essential identity and an authentic core that has been repressed by society. There is no essential core "natural" to us, and so there is no repression in the humanist sense.

There is an interesting sort of neodeterminism in this view. The subject or self is never determined by biology in such a way that

[23] Michel Foucault, "Why Study Power: The Question of the Subject," in *Beyond Structuralism and Hermeneutics: Michel Foucault*, ed. Hubert L. Dreyfus and Paul Rabinow, 2d ed. (Chicago: University of Chicago Press, 1983), 212.

[24] This term is principally associated with Derrida for whom it refers specifically to the process of unraveling metaphors in order to reveal their underlying logic, which usually consists of a simple binary opposition such as between man/woman, subject/object, culture/nature, etc. Derrida has demonstrated that within such oppositions one side is always superior to the other side, such that there is never any pure difference without domination. The term "deconstruction" has also come to mean more generally any exposure of a concept as ideological or culturally constructed rather than natural or a simple reflection of reality (see Derrida, *Of Grammatology*, trans. G. Spivak [Baltimore: Johns Hopkins University Press, 1976]; also helpful is Jonathan Culler's *On Deconstruction* [Ithaca, N.Y.: Cornell University Press, 1982]).

human history is predictable or even explainable, and there is no unilinear direction of a determinist arrow pointing from some fairly static, "natural" phenomena to human experience. On the other hand, this rejection of biological determinism is not grounded in the belief that human subjects are underdetermined but, rather, in the belief that we are overdetermined (i.e., constructed) by a social discourse and/or cultural practice. The idea here is that we individuals really have little choice in the matter of who we are, for as Derrida and Foucault like to remind us, individual motivations and intentions count for nil or almost nil in the scheme of social reality. We are constructs—that is, our experience of our very subjectivity is a construct mediated by and/or grounded on a social discourse beyond (way beyond) individual control. As Foucault puts it, we are bodies "totally imprinted by history."[25] Thus, subjective experiences are determined in some sense by macro forces. However, these macro forces, including social discourses and social practices, are apparently not overdetermined, resulting as they do from such a complex and unpredictable network of overlapping and criss-crossing elements that no unilinear directionality is perceivable and in fact no final or efficient cause exists. There may be, and Foucault hoped at one point to find them,[26] perceivable processes of change within the social network, but beyond schematic rules of thumb neither the form nor the content of discourse has a fixed or unified structure or can be predicted or mapped out via an objectified, ultimate realm. To some extent, this view is similar to contemporary methodological individualism, whose advocates will usually concede that the complex of human intentions results in a social reality bearing no resemblance to the summarized categories of intentions but looking altogether different than any one party or sum of parties ever envisaged and desired. The difference, however, is that while methodological individualists admit that human intentions are ineffective, post-structuralists deny not only the efficacy but also the ontological autonomy and even the existence of intentionality.

Post-structuralists unite with Marx in asserting the social dimension of individual traits and intentions. Thus, they say we cannot understand society as the conglomerate of individual intentions but, rather, must understand individual intentions as constructed within a social reality. To the extent post-structuralists emphasize social explanations of individual practices and experiences I find their work illuminating and persuasive. My disagreement occurs,

[25] Michel Foucault, "Nietzsche, Genealogy, History," in *The Foucault Reader*, ed. Paul Rabinow (New York: Pantheon, 1984), 83.

[26] This hope is evident in Michel Foucault's *The Order of Things: An Archaeology of the Human Sciences* (New York: Random House, 1973).

however, when they seem totally to erase any room for maneuver by the individual within a social discourse or set of institutions. It is that totalization of history's imprint that I reject. In their defense of a total construction of the subject, post-structuralists deny the subject's ability to reflect on the social discourse and challenge its determinations.

Applied to the concept of woman the post-structuralist's view results in what I shall call nominalism: the idea that the category "woman" is a fiction and that feminist efforts must be directed toward dismantling this fiction. "Perhaps . . . 'woman' is not a determinable identity. Perhaps woman is not some thing which announces itself from a distance, at a distance from some other thing. . . . Perhaps woman—a non-identity, non-figure, a simulacrum—is distance's very chasm, the out-distancing of distance, the interval's cadence, distance itself."[27] Derrida's interest in feminism stems from his belief, expressed above, that woman may represent the rupture in the functional discourse of what he calls logocentrism, an essentialist discourse that entails hierarchies of difference and a Kantian ontology. Because woman has in a sense been excluded from this discourse, it is possible to hope that she might provide a real source of resistance. But her resistance will not be at all effective if she continues to use the mechanism of logocentrism to redefine woman: she can be an effective resister only if she drifts and dodges all attempts to capture her. Then, Derrida hopes, the following futuristic picture will come true: "Out of the depths, endless and unfathomable, she engulfs and distorts all vestige of essentiality, of identity, of property. And the philosophical discourse, blinded, founders on these shoals and is hurled down these depths to its ruin."[28] For Derrida, women have always been defined as a subjugated difference within a binary opposition: man/woman, culture/nature, positive/negative, analytical/intuitive. To assert an essential gender difference as cultural feminists do is to reinvoke this oppositional structure. The only way to break out of this structure, and in fact to subvert the structure itself, is to assert total difference, to be that which cannot be pinned down or subjugated within a dichotomous hierarchy. Paradoxically, it is to be what is not. Thus feminists cannot demarcate a definitive category of "woman" without eliminating all possibility for the defeat of logocentrism and its oppressive power.

Foucault similarly rejects all constructions of oppositional subjects—whether the "proletariat," "woman," or "the oppressed"—as

[27] Jacques Derrida, *Spurs*, trans. Barbara Harlow (Chicago: University of Chicago Press, 1978), 49.
[28] Ibid., 51.

mirror images that merely recreate and sustain the discourse of power. As Biddy Martin points out, "The point from which Foucault deconstructs is off-center, out of line, apparently unaligned. It is not the point of an imagined absolute otherness, but an 'alterity' which understands itself as an internal exclusion."[29]

Following Foucault and Derrida, an effective feminism could only be a wholly negative feminism, deconstructing everything and refusing to construct anything. This is the position Julia Kristeva adopts, herself an influential French post-structuralist. She says: "A woman cannot be; it is something which does not even belong in the order of being. *It follows that a feminist practice can only be negative*, at odds with what already exists so that we may say 'that's not it' and 'that's still not it.' "[30] The problematic character of subjectivity does not mean, then, that there can be no political struggle, as one might surmise from the fact that post-structuralism deconstructs the position of the revolutionary in the same breath as it deconstructs the position of the reactionary. But the political struggle can have only a "negative function," rejecting "everything finite, definite, structured, loaded with meaning, in the existing state of society."[31]

The attraction of the post-structuralist critique of subjectivity for feminists is two-fold. First, it seems to hold out the promise of an increased freedom for women, the "free play" of a plurality of differences unhampered by any predetermined gender identity as formulated by either patriarchy or cultural feminism. Second, it moves decisively beyond cultural feminism and liberal feminism in further theorizing what they leave untouched: the construction of subjectivity. We can learn a great deal here about the mechanisms of sexist oppression and the construction of specific gender categories by relating these to social discourse and by conceiving of the subject as a cultural product. Certainly, too, this analysis can help us understand right-wing women, the reproduction of ideology, and the mechanisms that block social progress. However, adopting nominalism creates significant problems for feminism. How can we seriously adopt Kristeva's plan for only negative struggle? As the Left should by now have learned, you cannot mobilize a movement that is only and always against: you must have a positive alternative, a vision of a better

[29] Biddy Martin, "Feminism, Criticism, and Foucault," *New German Critique* 27 (1982): 11.

[30] Julia Kristeva, "Woman Can Never Be Defined," in *New French Feminisms*, ed. Elaine Marks and Isabelle de Courtivron (New York: Schocken, 1981), 137 (my italics).

[31] Julia Kristeva, "Oscillation between Power and Denial," in Marks and Courtivron, eds., 166.

future that can motivate people to sacrifice their time and energy toward its realization. Moreover, a feminist adoption of nominalism will be confronted with the same problem theories of ideology have, that is, Why is a right-wing woman's consciousness constructed via social discourse but a feminist's consciousness not? Post-structuralist critiques of subjectivity pertain to the construction of all subjects or they pertain to none. And here is precisely the dilemma for feminists: How can we ground a feminist politics that deconstructs the female subject? Nominalism threatens to wipe out feminism itself.

Some feminists who wish to use post-structuralism are well aware of this danger. Biddy Martin, for example, points out that "we cannot afford to refuse to take a political stance 'which pins us to our sex' for the sake of an abstract theoretical correctness. . . . There is the danger that Foucault's challenges to traditional categories, if taken to a 'logical' conclusion . . . could make the question of women's oppression obsolete."[32] Based on her articulation of the problem with Foucault we are left hopeful that Martin will provide a solution that transcends nominalism. Unfortunately, in her reading of Lou Andreas-Salome, Martin valorizes undecidability, ambiguity, and elusiveness and intimates that by maintaining the undecidability of identity the life of Andreas-Salome provides a text from which feminists can usefully learn.[33]

However, the notion that all texts are undecidable cannot be useful for feminists. In support of his contention that the meaning of texts is ultimately undecidable, Derrida offers us in *Spurs* three conflicting but equally warranted interpretations of how Nietzsche's texts construct and position the female. In one of these interpretations Derrida argues we can find purportedly feminist propositions.[34] Thus, Derrida seeks to demonstrate that even the seemingly incontrovertible interpretation of Nietzsche's works as misogynist can be challenged by an equally convincing argument that they are not. But how can this be helpful to feminists, who need to have their accusations of misogyny validated rather than rendered "undecidable"? The point is not that Derrida himself is antifeminist, nor that there is nothing at all in Derrida's work that can be useful for feminists. But the thesis of undecidability as it is applied in the case of Nietzsche sounds too much like yet another version of the antifeminist argument that our perception of sexism is based on a skewed, limited perspective and that what we take to be misogyny is in reality helpful rather than hurtful to the cause of women. The

[32] Martin, 16–17.
[33] Ibid., esp. 21, 24, and 29.
[34] See Derrida, *Spurs*, esp. 57 and 97.

declaration of undecidability must inevitably return us to Kristeva's position, that we can give only negative answers to the question, What is a woman? If the category "woman" is fundamentally undecidable, then we can offer no positive conception of it that is immune to deconstruction, and we are left with a feminism that can be only deconstructive and, thus, nominalist once again.[35]

A nominalist position on subjectivity has the deleterious effect of de-gendering our analysis, of in effect making gender invisible once again. Foucault's ontology includes only bodies and pleasures, and he is notorious for not including gender as a category of analysis. If gender is simply a social construct, the need and even the possibility of a feminist politics becomes immediately problematic. What can we demand in the name of women if "women" do not exist and demands in their name simply reinforce the myth that they do? How can we speak out against sexism as detrimental to the interests of women if the category is a fiction? How can we demand legal abortions, adequate child care, or wages based on comparable worth without invoking a concept of "woman"?

Post-structuralism undercuts our ability to oppose the dominant trend (and, one might argue, the dominant danger) in mainstream Western intellectual thought, that is, the insistence on a universal, neutral, perspectiveless epistemology, metaphysics, and ethics. Despite rumblings from the Continent, Anglo-American thought is still wedded to the idea(l) of a universalizable, apolitical methodology and set of transhistorical basic truths unfettered by associations with particular genders, races, classes, or cultures. The rejection of subjectivity, unintentionally but nevertheless, colludes with this "generic human" thesis of classical liberal thought, that particularities of individuals are irrelevant and improper influences on knowledge. By designating individual particularities such as subjective experience as a social construct, post-structuralism's negation of the authority of the subject coincides nicely with the classical liberal's view that human particularities are irrelevant. (For the liberal, race, class, and gender are ultimately irrelevant to questions of justice and truth because "underneath we are all the same." For the post-

[35] Martin's most recent work departs from this in a positive direction. In an essay coauthored with Chandra Talpade Mohanty, Martin points out "the political limitations of an insistence on 'indeterminacy' which implicitly, when not explicitly, denies the critic's own situatedness in the social, and in effect refuses to acknowledge the critic's own institutional home." Martin and Mohanty seek to develop a more positive, though still problematized, conception of the subject as having a "multiple and shifting" perspective. In this, their work becomes a significant contribution toward the development of an alternative conception of subjectivity, a conception not unlike the one that I will discuss in the rest of this essay ("Feminist Politics: What's Home Got to Do with It?" in Lauretis, ed. [n. 18 above], 191–212, esp. 194).

structuralist, race, class, and gender are constructs and, therefore, incapable of decisively validating conceptions of justice and truth because underneath there lies no natural core to build on or liberate or maximize. Hence, once again, underneath we are all the same.) It is, in fact, a desire to topple this commitment to the possibility of a worldview—purported in fact as the best of all possible worldviews—grounded in a generic human, that motivates much of the cultural feminist glorification of femininity as a valid specificity legitimately grounding feminist theory.[36]

The preceding characterizations of cultural feminism and post-structuralist feminism will anger many feminists by assuming too much homogeneity and by blithely pigeonholing large and complex theories. However, I believe the tendencies I have outlined toward essentialism and toward nominalism represent the main, current responses by feminist theory to the task of reconceptualizing "woman." Both responses have significant advantages and serious shortcomings. Cultural feminism has provided a useful corrective to the "generic human" thesis of classical liberalism and has promoted community and self-affirmation, but it cannot provide a long-range future course of action for feminist theory or practice, and it is founded on a claim of essentialism that we are far from having the evidence to justify. The feminist appropriation of post-structuralism has provided suggestive insights on the construction of female and male subjectivity and has issued a crucial warning against creating a feminism that reinvokes the mechanisms of oppressive power. Nonetheless, it limits feminism to the negative tactics of reaction and deconstruction and endangers the attack against classical liberalism by discrediting the notion of an epistemologically significant, specific subjectivity. What's a feminist to do?

We cannot simply embrace the paradox. In order to avoid the serious disadvantages of cultural feminism and post-structuralism, feminism needs to transcend the dilemma by developing a third course, an alternative theory of the subject that avoids both essentialism and nominalism. This new alternative might share the post-structuralist insight that the category "woman" needs to be theorized through an exploration of the experience of subjectivity, as opposed to a description of current attributes, but it need not concede that such an exploration will necessarily result in a nominalist position on gender, or an erasure of it. Feminists need to explore

[36] A wonderful exchange on this between persuasive and articulate representatives of both sides was printed in *Diacritics* (Peggy Kamuf, "Replacing Feminist Criticism," *Diacritics* 12 [1982]: 42–47; and Nancy Miller, "The Text's Heroine: A Feminist Critic and Her Fictions," *Diacritics* 12 [1982]: 48–53).

the possibility of a theory of the gendered subject that does not slide into essentialism. In the following two sections I will discuss recent work that makes a contribution to the development of such a theory, or so I shall argue, and in the final section I will develop my own contribution in the form of a concept of gendered identity as positionality.

Teresa de Lauretis

Lauretis's influential book, *Alice Doesn't*, is a series of essays organized around an exploration of the problem of conceptualizing woman as subject. This problem is formulated in her work as arising out of the conflict between "woman" as a "fictional construct" and "women" as "real historical beings."[37] She says: "The relation between women as historical subjects and the notion of woman as it is produced by hegemonic discourses is neither a direct relation of identity, a one-to-one correspondence, nor a relation of simple implication. Like all other relations expressed in language, it is an arbitrary and symbolic one, that is to say, culturally set up. The manner and effects of that set-up are what the book intends to explore."[38] The strength of Lauretis's approach is that she never loses sight of the political imperative of feminist theory and, thus, never forgets that we must seek not only to describe this relation in which women's subjectivity is grounded but also to change it. And yet, given her view that we are constructed via a semiotic discourse, this political mandate becomes a crucial problem. As she puts it, "Paradoxically, the only way to position oneself outside of that discourse is to displace oneself within it—to refuse the question as formulated, or to answer deviously (though in its words), even to quote (but against the grain). The limit posed but not worked through in this book is thus the contradiction of feminist theory itself, at once excluded from discourse and imprisoned within it."[39] As with feminist theory, so, too, is the female subject "at once excluded from discourse and imprisoned within it." Constructing a theory of the subject that both concedes these truths and yet allows for the possibility of feminism is the problem Lauretis tackles throughout *Alice Doesn't*. To concede the construction of the subject via discourse entails that the feminist project cannot be simply "how to make visible the invisible" as if the essence of gender were

[37] Teresa de Lauretis, *Alice Doesn't* (Bloomington: Indiana University Press, 1984), 5.
[38] Ibid., 5–6.
[39] Ibid., 7.

out there waiting to be recognized by the dominant discourse. Yet Lauretis does not give up on the possibility of producing "the conditions of visibility for a different social subject."[40] In her view, a nominalist position on subjectivity can be avoided by linking subjectivity to a Peircean notion of practices and a further theorized notion of experience.[41] I shall look briefly at her discussion of this latter claim.

Lauretis's main thesis is that subjectivity, that is, what one "perceives and comprehends as subjective," is constructed through a continuous process, an ongoing constant renewal based on an interaction with the world, which she defines as experience: "And thus [subjectivity] is produced not by external ideas, values, or material causes, but by one's personal, subjective engagement in the practices, discourses, and institutions that lend significance (value, meaning, and affect) to the events of the world."[42] This is the process through which one's subjectivity becomes en-gendered. But describing the subjectivity that emerges is still beset with difficulties, principally the following: "The feminist efforts have been more often than not caught in the logical trap set up by [a] paradox. Either they have assumed that 'the subject,' like 'man,' is a generic term, and as such can designate equally and at once the female and male subjects, with the result of erasing sexuality and sexual difference from subjectivity. Or else they have been obliged to resort to an oppositional notion of 'feminine' subject defined by silence, negativity, a natural sexuality, or a closeness to nature not compromised by patriarchal culture."[43] Here again is spelled out the dilemma between a post-structuralist genderless subject and a cultural feminist essentialized subject. As Lauretis points out, the latter alternative is constrained in its conceptualization of the female subject by the very act of distinguishing female from male subjectivity. This appears to produce a dilemma, for if we de-gender subjectivity, we are committed to a generic subject and thus undercut feminism, while on the other hand if we define the subject in terms of gender, articulating female subjectivity in a space clearly distinct from male subjectivity, then we become caught up in an oppositional dichotomy controlled by a misogynist discourse. A gender-bound subjectivity seems to force us to revert "women to the body and to sexuality as an immediacy of the biological, as nature."[44] For all her insistence on a subjectivity constructed through practices, Lauretis is clear

[40] Ibid., 8–9.
[41] Ibid., 11.
[42] Ibid., 159.
[43] Ibid., 161.
[44] Ibid.

that *that* conception of subjectivity is not what she wishes to propose. A subjectivity that is fundamentally shaped by gender appears to lead irrevocably to essentialism, the posing of a male/female opposition as universal and ahistorical. A subjectivity that is not fundamentally shaped by gender appears to lead to the conception of a generic human subject, as if we could peel away our "cultural" layers and get to the real root of human nature, which turns out to be genderless. Are these really our only choices?

In *Alice Doesn't* Lauretis develops the beginnings of a new conception of subjectivity. She argues that subjectivity is neither (over)determined by biology nor by "free, rational, intentionality" but, rather, by experience, which she defines (via Lacan, Eco, and Peirce) as "a complex of habits resulting from the semiotic interaction of 'outer world' and 'inner world,' the continuous engagement of a self or subject in social reality."[45] Given this definition, the question obviously becomes, Can we ascertain a "female experience"? This is the question Lauretis prompts us to consider, more specifically, to analyze "that complex of habits, dispositions, associations and perceptions, which en-genders one as female."[46] Lauretis ends her book with an insightful observation that can serve as a critical starting point:

> This is where the specificity of a feminist theory may be sought: not in femininity as a privileged nearness to nature, the body, or the unconscious, an essence which inheres in women but to which males too now lay a claim; not in female tradition simply understood as private, marginal, and yet intact, outside of history but fully there to be discovered or recovered; not, finally, in the chinks and cracks of masculinity, the fissures of male identity or the repressed of phallic discourse; *but rather in that political, theoretical, self-analyzing practice* by which the relations of the subject in social reality can be rearticulated from the historical experience of women. Much, very much, is still to be done.[47]

Thus Lauretis asserts that the way out of the totalizing imprint of history and discourse is through our "political, theoretical self-

---

[45] Ibid., 182. The principal texts Lauretis relies on in her exposition of Lacan, Eco, and Peirce are Jacques Lacan, *Ecrits* (Paris: Seuil, 1966); Umberto Eco, *A Theory of Semiotics* (Bloomington: Indiana University Press, 1976), and *The Role of the Reader: Explorations in the Semiotic of Texts* (Bloomington: Indiana University Press, 1979); and Charles Sanders Peirce, *Collected Papers*, vols. 1–8 (Cambridge, Mass.: Harvard University Press, 1931–58).

[46] Lauretis, *Alice Doesn't* (n. 37 above), 182.

[47] Ibid., 186 (my italics).

analyzing practice." This should not be taken to imply that only intellectual articles in academic journals represent a free space or ground for maneuver but, rather, that all women can (and do) think about, criticize, and alter discourse and, thus, that subjectivity can be reconstructed through the process of reflective practice. The key component of Lauretis's formulation is the dynamic she poses at the heart of subjectivity: a fluid interaction in constant motion and open to alteration by self-analyzing practice.

Recently, Lauretis has taken off from this point and developed further her conception of subjectivity. In the introductory essay for her latest book, *Feminist Studies/Critical Studies*, Lauretis claims that an individual's identity is constituted with a historical process of consciousness, a process in which one's history "is interpreted or reconstructed by each of us within the horizon of meanings and knowledges available in the culture at given historical moments, a horizon that also includes modes of political commitment and struggle. . . . Consciousness, therefore, is never fixed, never attained once and for all, because discursive boundaries change with historical conditions."[48] Here Lauretis guides our way out of the dilemma she articulated for us in *Alice Doesn't*. The agency of the subject is made possible through this process of political interpretation. And what emerges is multiple and shifting, neither "prefigured . . . in an unchangeable symbolic order" nor merely "fragmented, or intermittent."[49] Lauretis formulates a subjectivity that gives agency to the individual while at the same time placing her within "particular discursive configurations" and, moreover, conceives of the process of consciousness as a strategy. Subjectivity may thus become imbued with race, class, and gender without being subjected to an overdetermination that erases agency.

Denise Riley

Denise Riley's *War in the Nursery: Theories of the Child and Mother* is an attempt to conceptualize women in a way that avoids what she calls the biologism/culturalist dilemma: that women must be either biologically determined or entirely cultural constructs. Both of these approaches to explaining sexual difference have been theoretically and empirically deficient, Riley claims. Biological deterministic accounts fail to problematize the concepts they use, for example, "biology," "nature," and "sex" and attempt to reduce

48 Lauretis, ed. (n. 18 above), 8.
49 Ibid., 9.

"everything to the workings of a changeless biology."[50] On the other hand, the "usual corrective to biologism"[51]—the feminist-invoked cultural construction thesis—"ignores the fact that there really is biology, which must be conceived more clearly" and moreover "only substitutes an unbounded sphere of social determination for that of biological determination."[52]

In her attempt to avoid the inadequacies of these approaches, Riley states: "The tactical problem is in naming and specifying sexual difference where it has been ignored or misread; but without doing so in a way which guarantees it an eternal life of its own, a lonely trajectory across infinity which spreads out over the whole of being and the whole of society—as if the chance of one's gendered conception mercilessly guaranteed every subsequent facet of one's existence at all moments."[53] Here I take Riley's project to be an attempt to conceptualize the subjectivity of woman as a gendered subject, without essentializing gender such that it takes on "an eternal life of its own"; to avoid both the denial of sexual difference (nominalism) and an essentializing of sexual difference.

Despite this fundamental project, Riley's analysis in this book is mainly centered on the perceivable relations between social policies, popularized psychologies, the state, and individual practices, and she does not often ascend to the theoretical problem of conceptions of woman. What she does do is proceed with her historical and sociological analysis *without ever losing sight of the need to problematize her key concepts,* for example, woman and mother. In this she provides an example, the importance of which cannot be overestimated. Moreover, Riley discusses in her last chapter a useful approach to the political tension that can develop between the necessity of problematizing concepts on the one hand and justifying political action on the other.

In analyzing the pros and cons of various social policies, Riley tries to take a feminist point of view. Yet any such discussion must necessarily presuppose, even if it is not openly acknowledged, that needs are identifiable and can therefore be used as a yardstick in evaluating social policies. The reality is, however, that needs are terribly difficult to identify, since most if not all theories of need rely on some naturalist conception of the human agent, an agent who either can consciously identify and state all of her or his needs or whose "real" needs can be ascertained by some external process

[50] Denise Riley, *War in the Nursery: Theories of the Child and Mother* (London: Virago, 1983), 2.
[51] Ibid., 6.
[52] Ibid., 2, 3.
[53] Ibid., 4.

of analysis. Either method produces problems: it seems unrealistic to say that only if the agent can identify and articulate specific needs do the needs exist, and yet there are obvious dangers to relying on "experts" or others to identify the needs of an individual. Further, it is problematic to conceptualize the human agent as having needs in the same way that a table has properties, since the human agent is an entity in flux in a way that the table is not and is subject to forces of social construction that affect her subjectivity and thus her needs. Utilitarian theorists, especially desire and welfare utilitarian theorists, are particularly vulnerable to this problem, since the standard of moral evaluation they advocate using is precisely needs (or desires, which are equally problematic).[54] Feminist evaluations of social policy that use a concept of "women's needs" must run into the same difficulty. Riley's approach to this predicament is as follows: "I've said that people's needs obviously can't be revealed by a simple process of historical unveiling, while elsewhere I've talked about the 'real needs' of mothers myself. I take it that it's necessary both to stress the non-self-evident nature of need and the intricacies of its determinants, and also to act politically as if needs could be met, or at least met half-way."[55] Thus Riley asserts the possibility and even the necessity of combining decisively formulated political demands with an acknowledgment of their essentialist danger. How can this be done without weakening our political struggle?

On the one hand, as Riley argues, the logic of concrete demands does not entail a commitment to essentialism. She says: "Even though it is true that arguing for adequate childcare as one obvious way of meeting the needs of mothers does suppose an orthodox division of labor, in which responsibility for children is the province of women and not of men, nevertheless this division is what, by and large, actually obtains. Recognition of that in no way commits you to supposing that the care of children is fixed eternally as female."[56] We need not invoke a rhetoric of idealized motherhood to demand that women here and now need child care. On the other hand, the entire corpus of Riley's work on social policies is dedicated to demonstrating the dangers that such demands can entail. She explains these as follows: "Because the task of illuminating 'the needs of mothers' starts out with gender at its most decisive and inescapable point—the biological capacity to bear children—

[54] For a lucid discussion of just how difficult this problem is for utilitarians, see Jon Elster, "Sour Grapes—Utilitarianism and the Genesis of Wants," in *Utilitarianism and Beyond*, ed. Amartya Sen and Bernard Williams (Cambridge: Cambridge University Press, 1982), 219–38.

[55] Riley, 193–94.

[56] Ibid., 194.

there's the danger that it may fall back into a conservative restating and confirming of social-sexual difference as timeless too. This would entail making the needs of mothers into fixed properties of 'motherhood' as a social function: I believe this is what happened in postwar Britain."[57] Thus, invoking the demands of women with children also invokes the companion belief in our cultural conception of essentialized motherhood.

As a way of avoiding this particular pitfall, Riley recommends against deploying any version of "motherhood" *as such*. I take it that what Riley means here is that we can talk about the needs of women with children and of course refer to these women as mothers but that we should eschew all reference to the idealized institution of motherhood as women's privileged vocation or the embodiment of an authentic or natural female practice.

The light that Riley sheds on our problem of woman's subjectivity is three-fold. First, and most obviously, she articulates the problem clearly and deals with it head on. Second, she shows us a way of approaching child-care demands without essentializing femininity, that is, by keeping it clear that these demands represent only current and not universal or eternal needs of women and by avoiding invocations of motherhood altogether. Third, she demands that our problematizing of concepts like "women's needs" coexist alongside a political program of demands in the name of women, without either countermanding the other. This is not to embrace the paradox but, rather, to call for a new understanding of subjectivity that can bring into harmony both our theoretical and our political agendas.

Denise Riley presents a useful approach to the political dimension of the problem of conceptualizing woman by discussing ways to avoid essentialist political demands. She reminds us that we should not avoid political action because our theory has uncovered chinks in the formulation of our key concepts.

A concept of positionality

Let me state initially that my approach to the problem of subjectivity is to treat it as a metaphysical problem rather than an empirical one. For readers coming from a post-structuralist tradition this statement will require immediate clarification. Continental philosophers from Nietzsche to Derrida have rejected the discipline of meta-

[57] Ibid., 194–95.

physics in toto because they say it assumes a naive ontological connection between knowledge and a reality conceived as a thing-in-itself, totally independent of human practices and methodology. Echoing the logical positivists here, these philosophers have claimed that metaphysics is nothing but an exercise in mystification, presuming to make knowledge claims about such things as souls and "necessary" truths that we have no way of justifying. Perhaps the bottom line criticism has been that metaphysics defines truth in such a way that it is impossible to attain, and then claims to have attained it. I agree that we should reject the metaphysics of transcendent things-in-themselves and the presumption to make claims about the noumena, but this involves a rejection of a specific ontology of truth and particular tradition in the history of metaphysics and not a rejection of metaphysics itself. If metaphysics is conceived not as any particular ontological commitment but as the attempt to reason through ontological issues that cannot be decided empirically, then metaphysics continues today in Derrida's analysis of language, Foucault's conception of power, and all of the post-structuralist critiques of humanist theories of the subject. Thus, on this view, the assertion that someone is "doing metaphysics" does not serve as a pejorative. There are questions of importance to human beings that science alone cannot answer (including what science is and how it functions), and yet these are questions that we can usefully address by combining scientific data with other logical, political, moral, pragmatic, and coherence considerations. The distinction between what is normative and what is descriptive breaks down here. Metaphysical problems are problems that concern factual claims about the world (rather than simply expressive, moral, or aesthetic assertions, e.g.) but are problems that cannot be determined through empirical means alone.[58]

In my view the problem of the subject and, within this, the problem of conceptualizing "woman," is such a metaphysical problem. Thus, I disagree with both phenomenologists and psychoanalysts who assert that the nature of subjectivity can be discovered via a certain methodology and conceptual apparatus, either the epoch or the

---

[58] In this conception of the proper dimension of and approach to metaphysics (as a conceptual enterprise to be decided partially by pragmatic methods), I am following the tradition of the later Rudolf Carnap and Ludwig Wittgenstein, among others (Rudolf Carnap, "Empiricism, Semantics, and Ontology," and "On the Character of Philosophical Problems," both in *The Linguistic Turn*, ed. R. Rorty [Chicago: University of Chicago Press, 1967]; and Ludwig Wittgenstein, *Philosophical Investigations*, trans. G. E. M. Anscombe [New York: Macmillan, 1958]).

theory of the unconscious.[59] Neurophysiological reductionists likewise claim to be able to produce empirical explanations of subjectivity, but they will by and large admit that their physicalist
explanations can tell us little about the experiential reality of subjectivity.[60] Moreover, I would assert that physicalist explanations can
tell us little about how the concept of subjectivity should be construed, since this concept necessarily entails considerations not only
of the empirical data but also of the political and ethical implications
as well. Like the determination of when "human" life begins—
whether at conception, full brain development, or birth—we cannot
through science alone settle the issue since it turns on how we (to
some extent) choose to define concepts like "human" and "woman."
We cannot discover the "true meaning" of these concepts but must
decide how to define them using all the empirical data, ethical arguments, political implications, and coherence constraints at hand.

Psychoanalysis should be mentioned separately here since it
was Freud's initial problematizing of the subject from which developed post-structuralist rejection of the subject. It is the psychoanalytic conception of the unconscious that "undermines the
subject from any position of certainty" and in fact claims to reveal
that the subject is a fiction.[61] Feminists then use psychoanalysis to
problematize the gendered subject to reveal "the fictional nature
of the sexual category to which every human subject is none the
less assigned."[62] Yet while a theorizing of the unconscious is used
as a primary means of theorizing the subject, certainly psychoanalysis alone cannot provide all of the answers we need for a theory
of the gendered subject.[63]

As I have already stated, it seems important to use Teresa de
Lauretis's conception of experience as a way to begin to describe
the features of human subjectivity. Lauretis starts with no given
biological or psychological features and thus avoids assuming an

[59] I am thinking particularly of Husserl and Freud here. The reason for my
disagreement is that both approaches are in reality more metaphysical than their
proponents would admit and, further, that I have only limited sympathy for the
metaphysical claims they make. I realize that to explain this fully would require a
long argument, which I cannot give in this essay.

[60] See, e.g., Donald Davidson, "Psychology as Philosophy," in his *Essays on
Actions and Interpretations* (Oxford: Clarendon Press, 1980), 230.

[61] Jacqueline Rose, "Introduction II," in *Feminine Sexuality: Jacques Lacan and
the Ecole Freudienne*, ed. Juliet Mitchell and Jacqueline Rose (New York: Norton,
1982), 29, 30.

[62] Ibid., 29.

[63] Psychoanalysis must take credit for making subjectivity a problematic issue,
and yet I think a view that gives psychoanalysis hegemony in this area is misguided,
if only because psychoanalysis is still extremely hypothetical. Let a hundred flowers
bloom.

essential characterization of subjectivity, but she also avoids the idealism that can follow from a rejection of materialist analyses by basing her conception on real practices and events. The importance of this focus on practices is, in part, Lauretis's shift away from the belief in the totalization of language or textuality to which most antiessentialist analyses become wedded. Lauretis wants to argue that language is not the sole source and locus of meaning, that habits and practices are crucial in the construction of meaning, and that through self-analyzing practices we can rearticulate female subjectivity. Gender is not a point to start from in the sense of being a given thing but is, instead, a posit or construct, formalizable in a nonarbitrary way through a matrix of habits, practices, and discourses. Further, it is an interpretation of our history within a particular discursive constellation, a history in which we are both subjects of and subjected to social construction.

The advantage of such an analysis is its ability to articulate a concept of gendered subjectivity without pinning it down one way or another for all time. Given this and given the danger that essentialist conceptions of the subject pose specifically for women, it seems both possible and desirable to construe a gendered subjectivity in relation to concrete habits, practices, and discourses while at the same time recognizing the fluidity of these.

As both Lacan and Riley remind us, we must continually emphasize within any account of subjectivity the historical dimension.[64] This will waylay the tendency to produce general, universal, or essential accounts by making all our conclusions contingent and revisable. Thus, through a conception of human subjectivity as an emergent property of a historicized experience, we can say "feminine subjectivity is construed here and now in such and such a way" without this ever entailing a universalizable maxim about the "feminine."

It seems to me equally important to add to this approach an "identity politics," a concept that developed from the Combahee River Collective's "A Black Feminist Statement."[65] The idea here is that one's identity is taken (and defined) as a political point of departure, as a motivation for action, and as a delineation of one's

[64] See Juliet Mitchell, "Introduction I," in Mitchell and Rose, eds., 4–5.

[65] This was suggested to me by Teresa de Lauretis in an informal talk she gave at the Pembroke Center, 1984–85. A useful discussion and application of this concept can be found in Elly Bulkin, Minnie Bruce Pratt, and Barbara Smith, *Yours in Struggle: Three Feminist Perspectives on Anti-Semitism and Racism* (Brooklyn, N.Y.: Long Haul Press, 1984), 98–99. Martin and Mohanty's paper (n. 35 above) offers a fruitful reading of the essay in *Yours in Struggle* by Minnie Bruce Pratt entitled "Identity: Skin Blood Heart" and brings into full relief the way in which she uses identity politics. See also "The Combahee River Collective" (n. 19 above).

politics. Lauretis and the authors of *Yours in Struggle* are clear about the problematic nature of one's identity, one's subject-ness, and yet argue that the concept of identity politics is useful because identity is a posit that is politically paramount. Their suggestion is to recognize one's identity as always a construction yet also a necessary point of departure.

I think this point can be readily intuited by people of mixed races and cultures who have had to choose in some sense their identity.[66] For example, assimilated Jews who have chosen to become Jewish-identified as a political tactic against anti-Semitism are practicing identity politics. It may seem that members of more easily identifiable oppressed groups do not have this luxury, but I think that just as Jewish people can choose to assert their Jewishness, so black men, women of all races, and other members of more immediately recognizable oppressed groups can practice identity politics by choosing their identity as a member of one or more groups as their political point of departure. This, in fact, is what is happening when women who are not feminists downplay their identity as women and who, on becoming feminists, then begin making an issue of their femaleness. It is the claiming of their identity as women as a political point of departure that makes it possible to see, for instance, gender-biased language that in the absence of that departure point women often do not even notice.

It is true that antifeminist women can and often do identify themselves strongly as women and with women as a group, but this is usually explained by them within the context of an essentialist theory of femininity. Claiming that one's politics are grounded in one's essential identity avoids problematizing both identity and the connection between identity and politics and thus avoids the agency involved in underdetermined actions. The difference between feminists and antifeminists strikes me as precisely this: the affirmation or denial of our right and our ability to construct, and take responsibility for, our gendered identity, our politics, and our choices.[67]

Identity politics provides a decisive rejoinder to the generic human thesis and the mainstream methodology of Western political

---

[66] This point has been the subject of long, personal reflection for me, as I myself am half Latina and half white. I have been motivated to consider it also since the situation is even more complicated for my children, who are half mine and half a Jewish father's.

[67] I certainly do not believe that most women have the freedom to choose their situations in life, but I do believe that of the multiple ways we are held in check, internalized oppressive mechanisms play a significant role, and we can achieve control over these. On this point I must say I have learned from and admired the work of Mary Daly, particularly *Gyn/Ecology* (n. 6 above), which reveals and describes these internal mechanisms and challenges us to repudiate them.

theory. According to the latter, the approach to political theory must be through a "veil of ignorance" where the theorist's personal interests and needs are hypothetically set aside. The goal is a theory of universal scope to which all ideally rational, disinterested agents would acquiesce if given sufficient information. Stripped of their particularities, these rational agents are considered to be potentially equally persuadable. Identity politics provides a materialist response to this and, in so doing, sides with Marxist class analysis. The best political theory will not be one ascertained through a veil of ignorance, a veil that is impossible to construct. Rather, political theory must base itself on the initial premise that all persons, including the theorist, have a fleshy, material identity that will influence and pass judgment on all political claims. Indeed, the best political theory for the theorist herself will be one that acknowledges this fact. As I see it, the concept of identity politics does not presuppose a prepackaged set of objective needs or political implications but problematizes the connection of identity and politics and introduces identity as a factor in any political analysis.

If we combine the concept of identity politics with a conception of the subject as positionality, we can conceive of the subject as nonessentialized and emergent from a historical experience and yet retain our political ability to take gender as an important point of departure. Thus we can say at one and the same time that gender is not natural, biological, universal, ahistorical, or essential and yet still claim that gender is relevant because we are taking gender as a position from which to act politically. What does position mean here?

When the concept "woman" is defined not by a particular set of attributes but by a particular position, the internal characteristics of the person thus identified are not denoted so much as the external context within which that person is situated. The external situation determines the person's relative position, just as the position of a pawn on a chessboard is considered safe or dangerous, powerful or weak, according to its relation to the other chess pieces. The essentialist definition of woman makes her identity independent of her external situation: since her nurturing and peaceful traits are innate they are ontologically autonomous of her position with respect to others or to the external historical and social conditions generally. The positional definition, on the other hand, makes her identity relative to a constantly shifting context, to a situation that includes a network of elements involving others, the objective economic conditions, cultural and political institutions and ideologies, and so on. If it is possible to identify women by their position within this network of relations, then it becomes possible to ground a feminist argument for women, not on a claim that their innate capacities are being stunted, but that their position within the network lacks power and mobility and requires radical change. The position of women is relative and not innate, and yet neither is it "undecidable." Through social critique and analysis we can identify women via their position relative to an existing cultural and social network.

It may sound all too familiar to say that the oppression of women involves their relative position within a society; but my claim goes further than this. I assert that the very subjectivity (or subjective experience of being a woman) and the very identity of women is constituted by women's position. However, this view should not imply that the concept of "woman" is determined solely by external elements and that the woman herself is merely a passive recipient of an identity created by these forces. Rather, she herself is part of the historicized, fluid movement, and she therefore actively contributes to the context within which her position can be delineated. I would include Lauretis's point here, that the identity of a woman is the product of her own interpretation and reconstruction of her history, as mediated through the cultural discursive context to which she has access.[68] Therefore, the concept of positionality includes two points: first, as already stated, that the concept of woman is a relational term identifiable only within a (constantly moving) context; but, second, that the position that women find themselves in can be actively utilized (rather than transcended) as a location for the construction of meaning, a place from where meaning is constructed, rather than simply the place where a meaning can be *discovered* (the meaning of femaleness). The concept of woman as positionality shows how women use their positional perspective as a place from which values are interpreted and constructed rather than as a locus of an already determined set of values. When women become feminists the crucial thing that has occurred is not that they have learned any new facts about the world but that they come to view those facts from a different position, from their own position as subjects. When colonial subjects begin to be critical of the formerly imitative attitude they had toward the colonists, what is happening is that they begin to identify with the colonized rather than the colonizers.[69] This difference in positional perspective does not necessitate a change in what are taken to be facts, although new facts may come into view from the new position, but it does ne-

[68] See Teresa de Lauretis, "Feminist Studies/Critical Studies: Issues, Terms, Contexts," in Lauretis, ed. (n. 18 above), 8–9.

[69] This point is brought out by Homi Bhabha in his "Of Mimicry and Man: The Ambivalence of Colonial Discourse," *October* 28 (1984): 125–33; and by Abdur Rahman in his *Intellectual Colonisation* (New Delhi: Vikas, 1983).

cessitate a political change in perspective since the point of departure, the point from which all things are measured, has changed.

In this analysis, then, the concept of positionality allows for a determinate though fluid identity of woman that does not fall into essentialism: woman is a position from which a feminist politics can emerge rather than a set of attributes that are "objectively identifiable." Seen in this way, being a "woman" is to take up a position within a moving historical context and to be able to choose what we make of this position and how we alter this context. From the perspective of that fairly determinate though fluid and mutable position, women can themselves articulate a set of interests and ground a feminist politics.

The concept and the position of women is not ultimately undecidable or arbitrary. It is simply not possible to interpret our society in such a way that women have more power or equal power relative to men. The conception of woman that I have outlined limits the constructions of woman we can offer by defining subjectivity as positionality within a context. It thus avoids nominalism but also provides us with the means to argue against views like "oppression is all in your head" or the view that antifeminist women are not oppressed.

At the same time, by highlighting historical movement and the subject's ability to alter her context, the concept of positionality avoids essentialism. It even avoids tying ourselves to a structure of gendered politics conceived as historically infinite, though it allows for the assertion of gender politics on the basis of positionality at any time. Can we conceive of a future in which oppositional gender categories are not fundamental to one's self-concept? Even if we cannot, our theory of subjectivity should not preclude, and moreover prevent, that eventual possibility. Our concept of woman as a category, then, needs to remain open to future radical alteration, else we will preempt the possible forms eventual stages of the feminist transformation can take.

Obviously, there are many theoretical questions on positionality that this discussion leaves open. However, I would like to emphasize that the problem of woman as subject is a real one for feminism and not just on the plane of high theory. The demands of millions of women for child care, reproductive control, and safety from sexual assault can reinvoke the cultural assumption that these are exclusively feminine issues and can reinforce the right-wing's reification of gender differences unless and until we can formulate a political program that can articulate these demands in a way that challenges rather than utilizes sexist discourse.

Recently, I heard an attack on the phrase "woman of color" by a woman, dark-skinned herself, who was arguing that the use of this phrase simply reinforces the significance of that which should have no significance—skin color. To a large extent I agreed with this woman's argument: we must develop the means to address the wrongs done to us without reinvoking the basis of those wrongs. Likewise, women who have been eternally construed must seek a means of articulating a feminism that does not continue construing us in any set way. At the same time, I believe we must avoid buying into the neuter, universal "generic human" thesis that covers the West's racism and androcentrism with a blindfold. We cannot resolve this predicament by ignoring one half of it or by attempting to embrace it. The solution lies, rather, in formulating a new theory within the process of reinterpreting our position, and reconstructing our political identity, as women and feminists in relation to the world and to one another.

Department of Philosophy
Kalamazoo College

ABOUT THE CONTRIBUTORS

SUSAN HARDY AIKEN is associate professor of English at the University of Arizona. Several journals have published her essays and reviews on nineteenth-century literature, feminist criticism, and the fiction of Isak Dinesen. She is coeditor of *Changing Our Minds: Feminist Transformations of Knowledge* (Albany: State University of New York Press, 1988) and is now at work on the narrative of Isak Dinesen.

LINDA ALCOFF is author of "Justifying Social Science," *Hypatia* 2, no. 2 (Fall 1987). She is assistant professor of philosophy at Kalamazoo College. Her interests include feminist criticisms of epistemology and scientific methodology. Currently she is exploring the coherence concept of truth as an alternative to positivist and foundationalist epistemologies.

MARGARET ANDERSEN is the author of *Thinking about Women: Sociological Perspectives on Sex and Gender* (New York: Macmillan, 1987). She is associate professor of sociology at the University of Delaware and has consulted on several inclusive curriculum projects around the country.

KAREN ANDERSON is interested in the history of women's work and family roles. Currently she is writing on Mexican-origin, black, and American Indian women in the twentieth century. She is author of *Wartime Women: Sex Roles, Family Relations, and the Status of Women during World War II* (Westport, Conn.: Greenwood Press, 1981). She is associate professor of history, University of Arizona.

MARILYN J. BOXER has research interests in women workers in modern France and in women's studies. She is dean of the College of Arts and Letters and professor of women's studies at San Diego State University and is coauthor and editor with Jean Quataert of *Connecting Spheres: Women in the Western World, 1500 to the Present* (New York: Oxford University Press, 1987).

LYNN WEBER CANON is professor in the department of sociology and social work and associate director of the Center for Research on Women at Memphis State University. Her publications include *The American Perception of Class* (Philadelphia: Temple University Press, 1987), which she coauthored with Reeve Vanneman. The focus of her research is the intersection of race, class, and gender.

PHYLLIS L. CROCKER   is a practicing lawyer. She is author of "The Meaning of Equality for Battered Women Who Kill Men in Self Defense," *Harvard Women's Law Journal* 8 (Spring 1985).

BONNIE THORNTON DILL   does research in the area of race, class, and gender. She is director of the Center for Research on Women and associate professor of sociology at Memphis State University and has published widely in feminist readers and journals.

MYRA DINNERSTEIN   is coeditor of *Changing Perspectives on Meno-pause* (Austin: University of Texas Press, 1982). She is chairperson of women's studies and director of the Southwest Institute for Research on Women, University of Arizona. She is coeditor with Susan Hardy Aiken et al. of *Changing Our Minds: Feminist Transformations of Knowledge* (Albany: State University of New York Press, 1988).

BERENICE FISHER   is professor of educational philosophy at New York University, where she helped to create a women's studies program for the human service fields. Her essays on women's political activism, feminist pedagogy, women's friendships and disability, and women's work have appeared in a wide range of feminist publications.

ANNETTE HEMMINGS   is a dissertator in the department of educational policy studies at the University of Wisconsin—Madison. The article by her in this book is her first publication.

ELIZABETH HIGGINBOTHAM   is author of "Race and Class Barriers to Black Women's College Attendance," *Journal of Ethnic Studies* 13, no. 1 (Spring 1985). She is assistant professor of sociology at Memphis State University. Her research focuses on education and employment for women of color.

JUDY LENSINK   has research interests in nineteenth-century women's diaries. She has published "Expanding the Boundaries of Criticism: The Diary as Female Autobiography," *Women's Studies: An Interdisciplinary Journal* 14, no. 1 (1987) and has edited *Old Southwest/New Southwest: Essays on a Region and Its Literature* (Tucson: University of Arizona Press, 1987). Currently she directs the Writers of the Purple Sage Southwestern Literature Project for Tucson Public Library. She is a Ph.D. candidate in American studies, University of Iowa.

PATRICIA MACCORQUODALE   is coauthor of *Premarital Sexuality* (Madison: University of Wisconsin Press, 1979) and coeditor with Susan Hardy Aiken et al. of *Changing Our Minds: Feminist Transformations of Knowledge* (Albany: State University of New York Press, 1988). Currently she is writing on gender and ethnic identities in families and working on a project on gender and justice. She is associate professor of sociology at the University of Arizona.

ELIZABETH KAMARCK MINNICH   is professor of philosophy at the Union Graduate School. She has spoken and consulted on feminist transformation of the academy at over seventy-five schools and educational associations. She has published articles in *Feminist Studies, Soundings,* and *Women's Review of Books* and in anthologies, including *Learning Our Way* (Trumansburg, N.Y.: Crossing Press, 1983) and *Between Women* (Boston: Beacon Press, 1984).

MARY J. OATES   is a specialist in the education and occupational choices of Catholic women in America after 1850. She is professor of economics at Regis College and is author of "'The Good Sisters': The Work and Position of Catholic Churchwomen in Boston, 1870–1940," in *Catholic Boston: Studies in Religion and Community, 1870–1940,* ed. James M. O'Toole and Robert E. Sullivan (Boston: Archdiocese of Boston, 1985).

JEAN F. O'BARR   is director of women's studies at Duke University and a member of the political science department. She has published on women and Third World politics in a number of books and articles. Her interests also include contemporary feminism and women in higher education; she is the editor of *The Politics of Knowledge: Feminist Reconstructions for a New Academy* (Madison: University of Wisconsin Press, in press). She currently serves as editor of *Signs: Journal of Women in Culture and Society.*

GAIL PHETERSON   is research associate at the Institute for the Study of Social Change, University of California, Berkeley. She is author of *The Whore Stigma: Female Dishonor and Male Unworthiness* (The Hague: Ministry of Social Affairs and Employment, 1986). Her research interests include the psychohistory of women's oppression, alliance-building between women, and prostitution.

JOY K. RICE   is author of thirty articles, chapters, and books in the areas of women and continuing higher education and women and psychotherapy, including *Living through Divorce, A Developmental Approach to Divorce Therapy* (New York: Guilford, 1986). She is professor of educational policy studies and women's studies at the University of Wisconsin—Madison and a clinical psychologist in private practice.

RACHEL A. ROSENFELD   is associate professor of sociology and fellow of the Carolina Population Center at the University of North Carolina at Chapel Hill. Her research focuses on women's work and occupations, sex stratification, the contemporary women's movement, and education. She is the author of *Farm Women: Work, Farm, and Family in the United States* (Chapel Hill: University of North Carolina Press, 1986).

SALLY SCHWAGER   is research associate at the Harvard Graduate School of Education and director of the History Institute for Secondary School Teachers. She is currently completing a study of educational reform for women in nineteenth-century Boston.

M. ELIZABETH TIDBALL   is professor of physiology at George Washington University Medical Center. Her recent research publications include "Baccalaureate Origins of Recent Natural Science Doctorates," *Journal of Higher Education* 57, no. 6 (November/December 1986), and "Baccalaureate Origins of Entrants into American Medical Schools," *Journal of Higher Education* 56, no. 4 (July/August, 1985). Her research explores the positive relationship between women faculty and the achievement of women students.

SUSAN WILLIAMSON   is professor of mathematics at Regis College. Her long-standing research interest is the identity and organization of institutions of higher education. She presently serves on the executive committee of the Massachusetts Conference of the American Association of University Professors and works in the area of representation theory in mathematics.

ELISABETH YOUNG-BRUEHL   is author of *Hannah Arendt: For Love of the World* (New Haven, Conn.: Yale University Press, 1982). She is working on a biography of Anna Freud.

MAXINE BACA ZINN   has published extensively on family and gender among racial-ethnics. She is coauthor with D. Stanley Eitzen of *Diversity in American Families* (New York: Harper & Row, 1987) and is professor of sociology at the University of Michigan—Flint.

SIGNS ARTICLES OF RELATED INTEREST

Adler, Nancy E. "Women and Higher Education: Some Speculations on the Future." 3, no. 4 (1978): 912–15.

Barber, Elinor G. "Some International Perspectives on Sex Differences in Education." 4, no. 3 (1979): 584–92.

Barthel, Diane. "Women's Educational Experience under Colonialism: Toward a Diachronic Model." 11, no. 1 (1986): 137–54.

Bell, Susan Groag, and Millie Schwartz Rosenhan. "A Problem in Naming: Women Studies—Women's Studies?" 6, no. 3 (1981): 540–42.

Bem, Sandra Lipsitz. "Gender Schema Theory and Its Implications for Child Development: Raising Gender-aschematic Children in a Gender-schematic Society." 8, no. 4 (1983): 279–98.

Boris, Ellen. "Social Reproduction and the Schools: 'Educational Housekeeping': Archives." 4, no. 4 (1979): 814–20.

Brush, Lorelei R., Alice Ross Gold, and Marni Goldstein White. "The Paradox of Intention and Effect: A Women's Studies Course." 3, no. 4 (1978): 870–83.

Eccles, Jacquelynne S., and Janis E. Jacobs. "Social Forces Shape Math Attitudes and Performance." 11, no. 2 (1986): 367–80.

Estler, Suzanne E. "Women as Leaders in Public Education." 1, no. 2 (1975): 363–86.

Fellman, Anita Clair. "Teaching with Tears: Soap Opera as a Tool in Teaching Women's Studies." 3, no. 4 (1978): 909–11.

Ferber, Marianne A. "Citations: Are They an Objective Measure of Scholarly Merit?" 11, no. 2 (1986): 381–89.

Glazer, Nona Y. "Questioning Eclectic Practice in Curriculum Change: A Marxist Perspective." 12, no. 2 (1987): 293–304.

Graham, Patricia Albjerg. "Expansion and Exclusion: A History of Women in American Higher Education." 3, no. 4 (1978): 759–73.

Guttentag, Marcia, Lorelie R. Brush, Alice Ross Gold, Marnie W. Mueller, Sheila Tobias, and Marni Goldstein White. "Evaluating Women's Studies: A Decision-Theoretic Approach." 3, no. 4 (1978): 884–90.

Haaken, Janice. "A Historical Analysis of a Psychological Construct." 13, no. 2 (1988): 311–30.

Jones, Jennifer M., and Frances H. Lovejoy. "Discrimination against Women Academics in Australian Universities." 5, no. 3 (1980): 518–26.

Kaufman, Gloria. "Juan Luis Vives on the Education of Women." 3, no. 4 (1978): 891–96.

Kilson, Marion. "The Status of Women in Higher Education." 1, no. 4 (1976): 935–42.

Lightfoot, Sara Lawrence. "Family-School Interactions: The Cultural Image of Mothers and Teachers." 3, no. 2 (1977): 395–408.

Lobodzinska, Barbara. "The Education and Employment of Women in Contemporary Poland." 3, no. 3 (1978): 688–97.

Note.—The articles listed here appeared in various issues of *Signs*, from volume 1, number 2 through volume 13, number 2.

Martin, Elaine. "Power and Authority in the Classroom: Sexist Stereotypes in Teaching Evaluations." 9, no. 3 (1984): 482–92.

Shank, Michael H. "A Female University Student in Late Medieval Krakow." 12, no. 2 (1987): 373–80.

Strathern, Marilyn. "An Awkward Relationship: The Case of Feminism and Anthropology." 12, no. 2 (1987): 276–92.

Strober, Myra H., and Audri Gordon Lanford. "The Feminization of Public School Teaching: Cross-sectional Analysis, 1850–1880." 11, no. 2 (1986): 212–35.

Strober, Myra H., and David Tyack. "Why Do Women Teach and Men Manage? A Report on Research on Schools." 5, no. 3 (1980): 494–503.

Vinovskis, Maris A., and Richard M. Bernard. "Beyond Catharine Beecher: Female Education in the Antebellum Period." 3, no. 4 (1978): 856–69.

Yoon, Soon Young. "Women's Studies in Korea." 4, no. 4 (1979): 751–62.

INDEX

Abolition: blacks' work toward, 177; leaders, 162; teachers, 169, 174

Academic expenses, factor in rate of achiever production, 215–16, 215n. 11

Academic freedom, 34, 35, 36

Academic privilege, and women's movement, 84

Academics, women, distrust of, 245, 246

Academies, 161–67

Achievement: conditions for, among college graduates, 206; definition of, 206, 207, 216–17, 232–33; factors contributing to, 219, 224; images of, 250–51; and optimal environment for undergraduates, 219; professional, analysis of patterns, 156; relation to career patterns and baccalaureate origins, 216–17

Achiever production, success of small colleges, 211, 219

Achievers: absolute numbers produced in 1930, 197–98; among women's college graduates, 224; baccalaureate origins of, 206; distribution of by decade of graduation, 196; profile, 227–29, 230; rate of production of, 197, 199; record of production by women's colleges, 218. *See also* Success

Adams, Abigail, 160

Adams, John, 160

Addams, Jane, 239–40

Administration, college, and curriculum integration projects, 107

Administrators, male, 222

Admissions selectivity: factor in assessment of achiever production, 211, 213, 219; factor in success of Seven Sisters graduates, 224, 225, 230, 232

Advanced education available before 1900, 162

Affirmative action, 89

Ageism, and women's studies, 85

Ahlum, Carol, 74, 75

Albany, normal school, 176

Alice Doesn't, 274, 276, 277

New England: focus of studies of
education, 157; migration of
teachers from, 172–76; rural,
life-cycle patterns of women,
170
New Left, women's studies, 72
New York, life-cycle patterns of
women, 170
Nielsen, Linda, 134–35
Nietzsche, Frederick, 271, 280
Nixon, Richard, 118
Nominalism: and positionality,
287; denial of sexual difference,
278; gender blindness, 272;
post-structuralist concept of
woman, 269, 270
Non-elite institutions, 193
Nonfeminists, women's studies
scholarship, 44
Nonphysical harassment, sexual,
27. *See also* Sexual harassment
Non–Seven Sisters women's
colleges, 198, 201–2
Normal schools, 155, 156, 193
Normalcy, and dominant categories
of people, 140
North Carolina Central University,
"Common Differences"
conference, 137
Northern Rockies Project on
Women, 41
Norton, Mary Beth, 159–60, 161,
162
Norwegians, as teachers in Iowa,
180
Notable American Women, 162
Nursing homes, and women's
studies, 84
Nurturance: quality of women, 19,
265–66, 285; and role models,
239, 251, 252

Oates, Mary J., research on career
achievement, 181, 190, 214, 217,
218, 223–26, 228, 229, 231
Oberlin College, 174, 177, 183
Objectification, 120
Objectivity: academic demand for,
113; academic ideal, 121;
scientific, criticism of, 115;
value-free, pretext of, 95
Occupational categories, 204–5

Occupational choices, 195, 199–
200
Occupational distribution, of
college graduates, 199, 202
Occupational positions, basis for
inclusion in *Who's Who in
America*, 207
Oklahoma, schoolteachers, 177–78
Oklahoma Retired Teachers
Association, 178
On the Generation of Animals,
110
Ontology, and metaphysics, 281
Oppression; impact of, 144; and
women's studies, 75; male
denial of, 116–17; reactions to,
152; women's studies
commitment to fight, 85
Oppositional subjects, 269–70, 287
Organization of American
Historians, 41
Ortner, Sherry, 108
Otherness, 120

Painter, Rachel, 169
Palmer, Alice Freeman, 185
Palmer, Phyllis, 131
Palmieri, Patricia, 188, 189
Paradigms, in educational
curriculum, 53
Parochial schools, 181
Parsons, Elsie Clews, 187
Pateman, Carole, 110
Patriarchy: and gender blindness,
117; and progress, 240; and
success, 235; and values, 248;
essentialist definition, 262; in
education, 39, 44, 46, 53, 62
Peacefulness, as quality of women,
265–66, 285
Pedagogy: female academies, 166;
feminist, 52; reform, 193
Pennsylvania: dame schools, 159;
literacy rates, 160–61
Perkins, Linda, 176–77
Phase theories, curriculum
integration, 48–52
Phelps, Almira, 166
Philadelphia, eighteenth-century
grammar school, 159
Philadelphia Yearly Meeting, 159
Philosophy: and psychoanalysis,
22; history, masculinist canon,

Reagon, Bernice, 237
Reaganomics, impact on academic freedom, 103
Reason: and desire, 17; feminist attitudes toward, 13, 14
Reconstructing American Literature, 65
Reconstruction, and teaching opportunities for black women, 177
Recruitment, factor in success of Seven Sisters college graduates, 224
Reform, educational: female academy leaders, 166; nineteenth- and twentieth-centuries, 155–56; social movement, 70
Reformers, educational, 162
Register, Cheri, 80–81
Reinharz, Shulamit, 61
Religion, oppression, women's studies, 85
Religious commitment, incentive for teaching, 172, 173
Religious orders, membership of college presidents, 201
Religious training, and education of girls, 159
Report on the West Coast Women's Studies Conference, 77
Reproductive control, 287
Republican education, 157, 158–60, 161
Republican Motherhood, as ideology, 158, 159, 163, 165
Requirements, curricular, and women's studies, 90
Research: encouragement of by women's studies programs, 99; gains, 186–88; methods in social science, 60; on achievers, 206; opportunities for women, 187; scholarly, 127; universities, 189, 191–92
Resistance: curriculum integration projects, 107–22; feminist scholarship, 115
Respectability: academic, 111; of teaching as occupation, 175
Resources: differential, in women's and coeducational colleges, 232; materials, 64–67

Responsibility, and role modeling, 251, 252, 254
Reuben, Elaine, 82
Revolution, American, egalitarian rhetoric, 162
Rich, Adrienne, 15, 16, 38, 67–68, 78–79, 87, 88, 104, 117, 260, 261–62, 263, 264
Right wing, consciousness, 271
Rights, conflict of, in sexual harassment policy, 34
Riley, Denise, 277–80, 283
Roberts, J. R., 87
Role models: creation of, 242, 243–44, 249–52; historical dimension, 238–39, 240; implications of, 236, 249, 255; importance of criticizing, 235–36, 250, 254; political nature, 244; relation to reality, 245, 248, 256; responsibility, 253, 254; women, effect on students, 231, 232, 234, 235
Rose, Jacqueline, 20
Rosenberg, Rosalind, 186, 187, 192
Rosenfelt, Deborah, 77
Rossiter, Margaret, 187–88, 190, 191–92
Rowson, Susanna, 158, 160
Rural schools, difference from urban schools, 179, 180
Rush, Benjamin, 158, 160
Rush, Florence, 263, 265
Rutgers University, 26, 27, 28, 33

Sacramento State College, 1973 Women's Studies Conference, 76–77
Sage, 66
Sage College, 184. *See also* Cornell University
Salaries, of academic women, 167, 168, 174, 187
San Diego State College, 72, 78, 97
San Francisco State College, 96
Sanitary science, 186
Sarah Pierce's Academy, 161
"Saving the Life that Is Your Own: The Importance of Models in the Artist's Life," 237
Science: curriculum change, 62–64; female academies, 166